The American Darters

The American
DARTERS

ROBERT A. KUEHNE and
ROGER W. BARBOUR

THE UNIVERSITY PRESS OF KENTUCKY

Publication of this book was assisted by grants from the following:

Kentucky Nature Preserves Commission, Frankfort, Kentucky

High Point Farms, Inc., Springfield, Kentucky

Sport Fishery Research Foundation, Washington, D.C.

Scholarly publisher for the Commonwealth,
serving Bellarmine College, Berea College, Centre
College of Kentucky, Eastern Kentucky University,
The Filson Club, Georgetown College, Kentucky
Historical Society, Kentucky State University,
Morehead State University, Murray State University,
Northern Kentucky University, Transylvania University,
University of Kentucky, University of Louisville,
and Western Kentucky University.

Editorial and Sales Offices: Lexington, Kentucky 40506-0024

Library of Congress Cataloging in Publication Data

Kuehne, Robert A. (Robert Andrew), 1927-
    The American darters.

    Bibliography: p.
    Includes index.
    1. Darters (Fishes) 2. Fishes—North America.
I. Barbour, Roger William, 1919-   . II. Title.
QL638.P4K83   1983   597'.58   83-5934
ISBN 0-8131-1452-7

Contents

Acknowledgments

We started collecting and photographing darters in 1968 with the initial idea of preparing a color atlas of value to ourselves and colleagues. The decision to expand the project into a book came quickly, but serious writing efforts were not started until 1977. Over such a span of years we have become indebted to many people and organizations for a variety of favors. We trust we will be forgiven for any omissions in the following acknowledgments; certainly none were intended.

Generous support toward publication of the color plates was received from the Kentucky Nature Preserves Commission, the Sport Fishery Research Foundation, and High Point Farms, Inc. of Springfield, Kentucky. The University of Kentucky Research Foundation provided an initial grant. Our university department furnished typing and duplicating services through the interest and direction of Samuel Conti.

The help and encouragement given by Don Harker, James J. Schafer, James Small, and Doris Westerman are especially acknowledged.

Museum assistance was given by several individuals. Special thanks are due Reeve Bailey, Herbert Boschung, and Robert Miller in this regard, and Jeff Clayton, who acted as liaison with the U.S. National Museum. Other collections furnishing specimens were: Arkansas Southern State College, Mississippi State University, Northeast Louisiana State College, the University of Alabama, the University of Michigan Museums, and the University of Tennessee. George Becker and Gary Lutterbie furnished living and preserved specimens from Wisconsin.

Colleagues and former students who helped and often provided suggestions during trips include John E. Cooper, Wayne Davis, Carl Ernst, Bobby Jett, Victor Lotrich, James P. Schafer, and Kenneth Slone. James Barbour, Patricia Hudgins, and John Kuehne also learned more about seining darters than they may initially have intended.

In the field or during discussions colleagues often present facts and interpretations which one tends to adopt as his own. In particular, Branley Branson, David Etnier, Robert Jenkins, Henry Robison, Melvin Warren, and Jim Williams fell victim to this phenomenon. David Etnier allowed photographs to be taken of freshly caught snail darters.

A number of people dropped their pressing obligations to take us into the field. In particular we acknowledge Raymond Bouchard and University of Tennessee students, Neil Douglas and his Northeast Louisiana State College students, Robert Ross, and Jay Stauffer, Jr., for one or more days spent helping us.

For a variety of professional courtesies we thank Brooks Burr, Glenn Clemmer, Charles Cole, Bruce Collette, Carter Gilbert, Leslie Knapp, William Lewis, Larry Page, William Pflieger, James Ramsey, Donald Scott, Morgan Sisk, Franklin Snelson, Bill Yambert, and Ralph Yerger. Clark Hubbs reviewed, corrected, and informed on a number of preliminary accounts sent him.

Fishermen and landowners furnished help in many ways, including some that we hope have come through in the book as a public concern for our natural heritage. For example, we remember a Texas rancher, Mr. Baker, who gave us a graphic account of the vast changes in the springs, river flow, and vegetation that have occurred along the Devils River during his and his father's full life of ranching and sheep raising. He also directed us to one of the few permanent springs still supporting a population of the Rio Grande darter.

Roger Potts drafted the maps used to depict darter distributions. Faith Hershey Coskren drew the illustrations for the glossary. Extra typing was done by Judith Kuehne; much map work by Bernice Barbour.

We failed to obtain specimens or were unable to produce satisfactory color photographs of a few darters. We gratefully acknowledge the following persons, who generously provided slides of the indicated species for our color plates: Bruce Bauer, *Percina crassa* and *Etheostoma striatulum;* Raymond Bouchard, *Percina macrolepida;* R.T. Bryant, *Etheostoma aquali* and *Etheostoma fricksium;* Donald Distler, *Etheostoma australe;* Anthony Echelle, *Etheostoma pottsi;* J.P. Henley, *Etheostoma nianguae;* Robert Jenkins, *Etheostoma acuticeps;* and Patrick O'Neal, *Etheostoma boschungi.*

Introduction

The name darters might evoke the image of birds or butterflies, but in reality the darters are a group of tiny colorful freshwater fish. They are often seen darting about on the bottom of a shallow stream in short bursts of speed and coming to rest on their extended ventral fins. Numbering more than 140 species, the darters dwell only in the rivers, lakes, swamps, and springs of North America, from Arctic drainages in Canada to mountain streams of northern Mexico, everywhere enhancing the beauty and biological diversity of these waters.

Despite the attention created by recent environmental controversies over several of the rarest types, most people remain unaware that many of the common and most beautiful darters live in streams they pass almost daily. This book is intended to familiarize readers with the variety of darters, their distribution and natural history, and the startling colors developed in many species. For the professional ichthyologist or fisheries biologist, the presentation may only be a conveniently condensed version of information otherwise available from scattered sources. For other biologists and the increasing numbers of people with a strong interest in the natural world around them, we hope this book will foster an appreciation of the darters and provide a stimulus to attain a deeper understanding of this fascinating corner of nature.

Darters are diminutive members of the perch family, Percidae, which also contains 3 game fish familiar to many American fishermen: walleye, sauger, and yellow perch. These larger perch are rather long and slender, covered with toothed (ctenoid) scales, and equipped with long sharp teeth in both jaws. Their first dorsal fin is supported by sharp stiff spines, and the second dorsal by flexible rays. Rays support all the remaining fins, but the anal and pelvic fins may each have an initial spine or 2. All these larger species have moderately to well developed air bladders which give them considerable buoyancy. Darters are similar to these game fish but are usually more slender and are much smaller, ranging from about 2.5 cm to a maximum of only 16.8 cm. They have small teeth and either no air bladder or one of reduced size, which usually eliminates buoyancy. But in many other ways, both of external appearance and of internal characteristics, they remain perchlike.

Collette (1963) views the family Percidae as being composed of 4 tribes, and suggests that the darters, tribe Etheostomatini, are derived from the tribe Percini, which contains only the yellow perch of North America and 7 relatives in Europe or northern Asia. The American sauger and walleye are considered to be members of the tribe Luciopercini, which also contains 5 Eurasian species. Collette concludes that the latter tribe also has its offshoot, 4 or 5 European species placed in the tribe Romanichthyini. These also lack an air bladder and tend to live in shallow swift water, but they are not as small and certainly not as diverse or colorful as the darters.

Two basic selective forces may be responsible for these river fish exploiting the austere environment of riffles instead of remaining in the relative stability of pools. Shallow riffles are essentially free of large predators, so for that portion of its life spent there, an inhabitant is relatively free from attack. More importantly, riffles are zones of high food availability. Leaves, grass blades, and all sorts of organic debris entering a stream are most likely to be trapped among stones in riffles and there be processed by bacteria and fungi, thus creating a food supply for small aquatic insect larvae. Pool fishes must wait for such insects to wash into their environment, but fish adapted to small riffles readily attack this rich food supply at its source. Riffle fish also face disadvantages. They must expend more energy combating currents than do fish living in pools. They must retreat to deeper water during floods, extreme drought, and cold water temperatures, when they become too sluggish to contend with strong currents. In pools they are subject to predation, as are their young until they are large enough to fight strong currents. Minor secondary modifications, often behavioral in nature, have allowed some darters to succeed in additional habitats, such as pools of small streams, springs, weedy lakes, and swamps.

Exactly where and from what ancestral type the darters arose will probably never be precisely known, but their present center of species abundance is the Mississippi River basin, which is a fair candidate for the point of origin. Species abundance is further concentrated in the Ozark region and the interior low plateaus and ridge and valley areas south of the Ohio River. The Mississippi River has provided an escape route for all aquatic organisms during the repeated continental glaciations of the past million years. In fact, it may be that frequent isolation followed by mixing of populations has accelerated the rate of species formation in North American waters. By contrast, the north-flowing rivers of Europe did not provide convenient escape routes; in many of them, glaciers formed in the mountainous headwaters as well as in the northern regions near their mouths. With literally few places to hide (the Danube River being the notable exception) species number must have been greatly reduced. The difference that persists today is strikingly shown by the fact that the Duck River in Tennessee contains more species of strictly freshwater fish than does all of Europe eastward to the Ural Mountains. After minnows, darters are the most numerous fish in our rich North American fauna.

Darters do not occur in some parts of North America. Extreme northeastern United States and eastern Canada lack representatives, as do the lower reaches of streams draining to the Arctic Ocean. Except for introductions by man, darters neither reach nor cross the continental divide, with the exception of *Etheostoma pottsi,* members of which were transferred to a Pacific drainage by stream capture north of Durango, Mexico.

Arrangement of the book. Information in this volume is concentrated in the species accounts. These are grouped by subgenera within the 3 genera, and arranged phylogenetically in each case. Comments on each genus and its component subgenera precede the species accounts. The species are discussed in alphabetical arrangement within the subgenera. One unnamed and 30 named species of *Percina,* 7 named species of *Ammocrypta,* and 94 named species and 8 unnamed forms of *Etheostoma* are included. All these unnamed *Etheostoma* are in subgenus *Ulocentra;* 6 are illustrated and have range maps. Common names used are those sanctioned by Robins et al. (1980), or for exclusively Mexican species by Deacon et al. (1979). For knowledge of ranges in many cases we are indebted to Lee et al. (1980).

The **Description** section of each species account is based predominantly on the appearance of preserved specimens, which are those most often seen and examined by students and professional biologists. For a fuller treatment, the reader is generally given 1 or more references to consult. The appearance, proportions, and usually the color of a representative of a species can be seen in the appropriate **color plate,** which most often illustrates a breeding male. Sometimes additional characteristics are depicted in key illustrations. Counts presented for lateral line scales, fin spines and rays, and vertebral number are based on published studies, when available, or on small series we have examined. When sample size is large, the numerical range likely to be encountered is presented first, with maximum known variability in parentheses afterward. When not followed by parenthetical values, counts have been made on small samples and may not include the extremes to be encountered. Numbers of fin spines are given in roman numerals, and numbers of rays in arabic numerals. Lateral characteristics are described as viewed from a single side.

The **Distribution** section expands upon or clarifies details presented visually in the species range map. When subspecies are discussed, their differing ranges are described in this section. Stream captures and Pleistocene changes in drainage patterns are known to have been responsible for particular range characteristics of some species, and these may be discussed briefly or in detail. Range maps are deceptive when a species is found only at few spots within a large area; extreme cases of this are noted.

The **Natural History** section varies in length according to published information on a species. For those with little or no information beyond the original description, we often add our own field observations or impressions. Several species of darters have been the subjects of numerous studies; in such cases we have chosen enough representation to orient the serious student without exceeding certain practical considerations for account length. Scientific studies which have dealt with a number of species are not usually cited repetitiously.

The **Abundance** section notes species listed by Deacon et al. (1979) as endangered, threatened, or of special concern. Earlier lists, such as that of Miller (1972), will prove interesting to some readers, and numerous state lists may add more information, although many of the latter have been prepared with different criteria for evaluating rareness. We venture an opinion on the abundance of other forms and hope we have been neither too optimistic nor too pessimistic. A rule of thumb is that darters are less common today than in preindustrial times. Some few species, however, have spread or been introduced into totally new ranges in recent years, and some may be saved from extirpation within the coming decade or so

by cautious application of the same technique of introduction.

A brief section on **Name** has been included, and in virtually all cases a translation or approximation of the Latin name of species and subspecies is presented. In reality most darters have no accepted common names among fishermen or others who only encounter them from time to time. Many common names, especially of more recently described species, are contrived to conform to the conventionality that every fish should have one. Many readers will, we hope, come to appreciate the orderliness and consistency of scientific nomenclature and how it speeds the learning process in the long run. If one had to deal with the Spanish and French names of many of the darters as well as the English names, the value of scientific nomenclature would be even more apparent.

A glossary of terms, line drawings, and illustrated keys to aid in identification precede the species accounts. The **Glossary** will prove helpful in understanding terms used throughout the text as well as those occurring in the key. **Line drawings** illustrate and name body parts of darters and show details not easily captured in the black-and-white photographs used to illustrate the key.

The **Key** first separates the 3 genera of darters. Species of *Percina, Ammocrypta,* and *Etheostoma* are then keyed under genus headings. The shortcoming of any key is that it cannot adequately account for the variability encountered within a species, yet a key is the best way to make a tentative identification. Many major museums or universities have experts who can provide positive identification when this is important.

Examination of the **References** will reveal that little of the older taxonomic literature has been cited. Most of this is listed in the more basic recent literature we have included. Collette and Knapp (1966) present the citations of species descriptions up to that date, and Bailey et al. (1970) and Robins et al. (1980) bring one almost to the present in that regard.

Photography. Considerable thought and experimentation went into development of the tools and techniques we used for photographing darters, and we are indebted to many friends and colleagues for suggestions. Branley Branson is due a special thanks for giving us the basic techniques for treating the fish.

In preparing a fish for photographing by this technique, it is taken directly from the net and dropped into a container of cold 40 percent formalin which has been diluted to roughly half strength by the addition of crushed ice. The combination of low temperature and strong formalin kills the fish almost instantly; it becomes stiff within a few minutes and usually the fins are expanded as the fish expires. In some species more than others, the back arches and/or the opercles balloon out, producing an unnatural configuration. It appears that the low temperature slows the fading of the colors, but even so, some colors, such as the electric blues of some species, fade rapidly. The photograph needs to be taken as quickly as possible, ideally within 5 minutes.

As soon as the specimen has hardened sufficiently to remain essentially straight, it is impaled (we chose to show the left side) on a pair of sharpened steel wires arising some 15 cm above the background, and is photographed.

Fish, lights, and background are all movable laterally as a

unit, and the camera is movable vertically. This mobility is attained by use of a homemade 3-piece stand which is readily portable and which operates as well off the tailgate of a vehicle at stream-side as in the laboratory. Our basic camera stand is simply the modified remains of a discarded enlarger; only the upright was retained. It was fitted to a larger baseboard, and an adjustable camera base was attached in lieu of the original lamphouse and associated gear.

A support for a pair of electronic flash heads was constructed, consisting of a wooden base supporting at the back corners a metal rack to which the flash units are adjustably attached in such a manner as to light the impaled fish from above at approximately a 45-degree angle from each end. This wooden base also supports the background and fish-supporting unit.

The development of this latter unit went through a number of stages, largely in an effort to obtain a consistently clean black background. Too much extraneous light, water droplets, loosened scales, or other miscellaneous debris on the background degrades the quality of the photograph. To keep the background as clean and dark as possible in the field under the time constraints of rapidly fading colors, we evolved a multi-sectioned unit that works quite well.

As a base, we used a 30 x 45 cm rectangle of fiberglass ceiling tile 1 1/4 cm thick. In use, a piece of black velvet is spread smoothly over this base to reduce reflections and to facilitate keeping the background clean. Two spring steel wires, some 16 cm long and sharpened at each end, are pushed through the velvet and into the fiberglass, which holds them erect; their upper ends are approximately 15 cm above the velvet background. The pins are then surrounded by a light wooden box about 20 x 30 cm x 15 cm high, with neither top nor bottom, and painted flat black.

Atop this boxlike structure is placed an unattached 25 x 35 cm cover made of .63 cm (1/4 inch) plywood, also painted flat black. A rectangular cutout in the ratio of 1:1.5 (the ratio of a 35 mm frame) is made in the center of the cover, of a size to comfortably accommodate the fish to be photographed. We carry three covers with cutouts of 76 x 104 mm, 104 x 156 mm, and 128 x 192 mm; the two smaller sizes are more frequently used. A pair of thin cleats fastened to the bottom of the cover and pushed against an outside corner of the frame serve to center the cutout.

For lighting we use a battery-powered flash unit with 2 heads which divide the power between them 60-40. In order to get extra light on the anterior end of the fish, we always position it with the head toward the brighter flash. It also seems desirable to put some of this extra light on the dorsum of the fish, so the cutouts in the covers are angled 15 degrees to the light, and we position our specimen centrally in the opening.

Positioning the specimen under the camera and obtaining the desired image size are quickly done. A minimum of experience taught us the approximately correct distance from lens to subject, and with the camera at this point we simply grasp the base or the light-supporting uprights and, while looking through the stationary camera, move the background, fish, and lights as a unit to the proper position beneath the camera; this entails only a few seconds.

To photograph all our fishes at approximately the same

size on the film, we inked in a black line near each end of the focusing screen and filled the space between the lines with the image of the fish. Any reasonably good camera can be used for such work, but a close-focusing lens, an appropriate supplementary lens, a bellows, or a set of extension tubes is necessary. A good close-focusing lens, working down to a ratio of 1:1, is ideal. Any battery-powered flash units will suffice, but the 2 need to be interconnected, either directly or by a slave unit.

Darter Collecting. Because of mounting environmental concerns of more than a decade, darters seldom are free for the taking. In the United States, federal regulations forbid taking endangered species except by special permission of the Office of Endangered Species. Virtually every state has its own rules governing the collection of fishes and may give special protection to species not on the federal endangered list. Government regulations in Canada and Mexico also require justification and permits from appropriate ministries for collection of fishes. Transportation of live material across national borders may entail additional permissions. These regulations may appear to be a hindrance, but they are designed to protect species that are reaching critically low numbers. While we may be able to control collecting of rare species with some degree of success, the insidious environmental changes ultimately responsible for reduction in numbers are much more difficult to control and pose a problem of far greater magnitude. Some of the difficulties faced in trying to save our vanishing fishes are addressed by Williams and Finnley (1977).

It should be possible to obtain permission to take common darters for legitimate teaching and research purposes. Serious aquarium hobbyists should also usually be successful in obtaining permission to take common species for special display or for permanent acclimation to aquariums. Such enthusiasts

will likely play an important role in developing darter strains that eventually may thrive and reproduce in aquariums.

The majority of specimens we obtained for this book were caught with small-meshed seines, often with the help of students or colleagues. The latter were particularly helpful in suggesting appropriate collecting sites, and in many cases saved us hours of fruitless searching. Even so, a number of darters were difficult to collect and some have been illustrated here only through the kindness of others more fortunate than we in obtaining specimens. Virtually all species reach optimum coloration between February and June, a wet period during which rainfall may ruin any chance of catching the fish. Much of our material was taken during spring breaks from the University of Kentucky or on short weekend jaunts at appropriate times. All too often weather factors prohibited collecting or reduced our effectiveness drastically. On the other hand, good luck played a role in our catching a number of darters, and persistence paid off in getting others. Certainly the pride an angler feels in landing a near-record-size fish is the same as what we experienced when catching a *Percina macrocephala* or an *Etheostoma kanawhae*.

The few hundred darters needed for adequate photographic material were supplemented in many cases by additional specimens used to determine the counts included in the descriptive sections of the species accounts. Material borrowed from various collections cited elsewhere proved invaluable for those species we failed to capture or took in paltry numbers.

The American Darters is a book about darters, not a treatise on them. What remains to be discovered about these fishes must dwarf the information reported here and elsewhere. We hope that this volume stimulates in all its readers an awareness and appreciation of darters, and ultimately causes some to learn and contribute to a better understanding of them.

As controversy swirls about the preservation of a few species of darters, we should remember that conservation of these creatures has practical aspects. Darters play an important role in many aquatic habitats in North America, despite their modest size. They serve as subtle indicators of water quality, much as the mine canary once served to verify pure air.

Beyond practical considerations, however, darters are an integral and unique part of American natural history. Their diversity and complex patterns of distribution chronicle the recent geological development of our river systems. Their physical beauty, marvelously adaptive behavior, and finely tuned physiological adjustments to many specialized environments will, we trust, be matters for wonder and investigation for generations to come.

Glossary

Abundant. May be captured with ease throughout all or a significant portion of its range.

Air bladder. A gas-filled sac lying just beneath the backbone, providing buoyancy.

Anterior. Toward the front or head.

Anus. The ventral opening of the intestine; vent.

Basicaudal. Lying at the base of the caudal fin.

Belly. The portion of the ventral surface between the insertion of the pelvic fins and the anus.

Benthic. Pertaining to or occurring at the bottom of a stream or lake.

Branchiostegal ray. Gill ray.

Breast. The ventral surface between the gill membranes and the point of insertion of the pelvic fins.

Breeding tubercles. Hard conical or pointed extensions found on the body, fins, or head before and during the reproductive season, usually in adult males.

Brook. A very small narrow stream, usually considered to be smaller than a creek.

Caudal peduncle. That portion of the body between the posterior end of the anal fin and the origin of the caudal fin.

Cheek. The lateral surface of the head from the anterior margin of the eye to the groove separating the preopercle from the opercle.

Chin. The ventral surface of the lower jaw.

Chute. A portion of a stream with a strong current, deeper and with steadier flow than a riffle.

Congener. A species of the same genus or subgenus.

Conical. Cone shaped; usually used in reference to the head.

Creek. A stream larger than a brook and smaller than a river, usually considered to be wadable.

Crenulate. Scalloped.

Ctenoid. Having a comblike margin or supplied with small teeth (ctenii).

Dorsal. Pertaining to the back; toward the back.

Dorsolateral. Pertaining to both the back and the side.

Dorsum. The back.

Embedded scale. A scale partly covered by skin or mucus, usually smaller and more difficult to see than an exposed scale.

Endangered. In danger of extinction throughout all or a significant portion of its range.

Endemic. Confined or restricted to a given area, such as a state or province, or a spring or river.

Fall Line. A line roughly marking the boundary between the harder rocks and rolling uplands of the interior and the softer rocks and flatlands of the coastal plain.

Family. A taxonomic category used to designate a group of closely related genera that share a number of traits.

Frenum. A fleshy bridge connecting the snout and the upper jaw.

Fusiform. Spindle shaped.

Generalized. Of a species, possessing the morphology or behavioral characteristics of the majority of its congeners.

Genital papilla. A small fleshy protuberance just behind the anus containing the opening of the reproductive tract. It enlarges during the breeding season.

Genus (plural, **genera**). A group of species, presumably of common phylogenetic origin, separable from similar groups on the basis of one or more shared traits.

Gill membrane. A delicate structure located at the ventral margin of an opercle affording added protection to gills. Gill membranes may be separate from each other, narrowly joined, or broadly joined by accessory tissue across the midline.

Gill ray. One of the thin bony supports found on each gill membrane; known also as a branchiostegal ray.

Gradient. The rate of descent of a stream, important in determining maximum velocity, turbulence, substrate characteristics, and other related stream conditions.

Gravid. Of a female, carrying eggs, particularly when visibly distended by them.

Head length. The distance in a straight line from the tip of the snout to the posterior edge of the opercle.

Humeral spot. A darkened area just behind the opercle. It is formed on an enlarged scale but may include additional scales to form a vertical bar.

Hybrid. The offspring of 2 species.

Inferior mouth. A mouth located on the ventral surface of the head.

Infraorbital canal. A branch of the lateral line system lying in an arc beneath the eye and supplied with surface pores. It is interrupted when the canal is undeveloped beneath the eye; it is uninterrupted when the canal is continuous beneath the eye. (See Fig. 2.)

Interorbital pore. A pore often appearing on the supraorbital canal, often one of a pair.

Juvenile. An immature individual, lacking some adult characteristics.

Keel. A sharp median ridge.

Lacustrine. Pertaining to or living in lakes.

Lateral line. The portion of the lateral line system lying along the side of the body. It is complete when all the scales (or all but the last 1 or 2) bear pores; it may be incomplete to varying degrees, or absent in some cases.

Lateral line system. A submerged sensory canal lying along the side of the body and branching on the head, communicating with the surface via pores. It is made up of the lateral line and the preoperculomandibular, supratemporal, supraorbital, and infraorbital canals.

Lateral scale series. The number of scale rows between the opercle and the caudal fin base, counted whether they are pored or unpored.

Median. Along the midline, either dorsal or ventral. Of a fin band, lying midway between base and margin.

Melanophore. A black pigment cell, observed as a dark spot, contributing to the basic pattern.

Meristic. Divided into a number of parts, such as fin spines or fin rays.

Morphology. The form and structure of an organism or of any of its parts.

Naked. Lacking scales.

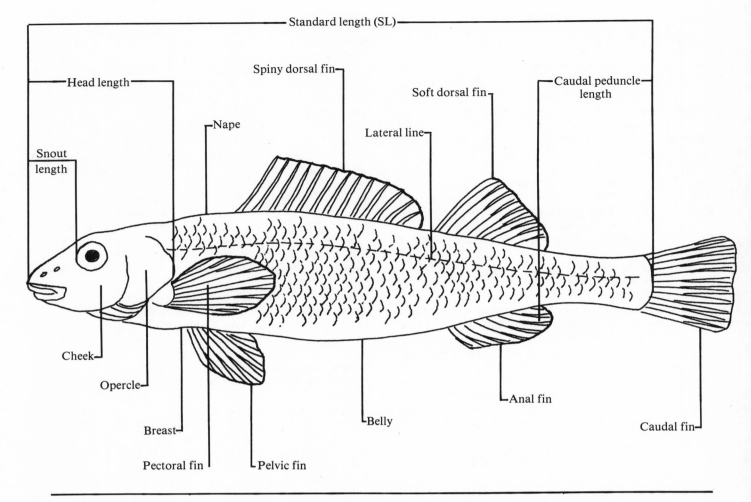

Fig. 1. Common external characteristics of darters

Nape. The area along the back from the head to the origin of the spiny dorsal fin.

Neoteny. Attainment of sexual maturity in an individual that retains juvenile or youthful traits.

Nomenclature. The system of names used in biological classification.

Nominate form. A subspecies entitled to carry the specific name, such as *Etheostoma maculatum maculatun,* or a subgenus entitled to carry the name of the genus, such as subgenus *Etheostoma* of genus *Etheostoma.*

Opercle. The structure covering the gills; known also as operculum.

Orbital. Pertaining to the eye.

Order. *See* stream order.

Origin. The anteriormost point of attachment or contact, as of a fin.

Papillose. Covered with papillae, which are fleshy nipple-like projections.

Phylogeny. The history of the development or evolution of a group of species.

Pleistocene. The most recently completed geological epoch, characterized by great climatic oscillations, particularly sequential advances and retreats of continental glaciers.

Posterior. Pertaining to the tail; toward the rear.

Premaxillary. The anterior most bone of each upper jaw.

Preopercle. A poorly defined area, here considered the posterior portion of the cheek.

Preoperculomandibular canal. A branch of the lateral line system extending downward along the margin of the preopercle and anteriorly onto the lower jaw.

Prepectoral area. The area immediately anterior to the insertion of the pectoral fin.

Range. The geographic region through which, or through portions of which, a species or subspecies is distributed.

Ray. A flexible segmented fin support, usually branched at the tip.

Reticulate. Resembling a network.

Riffle. A shallow turbulent area of a stream lying between quieter pools.

Rugose. With folds separated by deep grooves.

Saddle. A square to rectangular dark area on the back, sometimes extending onto the sides.

Scalation. The degree to which any part of the body is covered by scales; the pattern of scale distribution.

Serrate. Notched or toothed like a saw.

SL. Standard length.

Snout. That portion of the head anterior to the eye.

Spawning. The deposition of eggs and the behavior of both sexes during this act.

Special concern. A category for species that could become threatened or endangered by minor habitat disturbance or that require study to determine their status.

Species (plural, **species**). An interbreeding (or potentially interbreeding) natural population generally reproductively isolated from similar populations. Because of hybridization, no absolute definition suffices.

Spine. A stiff unsegmented and unbranched fin support.

Squamation. Scalation.

Squamous. Heavily scaled.

Standard length. The distance from the tip of the snout to the caudal fin base.

Stream. Any natural watercourse, regardless of size.

Stream capture. Any natural diversion of water from one stream basin to another.

Stream order. A stream unit determined by a classification which considers ultimate headwaters to be first order. The union of 2 first-order streams forms a second-order stream; order is subsequently increased only when streams of equal order fuse.

Striated. Marked by parallel streaks or lines.

Subgenus. An optional taxonomic category between genus and species used to indicate one or more species differing from congeners in having one of more unique traits.

Submarginal. Located just beneath the margin, as of a fin.

Subspecies. A taxonomically distinct aggregate of local populations occupying part of the total range of a species.

Substrate. The bottom of a stream or lake, ranging from soft sediment to solid bedrock.

Subterminal. Located near but not precisely at the end; as, a subterminal mouth, which does not lie at the tip of the snout.

Subtriangular. Approaching a triangular shape.

Supraorbital canal. A branch of the lateral line system lying in an arc above the eye and supplied with surface pores, including an interorbital pore.

Supratemporal canal. A branch of the lateral line system extending onto the dorsal surface of the head. It is interrupted when it fails to meet its counterpart; it is uninterrupted when it meets its counterpart. (See Fig. 3.)

Sympatric. Applying to 2 or more populations or species which occupy identical or overlapping geographic areas.

Taxonomy. The science of classification of organisms.

Terminal. At the edge or end. In reference to the mouth when jaws meet anteriorly, not overhung by the snout.

Threatened. Likely to become endangered in the foreseeable future in all or a significant portion of its range.

Type locality. The place of capture of the specimen designated as the type of a newly described species or subspecies.

Ventral. Pertaining to the lower surface of the body; toward the belly.

Vertebra. A segment of the backbone.

Vertebrate. Any animal with a backbone composed of bone or cartilage.

Villi. Small finger-like fleshy processes.

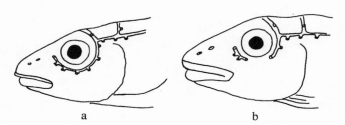

Fig. 2. Infraorbital canal; a: uninterrupted; b: interrupted

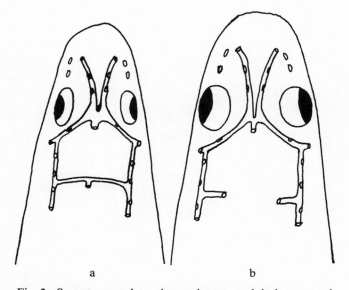

Fig. 3. Supratemporal canal; a: uninterrupted; b: interrupted

A Key to the
Darters

Genera

1a Body very slender, its maximum depth in the ratio of 1:7 or more to SL; body nearly covered with fine scales, or scales restricted to part of body; anal fin spine single; body rather translucent in life: *Ammocrypta*

1b Body deeper and less slender than above; body scaled, sometimes naked on belly; 1 or 2 anal fin spines; seldom very translucent (*E. vitreum* almost as slender and translucent as above, with 2 anal fin spines and fleshy villi surrounding anus)　　　　　　　　2

2a One or more large and heavily toothed scales between pelvic fins; belly usually partly naked in female, and usually with a row of enlarged toothed scales along midline in male; lateral line complete; 2 anal fin spines: *Percina*

2b No enlarged toothed scale between pelvic fins; belly midline usually with normal scales but sometimes naked; lateral line highly variable in number of pored scales; 2 (sometimes 1) anal fin spines: *Etheostoma*

Subgenera and Species of *Percina*
(Subgenera in parentheses)

1a Snout drawn to a point which extends well beyond inferior mouth (*Percina*)　　　28
1b Snout not drawn to a point which extends beyond mouth　　　　　　　　　　2

2a Gill membranes moderately, sometimes broadly, connected　　　　　　　3
2b Gill membranes separate or only slightly connected　　　　　　　　　10

3a Median caudal spot large, diffuse, and flanked above and/or below by fainter spots which may partly fuse with it (*Hadropterus*)　　　　　　　　　　4
3b Caudal fin base with a small median black spot; snout long and conical; spiny dorsal fin in adult males with a submarginal yellow or orange band (*Swainia*)　　　　7

4a Wavy, usually interrupted, dorsolateral band flanked by pale yellow or gold in most adults: *P. aurolineata*, page 27
4b No pronounced wavy dorsolateral band　　5

P1a

P2a　　　　　　　　P2b

P3a

P3b

P4a

P5a

P6b

P8a

P9a

P10a

5a Lateral line scales small, numbering 77-90; pectoral fin base freckled, or with densely packed pigment forming a dark spot: *P. lenticula,* page 28

5b Lateral line scales larger, numbering 46-77; pectoral fin not freckled and with no dark spot   6

6a Lateral blotches, particularly in male, forming vertical bands that extend far up on side: *P. nigrofasciata,* page 29

6b Lateral blotches, particularly in male, forming vertical bands that do not extend far up on side: *P. sciera,* page 30

7a Each gill membrane supported by 7 (rarely 6) rays; anterior lateral blotches vertically elongated, usually about twice as high as wide: *P. nasuta,* page 31

7b Each gill membrane supported by 6 (rarely 7) rays; anterior lateral blotches somewhat ovoid or partly fused into a lateral band   8

8a Lateral blotches tending to fuse into a horizontal band: *P. squamata,* page 34

8b Lateral blotches not tending to fuse into a horizontal band   9

9a Snout shorter, distance from front of eye to tip of snout equal to or less than distance from back of eye to posterior edge of opercle: *P. phoxocephala,* page 33

9b Snout longer, distance from front of eye to tip of snout greater than distance from back of eye to posterior edge of opercle: *P. oxyrhyncha,* page 32

10a Seven or more lateral blotches, most of which form vertical bands which fuse on back with counterparts *(Ericosma)*   11

10b Lateral markings variable in size and shape but not fusing on back with counterparts   12

11a Suborbital bar moderately developed; cheek, opercle, and breast in breeding male with orange or yellow [illustrated in 10a]: *P. evides,* page 43

11b Suborbital bar absent or scarcely developed; cheek, opercle, and breast in breeding male with green or blue: *P. palmaris,* page 44

12a A distinctive row of small black spots on upper side extending from head to soft dorsal fin (often continuing toward tail as a black line); lateral line scales small, numbering 84-95 *(Hypohomus): P. aurantiaca,* page 47

12b Upper side lacking distinctive row of black spots; lateral line with fewer than 84 scales 13

P12a

13a Scales on lower third of body with spines (ctenii) longer than elsewhere on body; prominent ventral caudal keel with long ctenii *(Odontopholis): P. cymatotaenia,* page 45

13b Scales on lower third of body without spines (ctenii) longer than elsewhere on body   14

P13a

14a Frenum present, broad and distinct *(Alvordius)*   15

14b Frenum absent, or present as a narrow bridge   23

15a Body slender, delicate; fins with little pigment; body markings mostly limited to a dark band from snout to opercle, where it joins about 8 partially fused lateral blotches: *P.* species, page 43

15b Body stocky to rather slender but not delicate; pigment variable but not as above   16

P15a

16a Pattern composed mostly of a series of oval spots on upper side, 9-11 larger oval lateral blotches, and a distinct caudal spot: *P. pantherina,* page 40

16b Body pattern not as above   17

17a Head long and rather pointed (approaching species of *Swainia*); upper jaw large; suborbital bar usually thin and faint: *P. macrocephala,* page 36

17b Head not so long and pointed; upper jaw smaller; suborbital bar moderately to well developed   18

P16a

P14a

P17a

P18a

P19a

P22a

P23b

P25a

18a Small but robust; breeding male with bright colors on body and fins: *P. roanoka,* page 42

18b Larger but less robust; breeding male without bright coloration   ▸   19

19a Several dorsal saddles interconnected by lateral extensions which isolate pale background as oval spots: *P. peltata,* page 41

19b Dorsal saddles not isolating pale background as oval spots   20

20a Lateral line scales usually 58 or more   21
20b Lateral line scales usually 57 or fewer   22

21a Cheek with some scales; opercle well scaled: *P. maculata,* page 37

21b Cheek usually scaled; opercle naked or with embedded scales: *P. gymnocephala,* page 36

22a Oval lateral blotches narrowly interconnected by a horizontal band: *P. notogramma,* page 39

22b Lateral blotches vertically elongated, confluent along lateral line: *P. crassa,* page 35

23a Anal fin not especially long; belly usually well scaled; adult male with a distinct row of enlarged midventral scales *(Cottogaster): P. copelandi,* page 48

23b Anal fin in adult male long, reaching closer to base of caudal fin than soft dorsal fin when both are pressed flat against body; much of belly naked in both sexes; enlarged belly scales rare to absent in adult male *(Imostoma)*   24

24a First dorsal saddle crossing nape just anterior to origin of spiny dorsal fin: *P. antesella,* page 49

24b When present, first dorsal saddle lying partly beneath spiny dorsal fin   25

25a Dorsal saddles weakly developed, partly obscured by dark pigment: *P. shumardi,* page 51

25b Dorsal saddles moderately to very distinct 26

26a Body slender, head rather small; pigmentation scattered, appearing rather pale: *P. ouachitae,* page 50

26b Body more robust, head larger; body darkly pigmented   27

27a Body very stocky; pectoral fin rather short (similar to next species): *P. tanasi,* page 53

27b Body stocky; pectoral fin not short: *P. uranidea,* page 54

28a Suborbital bar strikingly developed; vertically elongated lateral blotches seldom crossing back [illustrated in 1a]: *P. rex,* page 58

28b Suborbital bar weak or absent   29

29a Lateral blotches oval and partly fused into a lateral band: *P. burtoni,* page 54

29b Lateral blotches vertically elongated   30

30a Vertically elongated lateral bands usually dark, often expanded terminally; shorter bands often reaching below midline: *P. caprodes,* page 55

30b Vertically elongated lateral bands somewhat dusky, little if at all expanded terminally; shorter bands not extending below midline: *P. macrolepida,* page 57

P26a

P27b

P29a

P30a

P30b

A1a

A3a

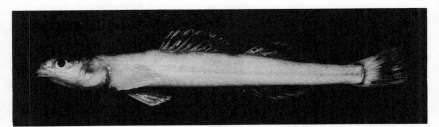

A3b

Subgenera and Species of *Ammocrypta*
(Subgenera in parentheses)

1a Four broad prominent dorsal saddles; frenum present; lateral line with 82-100 scales *(Crystallaria)*: *A. asprella,* page 59

1b No broad dorsal saddles; frenum usually absent; lateral line with 55-81 scales *(Ammocrypta)*   2

2a Side without dark blotches (sometimes with a thin dark lateral stripe)   3

2b Lateral blotches present   4

3a Spiny dorsal, soft dorsal, and anal fins in adult male with a median black band (not always simultaneously on all fins): *A. beani,* page 60

3b Spiny dorsal, soft dorsal, and anal fins in adult male with a black marginal and a black median band (not always simultaneously on all fins): *A. bifascia,* page 61

4a Small distinct opercular spine: *A. clara,* page 62

4b No opercular spine   5

5a Lateral blotches often vertically elongated; adult male usually with faint median and marginal dark bands in both dorsal fins: *A. vivax,* page 64

5b Lateral blotches oval or horizontally elongated; adult male lacking dark bands in dorsal fins   6

6a Usually 8-9 rows of scales beneath lateral line: *A. meridiana,* page 63

6b Usually 4-7 rows of scales beneath lateral line: *A. pellucida,* page 63

A4a

A5a

Subgenera and Species of *Etheostoma*

(Subgenera in parentheses)

Note: Unnamed snubnose darters are not included, nor are the recently named *E. baileyi, E. barrenense,* and *E. rafinesquei.*

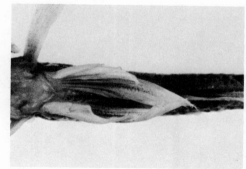

E1a

1a Male pelvic fins long, pointed, and forming a cup-shaped structure; lateral line incomplete with 0-9 pored scales; size less than 39 mm SL *(Microperca)*   92

1b Male pelvic fins not forming a cup-shaped structure (approaching this in *E. collis, E. saludae*); usually more than 9 pored scales in lateral series; adults usually exceeding 38 mm SL   2

2a Lateral line incomplete and arched anteriorly; shortest distance between lateral line and dorsal outline in the ratio of 1:4.5 or more to body depth *(Hololepis)*   87

2b Lateral line complete or incomplete, and straight or less arched (in a ratio of less than 1:4.5 to body depth)   3

E2a

3a Spines of first dorsal fin short and rather uniform in length, giving fin a low flattened silhouette; a combination of supratemporal canal interrupted, caudal peduncle rather deep, and pelvic fins rather closely set *(Catonotus)*   78

3b Spines of first dorsal fin of different lengths, giving a higher, more arched silhouette; supratemporal canal interrupted or uninterrupted, caudal peduncle deep or constricted, pelvic fins closely or widely set, but not in combination given above   4

4a Cheek, opercle, breast, gill membranes, nape, and dorsolateral portions of head scaled; anal spine single; lateral line incomplete *(Psychromaster)*: *E. tuscumbia,* page 69

4b Never with the above combination of traits   5

E4a

5a Head and snout long and conical, as in many *Percina;* anal fin rays usually 10-11; breeding male with conical tubercles on belly *(Litocara)*   6

5b Head and snout of various shapes but not as above; anal fin rays usually fewer than 10; belly tubercles, if present, not conical   7

6a Lateral line nearly complete, with 72-82 scales: *E. nianguae,* page 70

6b Lateral line nearly complete, with 52-69 scales [illustrated in 5a]: *E. sagitta,* page 71

E5a

E7a

E8a

E8b

E9a

E13a

7a Snout long, sloping downward from eye; lips heavy, mouth terminal; body usually with diagonal bands and 1 or more horizontal dorsolateral stripes; soft dorsal fin in adult male exceptionally elongated *(Allohistium)*: *E. cinereum,* page 72

7b Without the above combination of traits   8

8a Anal spine or spines thin, when both present the first scarcely thicker than the second, although first spine in mature male may have extra coating of opaque tissue *(Vaillantia, Doration, Ioa, Boleosoma)*   9

8b First anal spine thicker than second (second spine typically missing in *E. australe,* usually missing in *E. trisella)*   18

9a Lateral line incomplete, pored scales rarely reaching midpoint of soft dorsal fin *(Vaillantia)*   10

9b If lateral line incomplete, pored scales extending beyond midpoint of soft dorsal fin   11

10a Mature male with breeding tubercles on anal and pelvic fins [illustrated in 9a]: *E. chlorosomum,* page 108

10b Mature male apparently without breeding tubercles (similar to above species): *E. davisoni,* page 109

11a Lateral line incomplete, pores absent on last 5-10 scales *(Doration)*   12

11b Lateral line complete or pores absent only on last 1-3 scales   13

12a Lateral line usually with 53-62 scales; snout somewhat pointed; mouth rather large; frenum usually present: *E. jessiae,* page 100

12b Lateral line usually with 40-53 scales; snout rather rounded; frenum quite narrow or absent: *E. stigmaeum,* page 101

13a Anus encircled by fleshy villi *(Ioa)*: *E. vitreum,* page 107

13b Anus not encircled by fleshy villi *(Boleosoma)*   14

14a Lateral line scales 58-66; 2 anal fin spines: *E. perlongum,* page 105

14b Lateral line scales usually fewer than 58 (if more, usually with only 1 anal spine)   15

15a Usually 1 anal fin spine; breeding male without bright colors   16

15b Usually 2 anal fin spines; breeding male with some bright colors   17

16a Infraorbital canal usually interrupted; usually fewer than 9 lateral marks, often resembling letters X, V, or W (similar to next species but usually more slender): *E. nigrum,* page 102

16b Infraorbital canal usually uninterrupted; 9-11 lateral marks often resembling letters X, V, or W: *E. olmstedi,* page 104

17a Lateral line scales usually 36-39; suborbital bar moderately developed; soft dorsal fin in adult male somewhat elongated: *E. podostemone,* page 106

17b Lateral line scales usually 40-46; suborbital bar weak to absent; soft dorsal fin in adult male greatly elongated: *E. longimanum,* page 102

18a Gill membranes broadly connected (narrowly connected in *E. sellare,* with 4 prominent saddles) *(Etheostoma, Ulocentra)* 19

18b Gill membranes moderately connected, slightly connected, or separate 38

19a Each gill membrane typically supported by 6 rays (usually 5 in *E. zonale*); pectoral fin very expansive; snout rather blunt (very blunt in *E. blennioides*); frenum usually present *(Etheostoma)* 20

19b Each gill membrane typically supported by 5 rays (6 in *E. coosae*); pectoral fin usually expansive; snout blunt, usually overhanging mouth; frenum present or absent *(Ulocentra)* 33

20a Gill membranes slightly connected; cheek fully scaled: *E. sellare,* page 82

20b Gill membranes broadly connected; cheek naked or with few exposed scales 21

21a Back with 4 prominent saddles, 2 or more of which extend to or beneath lateral line 22

21b Back with more than 4 saddles or squarish blotches, not extending to lateral line 25

22a Side with several vertical bands, the posterior 3 meeting or almost meeting counterparts on ventral midline 23

22b Side with lateral blotches usually confluent with some dorsal saddles but not extending near ventral midline 24

23a Breast and opercle rather heavily scaled; saddles contrasting sharply with dorsum (similar to next species) [illustrated in 21a]: *E. tetrazonum,* page 84

23b Breast and opercle moderately scaled; saddles often not contrasting sharply with dorsum: *E. variatum,* page 86

E18a

E18b

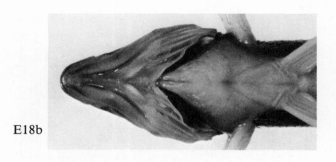

E19a

E20a

E21a

E24b

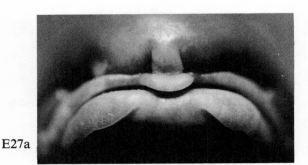

E27a

E28a

E30a

24a Snout blunt, anterior profile almost vertical: *E. blennius,* page 75
24b Snout rather pointed, sloping gradually to tip: *E. euzonum,* page 76

25a Dorsum with 5-6 saddles, usually smaller and less distinct than in species with 4 saddles   26
25b Dorsum with 5-9 small squarish saddles or blotches   27

26a Dorsum usually with 6 saddles; lateral line with 48-57 scales: *E. kanawhae,* page 79
26b Dorsum usually with 5 saddles; lateral line with 59-70 scales: *E. osburni,* page 80

27a Snout rounded, overhanging mouth, and usually with a terminal nipple (lacking in subspecies *gutselli*); adults large, often reaching 100 mm SL: *E. blennioides,* page 72
27b Snout less rounded and lacking terminal nipple; adults not reaching 100 mm SL   28

28a Side with 9-11 (6-13) rather uniformly spaced vertical bands which almost meet counterparts ventrally in male but are shorter and terminally pointed in female; each gill membrane typically supported by 5 rays: *E. zonale,* page 87
28b Side with pattern other than uniform vertical bands; each gill membrane typically supported by 6 rays   29

29a Cheek naked or with few scales; opercle with few to many scales   30
29b Cheek and opercle usually naked   31

30a Dark spots on cheek, opercle, prepectoral area, and often other parts of body and fins: *E. histrio,* page 77
30b Head, body, and fins without small dark spots: *E. rupestre,* page 81

E29a

31a Dorsal blotches 7, rarely 6; last 3-4 lateral blotches forming weak vertical bands: *E. thalassinum,* page 85

31b Dorsal blotches 6, rarely 5; last 3-4 lateral blotches not forming distinct vertical bands   32

32a Lateral line usually with 44-52 scales; fins tending to be spotted; adult coloration predominantly green: *E. inscriptum,* page 78

32b Lateral line usually with 48-58 scales; fins tending to be streaked with pigment along rays; adult coloration predominantly reddish brown: *E. swannanoa,* page 83

33a Frenum present, usually narrow but distinct   34

33b Frenum absent, snout separated from lip by deep groove   36

34a Two dorsal saddles anterior to origin of spiny dorsal fin: *E. atripinne,* page 89

34b One dorsal saddle entirely anterior to origin of spiny dorsal fin, a second often lying partially beneath fin   35

35a Breast usually with scales on posterior half; several interrupted horizontal stripes above lateral line: (in part) *E. etnieri,* page 93

35b Breast usually lacking scales on posterior half; lacking interrupted horizontal stripes above lateral line: *E. simoterum,* page 95

36a Six rays supporting each gill membrane; spiny dorsal fin in breeding male crossed by red band: *E. coosae,* page 92

36b Five rays supporting each gill membrane; breeding male with red spot near origin of spiny dorsal fin   37

37a Breast usually with scales on posterior half; several interrupted horizontal stripes above lateral line: (in part) *E. etnieri,* page 93

37b Breast usually lacking scales on posterior half; lacking interrupted horizontal stripes above lateral line: *E. duryi,* page 92

38a Caudal peduncle deep, laterally compressed, giving body a stout appearance *(Nothonotus)*   39

38b Caudal peduncle not deep nor very compressed, giving body a more slender appearance   53

39a Dorsum with 3-4 saddles, the first a broad yoke: *E. juliae,* page 115

39b Dorsum with neither distinct saddles nor broad yoke   40

40a Lateral line incomplete, pored scales ending beneath soft dorsal fin: *E. tippecanoe,* page 122

40b Lateral line complete or lacking fewer than 5 pored scales terminally   41

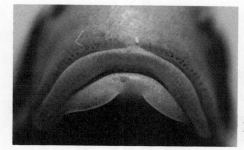

E33a

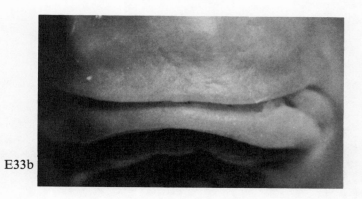

E33b

♀

♂

E38a

E42b

E46b

41a Dark horizontal stripes absent from side; breeding male with submarginal red band in spiny dorsal fin: *E. jordani,* page 114
41b Dark horizontal stripes on at least posterior part of body; breeding male with no submarginal red band in spiny dorsal fin, or with an interrupted band   42

42a Soft dorsal, caudal, and anal fins in male lacking a marginal or slightly submarginal dark band   43
42b Soft dorsal, caudal, and anal fins in male with a marginal or slightly submarginal dark band   46

43a Snout extremely pointed; opercle naked: *E. acuticeps,* page 109
43b Snout pointed; opercle with some scales   44

44a Wavy lines on cheek, best seen in male, and copper colored in life: *E. aquali,* page 110
44b No wavy lines on cheek   45

45a Snout rather pointed; fins in breeding male infused mostly with blue or green: *E. maculatum maculatum,* page 116
45b Snout somewhat less pointed; fins in breeding male infused mostly with red or orange: *E. maculatum sanguifluum,* page 116

46a Dark horizontal stripes developed on posterior third of body, not extending much anterior to origin of soft dorsal fin   47
46b Dark horizontal stripes developed on posterior half to two-thirds of body, extending anterior to origin of soft dorsal fin   50

47a Red spots on side surrounded by dark circles; belly fully scaled or almost so   48
47b Red spots on side not surrounded by dark circles; belly naked anteriorly   49

48a Lateral line usually with 55-61 scales; spiny dorsal, soft dorsal, and caudal fins in mature male with yellow or orange submarginal band; no broad green bands in above fins: *E. maculatum vulneratum,* page 116
48b Lateral line usually with 58-68 scales; spiny dorsal, soft dorsal, and caudal fins in mature male dominated by broad green bands: *E. microlepidum,* page 117

49a Up to 3 scales on cheek behind eye: *E. moorei,* page 118
49b Usually 6-9 scales on cheek behind eye: *E. rubrum,* page 119

50a Several dark marks on cheek and opercle contrasting with pale yellowish background: *E. rufilineatum,* page 121
50b No dark marks on cheek and opercle, which do not appear yellowish   51

51a Suborbital bar well developed: *E. bellum,* page 111

51b Suborbital bar absent or very faint   52

52a Lateral line usually with 53-59 scales (mean near 56); spiny dorsal, soft dorsal, caudal, and anal fins in breeding male with dull red or orange predominating: *E. camurum,* page 112

52b Lateral line usually with 56-66 scales (mean near 61); spiny dorsal, soft dorsal, caudal, and anal fins in breeding male with a green band; spiny dorsal fin sometimes with interrupted red band: *E. chlorobranchium,* page 113

53a Anterior part of lateral line slightly arched upward, the least distance between it and base of spiny dorsal fin in the ratio of 1:4.5 (or a little less) to body depth at that point *(Villora)*   54

53b Anterior portion of lateral line straight or somewhat arched upward, the least distance between it and base of spiny dorsal fin in the ratio of 1:4.0 or less to body depth at that point (sometimes about 1:4.5 in *E. exile*)   55

54a Lateral line with 0-4 unpored scales posteriorly: *E. okaloosae,* page 124

54b Lateral line usually with 7-15 unpored scales posteriorly [illustrated in 53b]: *E. edwini,* page 123

55a Anal fin with single thick spine *(Austroperca)*: *E. australe,* page 129

55b Anal fin with 2 spines, or rarely 1 spine   56

56a Upper half of body rather uniformly dark, lower half much lighter but rather blotchy and stippled; broad dark suborbital bar; breeding male with reddish orange horizontal band on lower side (poorly developed in *E. trisella* and often developed in *E. exile,* not in this subgenus) *(Ozarka)*   57

56b Body and head not pigmented as above; suborbital bar seldom broad and dark; reddish horizontal band on side rarely present *(Oligocephalus)*   61

57a Anal spine usually single; lateral line usually complete: *E. trisella,* page 128

57b Two anal spines; lateral line incomplete   58

58a Lateral line usually with 30 or more pored scales   59

58b Lateral line usually with fewer than 30 pored scales   60

59a Suborbital bar narrower than eye; body deeply rounded: *E. punctulatum,* page 127

59b Suborbital bar wider than eye; body not deeply rounded: *E. boschungi,* page 125

E53b

E56a

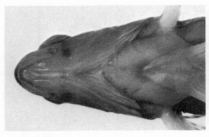

E61a

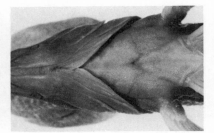

E61b

E77b

E80a

E86a

E87a

60a Basicaudal spots well developed, sometimes fused; cheek and prepectoral area naked: *E. pallididorsum,* page 126

60b Basicaudal spots weakly developed; cheek and prepectoral area with few embedded scales: *E. cragini,* page 125

61a Gill membranes moderately (occasionally slightly) joined, margin of connecting tissue concave   62

61b Gill membranes slightly connected to separate, margin of connecting tissue meeting at sharp angle   65

62a Lower cheek, opercle, and breast with several dark spots or dashes: *E. mariae,* page 139

62b Lower cheek, opercle, and breast without dark spots and dashes   63

63a Lateral line scales pale, producing effect of thin yellow stripe in life, contrasting with darker side: *E. parvipinne,* page 140

63b Lateral line scales not so pale as to produce the above effect, though pale stripe may be weakly developed   64

64a Usually last 1-4 lateral line scales unpored; gill membranes usually moderately connected: *E. fricksium,* page 134

64b Usually last 7-8 lateral line scales unpored; gill membranes often slightly connected: *E. hopkinsi,* page 136

65a Lateral line with slight upward arch beneath origin of spiny dorsal fin   66

65b Lateral line without upward arch beneath spiny dorsal fin   67

66a Indistinct basicaudal dark spot sometimes flanked beneath by a weak spot: *E. exile,* page 133

66b Small distinct basicaudal dark spot flanked above and below by a spot of almost equal intensity: *E. ditrema,* page 132

67a Both supratemporal canal and infraorbital canal usually interrupted   68

67b Supratemporal canal uninterrupted; infraorbital canal interrupted or uninterrupted   71

68a Opercle without scales (weakly scaled in some *E. lepidum*)   69

68b Opercle scaled   70

69a Usually more than 48 lateral line scales; margin of spiny dorsal fin in breeding male blue to green: *E. lepidum,* page 137

69b Usually fewer than 48 lateral line scales; margin of spiny dorsal fin in breeding male not blue or green: *E. pottsi,* page 141

70a Lateral line usually with 35-42 scales: *E. nuchale,* page 140
70b Lateral line usually with 44-58 scales: *E. grahami,* page 135

71a Infraorbital canal usually interrupted 72
71b Infraorbital canal usually uninterrupted 73

72a Usually 8 or more dorsal blotches; suborbital bar rather weak; breeding male with orange on gill membranes: *E. spectabile,* page 143
72b Usually 6-7 dorsal blotches; suborbital bar rather distinct; breeding male with blue or green on gill membranes or breast: *E. luteovinctum,* page 138

73a Cheek in male well covered with exposed scales; cheek in female sparsely covered with scales, exposed or partly embedded 74
73b Cheek in male occasionally naked but usually with some exposed scales near eye and embedded scales elsewhere; cheek in female naked or with few scales, exposed or embedded 75

74a Humeral spot small and distinct; spiny dorsal fin in breeding male with a wide reddish orange band: *E. collettei,* page 132
74b Humeral spot faint to absent; spiny dorsal fin in breeding male with a narrow reddish orange band: *E. asprigene,* page 130

75a Side, especially in male, with narrow dark vertical bands, those on caudal peduncle meeting or almost meeting counterparts, thus encircling body: *E. caeruleum,* page 131
75b Side variously marked, sometimes with weak vertical bands which do not encircle caudal peduncle 76

76a Suborbital bar prominent; breeding male with prominent red spots on body: *E. whipplei,* page 145
76b Suborbital bar weak to absent; breeding male with no prominent red spots on body 77

77a Side with series of tiny blotches, often forming weak vertical bands on caudal peduncle: *E. radiosum,* page 142
77b Side with small dark spots tending to form horizontal stripes: *E. swaini,* page 145

78a A large iridescent patch on cheek; breeding male colorful 79
78b No iridescent cheek patch; breeding male without bright colors 83

79a Body with distinct horizontal bands 80
79b Body lacking distinct horizontal bands 81

80a Horizontal bands formed by pigment concentrated along midline of scales involved: *E. virgatum,* page 155
80b Horizontal bands formed by pigment both along midline and on outer margin of scales involved; bands resembling a series of a dots: *E. striatulum,* page 154

81a Suborbital bar distinct: *E. barbouri,* page 146
81b Suborbital bar absent or indistinct 82

82a Lateral line usually with more than 13 pored scales; last few lateral blotches not tending to form vertical bands: *E. obeyense,* page 151
82b Lateral line with 13 or fewer pored scales; last few lateral blotches tending to form vertical bands: *E. smithi,* page 152

83a Tips of dorsal fin spines knobbed in breeding male (and in female in *E. kennicotti*) 84
83b Tips of dorsal fin spines not knobbed; in breeding male tips of dorsal fin spine usually with posteriorly directed extensions 85

84a Lower jaw jutting slightly beyond upper jaw; spiny dorsal fin in adult male with strong dark basal band, marginal band weak or absent: *E. flabellare,* page 147
84b Lower jaw not jutting beyond upper jaw; spiny dorsal fin in adult male with strong dark marginal to submarginal band: *E. kennicotti,* page 149

85a Three vertically arranged dark basicaudal spots (obscure in some adults): *E. squamiceps,* page 153
85b Sometimes a single faint basicaudal spot but never 3 vertically arranged spots 86

86a Soft dorsal fin rays in breeding male terminally knobbed and protruding far beyond margin of fin membranes: *E. neopterum,* page 150
86b Soft dorsal fin rays in breeding male not knobbed, not protruding beyond margin of membranes: *E. olivaceum,* page 151

87a Margin of preopercle finely serrate: *E. serriferum,* page 160
87b Margin of preopercle not serrate 88

E89a

E90a

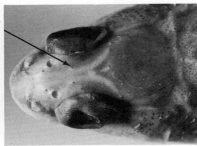

E91a

88a Infraorbital canal interrupted: *E. gracile,* page 158

88b Infraorbital canal uninterrupted   89

89a Ten preoperculomandibular pores; much like *E. gracile*: *E. zoniferum,* page 160

89b Nine preoperculomandibular pores   90

90a Breast fully scaled; interorbital pores absent: *E. fusiforme,* page 157

90b Breast variably naked to about 80% scaled; interorbital pores absent, single, or paired   91

91a Interorbital pore or pores present; 1 or 2 anal fin spines: *E. saludae,* page 159

91b Interorbital pores usually absent: 1 anal fin spine: *E. collis,* page 156

92a Cheek scaled: *E. proeliare,* page 163

92b Cheek naked   93

93a Anal spine almost always 1: *E. fonticola,* page 161

93b Almost always 2 anal spines: *E. microperca,* page 162

Percina
and Its Subgenera

Percina is the most generalized of the 3 darter genera. It comprises 31 species plus several forms perhaps worthy of specific recognition. *Percina* is easily separated from *Ammocrypta,* whose members are much more slender, finely scaled, and translucent. Some species of *Percina* and *Etheostoma* share traits, however; they are best separated by the fact that males of *Percina* have a single row of modified scales between the breast and anus, or are unscaled along the ventral midline (Page, 1976a). In some *Etheostoma* the anterior portion of the belly is naked but the remainder is fully scaled.

Additional characteristics of *Percina* include: Adult size moderate to large, 45-169 mm SL. Body moderately slender to robust, often fusiform. Lateral line complete, almost straight, with 49-90 pored scales, one or more of which may extend onto the caudal fin. Males of many species and females of some with enlarged toothed scales between the pelvic fins, on the center of the breast, and occasionally elsewhere on the breast. Top of the head flat or very little arched. Head usually somewhat conical, or quite so. Premaxillary frenum present (usually absent in *P. copelandi*). Mouth moderate to large, horizontal to slightly oblique, usually terminal but sometimes subterminal due to elongated snout. Gill membranes usually separate, sometimes moderately connected. Supratemporal and infraorbital canals complete. Two anal spines. Anal fin often expansive. Breeding tubercles in males of some species. Body and/or fins of males brightly colored in some species. Subdued colors in fins or on body of females in a few species. Air bladder usually reduced, occasionally well developed.

The majority of *Percina* are river darters which prefer moderate current and sand, gravel, or bedrock substrate. Most species enter the deeper portions of riffles and a few enter the shallow turbulent areas favored by so many *Etheostoma*. A few species are closely associated with aquatic plants or are at least most abundant within and adjacent to vegetation. We have often encountered *P. caprodes, P. maculata,* and *P. nigrofasciata* in streams as small as third order, but fourth- or fifth-order streams are the smallest entered by most *Percina*.

The geographic range of *Percina* is intermediate between those of *Ammocrypta* and *Etheostoma*. The enormous north-south extent is accounted for by the subgenus *Percina,* and most of that by the single form *P. caprodes. P. macrolepida* barely enters Mexico, whereas 2 species of *Etheostoma* occur far to the west in that country. A few *Etheostoma* but no *Percina* extend across the Great Plains, down the length of the Florida peninsula, and into New England. *P. caprodes* may extend farther down the St. Lawrence than either *Etheostoma* or *Ammocrypta,* but darters occur sporadically in that area. *Percina* is well represented in Atlantic drainages by 7 species.

Observations on a number of species in *Percina* indicate that probably all members display generalized spawning behavior. Territoriality and male combat are weakly if at all developed, except perhaps for intimidation of small males by large ones. The precise role of male coloration needs clarification for those few *Percina* in which it develops. Males seem to gather at favorable spawning sites to follow any gravid female entering the area. As a female burrows into the substrate to lay a number of eggs, she is mounted by an attendant male who bends the posterior end of the body around to fertilize the eggs. Females usually spawn several times, presumably with various males. We may surmise that the enlarged modified scales of male *Percina,* generally best developed in breeding specimens, stimulate the female to release eggs or give the male a more secure grip, but their exact function needs elucidation.

Early taxonomists treated the darters as a large assemblage of genera, distinguished by one or a few traits. Inadequate numbers of specimens sometimes led to errors in interpretation. What we now consider to be the genera *Percina* and *Etheostoma* resembled a graded series, intermediate ones of which might contain species of either genus. Bailey and Gosline (1955), relying heavily on the presence of modified belly scales, simplified the picture by placing all species with that trait in *Percina,* with 8 subgenera to reflect internal relationships. Several of these subgenera were adequately characterized only much later by Page (1974a). He added the subgenus *Odontopholis,* switched subgeneric positions of 2 species, and employed both numerical taxonomy and electrophoretic evidence to arrange the subgenera phylogenetically. We follow this classification, which has gained wide acceptance.

Hadropterus and *Swaina* are the most primitive subgenera. Both possess moderately well connected gill membranes and a nearly complete row of enlarged midventral scales. Breeding tubercles are absent, and body and fins lack bright colors (somewhat developed in *P. phoxocephala*). Members of *Hadropterus* are rather blunt snouted and bear 3 vertically arranged spots at the base of the caudal fin. The 2 ventral spots may be partly fused. Members of *Swaina* have a single caudal spot and elongated conical snouts.

Three species of *Hadropterus* occur in Gulf Coast rivers east of the Mississippi. Two of these are quite rare, *P. aurolineata* and *P. lenticula,* the largest and perhaps most primitive of all darters. *P. nigrofasciata* is widespread and abundant along the Gulf and southern Atlantic coasts. The only species to extend beyond these confines is *P. sciera,* which is locally common in much of the Ohio basin, the lower Mississippi system, and western Gulf Coast rivers.

Members of *Swaina* are confined to the Mississippi River basin. *P. phoxocephala,* a species living in streams with moderate gradient, is widespread; the other species are found on the edge of its range in streams of higher gradient. *P. nasuta* is the Ozark representative, and *P. squamata* is that of the upper Cumberland and Tennessee basins. *P. oxyrhyncha* is confined to upland tributaries of the Ohio River from the Kentucky River upstream; its range encompasses principally the headwater tributaries of the ancient Teays River, a preglacial trunk stream largely replaced by the modern Ohio.

Alvordius is a loosely knit subgenus whose members

remain generalized in that they lack breeding tubercles or bright coloration (except *P. roanoka*). But the large midventral scales of males are few and breast scales are absent, reduced to a central scale, or are small and partly embedded. Breast scales usually are absent in females, which also lack scales on the anterior part of the belly. *Alvordius* lacks highly specialized features.

In the Mississippi River basin, *P. maculata* is the widespread and abundant species in *Alvordius,* extending also into the St. Lawrence system and Arctic drainages just north of Minnesota. The Ozark representative, *P. pantherina,* is both rare and quite localized, as is an unnamed representative of the upper Mobile basin. *P. macrocephala* also is rare but was once widely distributed in the Ohio basin. *P. gymnocephala* is a common species in the upper Kanawha River (ultimate headwaters of the preglacial Teays River), where it replaces *P. maculata.*

Four additional *Alvordius* dwell in the montane and Piedmont sections of Atlantic Coast rivers, seldom occurring below the Fall Line. They are a successful and rather closely related assemblage. *P. peltata* is the most widespread but *P. roanoka* is easily the most abundant. The latter is the most advanced *Alvordius*—small, colorful, and invasive of shallow riffles of small streams as well as those of large rivers. *P. crassa* is quite similar to *P. roanoka,* while *P. notogramma* more closely resembles *P. maculata.*

Ericosma contains 2 species, *P. evides* and *P. palmaris,* separable from all other *Percina* by the presence of broad vertical bands on each side which fuse with their counterparts on the back. Like *Alvordius,* these species are generalized in regard to scalation but develop breeding tubercles as well as handsome coloration. *P. evides* is a species of the Ohio basin, northern Ozarks, and upper Missisippi basin. *P. palmaris* is restricted to the northeast uplands of the Mobile River system. Neither is officially considered to be rare, but *P. evides* occurs spottily, *P. palmaris* is very restricted, and neither is more than locally common.

Odontopholis consists of *P. cymatotaenia* in Missouri and an eastern representative in Kentucky and Tennessee which we refer to this species. Primitive traits are the absence of breeding tubercles or bright coloration, high vertebral counts, and heavy scalation on the head. But special traits, some extreme, also typify *Odontopholis.* The belly in females is fully scaled. Large males have a slightly elevated ridge along the belly but only the interpelvic scale and sometimes the first few scales posterior to it are toothed and enlarged. Scales on the ventral third of the body in both sexes are unusually spiny. Both sexes possess a ventral caudal keel, which in mature males becomes almost semicircular and bears protruding spines on each scale. The exact function of this structure has not been clarified. Aquarium-held specimens caught in Kentucky swim leisurely through open water, indicating that the air bladder is functional.

P. cymatotaenia from Kentucky are most easily taken where aquatic vegetation grows at the margin or foot of a riffle. Sticks, leaves, and other debris in quiet water also seem to afford habitat to this species.

Hypohomus is primitive in its large size, many vertebrae, and numerous lateral line scales. Belly scalation is similar to that in *Odontopholis,* except that prominent, toothed scales are absent from the ventral third of the body. A ventral caudal keel is very weakly developed. Breeding tubercles and bright coloration are present in males. *P. aurantiaca* survives in deep portions of riffles and turbulent pools and is the most highly adapted *Percina* for such austere habitats.

Cottogaster contains widely disjunct populations referred to *P. copelandi.* One or more of these may deserve specific status. Lack of breeding colors and the presence of modified belly scales are generalized traits. But breeding tubercles are present, a frenum is usually absent, size is small, the number of spines and rays in the fins is reduced, and lateral line scales are few. In general appearance no other *Percina* is so similar to *Etheostoma.*

Imostoma is a subgenus distinguishable from other *Percina* by an extreme elongation of the anal fin in males. The only primitive trait of *Imostoma* is the absence of bright coloration. Breeding tubercles, lack of midventral scales, and absence or reduction of the frenum are advanced traits. Closely set eyes are a specialized trait whose significance has not been established. *P. shumardi* best displays the preference of *Imostoma* for big rivers; it occurs in major streams directly tributary to the Ohio and Mississippi rivers and even enters southern Canada. *P. ouachitae* lives in the southern Mississippi basin, often entering much smaller streams than do other species of *Imostoma. P. uranidea* and *P. tanasi* are the upland forms found in the Ozarks and Tennessee basin. The latter 2 species are listed by Deacon et al. (1979) as threatened. The other 3 members are faring better but are common only locally. Based on evidence from *P. tanasi, Imostoma* may display downstream and upstream migrations of young which are very specialized. Snails constitute a surprisingly large part of the diet in *P. tanasi,* and other *Imostoma* may be equally specialized.

Species in subgenus *Percina* are easily recognized by the pointed snout which protrudes noticeably beyond the mouth. Most other traits of this subgenus are generalized. A brief characterization is: large size, exceeding 100 mm SL; high numbers of lateral line scales, fin spines, fin rays, and vertebrae; gill membranes separate to slightly connected; midventral belly scales in males enlarged (missing in some individuals); midline of belly naked in females; upper side with narrow vertical bands, separate from or connected with broader vertical bands or prominent blotches on the side; usually a distinct spot at the caudal fin base; male breeding tubercles confined to ventral scales; and bright breeding colors absent but an orange or red band in the spiny dorsal fin of males of some species.

P. caprodes is the most widely distributed of all darters and occupies the heart of the collective ranges of its subgeneric relatives. Should additional species be recognized in the subgenus, it will be because they are elevated from the status of mere variants or subspecies of *P. caprodes.* The ultimate validity of species within the *caprodes* complex awaits testing by experimental approaches, traditional taxonomy having gone as far as it can at present. Remaining species within the subgenus form a familiar fringing pattern. *P. rex* is extremely localized in the upper Roanoke River, and *P. burtoni* is almost equally restricted in the upper Tennessee River system (once recorded from the Cumberland basin). The rarity of these 2 species is recognized by Deacon et al. (1979). *P. macrolepida* is fairly common and widespread along the western Gulf Coast. The Mobile River system contains 1 or more members of the subgenus *Percina* whose taxonomy requires attention.

In summary, the genus *Percina* is almost certainly a single phyletic group, and the subgenera are a satisfactory means of treating related species within the genus. The arrangement of the subgenera in a sequence from primitive to advanced is arbitrary in some regards, and unanimity of opinion may never be achieved. Most subgenera comprise 1 or 2 abundant and widespread species at the center of the subgeneric range and additional species, restricted and sometimes rare, along the margins of this range. Species pairs in the upland streams east and west of the middle Mississippi basin occur in several subgenera, as do pairs found in the Tennessee and Mobile basins. Ross (1971) discusses the ancient stream capture that diverted the upper Tennessee, once a component of the Mobile basin, into its present association with the ascending arm of the Tennessee. We suggest that smaller piracies and drainage realignments following that major change may be equally important in understanding present similarities and differences between the basins.

Since the settlement of North America, its major rivers have shifted from being the most stable of aquatic habitats to the most perturbed. Irrigation, navigation, damming, dredging, siltation, and industrial or domestic pollution have so far spared a number of small rivers, but sooner or later have exerted their cumulative impact on our major waterways. As a group primarily adapted to large streams, *Percina* darters have suffered from these changes. Nine named and 2 unnamed forms are listed as endangered, threatened, or of special concern by Deacon et al. (1979). Most of the remainder are far from abundant anywhere, and all tend to be found in isolated enclaves within their total range. Were we to construct a list of truly abundant *Percina*, included would be only *P. caprodes, P. maculata, P. nigrofasciata,* and *P. roanoka.*

Future practical efforts might be directed at obtaining better knowledge of the life histories and movements of *Percina* in hope of ultimately saving forms from extinction. Basic research in the taxonomy of *Percina* is drawing to a close, but many fascinating things remain to be discovered about the genus through the experimental fields of biology and ethology. In turn, these darters may be useful experimental systems for studying a number of fundamental processes in biology. The beauty of many of these darters speaks for itself.

Percina aurolineata Suttkus & Ramsey   Plate 1
Goldline Darter   Subgenus *Hadropterus*

Description. A moderate sized slender darter with a maximum SL of 74 mm. It is recognizable as a member of subgenus *Hadropterus* by rather broadly joined gill membranes, 3 vertically set dark spots at the caudal fin base, absence of breeding tubercles, and a nearly complete row of enlarged scales on the

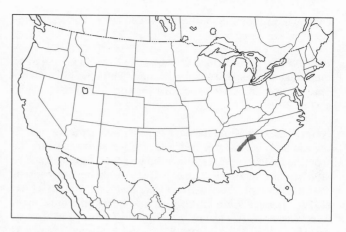

Distribution of *Percina aurolineata*

midline of the belly in males. It differs from other *Hadropterus* in the pattern of the back.

Back has 2 wavy dorsolateral bands narrowly interrupted at various points, running from head to end of soft dorsal fin. These frame the yellowish back, which may have dark blotches or a middorsal stripe. A midlateral band connects 7-9 black oval or rectangular blotches. Prominent preorbital bar fails to meet counterpart on snout. Suborbital bar is faint to absent. Postorbital bar is often continuous with midlateral band. Lower 2 caudal fin spots may fuse. In females ventral surface of head and body are pale, but in males they are dusky.

Males have a well developed dark marginal band and a broader one just above clear base of spiny dorsal fin; dusky soft dorsal fin repeats this pattern. In females similar banding is confined mostly to dorsal spines and to basal portion of soft dorsal fin. Caudal fin in both sexes usually has 3 wavy vertical bands. Anal and pectoral fins are dusky in mature males and little pigmented in other specimens. Pectoral fins are darkened basally, most noticeably in mature males.

Midventral line in males usually bears a row of moderately enlarged scales, while that in females varies from fully scaled to naked anteriorly. Exposed or partly embedded scales occur on breast, prepectoral area, cheek, nape, and dorsolateral portion of head in males; opercular scales are exposed. Scales on these areas in females are smaller and more frequently embedded. Lateral line has 64-72 (59-74) pored scales, the last 1-3 on caudal fin proper. Fin counts are: dorsal XII-XIV, 10-11 (10-13); anal II, 8-9 (7-10); pectoral 13-14 (12-15). Vertebrae number 41-43 (40-44).

Breeding males may develop more yellow or orange on upper body than is shown in color plate. Dorsolateral wavy bands become amber, as do some spots on head. Belly becomes pale bluish green; chin, throat, and ventral portion of cheek become blue. Orange develops in median part of both dorsal fins and faintly at base of soft dorsal and in caudal and anal fins. Breeding tubercles are absent; genital papilla presumably is a short flattened tube, but specimens were not examined by us. Breeding females develop some yellow on lips, upper side, and possibly cheek and caudal fin. Genital papilla is presumably a short rounded tube, but specimens were not examined by us.

Distribution. Found in the Coosawattee River in Georgia and the Cahaba River in central Alabama. This species probably once enjoyed much broader distribution within the Mobile basin.

Natural History. Goldline darters have been captured only in the rapids of rivers over bedrock or other substrates ranging from boulders to gravel. According to Suttkus and Ramsey (1967), collecting sites characteristically abound in beds of *Podostemum* or the water willow, *Justicea.* Bryant et al. (1979) caught additional Georgia specimens in similar habitats. Darter associates are *Etheostoma jordani* and *Percina palmaris* in the Coosawattee River, and *E. jordani, E. rupestre, E. stigmaeum, P. copelandi, P. lenticula, P. nigrofasciata, P. shumardi,* and perhaps others in the Cahaba River.

Abundance. Carters Reservoir now occupies much of the Coosawattee River that was favorable habitat for the goldline darter. Urbanization and pollution in the upper Cahaba pose a continuing, perhaps growing, threat. Undoubtedly the construction of reservoirs elsewhere in the upper Mobile basin, coupled with various forms of pollution, has contributed to the precarious position of this handsome darter, which is accorded threatened status by Deacon et al. (1979).

Name. *Aurolineata* means gold lined.

Percina lenticula Richards & Knapp   Plate 1
Freckled Darter   Subgenus *Hadropterus*

Description. Apparently the largest of all darters, with a maximum SL of 169 mm. Recognizable as *Hadropterus* by moderately joined gill membranes and 3 vertically arranged caudal spots (the lower 2 often fused), it is distinguished from other members of the subgenus by small scales and usually a distinct curved suborbital bar. Frenum is narrow. Air bladder is well developed.

Dorsum has 8 dark blotches, each partly surrounded by a pale area. About 8 dark lateral blotches are often connected by a horizontal band; the posterior 4 or 5 blotches are expanded into vertical bands. Smaller spots on body may be numerous enough to partially obscure side pattern. Pelvic fin base and prepectoral area are dark, the latter resembling freckles. Belly is clear to dusky, and may have a dark stripe along midline.

Preorbital bar often meets counterpart on snout; postorbital bar lies just beneath a second band which extends diagonally upward toward nape. Suborbital bar is rarely weak or absent, usually seen as a distinct posteriorly recurved band. Breast and ventral part of head are stippled or lightly spotted.

Basal, median, and marginal dark bands extend the length of spiny dorsal fin in large individuals but are weakly developed in small specimens. Three or 4 bands cross soft dorsal

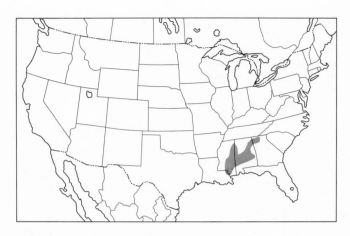

Distribution of *Percina lenticula*

fin; pronounced darkening forms a spot at anterior base of fin in most specimens. Two or 3 vertical dark caudal bands and a like number of horizontal anal bands are best developed in large specimens. Sometimes bands, but more often blotches, characterize pelvic fin. Two or 3 vertical bands of variable intensity develop in pectoral fin.

Embedded to partly embedded scales are found on cheek, opercle, nape, and dorsolateral portion of head. One or more enlarged scales are set between pelvic fins; remainder of breast and prepectoral area are naked to lightly scaled. Belly is completely scaled in females and has a midventral row of somewhat enlarged scales in males. Pored lateral line scales number 80-86 (77-90), the last 2-6 extending onto caudal fin. Fin counts are: dorsal XII-XIV, 13-14; anal II, 9-10; pectoral 14-15. Vertebrae number 42-44.

Adult males are patterned much like our illustrated specimen (the individual of record size), but yellow coloration may be much livelier. Large mature females are so darkened as to obscure body pattern; their fins are more boldly banded than those of large males. Genital papilla has not been described for either sex. Juveniles are characterized by reduced pigmentation, particularly in fins.

Distribution. Initially described from the Etowah and Cahaba rivers of the Mobile basin in Georgia and Alabama, and now known to occur elsewhere within that basin both above and below the Fall Line. The species also occurs in the Pascagoula and Pearl drainages in Mississippi and Louisiana.

Natural History. Little information has been published on the freckled darter. Suttkus and Ramsey (1967) obtained specimens from deep swift water, as did Douglas (1968). The latter used electrofishing gear and fine-mesh hoop nets to collect in areas too deep and swift for seines. Bryant et al. (1979) found a juvenile in vegetation within a gently flowing riffle, where individuals may reside until able to face the austere habitat of adults. Apparently a species of medium to large rivers exclusively, *P. lenticula* is particularly vulnerable to channelization projects, dams, serious pollution problems, and other disturbances. The large air bladder suggests that this may be a more open water fish than the typical darter.

Richards and Knapp (1964) indicate that this species is most closely related to *P. sciera,* which also sometimes has a weak suborbital bar. They state that entry of ancestral stock from the Mississippi basin is a more likely origin of Mobile basin stocks than stream capture from the Tennessee River system. Subsequent discovery of *P. lenticula* in the Pearl and Pascagoula rivers strengthens the first possibility.

Abundance. Few specimens of *Percina lenticula* have been taken, and collecting sites are few. In part this may be due to difficulty of capture, but the situation is serious enough to cause Deacon et al. (1979) to list the species as threatened.

Name. *Lenticula* means freckled and refers to the spots at the pectoral fin base.

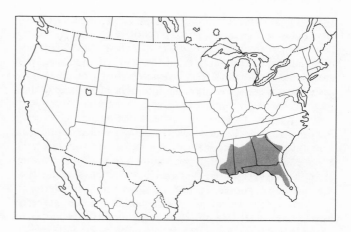

Distribution of *Percina nigrofasciata*

Percina nigrofasciata (Agassiz) Plate 1
Blackbanded Darter Subgenus *Hadropterus*

Description. A rather large and robust darter with a maximum SL of 93 mm. Recognized as a *Hadropterus* by the moderately joined gill membranes and by 3 vertically set caudal spots, this species lacks the pale dorsum of *P. aurolineata* and the distinct suborbital bar of *P. lenticula.* Blotches on the side of *P. sciera* are oval, while those of *P. nigrofasciata* appear as narrow vertical bars; young specimens of these 2 species are easily confused.

Dorsum has 7 or 8 small blotches of variable intensity, often broken into spots in females. Eleven to 16 vertically elongated bars on side usually are connected by a midlateral band. Bars on caudal peduncle are more ovoid, with ventral extensions that may fuse with counterparts from other side. Small spots and reticulations characterize upper side in both sexes and lower side in females. Belly in males is lightly to heavily stippled.

Preorbital bar meets or almost meets counterpart on snout. Suborbital bar is variably absent to moderately developed. Postorbital bar usually appears virtually continuous with midlateral band. Entire lower half of head is pale, though often lightly stippled with small black spots.

Dorsal spines are often clear but may be alternately light and dark, particularly in females. Spiny dorsal fin membranes are virtually clear in females and young, and stippled in males, more heavily near base. Soft dorsal fin is pale in females and young but variably dusky in males. Usually 3 weak vertical bands are found on caudal fin, and may be partly obscured by dusky membranes in mature males. Anal fin in females is clear to lightly stippled; that in males is more heavily stippled, especially toward base. A few dark spots near base constitute pelvic fin pigmentation in females; membranes in males may be somewhat dusky. Pectoral fin is little pigmented in either sex. A distinct prepectoral spot is usually best developed in females.

Opercle is well scaled; cheek scales may be partly embedded or absent ventrally. Nape is well scaled; a few scales may extend forward onto head. Breast varies from naked to partially covered with small embedded scales. One or more large scales lie between insertions of pelvic fins. Slightly enlarged scales lie along belly midline in males; this area usually is naked in females. Lateral line contains 50-62 (46-71) pored scales, 1 to 4 of which may extend onto caudal fin. Fin counts are: dorsal XI-XIII (IX-XV), 11-12 (10-13); anal II, 9 (7-10); pectoral usually 14. Vertebrae number 39-41.

Breeding males are characterized by darkening of fins and body and an accentuation of vertical banding on body. Although a bluish green sheen develops on upper body, and green and gold casts may be seen on cheek and opercle, males are not otherwise colorful. Genital papilla is a small somewhat flattened cone with fingerlike villi at tip. Breeding females become more strongly pigmented and may develop irregularly shaped markings between lateral blotches. Genital papilla is a conical tube with distinct grooves and terminal villi.

Crawford (1956) recognized 8 races of subspecies *P. n. nigrofasciata,* each associated with part or all of a major river basin and distinguished by slight differences in scalation and body proportions. He named the subspecies *P. n. raneyi* on the basis of greater differences in scales and body proportions, including a more pointed snout. Subspecies *raneyi* has 60-67 (54-71) lateral line scales; subspecies *nigrofasciata* has 50-61 (44-66).

Distribution. Occurs from the lowermost Mississippi River tributaries in Louisiana and Mississippi eastward through all major Gulf Coast drainages to the Suwannee, and along the Atlantic Coast drainages from the Kissimmee River in Florida to the Edisto River in South Carolina. Subspecies *raneyi* is confined to the upper Savannah River of Georgia and South Carolina, with possible intergrades in the Altamaha basin and the lower Savannah. Guillory (1976) indicates that the blackbanded darter may have been extirpated from lower tributaries of the Mississippi.

Natural History. In the Coastal Plain portions of its range the blackbanded darter is usually the most abundant *Percina* and often the most common of all darters. It inhabits areas of slow to steady current around snags, beds of vegetation, gravelly chutes, and over gravel in typical riffle habitat. Apparently more than any other *Percina, P. nigrofasciata* enters creeks of small size but probably attains greater abundance in large creeks and small rivers. The invasion of tiny streams may be associated with the fact that this species has few other darters to act as competitors. On the Atlantic coast *Etheostoma olmstedi* is its most frequent associate, and along the Gulf coast *E. swaini* is. Blackbanded darters also fare well above the Fall Line, even as a component of the rich darter fauna of the Mobile basin. Although more common in quieter runs, they are nonetheless captured over gravel and rubble-strewn riffles inhabited by *E. coosae, E. jordani,* and other upland darters.

Some excellent life history information has been gathered by Mathur (1973). He observed aquarium-held specimens to prefer gravel substrate and to darken or blanch rapidly as conditions demanded. He demonstrated that the number of eggs produced per female was correlated linearly with body weight and exponentially with total body length. This discovery may be useful to clarify the great discrepancies among reports of the egg complement of other species of darters. Mathur observed a long breeding season, February to April in Louisiana and early May to early June near Auburn, Alabama. Natural hybridization between *P. nigrofasciata* and *P. sciera* is reported by Suttkus and Ramsey (1967). Additional studies are justified for this adaptable species.

In our trips to southern streams we became well acquainted with the blackbanded darter, noting the subtle differences it exhibits from one major basin to the next.

Abundance. This is one of the most abundant and successful darters.

Name. The common name, blackbanded, is a direct translation of the trivial epithet, *nigrofasciata*. E.C. Raney is the noted ichthyologist of Cornell University.

Percina sciera (Swain)   Plate 1
Dusky Darter   Subgenus *Hadropterus*

Description. A fairly large and robust darter, the biggest individuals somewhat in excess of 90 mm SL. Recognized as a *Hadropterus* by the moderately joined gill membranes and 3 vertically set caudal spots, it is easily distinguished from *P. aurolineata* with its pale dorsum and from *P. lenticula* with its strong suborbital bar. Though young specimens may be confused with *P. nigrofasciata* because of poorly developed markings, adults have oval blotches along the sides rather than the vertically elongated ones which characterize *P. nigrofasciata*.

Back is crossed by 8 small and usually indistinct saddles. On upper side, margins of scales are often darkly edged to produce a cross-hatched, dusky appearance. First 1 or 2 of the 7 or 8 lateral blotches are much smaller than the rest. Blotches tend to be connected by a lateral band. Lower side and belly in females lack markings; those of males may be stippled lightly. Humeral region is dark. Bottom pair of 3 caudal spots are

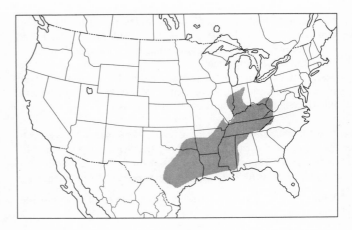

Distribution of *Percina sciera*

often fused; dorsal spot almost fuses with its counterpart from other side.

Preorbital bar of variable intensity usually fuses with counterpart on lip. Postorbital bar broadens from cheek across opercle and joins midlateral band. Suborbital bar may be absent or represented by a spot. Prepectoral region is stippled.

Spiny dorsal fin bears a narrow marginal to submarginal band and a broader band, both more apparent in males than in females. Rays of soft dorsal fin are darkened to form a marginal band. A similar but weaker band near base of soft dorsal is strengthened by stippled membranes. Three wavy vertical bands are weakly to moderately developed in caudal fin. Anal fin usually has faint pigmentation submarginally and basally. Pelvic fin ordinarily lacks pigmentation. Pectoral fin has 4 or 5 faint vertical bands.

Cheek and opercle are scaled; lower cheek scales may be embedded. Scales on anterior part of nape may be embedded, as are the few which may extend forward on head. One or more enlarged scales lie between pelvic fin bases; partly embedded scales are scattered over breast. Scales along midventral line in males are somewhat larger than normal; belly midline is naked in females. Last 1 or 2 scales of lateral line may extend onto caudal fin. Lateral line consists of 66-72 (63-78) scales in subspecies *apristis* and 59-68 (56-74) in nominate subspecies. Fin counts are: dorsal XI-XIII (X-XV), 10-13; anal II, 8-9 (7-10); pectoral 13-14 (12-15). Vertebrae number 40-41 (39-42).

Breeding males may develop a bluish sheen on back and a little yellow on body. All fins but pectoral are variably darkened. Males of subspecies *apristis* may develop a submarginal orange band in spiny dorsal fin. Genital papilla is a small, conical tube which may be longitudinally grooved and have villi at tip. Body pattern in adult females is sharp by comparison with males, being little obscured by dusky quality. Midlateral band may be weak, leaving lateral blotches virtually separate. A little yellow may develop on body. Genital papilla is a conical tube, deeply grooved at tip.

Hubbs (1954) recognized subspecies *apristis* but declined to name additional subspecies, although some differences were noted between Wabash and Ozark populations.

Distribution. Occurs in the lower Mississippi valley, extending westward into central Texas and southeastern Oklahoma and eastward into the Tombigbee and Black Warrior arms of the Mobile drainage. The species does not extend up the Missouri or upper Mississippi rivers but is common throughout the lower Ohio River basin, attaining its upstream limits in the lower reaches of tributaries in Ohio and West Virginia. The northern limits are the headwaters of the Wabash river.

Subspecies *apristis* is restricted to the Guadalupe River of Texas and its tributaries, the San Marcos and Blanco rivers. It is confined to the main channels of these streams and is absent from the headwaters of the Guadalupe and Blanco and from the entire San Antonio River. Subspecies *sciera* does not occur in the Guadalupe.

Natural History. The dusky darter lives in medium to large streams of moderate to low gradient as long as they are not highly turbid. During spring and early summer it is most frequently found in riffles over coarse clean gravel at depths of 20 cm or more. Specimens may be captured in or adjacent to aquatic vegetation when it is present. During hot weather dusky darters may retreat to quieter, deeper pools, especially where debris or vegetation affords protection. Frequent associates are *P. maculata, P. caprodes,* and *P. phoxocephala.* In upland streams, common associates are *Etheostoma blennioides, E. caeruleum, E. spectabile,* and *E. flabellare. E. asprigene, E. histrio,* and *P. ouachitae* are more likely lowland associates.

Many aspects of the life history of the dusky darter have been studied in Illinois by Page and Smith (1970). Males are ready to breed at 1 year of age. Few individuals of either sex reach 3 years of age, and 4 years is the maximum. Winter apparently is spent in deep pools; riffles and shallows yield no specimens from November through March. Spawning time varies but seems most often to be in June. Though not directly observed, spawning probably occurs over loose gravel. Some male-to-male aggressiveness was observed in aquariums, but clearly defended territories were not established. Heaviest feeding occurred in May, apparently just before spawning. The darters feed almost entirely on larval insects that dwell in riffles, partcularly midges and blackflies; mayflies and caddisflies predominate briefly during summer. There was no evidence of predation upon dusky darters by spotted bass, which were common in the study area used by Page and Smith. They observed that leeches were common parasites of adults. Adults dwell on the bottom much of the time. The young swim about in shallow open water, sometimes entering tributaries not visited by adults.

Natural hybrids between *P. sciera* and *P. caprodes* and even *Etheostoma spectabile* were reported by Hubbs and Laritz (1961). Suttkus and Ramsey (1967) report hybridization with *P. nigrofasciata.* Egg complements have been reported by Brown (1955) and Hubbs and Johnson (1961).

Abundance. The dusky darter is one of the species best adapted to lowland rivers, and occurs abundantly in much of its range. It is not limited by the Fall Line, reaching the lower courses of some Ozark streams, and many Ohio basin tributaries of moderate gradient. With such a variety of habitats, there is little danger of extirpation. Former avenues of dispersal like the Ohio River no longer serve in that capacity, however, resulting in some shrinkage and fragmentation of range. Western populations have been adversely affected by drought and pollution.

Name. *Sciera* means dusky. *Apristis* means without saw, referring to the few, if any, serrations on the preopercle.

Percina nasuta (Bailey)   Plate 1
Longnose Darter   Subgenus *Swainia*

Description. A rather large darter with a maximum SL of at least 80 mm. A small dark spot at the caudal fin base, elongated head and snout, and moderately joined gill membranes (slightly joined in some individuals) place this species in subgenus *Swainia.* It differs from *P. oxyrhyncha* in having narrower, more intense, and more elongated lateral blotches, and in more frequently having 7 rather than 6 branchiostegal rays. The lateral markings of *P. squamata* are much less distinct; the snout of *P. phoxocephala* is blunter.

About 14 marks lie along dorsum. Those anterior to second dorsal fin are narrow bands which often join ventrally with markings on side. Posterior marks are squarish saddles. A faint lateral band may connect 10-14 vertically elongated lateral blotches. Lower parts of body lack a pattern but may be stippled. A narrow, dark humeral mark is present.

A dark preorbital bar remains narrowly separated on lip from counterpart. A less well defined postorbital bar extends across cheek and opercle. Suborbital bar is undeveloped. Chin, throat, and breast usually are lightly stippled.

Spiny dorsal fin bears a narrow marginal dark band and a broader basal band, but neither is intense. Rays of soft dorsal fin are alternately dark and light, producing a weakly banded effect. Three or 4 similar bands are set vertically on caudal fin. Both anal rays and membranes are somewhat stippled basally. Pelvic fin is entirely clear and pectoral fin rays are a little darkened basally.

Cheek scales are small and may be embedded and difficult to see. Opercle has a patch of larger exposed scales. Nape is finely scaled and may be naked anteriorly. An enlarged scale between pelvic fins and another in middle of breast are rarely accompanied by a few small embedded scales on rest of breast. Males have a midventral row of slightly enlarged scales, while those of females are normal in size. Anterior portion of belly is naked in both sexes. Lateral line consists of 73-83 pored scales, the last 1 or 2 located on caudal fin base. Fin counts are: dorsal XI-XIV, 11-13; anal II, 8-9; pectoral 13-15. Vertebrae number 40-41.

A yellowish to reddish orange submarginal band in spiny dorsal fin of males may be accompanied by traces of color in soft dorsal fin, caudal fin, and on head and nape. Body pattern may become more distinct. Genital papilla is short and flattened. Mature females may have a weak orange band in spiny dorsal, but little if any additional coloration. Genital papilla is a short rounded tube, pointed at tip.

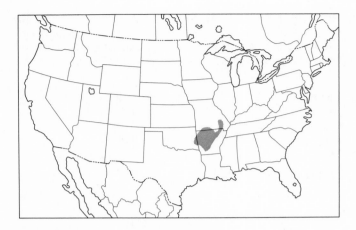

Distribution of *Percina nasuta*

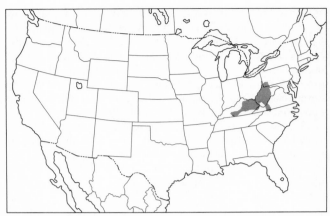

Distribution of *Percina oxyrhyncha*

Distribution. Inhabits portions of the Ozark-Ouachita uplands in southern Missouri, Arkansas, and extreme eastern Oklahoma. In Missouri *P. nasuta* has been captured in St. Francis River and at several sites in the White River. It is fairly widespread in the White River system within Arkansas, and again in the headwaters of the Ouachita River basin in southwestern Arkansas. In the Arkansas River basin it appears at a few spots in western Arkansas and eastern Oklahoma, sympatrically with *P. phoxocephala* in at least one case (Blair, 1976).

Natural History. The longnose darter is a river species that has been recorded from both riffles and quieter water. Bailey (1941) noted the presence of quiet water and aquatic vegetation at the capture site of his type specimens. Pflieger (1975) reported capture on riffles, in quiet vegetated water, and also in Lake Wappapello, which suggests that this may be one of the few darters able to persist in impoundments.

It is probably the most generalized member of subgenus *Swainia,* based on the consistent presence of an additional branchiostegal ray. Geographically it is widely separated from its eastern upland counterparts, *Percina oxyrhyncha* and *P. squamata*. These 3 species seem to represent a stock somewhat older than that from which *P. phoxocephala* has developed.

Abundance. The longnose darter has proved to be more widespread and common than was initially thought, although it is far from being abundant and deserves careful monitoring.

Name. *Nasuta* means long nose.

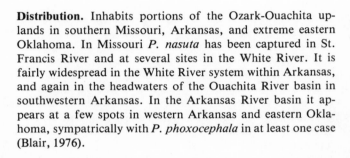

Percina oxyrhyncha (Hubbs & Raney)   Plate 1
Sharpnose Darter   Subgenus *Swainia*

Description. A rather large darter reaching 93 mm SL. A dark basicaudal spot, elongated head and snout, and moderately joined gill membranes place it in the subgenus *Swainia*. Most like *P. nasuta,* it usually lacks the seventh branchiostegal ray

found in that species and has broader, less intense, and less elongated lateral blotches. Lateral markings of *P. squamata* are less distinct; snout of *P. phoxocephala* is blunter.

Back is crossed by up to 16 narrow bands, which may be interrupted at midline and may connect to diagonal markings on upper side to form a reticulated pattern. Eleven to 14 lateral blotches vary from vertically elongated to almost square on caudal peduncle; elongated blotches are connected by a dull midlateral band. Upper side appears finely cross-hatched, while lower side and belly are pale. Humeral bar is long and very distinct.

Preorbital bar usually fuses with counterpart on upper lip. Postorbital bar is narrow on cheek, broadening on opercle. Suborbital bar is weakly present only in some mature individuals. Chin, throat, and breast are pale.

Stippling in dorsal fin membranes produces a marginal or submarginal dark band and a broader basal band. Rays of soft dorsal fin are alternately light and dark, producing several very weak bands. Several similar bands occur on caudal fin. Anal and pelvic fin membranes may be stippled near base. A little dark pigment is scattered along pectoral fin rays.

Cheek scales are few and mostly embedded; opercular scales are more numerous but most still are embedded. A large scale in center of breast is often flanked by small embedded scales. One or 2 large scales lie between pelvic fins. Belly in females may be normally scaled but often is partly naked. Enlarged scales lie along midline of belly in males. Lateral line contains 72-81 scales. Fin counts are: dorsal XI-XIV, 13-14; anal II, 8-9; pectoral 13-14. Vertebrae number 42-43.

Breeding coloration of males is adequately depicted in color plate. Genital papilla is short, flattened, and longitudinally grooved. Females may develop subdued body coloration and an orange submarginal band in spiny dorsal fin. Genital papilla is a short nearly round tube.

Distribution. Was initially thought to be restricted to the upper Monongahela River basin and the Kanawha River above the Falls (New River). Other southern tributaries of the Ohio River (the lower Kanawha, Little Kanawha, Big Sandy, Licking, and upper Kentucky rivers) are now known to harbor the species (Hocutt and Hambrick, 1973). This distribution suggests that the sharpnose darter is a relict of the ancient Teays drainage system, but additional records from the Green River basin indicate further dispersal. *Percina squamata* and *P. nasuta* are its counterparts in the upper Cumberland-Tennessee basins and Ozark-Ouachita uplands. The intervening regions are occupied by *P. phoxocephala,* whose range reaches or slightly overlaps that of the 3 above forms. The possibility of hybridization and the careful delineation of the contact region of *P. oxyrhyncha* and *P. phoxocephala* needs closer study.

Natural History. The sharpnose darter inhabits strong riffles of upland streams with moderate to fairly high gradients. Hubbs and Raney (1939) reported it to live under large stones or in sandy riffles and vegetation. We observed greater abundance in rubble and gravel riffles of rivers where aquatic vegetation occurs. This darter usually lives in the central portion of a riffle at depths of a ⅓ to ½ m. Associates may include *Percina copelandi, P. evides, P. caprodes, P. maculata, Etheostoma blennioides, E. flabellare, E. caeruleum, E. zonale,* and occasionally additional species.

P. roanoka has been introduced into the darter-poor upper Kanawha basin, where it has spread rapidly and hybridized with *P. oxyrhyncha.* This situation has been discussed by Hocutt and Hambrick (1973).

Food preference, behavior, and life history studies need to be conducted for this species.

Abundance. Construction of reservoirs and widespread surface mining have combined to reduce greatly the suitable habitat for the sharpnose darter. Canalization of the Ohio River has isolated the species in each major tributary it occupies. It is not rare or endangered because it persists in several places unlikely to be affected by these problems. But much excellent habitat has been lost or badly degraded, as in the Licking River, where 14 species of darters (including 6 species of *Percina*) could predictably be obtained before the construction of Cave Run Reservoir. A good collection now contains half that number, though it remains unknown whether or not any one form has been totally eliminated from the river.

Name. *Oxyrhyncha* means sharp nose, in exact agreement with the common name of the species.

Percina phoxocephala (Nelson)　　　　　　Plate 2
Slenderhead Darter　　　　　　　　Subgenus *Swainia*

Description. A moderate sized darter reaching 80 mm SL. The small dark spot at the caudal fin base, elongated head and snout, and moderately joined gill membranes place this species in subgenus *Swainia.* This is the stoutest member of the group and also differs from the other 3 in having a less elongated snout.

Dorsum supports 11-16 small blotches. Anterior to spiny dorsal fin, blotches fuse into reticulations on upper side. Pos-

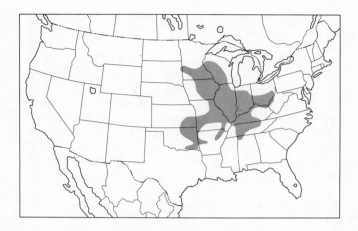

Distribution of *Percina phoxocephala*

teriorly, blotches are separate spots, hardly qualifying as saddles. Eleven to 13 (maximally 15) small lateral blotches are connected by a faint horizontal band. Lower side and belly are pale to lightly stippled. Humeral bar is rather small.

Preorbital bar may fuse with counterpart on lip. Postorbital bar is narrow on cheek, broader across opercle. Suborbital bar varies from absent to a stippled area beneath eye. Chin, throat, and breast are lightly to moderately stippled.

A narrow marginal to submarginal dark band in spiny dorsal fin membranes is matched by a broader band near base. Alternating light and dark rays of soft dorsal fin produce several weak horizontal bands; associated membranes are darkly stippled at base. Caudal fin rays are darkened to produce several weak vertical bands. Anal and pelvic fin membranes are lightly stippled; a little darkening occurs along edges of pectoral fin rays.

Cheek may be naked (Cross, 1967) but usually supports a number of small, often embedded, scales. Opercle is scaled. Nape is partly to fully scaled. Small embedded scales usually lie posterior to large central scale on breast. In females belly is fully scaled or is naked just posterior to pelvic fins. In males a row of enlarged scales lies along belly. Lateral line contains 64-74 (59-79) scales. Fin counts are: dorsal XII-XIV, 12-15; anal II, 8-9; pectoral usually 13-14. Vertebrae number 38-40.

P. phoxocephala is the only colorful species in subgenus *Swainia.* Coloration of breeding males is fairly well depicted in color plate. Genital papilla is short and flattened with some longitudinal grooves. Green and yellow on body of breeding females is faintly imitative of males, but orange dorsal fin stripe may be moderately developed. Genital papilla is a somewhat flattened tube, grooved and pointed at tip.

Distribution. Occurs in much of the Mississippi River basin. It is found in the upper Mississippi and Minnesota river basins in Minnesota and South Dakota through Wisconsin, Iowa, and Illinois. As noted by Bailey and Allum (1962), it apparently arrived in Minnesota too late to enter the Red River of the North and establish a Canadian distribution. Pflieger (1971) indicates that the upper Arkansas populations in Kansas and Oklahoma may have entered via stream capture of Missouri basin streams rather than by ascent of the mainstream of the Arkansas River. This darter is rare in Arkansas but common in the Red River system of extreme southeastern Oklahoma.

The slenderhead darter invades the lower and middle reaches of the Tennessee and Cumberland rivers, but is absent or rare in upper portions of these rivers. Above the Falls of the Ohio there is some question as to the distributional boundary between slenderhead darters and *P. oxyrhyncha*. Most collections from Ohio (Trautman, 1957) and the lower Kentucky River (Horseman and Branson, 1973) include only *P. phoxocephala*, but it gives way to *P. oxyrhyncha* in West Virginia and high gradient streams of eastern Kentucky.

Natural History. The slenderhead darter inhabits medium sized creeks to large rivers with strong flow and gravel, rubble, or bedrock riffles. Small individuals may enter tributaries. Smith, Lopinot, and Pflieger (1971) occasionally found this species in the upper Mississippi channel. Associated darters in its range include *Percina caprodes, P. maculata, P. sciera, Etheostoma blennioides, E. caeruleum, E. zonale,* and others.

Karr (1963), Thomas (1970), and Page and Smith (1971) agree that dipteran, mayfly, and caddisfly larvae constitute the principal food of this species, larger individuals usually consuming greater percentages of mayfly and caddisfly larvae. Both sexes are reproductively mature at 1 year of age. Spawning has not been described, but probably occurs over gravel riffles. In Illinois the spawning season is late May to mid-June; in Kansas spawning occurs from late March to early May (Cross, 1967). The species is short lived, apparently not more than 3 years. Reproductive behavior remains undescribed.

Abundance. Rather common in some parts of its range, the slenderhead darter is in no danger of extirpation. P.W. Smith (1979) and Trautman (1957) both noted considerable range shrinkage in Illinois and Ohio, where siltation associated with agricultural practices has covered the gravel riffles of many rivers.

Name. *Phoxocephala* means tapered head.

Percina squamata (Gilbert & Swain)   Plate 2
Olive Darter   Subgenus *Swainia*

Description. A rather large darter reaching at least 93 mm SL and recognizable as a member of subgenus *Swainia* by a small basicaudal spot, elongated head and snout, and moderately joined gill membranes. The snout is much sharper than that of *P. phoxocephala* and the lateral blotches tend to fuse into a band, unlike *P. nasuta* and *P. oxyrhyncha*.

Ten to 15 dorsal blotches and 12-13 lateral blotches are best developed in small individuals, but dorsal pattern becomes less distinct in adults, and lateral blotches tend to fuse into a midlateral band. Scales are darkly edged on upper

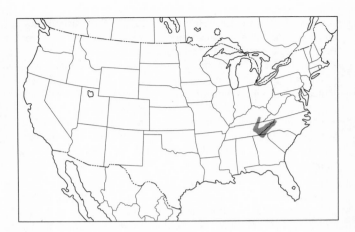

Distribution of *Percina squamata*

side, becoming steadily less so on lower side and belly. Dark humeral bar is small.

Broad, dark preorbital bar usually meets counterpart on lip. Postorbital bar is narrow across cheek and expands on opercle. Suborbital bar is absent or represented by light stippling, but lower cheek may bear 1 or more faint horizontal bands. Chin, throat, prepectoral area, and breast are lightly stippled.

Membranes of spiny dorsal fin are stippled to produce a broad dark band near the base and a narrow marginal band. Alternating light and dark zones in rays of soft dorsal fin produce several very weak bands; membranes of this fin are stippled at base but tend to become clear marginally. Darkening in and adjacent to caudal fin rays produces 3 or 4 vertical bands. Anal fin membranes are clear or stippled basally. Pelvic and pectoral fins usually lack pigmentation.

Cheek bears a patch of small, sometimes embedded, scales. Opercle is well scaled. Nape is covered with small, often embedded, scales. One or more large scales occur between pelvic fins and another is in center of breast, which may also support numerous small embedded scales. Belly in females is fully scaled, while that in males has a midventral row of enlarged scales. Lateral line consists of 71-84 scales, 1 or 2 of which may extend onto caudal fin. Fin counts are: dorsal XII-XV, 12-15; anal II, 8-10; pectoral 13-15. Vertebrae number 42-44.

Males may become brighter than is suggested by color plate. A submarginal orange band in spiny dorsal fin and traces of orange in soft dorsal and caudal fins contrast with olive green hues on body. Females have a dull orange band in spiny dorsal fin, and body hues similar to those in males. Young and nonbreeding specimens often appear a drab brown. Male genital papilla is short and flattened; that of females is a rounded tube, pointed at tip.

Distribution. Confined to the headwaters of the Tennessee River system and the Cumberland River basin below the falls, primarily in the Rockcastle River and the Big South Fork. Within the Tennessee basin it has been taken from the French Broad, Watauga, Nolichucky, Hiwassee, and Emory rivers in Tennessee, North Carolina, and Georgia.

Natural History. The olive darter is a river inhabitant, characteristic of strong chutes with rubble and boulders in high-gradient streams, or in the deeper downstream portions of gravel riffles in streams of moderate gradient. In the Rockcastle River we have encountered a few olive darters in shallow pools with clean substrates of bedrock or gravel. A juvenile from a moderate sized creek is the only specimen we have encountered outside a principal river. Reservoirs and stripmine siltation have been reducing suitable habitat in Kentucky and Tennessee.

Percina caprodes is the only common associate of the olive darter, but nearby riffles may yield a diverse assemblage of darters.

Abundance. Even allowing for difficulty of capture, the olive darter is nowhere abundant, most collections consisting of only 1 or 2 individuals. This species should be carefully monitored for possible endangerment.

Name. *Squamata* means scaly, and refers to the presence of scales over the breast, cheeks, and opercles of the olive darter.

Percina crassa (Jordan & Brayton) Plate 2
Piedmont Darter Subgenus *Alvordius*

Description. A moderate sized member of this subgenus, reaching a maximum SL of about 75 mm. Separated gill membranes, an incomplete row of large spiny belly scales, and absence of male breeding tubercles mark *P. crassa* as a member of subgenus *Alvordius*. It is most similar to *P. roanoka*, which however has brightly colored males. *P. crassa* lacks the distinctive dorsal patterns which characterize *P. notogramma* and *P. peltata*. Side blotches are more vertically elongated than those found in the remaining species of *Alvordius*.

Usually 7 squarish saddles lie along back. Side supports 7-9 vertically elongated oval blotches joined by a midlateral band. Dorsal and lateral markings tend to be interconnected by a zigzag pattern of lines on upper side. Lower side and belly vary from pale to stippled. Caudal spot is usually diffuse and vertically elongated. A dark humeral mark may be partly hidden by pectoral fin.

Preorbital bar extends onto snout. Suborbital bar crosses cheek and may almost meet counterpart on ventral midline. A postorbital spot is present. Chin, throat, and breast are lightly stippled in females, more heavily so in males.

Spiny dorsal fin of males has a basal and a submarginal band, while that of females is weakly pigmented. In both sexes soft dorsal fin is crossed by 2 or 3 weak diagonal bands; caudal fin is similarly marked with vertical bands. Particularly in males, anal and pelvic fins are somewhat darkened basally. Pectoral fin is pale and lacks pattern.

Cheek is naked; opercle has a few embedded scales. Nape is naked anteriorly and remainder bears small scales, sometimes partly embedded. Breast and anterior portion of belly are naked. Posterior portion of breast is naked along midline in females but bears a row of much enlarged scales in males.

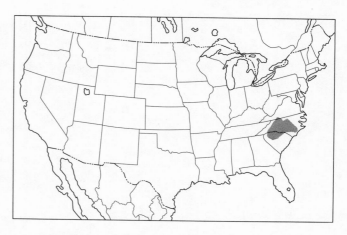

Distribution of *Percina crassa*

Lateral line is complete, with 47-53 (44-58) scales. Fin counts are: dorsal XI-XII (X-XIII), 11-13; anal II, 8-9 (7-10); pectoral 13-15. Vertebrae usually number 41-42.

Though not brightly colored, breeding males do have a yellow band in spiny dorsal fin not shown in color plate. Body and fins, particularly spiny dorsal, darken considerably. Genital papilla is a short, flattened tube. Females are never brightly colored. We have not seen genital papilla of a breeding female.

P. crassa is difficult to distinguish from *P. roanoka* except by the more pronounced suborbital bar and lack of breeding coloration. Females and immature specimens are especially hard to separate. Mayden and Page (1979) report that montane populations of *P. crassa* from the Pee Dee and Santee drainages have high lateral line scale counts, but they do not propose subspecific recognition.

Distribution. Found in the Cape Fear, Pee Dee, and Santee basins of Virginia, North Carolina, and South Carolina, most commonly in the Piedmont and montane zones.

Natural History. The Piedmont darter is a riffle species of moderate to large streams and occurs over a variety of substrate from sand to cobbles. It seems to avoid very strong currents. More extensive collecting may reveal it to inhabit pools and quiet water to a greater degree than *Percina roanoka*. Much more information needs to be gathered on *P. crassa*.

Abundance. A better idea of the abundance and status of *Percina crassa* is needed. We found it difficult to obtain compared with *P. roanoka* in adjacent streams to the north. A wide distribution pattern within its range suggests that the survival of *P. crassa* is not of great concern at present.

Name. *Crassa* means thick and refers to the rather stocky appearance of this species. However, the name is also applicable to *Percina roanoka*, until recently treated as a subspecies of *P. crassa*.

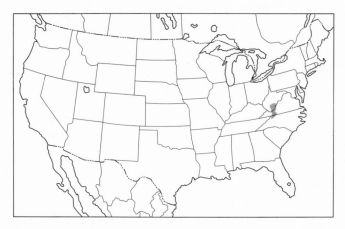

Distribution of *Percina gymnocephala*

Percina gymnocephala Beckham   Plate 2

Appalachia Darter   Subgenus *Alvordius*

Description. A rather large representative of this subgenus reaching a maximum SL of about 80 mm. Separated gill membranes, an incomplete row of large spiny belly scales, and absence of breeding tubercles place it in subgenus *Alvordius*. It appears similar to *P. peltata* and *P. notogramma* but lacks their distinctive dorsal patterns. It is very difficult to distinguish from *P. maculata* and may yet prove to be simply a variant of that species; primarily *P. gymnocephala* has reduced head scalation compared with *P. maculata*.

There usually are 7 uniformly spaced, squarish dorsal saddles and wavy V-shaped markings on upper side. Six to 8 large lateral blotches are narrowly joined by a longitudinal dark band. A vertically elongated caudal spot appears to be partly fused to last lateral blotch. Lower side and belly vary from clear to lightly stippled. A faint prepectoral mark and a distinct humeral band complete body markings.

A poorly defined preorbital bar extends to tip of snout. Suborbital bar is well developed. Postorbital bar appears merely as darkened areas on opercle and part of cheek. Chin, throat, and gill membranes are lightly stippled. Breast is clear.

A broad basal band in spiny dorsal fin is strongest anteriorly, while marginal band is darker toward posterior end; bands are poorly defined in some specimens. Soft dorsal fin is darkened near anterior base and may have 3 weak horizontal bands. There are 3 or 4 vertical caudal bands. Anal fin is dark basally; pelvic fin is pale; pectoral fin has about 5 weak vertical bands.

Cheek normally is naked; opercle is naked or has a few embedded scales dorsally. Nape may be virtually naked but more often has a few small embedded scales at anterior and posterior ends. Belly is naked anteriorly in both sexes; posteriorly, midline is naked in females and supplied with enlarged scales in males. Lateral line consists of 61-68 (56-72) scales. Fin counts are: dorsal XII-XVI, 10-13; anal II, 7-10; pectoral 13-15. Vertebrae usually number 44 or 45.

Mature males appear similar to specimen in color plate.

Genital papilla is a flattened tube, longitudinally grooved near tip. Genital papilla of mature females is a large flattened tube, longitudinally grooved along most of its length.

Distribution. Restricted to the Kanawha River system above the falls. It has been taken from the Gauley and Greenbrier rivers in West Virginia but most specimens have come from the Blue Ridge region of Virginia and North Carolina.

Natural History. Beckham (1980) indicates that Appalachia darters are found in riffles during spring and early summer but then retreat to quiet pools for the remainder of the year. *Etheostoma blennioides, E. flabellare, E. kanawhae,* and *P. oxyrhyncha* are darter associates.

We have taken this darter on several occasions. Females from the Little River, Virginia, appeared to have spawned by mid-May, but males retained a darkened appearance. Life history information is needed.

Abundance. The Appalachia darter is locally common and seems in no danger of extirpation.

Name. *Gymnocephala* means lightly clad head, referring to the reduced scalation of the head and nape.

Percina macrocephala (Cope)   Plate 2

Longhead Darter   Subgenus *Alvordius*

Description. Probably the largest darter of subgenus *Alvordius,* reaching just over 100 mm SL. Easily distinguished from other members of the subgenus by its elongated head and snout, it nonetheless possesses the combination of separate (or nearly separate) gill membranes, an incomplete row of enlarged belly scales, and absence of male tuberculation which characterize *Alvordius*.

Dorsal pattern is variable. There may be a middorsal stripe on nape which sometimes continues along base of both dorsal fins. A parallel stripe on upper side of body is often present as well. Alternatively, nape may have 2 dark oval spots, and up to 10 additional poorly defined spots may be evenly distributed along back. Eight to 12 lateral blotches are connected by a broad midlateral band which sometimes almost obliterates their distinctness. Lateral line usually appears as a pale stripe within dark band, particularly anteriorly. Lower side varies from pale to blotchy, and belly is pale. Dark midcaudal spot usually continues ventrally as a band.

Conspicuous preorbital bar meets counterpart on lip, which may itself be darkened. Suborbital bar may be complete or reduced to a posteriorly recurved mark on lower cheek. Postorbital spot has a narrow line which continues across cheek and onto opercle. Chin and gill membranes vary from stippled to unmarked. Breast is unpigmented.

Spiny dorsal fin has a dark submarginal band and another band near base. Darkening of rays produces 3 or 4 weak bands in soft dorsal; several wavy vertical bands are similarly produced in caudal fin. Anal fin usually is stippled basally. Pelvic fin is clear or lightly stippled on rays. Weak vertical

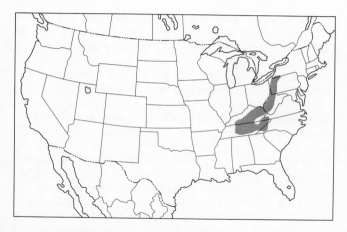

Distribution of *Percina macrocephala*

that basin. Additional populations may exist but need documentation.

Natural History. The longhead darter is generally found in pools or chutes of moderate sized streams which also have moderate gradients. It is most often encountered in steady currents above or below riffles over a variety of clean substrate varying from weed beds to exposed bedrock. We have encountered only a few individuals, always at depths of ½ to 1 m. Lack of life history information will be hard to remedy because of the infrequency of capture.

Abundance. Deacon et al. (1979) list the longhead darter as threatened. The scattered nature of present populations suggests that they are mere remnants of a formerly extensive distribution. Recent developments give little encouragement that the trend toward actual endangerment will not continue.

Name. *Macrocephala* means big head.

bands in pectoral fin are produced by pigment adjacent to rays.

Cheek varies from naked to scaled, but usually such scales are embedded. Opercle has exposed scales or at least a few embedded ones. Nape also is variable; in extreme cases it is naked or covered with small scales, but usually is naked anteriorly and scaled posteriorly. Occasionally breast has a few small embedded scales but normally only 1 or 2 enlarged scales between pelvic fins. Belly is naked anteriorly in both sexes. Males have typical row of enlarged spiny scales on posterior part of belly. Many species of *Percina* have a few scales on base of caudal fin, a trait quite pronounced in *P. macrocephala*. Lateral line consists of 70-90 scales but local populations display only part of such wide variation. Fin counts are: dorsal XII-XV (XI-XVI), 12-13 (11-14); anal II, 5-6; pectoral 13-14 (12-15). Vertebrae number 44 or 45.

Breeding males darken enough to obscure much of their body pattern but do not develop coloration. Genital papilla is a semicircular flap. Mature females may darken but retain normal pattern. We have not seen genital papilla of a breeding female.

The discontinuous populations of *P. macrocephala* differ from one another in several ways. Those of upper Ohio River basin are deepest bodied and have best defined lateral blotches. Snout tends to be longest in Green River specimens, which also produce highest lateral line scale counts. Tennessee River basin specimens have low scale counts, often are rather small, and like Green River stock have a band which may obscure lateral blotches. Detailed characteristics of the species have been well presented by Page (1978).

Distribution. Has been taken sporadically from the major southern tributaries of the lower Ohio River as well as various upstream tributaries in Ohio, West Virginia, Pennsylvania, and New York. It may be caught with a degree of certainty in the upper Allegheny basin, in a few small tributaries of the Ohio such as Kinniconick Creek in Kentucky, and in the Little River near Knoxville, Tennessee. Green River collecting sites were adversely affected by construction of Barren River and Green River reservoirs, though the species probably persists in

---

Percina maculata (Girard)   Plate 2
Blackside Darter   Subgenus *Alvordius*

Description. A moderate sized member of *Alvordius* usually no larger than 65 mm SL but reaching 80 mm SL. Typically for the subgenus, it has separate or slightly joined gill membranes, an incomplete midventral row of enlarged scales, and no breeding tubercles. It is difficult to distinguish from *P. gymnocephala,* which has reduced head and nape scalation. *P. maculata* tends to have more elongated lateral blotches than either *P. peltata* or *P. notogramma* and lacks their special dorsal patterns.

Eight or 9 weak and poorly separated dorsal blotches tend to be joined with wavy lines on upper side to produce a slightly reticulated effect. Five to 8 horizontally elongated lateral blotches are connected by a midlateral band. Lower and ventral body surfaces may be unmarked or stippled. A narrow humeral bar usually extends downward behind pectoral fin. Midcaudal spot is small but fairly prominent.

Preorbital bar does not meet counterpart on lip, which is dark except for a narrow median gap in many individuals. Suborbital bar extends downward and posteriorly across pale cheek. Postorbital bar is weak on cheek and fuses into dark upper opercle. Chin, throat, and breast vary from unpigmented to lightly stippled.

Spines of first dorsal fin are alternately light and dark; membranes are stippled at base and become clear at fin margin. A dark spot appears at anterior base of fin in many individuals, particularly males. Darkened portions of soft dorsal fin rays produce several weak bands, sometimes strengthened by corresponding stippling of fin membranes. Alternatively, membranes may be stippled uniformly from base almost to fin margin. Caudal rays are darkened to produce 4 or 5 vertical bands. Remaining fins often appear clear but may have a little pigmentation.

Cheek is lightly to moderately well scaled, and opercle is

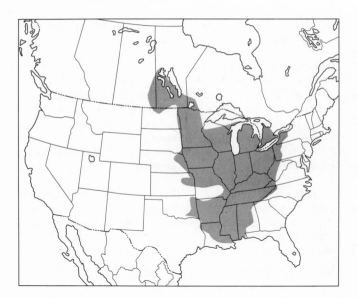

Distribution of *Percina maculata*

almost completely scaled. Nape varies from scaled to naked anteriorly and has only small embedded scales toward spiny dorsal fin. Breast in males usually bears a central enlarged scale and 1 or 2 similar scales between pelvic fins. Females may possess an interpelvic scale; anterior portion of belly and posterior midline are naked. Posterior portion in males bears enlarged, spiny scales. Lateral line contains 58-77 scales, though a local population does not show the full range of variation. Fin counts are: dorsal XII-XIV (XII-XV), 12-13 (11-15); anal II, 8-10 (8-12); pectoral 13-14 (12-15). Vertebrae number 42-43 (40-44).

Breeding males darken but do not develop bright coloration, as shown in color plate. Black spot in spiny dorsal fin is very prominent in breeding males. Genital papilla is a rather flattened tube with many longitudinal grooves at maximal development. Body of breeding females may darken enough to accentuate pattern. Genital papilla is a rounded tube, somewhat pointed at tip. Small individuals are poorly marked and may be confused with *P. sciera*, *P. gymnocephala*, and perhaps other darters.

Distribution. Is widespread in the Mississippi River basin from Louisiana to the headwaters in Minnesota. To the west, *P. maculata* just enters the Dakotas, Nebraska, and northeast Kansas. Essentially absent from the northern Ozarks, it is again present in much of Arkansas and enters eastern Oklahoma and northeastern Texas. The blackside darter occupies most of the Ohio River basin and has invaded the lower Great Lakes drainages of Wisconsin and Michigan. It extends eastward in southern Ontario to Lake Ontario and has also invaded Canada through Red River of the North. It achieves its westernmost limits in the Souris River of Saskatchewan and its northernmost limits in central Manitoba.

Natural History. The blackside darter is a common, sometimes abundant, inhabitant of medium-sized creeks and small to medium-sized rivers of low to moderate gradient. It may be found in a variety of habitats, including gravel riffles, chutes with steady flow, and pools. The species usually avoids big rivers, although Smith, Lopinot, and Pflieger (1971) did report strays in the upper Mississippi River. Because of its presence in a variety of stream types and local habitats, it has been captured with the majority of darters characteristic of the local fauna. Having retained a partially developed air bladder, this species often swims in midwater and may even leap out of the water to capture flying insects (Trautman, 1957). It seems better suited to slowly rather than rapidly flowing water.

Since the early years of this century (Forbes and Richardson, 1920), the blackside darter has received attention in Illinois. Some of this information is summarized by Larimore and Smith (1963). Larimore, Childers, and Heckrotte (1959) found the blackside darter to be one of the first species to reinvade small drought-stricken streams of that state. Thomas (1970) conducted a partial life history of *P. maculata* in Illinois and found it to be the only abundant *Percina* in the headwaters of the Kaskaskia River, reaching densities of about 260 fish per surface acre. In the middle reaches of that river it was replaced by *P. phoxocephala* as the dominant darter, while the lower end of the river was dominated by *P. shumardi*. Thomas found that blackside darters move into small headwater streams in winter or spring and migrate out again in summer. He determined that April is the month of maximal spawning, and that the young grow rapidly the first year and shift their diet from predominantly dipterans to a preponderance of mayfly larvae in summer. The species was found to take a great variety of food items, particularly in summer. Thomas's data indicate a lifespan of 4 years. Karr (1963) found an Iowa population that also lived to 4 years. Males and females grow at similar rates throughout life. Page (1976b) reported hybrids between *P. maculata* and *P. phoxocephala*, *P. caprodes*, and *Etheostoma gracile*.

Petravicz (1938) and Winn (1958a, b) describe various aspects of the breeding behavior of blackside darters. Reproduction occurs in April and May in Michigan and starts with the upstream migration of males into spawning pools and raceways. Depths of 30-60 cm and bottoms composed of sand and gravel are favored. Some ritualistic fighting occurs between males but fixed territories are not held and defended. Egg-laying starts at a minimal temperature of 16°C. A female moves from a downstream pool into the spawning area and is joined by males. She burrows into gravel or sand, which seems to stimulate a male to mount her and fertilize the eggs produced. The spawning act is repeated, usually with various males, until a complement of as many as 1,700 eggs has been laid. During spawning the male may show flashes of green or gold instead of the dark drab pigmentation otherwise seen.

Scott and Crossman (1973) state that in Ontario the blackside darter lives in turbid streams, an observation not stressed in the literature. We have noted the blackside darter, along with *Etheostoma virgatum*, to be the first darter to reinvade silted stripmine streams in the Rockcastle basin of Kentucky.

Abundance. The blackside darter remains one of the most abundant species. Cross (1967) recounts the sporadic occurrence of this species in Kansas, a condition that apparently holds along the entire western fringe of its range in the United States. Trautman (1957) observed that early collections from Ohio often contained large numbers of blackside darters, while more recent ones have tended to contain very few individuals. Similarly, Pflieger (1975) and P.W. Smith (1979) state that prairie streams of Missouri and Illinois have suffered reductions. Certainly some local reductions and losses have occurred.

Name. *Maculata* means spotted and refers to the lateral blotches.

Percina notogramma (Raney & Hubbs)   Plate 3
Stripeback Darter   Subgenus *Alvordius*

Description. A moderate sized member of its subgenus reaching at least 69 mm SL. Separate gill membranes, an incomplete row of large spiny belly scales in males, and absence of breeding tubercles place it in subgenus *Alvordius*. It looks like *P. maculata* and *P. peltata* but differs notably in that the dorsal saddles appear as dark blotches within a uniformly lighter background.

Seven or 8 small dorsal saddles are found from origin of spiny dorsal fin to base of caudal fin. Midline of nape is darkened by 2 elongated markings which have oblique extensions to a zigzag line located on upper side of body. This line tends to break up into a series of faint spots posterior to spiny dorsal fin. Side bears 6-8 large oval spots usually interconnected at level of lateral line. On anterior half of body, lateral blotches extend downward onto lower side, which is otherwise little pigmented. A pale spot usually lies above dark midcaudal spot, and the 2 may fuse into a vertical bar.

Broad preorbital bar meets counterpart on lip, which itself is somewhat darkened. Suborbital bar is curved posteriorly and contrasts well with pale cheek. Postorbital bar is narrow along upper cheek and expands on opercle. A narrow line above parallels postorbital bar. Chin, throat, and breast are pale.

A broad basal band in spiny dorsal fin is so darkened anteriorly as to form a distinguishable spot; a narrow diffuse marginal band is more prominent posteriorly. Pigment on and adjacent to soft dorsal fin rays produces 3-5 weak horizontal bands. Usually 4 similar bands are vertically arranged on caudal fin. Anal and pelvic fins are somewhat darkened basally. Pectoral fin is weakly banded.

Cheek has a few scales, mostly embedded; opercle is scaled. Nape is naked anteriorly and usually bears only a few partly embedded scales near base of spiny dorsal fin. Breast may be naked or may support a central spiny scale and a similar one between pelvic fins. Anterior portion of belly is naked in both sexes. In females remainder of belly is either fully scaled or naked along midline. Males have an incomplete row of enlarged spiny scales along posterior midline of belly. Lateral line contains 49-67 scales. Fin counts are: dorsal XIII-XV (XI-XVI), 11-14; anal II, 8-10; pectoral 13-15. Vertebrae number 40-45.

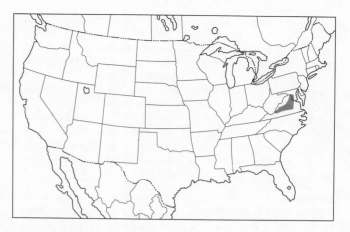

Distribution of *Percina notogramma*

Bright breeding coloration does not develop, but greater amounts of yellow highlights may be seen on opercle and fins than show in color plate. Fins of males are much darkened, and lateral blotches appear almost like a single dark band. Male genital papilla is a short, flattened tube, sometimes terminally grooved. Female genital papilla is longer, less triangular, and grooved at end.

Raney and Hubbs (1948) noted differences between upper James River populations and those elsewhere. Hogarth and Woolcott (1966) recognize the differences formally in describing subspecies *P. notogramma montuosa*. This form usually has 58-67 lateral line scales and 42-45 vertebrae, versus 49-64 scales and 40-43 vertebrae for the majority of *P.n. notogramma*.

Distribution. Occurs from the Patuxent River in Maryland southward to the James River in Virginia and the adjacent border of West Virginia. The species is absent in the sluggish lower reaches of these Chesapeake Bay streams. The population of each major drainage differs slightly from the others but the upper James River population is easily the most distinct. Hogarth and Woolcott (1966) feel it may have developed in response to the particularly cold Pleistocene temperatures experienced in its upland habitat. Distribution of the stripeback darter was probably facilitated at times of lower sea levels, which linked all Chesapeake Bay streams with the Susquehanna River.

Natural History. The stripeback darter usually inhabits streams of moderate size and gradient. It does not live in brooks but is taken in the mainstream rivers within its range. Stony riffles are preferred springtime habitat, especially where aquatic vegetation forms weedbeds. We have only taken specimens from such a weedy run and from strongly flowing channels just below riffles. Raney and Hubbs (1948) indicate that stripeback darters move into pools adjacent to riffles in summer. Darter associates are few. In the upper James River, *Percina roanoka* and *Etheostoma longimanum* inhabit the same riffle zones. Elsewhere, *E. olmstedi* or *P. peltata* may occur with *P. notogramma*.

The stripeback darter resembles and is related to *P. peltata*. Differences in behavior between the 2 might be presumed to be small, but a detailed study of the stripeback darter is still a worthwhile undertaking. Loos and Woolcott (1969) report hybridization of these species and introgression from *P. peltata* to *P. notogramma* in the York River system, apparently prompted by human disturbance of breeding sites. The variation within stripeback darters may be in part a result of past introgression. Loos and Woolcott observed the stripeback darter to spawn in shallower water than *P. peltata* and to possess behavior which they interpret to be more specialized than that of *P. peltata*.

Abundance. It is doubtful that this species is in danger of extirpation. Much of its range, however, lies within or adjacent to the eastern American megalopolis and is threatened with degradation or despoiling.

Name. *Notogramma* means line-back. *Montuosa* means of the mountains.

Percina pantherina (Moore & Reeves) Plate 3
Leopard Darter Subgenus *Alvordius*

Description. A moderate sized member of subgenus *Alvordius* reaching at least 72 mm SL. It has the subgeneric traits of separate gill membranes, an incomplete row of enlarged belly scales, and no breeding tubercles, and is unique among members of *Alvordius* in the prominence of lateral blotches unmodified by much additional patterning.

There are 10-13 middorsal spots and additional ones on upper side, some with vertical extensions to dorsal spots. Lateral extensions of 1 or both of spots on nape create the appearance of chevrons when viewed from above. A prominent midlateral series of 9-11 rounded blotches are connected by a thin pale lateral band. Small, less intense, spots may lie between several of principal lateral blotches. Upper half of body is uniformly dusky while lower half is pale. A narrow dark humeral bar is present, and caudal spot is distinct.

Broad preorbital bar darkens on snout and lip but does not quite converge with counterpart. Weak suborbital bar is directed downward and a bit posteriorly. Postorbital spot may have a posterior extension just reaching large dark spot on upper opercle. Chin, throat, and breast are pale.

Membranes of spiny dorsal fin are stippled, sometimes heavily so, almost to margin. Rays of soft dorsal fin are margined in black; membranes are darkened basally. About 3 broad indistinct vertical bands occur in caudal fin. Stippling in anal and pelvic fins is rather limited and confined to base. Pectoral fin rays have darkened margins but fin still appears quite pale.

Cheek scales may be exposed but usually are embedded. Opercle is well scaled. Nape is often naked anteriorly and usually has only tiny partly embedded scales elsewhere. There is a single large breast scale and 1 to several scales between pelvic fins. Lateral line contains 81-95 scales. One to 3 pored scales

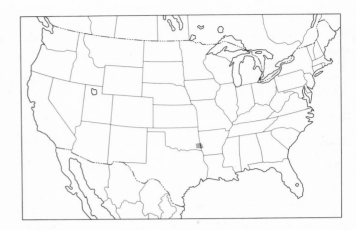

Distribution of *Percina pantherina*

may extend onto base of caudal fin. Fin counts are: dorsal XIII-XVI, 11-14; anal II, 9-11; pectoral 13 or 14. Vertebral number is not known.

Bright colors do not develop on breeding males, which may however develop spots of yellow or orange on both dorsal fins and green body hues to a degree not shown in color plate. Male genital papilla is a short pointed tube. Female genital papilla has not been observed in mature specimens.

Distribution. Is narrowly confined to the Little River system of southeastern Oklahoma and southwestern Arkansas, where it is restricted to separate headwater components of that system.

Natural History. The leopard darter occurs in moderate sized streams with gradients sufficient to produce riffles predominated by gravel, rubble, or boulders. Moore and Reeves (1955) state that it occurs in swift gravelly riffles with *Percina copelandi, P. sciera, P. phoxocephala, Etheostoma nigrum,* and *E. radiosum*. The related species *P. maculata* occurs in lower reaches of the Little River where murkiness and slow flow prevail, but apparently is not likely to be closely associated with the leopard darter. Eley, Randolph, and Miller (1975) give a good synopsis of the status of this darter. We have not seen a live specimen of the leopard darter.

Abundance. Several reservoirs have destroyed habitat, impeded the movements of *P. pantherina,* and reduced it to isolated and vulnerable populations. Robison, Moore, and Miller (1974) list the leopard darter as rare and endangered in Oklahoma, and Robison (1974a) does the same for Arkansas. Deacon et al. (1979) list the species as threatened.

Name. *Pantherina* means little panther and refers imaginatively to the leopardlike spots on the body of this darter.

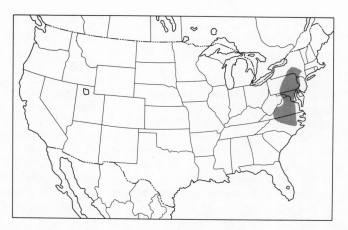

Percina peltata (Stauffer)   Plate 3
Shield Darter   Subgenus *Alvordius*

Description. A moderate sized species of subgenus *Alvordius* reaching at least 65 mm SL. Separate gill membranes, an incomplete row of enlarged scales on the belly, and absence of breeding tubercles mark it as an *Alvordius* type. It usually has fewer scales than *P. maculata* and differs from *P. notogramma* in the appearance of the dorsum.

Back usually supports 8 saddles which are connected by narrow extensions, enclosing pale portions of back as 5-7 oval spots. Six to 8 squarish lateral blotches are variable in size. Lower side is pale to stippled, and belly is pale. Some darkening occurs on ventral caudal peduncle and along anal fin base. Caudal spot may extend somewhat ventrally. Humeral mark is narrow and rather faint.

Broad preorbital bar is connected to counterpart by pigmentation on upper lip. Posteriorly curved suborbital bar is moderately to well developed. Narrow postorbital bar extends diagonally upward across cheek and may be paralleled by a second stripe beneath. Chin usually is stippled, as is breast.

Spiny dorsal fin is edged with a dusky band; vertical slashes of pigment in membranes produce a more prominent basal band. Rays of soft dorsal fin are alternately dark and clear, producing several weak bands; membranes are stippled basally. About 4 vertical bands cross caudal fin. Anal fin is stippled basally. Pelvic fin is very lightly stippled. Pectoral fin is weakly banded.

Cheek is naked or bears some embedded scales. Opercle usually has some exposed scales as well as embedded ones. Nape is naked or has small embedded scales near spiny dorsal fin. A large spiny scale usually occurs in middle of breast in males, and another is set between pelvic fins. Anterior portion of belly and remaining midline are naked in females. Posterior midline in males has enlarged spiny scales. Lateral line contains 52-61 (49-66) scales. Fin counts usually are: dorsal XII-XIII, 11-14; anal II, 8-10; pectoral 13-14. Vertebrae number 42-44.

All dark markings of head and body are intensified and often green in breeding males, and pattern may sharpen in females, but bright colors are absent in all cases. Genital papilla in males is a short flat tube with terminal knob. Papilla is larger in females, lacks knob, and is grooved.

Two subspecies, *P. p. peltata* and *P. p. nevisense,* are considered valid by Jenkins, Lachner, and Schwartz (1971). The latter form tends to have more cheek scales and more interconnected lateral blotches than the nominate subspecies.

Distribution. Occurs in Atlantic Coast streams from the Hudson southward to the Neuse basin in North Carolina. The subspecies *nevisense* occupies those drainages from the Neuse northward to the Roanoke.

Natural History. Shield darters live in rivers and many tributaries of moderate size and gradient but avoid small streams. Specimens seem to prefer riffles or the area immediately upstream rather than the foot of riffles or quiet water. During

Distribution of *Percina peltata*

summer and autumn, individuals of all sizes may take shelter or find food in beds of *Potamogeton* or other rooted aquatic plants.

New (1966) chose the shield darter for field and laboratory studies that spanned several years. He incorporated innovative control of light and temperature, as well as photographic techniques. Field observations revealed there to be no migrations of shield darters, fish tending to spend their lives closely confined to their spawning grounds. Males are ripe from September to June but females develop ripe eggs and breed when water temperature reaches 10°C, from mid-April to the end of May in New York. Males establish territories in gravel and sand riffles, where cobbles and boulders also occur. Display and chasing seldom if ever result in fights except when fish are artificially crowded in aquarium situations. A female enters breeding areas and breeds promiscuously. A male, sometimes not even the one holding the territory, mounts the female's bent body in such a fashion that her erect soft dorsal and his anal and caudal fins interlock. The male rubs the female's back as they inch forward, quiver, and deposit eggs and sperm beneath the gravel. From 15 to 25 eggs may be the complement of such an act, but New was unable to make exact counts. Several hundred eggs are probably deposited over 2 or 3 days by a breeding female. By this time her back may be rubbed bare by the spiny ventral scales of her mates. New concludes that the spawning pattern of the shield darter is quite generalized.

Darter associates are virtually limited to *Etheostoma olmstedi* in the north, but southward include *Percina crassa, P. notogramma,* and *P. roanoka,* as well as regionally common *Etheostoma.* Loos and Woolcott (1969) found evidence through hybridization of introgression from *P. peltata* to *P. notogramma* in the York River basin.

Abundance. Enough quality habitat exists at present to guarantee the continued success of the shield darter. It has an unusually large range for an eastern darter.

Name. *Peltata* means shield and refers to the dorsal pattern. *Nevisense* means birthmark, probably referring to the lateral blotches.

Percina roanoka (Jordan & Jenkins)   Plate 3
Roanoke Darter   Subgenus *Alvordius*

Description. A small robust member of *Alvordius* reaching a maximum size of about 60 mm SL. It is a typical member of the subgenus by virtue of separate gill membranes, no breeding tubercules, and an incomplete row of enlarged scales on the belly, but is a bit stockier than its relatives and is the only *Alvordius* to attain bright breeding coloration.

Back is crossed by 6 or 7 saddles, anterior ones being laterally connected by horizontal bands on upper side, resulting in several isolated pale spots on dorsum, somewhat like those of *P. peltata*. Posteriorly, saddles become small and disconnected. Nine to 11 vertically elongated lateral blotches are narrowly connected by a midlateral stripe; several extend far ventrally, but lower side and belly are otherwise pale to stippled. Dark humeral bar sometimes is partly fused with first lateral blotch. A basicaudal spot, distinct in small specimens, tends to fuse partially with adjacent lateral blotch in adults.

Preorbital bar fuses with counterpart on upper lip. Suborbital bar is rather short, broad, and diffuse. A postorbital spot is present and in some individuals expands into a bar extending across cheek and opercle. Chin, throat, and breast are lightly stippled in females, more heavily stippled in males. There is a narrow black submarginal band in spiny dorsal fin; a similar broad basal band is best developed in males. Rays and membranes of soft dorsal fin are darkened to produce at least 3 horizontal bands; caudal fin has similar vertical bands. Anal, pelvic, and pectoral fins are clear to lightly pigmented in females, but anal and pelvic fins in particular are dark in mature males.

Cheek is naked and opercle has a few scales, some partly embedded. Most of nape is naked, but embedded or exposed scales appear just in front of spiny dorsal fin. Most individuals have a large spiny scale in middle of breast and another between pelvic fins. Midline of belly is naked in females. In males, posterior midline has enlarged spiny scales. Lateral line has 40-50 (38-54) scales. Fin counts are: dorsal X-XI (IX-XII), 10-11 (9-12); anal II, 7-9; pectoral 13-15. Vertebrae number 39-40 (37-41).

Breeding males are brightly colored, as shown in color plate. Genital papilla is a short flattened tube. Breeding females may develop a green to yellow cast but are not brightly pigmented. Genital papilla is a fleshy tube, thick at base and tapering to a weakly grooved terminal flap.

Mayden and Page (1979) have noted higher lateral line scale counts, more dorsal rays, and somewhat modified belly scales in montane populations of *P. roanoka* compared with those from the Piedmont and Coastal Plain.

Distribution. Principally inhabits the Roanoke, Neuse, and Tar River basins in Virginia and North Carolina. Populations now present in the upper New River basin of Virginia and West Virginia are said by Robert Ross (personal communication) to be bait introductions. Hocutt and Hambrick (1973) attribute it to the same cause. While human introduction into Craig Creek of the James system cannot be ruled out, Lachner

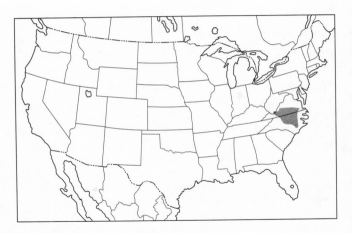

Distribution of *Percina roanoka*

and Jenkins (1971) suggest that stream piracy was involved in species transfers at this point. By whatever means, the Roanoke darter is one of the few darters known to be rapidly expanding its range.

Natural History. The Roanoke darter is an inhabitant of fast current over a variety of substrates ranging from sand and gravel to cobble mixed with other sediments. This species invades rather small streams as well as the main channels of principal rivers within its range. In some riffle situations it exceeds all other darters in abundance, but usually is less abundant than one or more species of *Etheostoma*. In the James, New, and upper Roanoke rivers, the Roanoke darter lives in streams of high gradient under essentially montane conditions. In the Tar, Neuse, and lower Roanoke rivers, this species exploits stream habitat of low to moderate gradient where riffle habitat exists. In the upper Roanoke River we have found females fully ripe as late as June 3, and males in good coloration at the same time. The height of the breeding season appears to be earlier in lowland streams. Hobson (1979) reports that in the upper Roanoke basin juveniles live in pools while adults choose riffles. He found that breeding occurs in late May and early June. Individuals grow most in their first year, and life span is estimated to be 3 years. Larval stages of mayflies, blackflies, and midges are the main food items, and these are taken during daylight hours.

Hocutt and Hambrick (1973) found considerable hybridization between the introduced population of Roanoke darters and the native *P. oxyrhyncha* in the New River. This situation will be interesting to follow. The speed with which Roanoke darters spread may give us a time reference for dispersal rates among small stream fishes.

Bailey and Gosline (1955) treat this darter as *P. crassa roanoka*. Mayden and Page (1979) restore full species recognition and also contribute a firmer understanding of other members of *Alvordius* in Atlantic drainages.

Abundance. The Roanoke darter is one of the most adaptable and successful species of darters.

Name. *Roanoka* is obviously a reference to the Roanoke River in which this species occurs.

Percina species
Upper Mobile Basin form

Plate 3

Subgenus *Alvordius*

Description. A delicate member of subgenus *Alvordius,* and the smallest, at maximum length a little over 50 mm SL. Sharing the subgenus traits of separate (or slightly connected) gill membranes, lack of breeding tubercles, and enlarged belly scales, it is easily separated from other members of the subgenus on the basis of size and the full-length lateral band.

Upper half of body is a dusky tan in contrast to pale ventral half. A thin middorsal line extends from head to end of soft dorsal fin. There are several weakly developed dorsal saddles. A weak dorsolateral band extends from head at least as far as origin of soft dorsal fin. A striking dark lateral band extends from snout to caudal fin base, expanding into a series of 7 or 8 blotches on the body. Pale lower side and belly are virtually white but lightly sprinkled with tiny stipples.

If present, preorbital and postorbital bars are incorporated in midlateral band. Suborbital bar is lacking. Chin and throat are lightly stippled. Breast is more densely stippled.

Dorsal spines are clear, but basal and marginal bands in spiny dorsal fin are produced by darkening of membranes. This fin is particularly low and arched. Margins of soft dorsal, caudal, and anal fins are darkly edged but otherwise pale. Dorsal and ventral keels of modest proportion extend from slender peduncle onto caudal fin. Lightly stippled pelvic fins are slender and sometimes overlap at tips. Pectoral fin rays bear touches of pigment along their margins, but fin appears almost transparent.

Cheek and opercle are scaled. Nape is finely scaled posteriorly but becomes naked near head. Breast bears a few tiny scales and 1 large spiny interpelvic scale. Belly lacks scales anteriorly; males have a series of enlarged spiny scales on midline. Complete lateral line contains 66-74 scales. Fin counts are: dorsal XII-XV, 10-12; anal II, 8-10; pectoral 13-14. Vertebral numbers are not known.

Though striking because of intense tonal contrasts between dark lateral band and tan above or white beneath, this undescribed species apparently lacks bright breeding colors. Male genital papilla is a small triangular flap, stippled at base. Female genital papilla has not been observed in mature specimens.

Distribution. Has been taken in the Conasauga River in Tennessee and immediately downstream in Georgia. A subspecies of this unnamed darter is apparently confined to the Sipsey Fork of the Black Warrior River in Alabama.

Natural History. Little can be said about this species other than that it occurs in slowly flowing reaches of rivers with sandy bottoms and depths of 1/2 m or more. Apparently it is not an inhabitant of creeks. We are greatly indebted to David Etnier for aid in obtaining the specimen we photographed.

Abundance. This species' precarious situation in Alabama is discussed by Ramsey (1976). Though unnamed, it is mentioned by Deacon et al. (1979) as threatened.

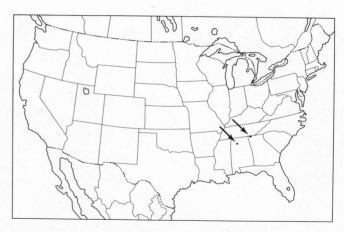

Distribution of *Percina* sp., subgenus *Alvordius*

Percina evides (Jordan & Copeland)
Gilt Darter

Plate 3

Subgenus *Ericosma*

Description. A moderate sized darter of robust appearance reaching a maximum size of at least 65 mm SL. It is easily recognized as a member of subgenus *Ericosma* by the broad bands crossing the back in association with bright breeding colors and breeding tubercles in adult males. It differs from its only congener, *P. palmaris,* in possessing a strong suborbital bar.

In adults, 7-9 dark bands cross back and join a like number of darker lateral blotches, which are joined by a midlateral band. Faint ventral extensions of some vertical bands constitute the only pattern of lower body. Scales on lower part of body may be finely stippled along margins to produce a dusky appearance, especially in males. Prepectoral area often is dusky.

Diffuse preorbital bar tends to merge into darkened snout and upper lip. Suborbital bar stands out strongly against pale cheek and extends almost to ventral midline in many cases. Horizontally elongated postorbital bar may end on upper cheek or fuse into darkened part of upper opercle. Chin, throat, and breast are lightly stippled in males but may be pale in females. A large dark patch occurs on head behind eyes.

Dark pigments are variably distributed in spiny dorsal fin. Spines are clear, and in females membranes may simply grade from stippled at base to clear at margin, or females may have a basal and a submarginal band. In males, pigment in membranes is most concentrated in a broad median band if not uniformly distributed. Each ray of soft dorsal fin has a darkened spot near base, while membranes are moderately stippled at base and become clear at margin. Caudal fin rays are narrowly edged in black with no additional pattern present. Anal fin rays are similarly marked near base. Pelvic fin is clear to stippled on membranes. Pectoral fin rays are narrowly and faintly edged in black.

Cheek is naked or has a few embedded scales behind eye. Opercle bears a few exposed scales and sometimes additional

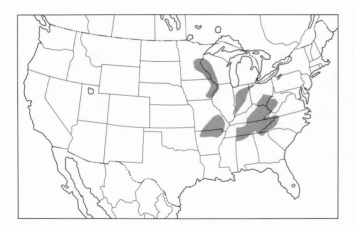

Distribution of *Percina evides*

partially embedded ones. Nape is well scaled posteriorly but grades to embedded scales anteriorly and sometimes is naked. A large spiny scale is found in center of breast and another between pelvic fins. Midline of belly usually is naked in females, and lined with a row of enlarged spiny scales in males. Lateral line contains 56-76 scales, higher counts tending to be found in western parts of range. Fin counts are: dorsal XII-XIV (XI-XV), 11-12 (10-14); anal II, 8-9 (7-10); pectoral 14-15 (13-16). Vertebrae number 38-39 in specimens studied in Indiana and 40-41 in Georgia.

As shown in color plate, breeding males are brightly colored. Green or blue may be more prominently developed on body than shown in our specimen. Breeding tubercles are abundantly distributed on ventral surface of each pelvic ray and dorsal surface of first 3 pelvic rays. Conspicuous tubercles occur on anal spines and rays and a few on ventral caudal fin rays. Enlarged midventral belly scales contain up to 3 tubercules each, apparently a unique situation among darters. Several additional rows of scales on belly and caudal peduncle are tuberculate, and a few tubercles may occur as far up as lateral line. Small tubercles develop on head pores of lateral line system and continue onto chin, opercle, and branchiostegal rays. *P. evides* is probably the most tuberculate species of the genus. Male genital papilla is a short triangular flattened tube, usually sprinkled with dark spots. Coloration in females consists of dull yellow on lower body and on submarginal band in spiny dorsal fin. Genital papilla is a semicircular grooved pad, pointed at tip.

Variation of scale counts and perhaps other characteristics may warrant recognition of subspecies of the gilt darter.

Distribution. Occurs in the upper Ohio River basin of New York and Pennsylvania and in most of the major southern tributaries of that river. It was never common in Ohio (Trautman, 1957) and is recorded again in Indiana for the first time in 46 years by Margulies, Burch, and Clark (1980). The species has been taken in scattered spots within the upper Mississippi River basin and again in the eastern Ozarks of Missouri and Arkansas, where it is locally common.

Natural History. The gilt darter inhabits fairly clear rivers of various size. Clay (1975) collected it in large creeks in Kentucky. It favors moderate current from the middle to lower portions of clean gravelly riffles and may also be found in clean pools with moderate current. Because of its strong preference for clear streams, it usually has a number of associates, often the bulk of the regional darter fauna.

Little is known about the habits of the gilt darter. We have only captured it in Missouri, Tennessee, and Kentucky, where males retain bright coloration well into summer. Pflieger (1975) suggests a late breeding season, based on his observations in Ozark streams.

Abundance. The gilt darter seems to be a dwindling species throughout much of its range. Harlan and Speaker (1956) report that no Iowa records exist for this century, and Gerking (1945) noted population declines in Indiana. Though not yet listed as rare and endangered, the gilt darter is nonetheless rare in many parts of its range and should be a species of concern. Populations in the upper Tennessee River system and the Ozarks seem to offer the best hope for persistence of this handsome fish.

Name. *Evides* means comely and is quite appropriate.

Percina palmaris (Bailey)   Plate 4
Bronze Darter   Subgenus *Ericosma*

Description. A robust darter of above average size, reaching 78.4 mm SL in our largest specimen. It is recognized as a member of subgenus *Ericosma* by the broad bands crossing the back, along with the bright breeding colors and tubercles in adult males. It differs from its congener, *P. evides,* in lacking a sharp suborbital bar.

Eight to 10 broad vertical bands cross back, merge with a like number of interconnected lateral blotches, and continue onto lower side. There may be additional isolated dark spots and zigzag lines on upper side. Broad bands may not cross back in females, some having instead small dorsal saddles and a reticulate pattern on upper side. Lower side and belly are pale but stippled. Darkened humeral area is often fused above with a dark blotch on nape. Prepectoral area is often dusky. A diffuse midcaudal spot is flanked above and below by pale oval spots.

Rather narrow preorbital bar fails to meet counterpart on snout but may be joined by blackening on upper lip. Suborbital bar is absent or vaguely suggested by heavier than normal stippling on cheek. Postorbital bar crosses cheek and fuses into dark upper part of opercle. Especially in females, there may be an additional line running diagonally upward from eye. Chin, throat, and breast in females are lightly stippled, in males are more darkly pigmented.

Dorsal fin spines of males are overlain with stippling. Membranes are darkened to form a narrow marginal band and a more prominent median band. Clear areas at base of membranes appear as small windows. In females dorsal fin spines are alternately light and dark, and membranes form much weaker marginal and median bands than in males. Soft dorsal fin in males is similar to spiny dorsal except that marginal band is absent. Soft dorsal fin of females also resembles its spiny counterpart, although banding is quite weak. Caudal fin appears to be square-cut at end. In males caudal rays are darkened along their full length, partly obscuring the 3 vertical bands. These vertical band are more distinct in females, which have little continuous pigment along caudal rays. Anal fin is little pigmented except for stippling of membrane base in males. Pelvic fin is similarly pigmented. Pectoral fin rays are slightly darkened in males, clear in females.

Cheek supports a large patch of small scales, some of which may be partly embedded. A small group of larger opercular scales may be difficult to see due to embedding. Nape is well scaled posteriorly but scales may be embedded near head. Breast of females may be naked or have a few embedded scales on posterior half. Breast of males contains a few enlarged scales along midline from center back to a patch of large interpelvic scales, as well as a few embedded scales to either side of midline. Belly of females usually is naked anteriorly and fully scaled posteriorly. Males are similar except for a row of enlarged scales along belly midline. Lateral line contains 59-69 (57-73) scales. Fin counts are: dorsal XII-XIII (XI-XIV), 11-12 (10-13); anal II, 8-9 (7-10); pectoral 13-15. Vertebrae number 40-42.

As with a number of species of darters, mature males have longer and more expansive fins, especially soft dorsal and anal fins. Denoncourt (1976) has shown in addition that modal number of rays in fins is 1 greater in males than in females. Breeding males are handsomely colored, as shown in color plate. Fleshy tubercular ridges occur on anal, pelvic, and pectoral fins from March through June (Denoncourt, 1976). Additional tubercles are on ventral scales of caudal peduncle. Male genital papilla is a small conical projection with 1 to several terminal grooves. Breeding females lack bright colors but are nonetheless striking with green and yellow highlights on body, head, and fins. Female genital papilla is a semicircular grooved pad.

Distribution. Restricted to the Coosa and Tallapoosa arms of the Mobile basin, where it is reported only above the Fall Line in Alabama, Georgia, and Tennessee.

Natural History. The bronze darter inhabits small rivers and their principal tributaries. Boschung (1961) lists it as a species characteristic of tributaries of the Coosa River. Clear to slightly murky streams with riffles composed of rubble, gravel, and clean sand may yield bronze darters from deeper, strongly flowing zones (Bailey, 1940). We took 2 adults in a creek from beneath undercut banks with steady current and a substrate of gravel and sand.

Percina copelandi, P. nigrofasciata, Etheostoma coosae, and *E. jordani* are common associates. Unnamed forms of subgenus *Ulocentra* from the Coosa and Tallapoosa drainages also occur with the bronze darter, and some rare species such as *P. antesella, P. aurolineata,* and *P. lenticula* occur within its range. Ecological and life history information on this species is limited. Wieland (1980) found a single afternoon feed-

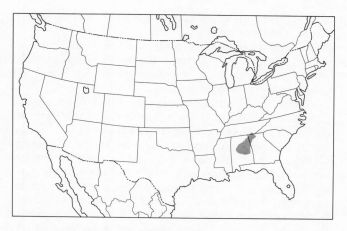

Distribution of *Percina palmaris*

ing peak for bronze darters, males and females alike taking mayflies, blackflies, midges, caddisflies, stoneflies, and snails. Crawford (1954) found variability within the species insufficient to erect subspecies. Denoncourt (1976) reports differences between Coosa and Tallapoosa River populations.

Abundance. The bronze darter has lost valuable habitat to reservoirs and is probably abundant in few streams. Its status bears close watching, though it is not at present threatened.

Name. *Palmaris* means prize, a name choice left to the imagination of the reader by Bailey (1940).

Percina cymatotaenia (Gilbert & Meek)   Plate 4
Bluestripe Darter   Subgenus *Odontopholis*

Description. A darter of moderate size and robustness, reaching 65.1 mm SL in our largest specimen. This species and the subgenus *Odontopholis* are unique in having a distinct keel at the ventral contact between the caudal peduncle and caudal fin. Several other species in *Percina* have the suggestion of a keel but in this case it is semicircular in adult males and covered with scales bearing exceptionally long spines. The bluestripe darter is named from Missouri but we include here the Kentucky and Tennessee populations, as well. If, as several ichthyologists feel, the eastern form is a distinct species, then the name *P. cymatotaenia* will apply only to specimens west of the Mississippi River.

A dark middorsal stripe extends from head to end of spiny dorsal fin or beyond. Expansions of the stripe are far too slight to be viewed as dorsal saddles. An additional interrupted wavy dorsolateral band may be found to either side of midline stripe. Remainder of dorsum is pale to dusky and contrasts markedly with a very broad black lateral band with 8-10 expansions, the first 2 of which are poorly defined. Lateral line runs through this band as a thin pale line. A small black midcaudal spot is usually flanked above and below by pale areas. Lower parts of body are basically pale but in adults become stippled and mottled.

Preorbital bar meets counterpart on snout and seems to continue as dark pigment through eye; postorbital bar joins with lateral band. Head is dusky above level of eyes and very pale but mottled or stippled below.

Spines in first dorsal fin bear several dark spots, most of pigment lying adjacent to rather than in spine; membranes are darkly stippled to produce marginal and basal bands. Darkening of soft dorsal fin rays produces 2-4 faint bands; membranes are lightly stippled at base and gradually become unmarked at margin. Caudal fin membranes are virtually clear, and rays are spotted to produce several dark wavy bands. Large anal fin is distinctly notched between second spine and first ray; spots on and adjacent to rays are the only markings. Both pelvic and pectoral fins have dark spots produced by pigment on rays and adjacent portions of membranes.

Cheek is well scaled though some scales may be partly embedded. Opercle and nape are scaled and there is some encroachment of scales onto dorsolateral portion of head. One or more enlarged scales lie between pelvic fins. Breast is variably sprinkled with large scales or a few small embedded ones, but scales are not present on anterior margin of breast or prepectoral area. A few scales may be missing from belly just posterior to pelvic fins, but remainder is essentially fully scaled in both sexes. Large males may have a few enlarged scales immediately anterior to anus. Lateral line usually has 64-75 scales. Often several rows of tiny scales extend onto base of caudal fin. A distinct ventral keel lies at junction of body and caudal fin. Keel is moderately developed in females and in males may be so enlarged as to appear semicircular. Fin counts are: dorsal XII-XIV (XI-XV), 11-12 (10-14); anal II, 9-10 (8-13); pectoral usually 12-13. Vertebral counts of 43-45 are known but range may be greater.

Though not brightly colored, as seen in color plate, the bluestripe darter is handsomely marked, particularly in large specimens. Midlateral band may be bluish black in breeding individuals, accounting for the common name. In breeding males, scales on ventral keel stand away from body and several long spines on each may be directed vertically away from body. Anal fin is expansive, usually reaching caudal keel when pressed against body. Breeding tubercles are not present. Male genital papilla is a short triangular flap, longitudinally grooved at tip. Mature females also are strikingly marked, body and fins appearing quite blotchy and spotted. Size of ventral keel and length of spines on them are reduced. Genital papilla is short, somewhat squarish, and flattened, and is grooved and bilobed terminally. Even in juveniles, mid-dorsal stripe, lateral band, and caudal spot are conspicuous.

Information given in this description comes almost exclusively from Kentucky specimens.

Distribution. Described from Missouri; known originally from the Osage and Gasconade systems. Clay (1975) lists it in Kentucky from the Green and Kentucky rivers.

That the Kentucky records constitute a new species has been stated by Collette (1965), Page (1974a), and emphatically by Burr (1980). Morphological evidence may prove this idea correct, but zoogeographic evidence speaks against it in that

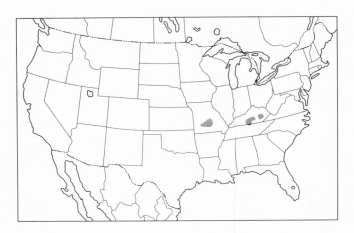

Distribution of *Percina cymatotaenia*

there are at present no endemic fishes shared exclusively by the Kentucky and Green rivers. *Percina cymatotaenia* is not a headwater species and could not have been transferred by stream capture without other fishes having been exchanged also. What we may see in this case is relict populations of a once widely distributed darter.

Natural History. The bluestripe darter occurs in streams of moderate size and gradient, where it lives in quiet backwaters that are relatively free of silt. Aquatic vegetation and woody debris that afford some cover are favorite haunts. In May these darters may be encountered in moderately swift water just below and marginal to strong riffles, where presumably they gather to spawn. Bluestripe darters are often taken with *Percina maculata,* which also avoids strong currents. In aquariums they rest among aquatic vegetation or swim freely and easily through open waters. Their air bladder must be well developed, in contrast to most darters.

Because the bluestripe darter lacks breeding tubercles, there is a good possibility that the specialized caudal keel of males plays a distinctive role in mating behavior. In well developed males there also are fleshy spinelike extensions along the base of the anal fin. A thorough life history study of this species is needed.

Abundance. Pflieger (1971, 1975) indicates that the bluestripe darter was locally abundant and more widespread in Missouri before 1900 than now, and that the species may only persist there in the Gasconade and Niangua rivers. Branson (1977) cites the threat of stripmining to the bluestripe darter in eastern Kentucky. During the past 10 years we have found the species more difficult to obtain in the upper Green River and to some extent in the Red River of the Kentucky basin. Our general impression is one of a species with continuously less success and one worthy of concern if not threatened status in Kentucky and Tennessee. Based on the Ozark populations alone, Deacon et al. (1979) consider the species to be threatened.

Name. *Cymatotaenia* can be translated as wavy stripe and refers to the beautiful lateral band.

Percina aurantiaca (Cope)   Plate 4
Tangerine Darter   Subgenus *Hypohomus*

Description. A large robust darter often exceeding 100 mm SL and known to reach 133 mm SL. It is unique among *Percina* in several ways, including having 84 or more lateral line scales, the absence or virtual absence of enlarged midventral scales, the presence of a series of dark spots along the upper side, and bright male coloration.

Dusky back is marked by a middorsal dark stripe extending from head to about end of soft dorsal fin. Stripe may be expanded at numerous points. A broad dark lateral band with 8-10 expansions extends full length of body. Upper side has a distinctive series of black spots extending from behind head to beneath soft dorsal fin. By contrast, lower side and ventral body surface are pale except for some faint ventral extensions of lateral band. A broad diffuse humeral bar is partially hidden behind pectoral fin. There is a prominent midcaudal spot.

Orbital bars are essentially replaced by a narrow continuation of lateral band forward to snout. Cheek is pale except for stippling on scale margins. Chin and throat are lightly stippled, breast more intensely so. Gill membranes are narrowly connected in most cases but moderately connected in some.

Dorsal fin spines are clear to slightly amber. Fin supports a narrow marginal band and a broad band near base. Rays of soft dorsal fin are clear and membranes stippled to produce bands similar to but fainter than those of spiny dorsal. Caudal fin is short and deep, an appearance enhanced by a small ventral keel on caudal peduncle in males. Caudal fin rays are darkened marginally and membranes are virtually clear. Anal fin has 2 weak bands in females, but a denser, more uniform distribution of melanophores in males. Pelvic fin is moderately stippled in males but lacks basal pigmentation in females. Rather short pectoral fin is weakly pigmented, mostly with dark flecks near tip.

Cheek is well covered with scales, some of which may be embedded. Opercle is heavily scaled. Nape scales are exposed posteriorly and exposed or embedded near head, which also bears a few scales adjacent to nape. Breast and lower prepectoral area vary from well scaled to scaled only in patches. Belly often is naked immediately behind pelvic fin insertions; remainder is fully scaled in both sexes except for a few slightly enlarged scales before anus in some males. Lateral line contains 84-95 scales. Fin counts are: dorsal XIII-XV (XII-XVI), 13-15 (11-15); anal II, 10-12; pectoral usually 14-15. Vertebrae number 44-45.

As seen in color plate, breeding males develop bright coloration. In young males this starts as an orange patch on gill membranes. At maximum development even lips and lower surfaces of body are orange to reddish orange. Genital papilla is a small triangular flap, deeply grooved at tip. Denoncourt (1976) indicates that breeding tubercles are similar to those of *P. palmaris,* but they await detailed description. Breeding coloration in females is subdued compared to males, but dull yellow appears on both fins and body. Female genital papilla is a short rounded tube.

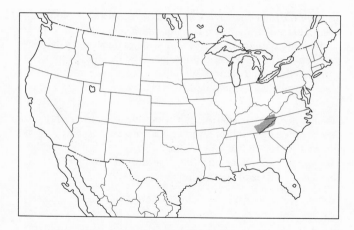

Distribution of *Percina aurantiaca*

Distribution. Found in large tributaries of the Tennessee River in Georgia, North Carolina, Tennessee, and Virginia. Collecting sites are quite scattered and only a few in Tennessee seem to support the species in large numbers.

Natural History. The tangerine darter inhabits rivers of moderate to steep gradient, often in currents and at depths which preclude capture with seines. Adults apparently spend the winter in deep pools and congregate during spring in waters of intermediate depth downstream from swift chutes and rapids. Females remain in such habitat until autumn except to spawn in shallower rubble and gravel areas from mid-May to mid-June. Males usually remain in very swift water from July to October. The young choose shallow and comparatively quiet areas marginal to the main channel, where they may be associated with many other species of the rich Tennessee basin fauna. Adults are found in association mostly with *Percina burtoni, P. caprodes,* and *P. evides. Etheostoma acuticeps, E. chlorobranchium,* and *E. swannanoa* utilize the same habitat, and *E. simoterum* and *E. rufilineatum* may be abundant in shallow riffles nearby. No other darter in the upper Tennessee basin seems so well suited to torrential flow.

Observation or capture of tangerine darters poses a major challenge. Howell (1971) used scuba diving techniques to observe this species and employed a special cyanide collecting technique that prevented fish mortality. Howell's studies showed that tangerine darters are long lived, up to 4 years, but that growth is rapid only in the first year. Adults feed heavily on immature insects associated with riverweed, *Podostemum ceratophyllum,* and on insect larvae living among gravel and rubble. Young and juvenile specimens feed on small crustacea, diptera larvae, and baetid mayflies that frequent the stream margin.

Territoriality and elaborate courtship were not observed by Howell. In fact, a male seems to be stimulated to spawn when a female comes to rest motionlessly over clean gravel. Quivering may accompany the spawning act when the male is mounted over the female in typical *Percina* fashion, but there seems to be no complex ritual. Females spawn several times with a male and presumably spawn with more than one mate. Parental care was not observed.

David Etnier employed the cyanide technique to obtain the individual illustrated in our color plate. He states that large individuals will strike a fly, and with patience may be captured in such a manner. Dahlberg and Scott (1971) report the same method of capture. We have caught only rather small specimens by conventional seining methods.

Abundance. The tangerine darter remains common only at a few sites where siltation and various forms of domestic or industrial pollution are no problem. The status of this spectacular darter should be carefully monitored, though it is not listed as a species of special concern.

Name. *Aurantiaca* means orange colored.

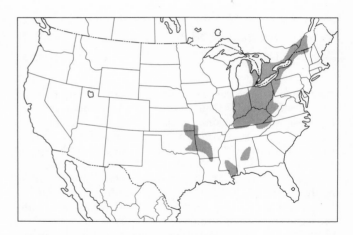

Distribution of *Percina copelandi*

Percina copelandi (Jordan)   Plate 4
Channel Darter   Subgenus *Cottogaster*

Description. A small and delicate *Percina* seldom exceeding 60 mm SL and usually less than 50 mm SL. It is similar to the majority of forms in the genus in having enlarged belly scales in males, but differs from all others in lacking a frenum, or in rarely having a quite narrow one. Juveniles are weakly marked and may be confused in the field with johnny darters, *Etheostoma nigrum*.

Back supports 5-9 blotches, in no case particularly darkened. Dusky cross-hatched appearance of back and upper side is due to darkening of most scale margins. Midlateral series of 8-18 horizontally elongated small blotches tend to be interconnected by a faint narrow band. Lower half of body is free of pattern and usually pale. A small basicaudal spot may be faint and joined to last midlateral blotch.

Well defined preorbital bar meets counterpart on snout. Additional pigment occurs on upper lip. A dorsal extension of bar may be found just anterior to each nostril. Suborbital bar may be absent in juveniles, is present as a large spot in females, and may be quite long and narrow in males. Dashes on cheek replace postorbital bar. Chin usually has a patch of small spots, but throat and breast are virtually without pigment.

Spiny dorsal fin is weakly pigmented in females, but has a broad dark band above base and a narrow marginal band in males. Soft dorsal fin rays are darkened at 3 or 4 points along their length; darkening of membranes grades from base to nearly clear fin margin. Pigmentation in males greatly exceeds that in females. Caudal fin membranes are little stippled but rays are darkly edged. Anal fin may be almost clear or rather well darkened toward base of each membrane. Second anal spine is particularly clear and translucent. Pelvic fins are widely separated, rounded, and often somewhat cupped; membranes are darkened basally in males but are almost clear in females. Pectoral fin margins are a bit darkened but fin appears to be pale.

Cheek is naked in most populations, weakly scaled (small and embedded) in a few. Opercle is scaled. Nape is scaled near dorsal fin but variably scaled to naked toward head. Breast is naked except for 1, rarely 2, enlarged scales between pelvic fins of most individuals and in some cases a scale in center of breast. Belly is naked anteriorly in both sexes and along midline to anus in females. In males this posterior line is occupied by a row of enlarged spiny scales. Lateral line consists of 43-61 scales, but most commonly 48-52 through most of the species range. Fin counts are: dorsal X-XI (IX-XII), 11-12 (10-14); anal II, 7-9; pectoral 13-14 (12-15). Vertebrae number 38-39 (37-40).

Breeding males lack bright coloration but may develop intense darkening of fins and body, more so than shown in color plate. A greenish sheen may appear on upper body and blue on lower side. Male genital papilla is a short tapered tube. Male tuberculation was not found by Collette (1965) but since has been reported (but not described) by Page (1974a) and Denoncourt (1976). Breeding females have sharper patterns than nonbreeding counterparts. Female genital papilla is a slender tube.

The channel darter is variable and may constitute several species, or at least distinct subspecies. Cross (1967) states that cheeks are scaled in Kansas specimens, lateral line counts are 55-61, and lateral blotches are low in number. Populations isolated in the Mobile basin are distinct, as illustrated in Smith-Vaniz (1968). Deacon et al. (1979) list the Pearl River form as an unnamed species. Ramsey et al. (1980) mention the Cahaba River population as being an unnamed species.

Distribution. Principally found in the Ohio River basin, within which this species occurs sporadically. Extending into the Great Lakes and St. Lawrence drainage, it occurs in Michigan along Lake Huron and eastward along both shores of Lake Erie. Scattered records exist for the lower St. Lawrence as far as the Nicolet and St. François rivers in Canada and Lake Champlain in the United States. Channel darters occur again in the Arkansas, Ouachita, and Red rivers of southeastern Kansas, southwestern Missouri, eastern Oklahoma, Arkansas, and northern Louisiana. Other isolated distributional segments are found in the Pearl and Pascagoula rivers of Mississippi and Louisiana, and in the Black Warrior, Cahaba, and Coosa rivers in Alabama.

Natural History. The channel darter generally inhabits rivers and large creeks in areas of moderate current, usually over sand and gravel substrates. Such conditions are usually found at the lower ends of riffles or at the edges of deep channels. Seasonally these darters may move into the slower current of pools or somewhat upstream where scattered rubble affords spawning sites. They may be collected with all regional darters except those with strong preference for small streams. Trautman (1957) reports that channel darters most often remain at depths approaching 1 m during the day but invade shallow water at night. Trautman (1957), Hubbs and Lagler (1947), and Scott and Crossman (1973) all report that the channel darter inhabits lakes, including Lake Erie, in the northeastern part of its range.

Winn (1953) describes the reproductive behavior of channel darters in a Michigan stream. Males occupy territories as small as 1 sq m downstream from stones located in moderate current, usually near shore. A female entering such a territory is courted by the male or at least is directed toward the center of the territory. The female burrows into clean gravel behind the stone and is mounted by the male with his caudal fin placed against hers. Winn was able to collect 4-10 eggs from single spawnings. The female repeats the process with various males until as many as 400 eggs may have been laid. This breeding activity occurs in July at water temperatures of about 20° or 21°C. Cross (1967) found Kansas specimens to be spent by early June, and surmised that late April and early May are the spawning time in that state.

Several authors have reported chironomids and small crustacea to be the most important food items of *P. copelandi*. Turner (1921) reports mayflies as a component of the diet, and Cross (1967) indicates that caddisflies also were taken. Hoffman (1967) and Bangham and Hunter (1939) found low parasite infestation rates in the channel darter.

We have never taken channel darters in large numbers except in the Licking River of Kentucky. The preferred habitat here fits that described by various other writers who have discussed the channel darter.

Abundance. The species is still too well distributed to be classified as rare or endangered, but channel darters are distributed quite sparingly over much of their range, and are quite rare locally. Deacon et al. (1979) list the Pearl River representative as threatened.

Name. Named for H.E. Copeland, who discovered the fish near Indianapolis, Indiana.

Percina antesella Williams & Etnier   Plate 4
Amber Darter   Subgenus *Imostoma*

Description. A rather small and delicate appearing member of this subgenus unlikely to exceed 60 mm SL. This darter is easily recognized as an *Imostoma* by the combination of nearly separate gill membranes, lack or virtual lack of a frenum, eyes closely set high on the head, scarcity of belly

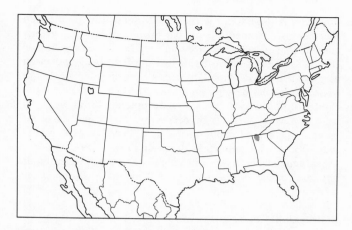

Distribution of *Percina antesella*

scalation, elongated anal fin in males, and the presence of numerous breeding tubercles on the lower body of males. It differs from other members of its subgenus in that the first dorsal saddle lies wholly anterior to the spiny dorsal fin.

Back is dusky and somewhat speckled, usually tan or reddish brown in life. The first of 4 dorsal saddles is darkest and most isolated. All saddles extend downward on upper side but usually fail to join directly with lateral markings, which consist of irregularly shaped blotches connected along midline by numerous stipplings. Blotches and midlateral band tend to be much better defined on posterior half of body. Lower side is pale, blotched, and suffused with some yellow in life. Belly is pale and unmarked. A small midcaudal spot is usually present.

Head is quite dark above eye level and basically pale below. Rarely a narrow frenum is present. Preorbital bar is not apparent. Posteriorly recurved suborbital bar stands out boldly against cheek. A postorbital spot is found well behind eye. Throat usually is darkened at junction of gill membranes. Breast is pale.

Spiny dorsal fin supports weak marginal and basal bands produced principally by darkening in membranes. Each ray of soft dorsal fin has 4 or 5 darkened areas which produce a faintly banded appearance. Caudal and pectoral fins are similarly marked and appear to be vertically banded. Ventralmost caudal rays are bent downward in a weak keel, unlike other species in subgenus *Imostoma*. Anal and pelvic fins are stippled but not distinctly banded.

Cheek is unscaled and opercle scaled, at least in a dorsal patch. Nape is scaled posteriorly but either is naked or has embedded scales anteriorly. Males usually have 2 enlarged scales between pelvic fins and several smaller scales just anterior to them and along midline. Minute embedded scales may be scattered elsewhere on breast. Anterior part of belly is naked in both sexes, and midline remains so in females. Males have a row of elongated toothed scales along belly midline. Lateral line is complete with 51-66 scales. Fin counts are: dorsal IX-XI, (13-15); anal II, 8-10; pectoral 13-15. Vertebrae number 38-40.

Golden hues on body, head, and bases of pectoral and pelvic fins of breeding males have given the common name to *P.*

antesella. Although not particularly bright, it is the showiest member of an otherwise somber group. Anal fin is greatly elongated. Tubercles that are small for *Imostoma* develop on several scale rows on posterior two-thirds of belly and as far as anal fin origin. Small tubercles may develop on breast scales. Tubercles develop also on caudal keel, ventral rays of caudal fin, outer two-thirds of anal spines and rays, and dorsal and ventral surfaces of pelvic rays and rarely of pelvic spine. Male genital papilla is not described. Body of females may be somewhat golden. Williams and Etnier (1977) report a gravid female which was unusual in having small tubercles on anal and pelvic fins. Female genital papilla is an elongated round tube.

Distribution. Taken in the Mobile basin only from very restricted localities in the headwaters of the Coosa River system, including the Conasauga and Etowah rivers in northwestern Georgia and southeastern Tennessee.

Natural History. The amber darter usually inhabits riffles with moderate current at depths up to 1/2 m or a little more over gravel and sand. Little is known beyond the description published by Williams and Etnier (1977). Etnier furnished us a relatively freshly caught female for the color plate.

Abundance. Williams and Etnier (1977) state that the first specimens were taken from an Etowah River tributary in 1948 but that additional collecting since 1966 has not produced more material and the species is now presumed to have been extirpated there by the construction of Alatoona Reservoir and by poor land management in the Etowah basin. Specimens have been taken at regular intervals since 1968 from the Conasauga River, where a stable population remains at least in Bradley and Polk counties, Tennessee, and for several miles downstream into Georgia. Since the known collecting sites are so restricted, Deacon et al. (1979) have listed the amber darter as threatened.

Name. *Antesella* literally means anterior saddle, and refers to the unique position of the first dorsal saddle in comparison with other *Imostoma* darters.

Percina ouachitae (Jordan & Gilbert)   Plate 5
Saddleback Darter   Subgenus *Imostoma*

Description. A slender delicate member of *Imostoma* probably exceeding 60 mm SL in a few cases. It is placed in *Imostoma* by having separate to slightly joined gill membranes, a quite narrow frenum (sometimes absent); eyes closely set high on the head, scarcity of belly scalation, an elongated anal fin in males, and the presence of numerous breeding tubercles. It is the least pigmented member of the subgenus. As with other *Imostoma*, *P. ouachitae* has especially numerous small teeth in both jaws.

Dorsum is basically pale, but blackened scales produce a cross-hatched effect. Small irregular blotches may develop. The first of 4 dorsal saddles lies beneath origin of spiny dorsal

fin and is the palest member; all tend to be constricted at midline and expanded on upper side. Most individuals have suggestion of a fifth saddle at junction of body and caudal fin. Upper side is cross-hatched, these markings sometimes fusing into zigzag lines. A dark spot may be on nape just behind head. Side is marked with 8-10 vertically elongated blotches that extend well downward. There is little indication of a midlateral band. Belly lacks markings. Many individuals have a tiny midcaudal spot.

Stippling between eyes actually continues downward into eyes. Narrow preorbital bar does not meet counterpart on snout. Broad, long, and somewhat diffuse suborbital bar crosses cheek. Postorbital bar may be complete or reduced to a spot behind eye. A narrow dark band may extend from eye backward and upward toward nape. Opercle is heavily stippled dorsally, becoming pale ventrally. There is a small dark patch on chin and another at junction of gill membranes. Breast is pale; prepectoral area is stippled.

Spines of first dorsal fin are clear and membranes stippled to produce a weak marginal band and a somewhat better developed one just above base. Rays and adjacent membranes of soft dorsal fin have 2 or 3 darkened areas, creating weak banding. Similarly, caudal fin has 2 or 3 faint wavy vertical bands. Anal fin is quite pale; when depressed to body it extends almost to base of caudal fin. Short slightly cupped pelvic fin may be clear to slightly stippled. Pectoral fin rays are marginally darkened but insufficiently to produce a distinct pattern.

Cheek may support exposed scales or only a few partly embedded scales behind eye. Opercle is scaled and nape is completely scaled, but scales near head may be embedded. One to 3 enlarged scales lie between pelvic fins. Breast may otherwise be naked or supplied with only a few embedded scales. Anterior portion of belly is naked in both sexes, and remainder of ventral midline is naked in females. Several elongated, spiny, slightly enlarged scales occur along posterior half of ventral midline in males. Scales in humeral region usually stand out from body. Lateral line consists of 48-59 (46-62) scales. Fin counts are: dorsal X-XI (IX-XII), 12-15; anal II, 10-11 (9-12); pectoral usually 14-15. Vertebrae number 38-40.

Body may darken in breeding males but coloration does not appear, as shown in color plate. During peak development, usually in February and March, tuberculation is so widespread as to be exceeded only by *P. evides* among all darters. Tubercles may be present on almost all ventral body scales, on lower half to three-quarters of each anal ray, and on ventral surface of each pelvic ray and pelvic spine. Ventral caudal fin rays are tuberculate, as are ventral 2-5 pectoral rays in some cases. Additional tubercles occur on breast, infraorbital and preoperculomandibular canals, cheek, opercle, lower jaw, and branchiostegal rays. Male genital papilla is a short tapered flattened tube with lateral grooves and terminal papillae. Breeding females are little changed in appearance except for increase in girth. Female genital papilla is an elongated tube.

Distribution. Occurs in the Ouachita River basin of Arkansas and Louisiana and in lowland components of the White and

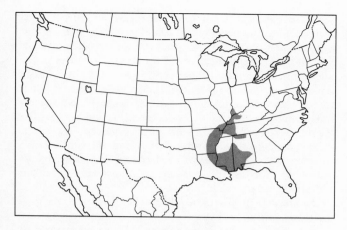

Distribution of *Percina ouachitae*

St. Francis rivers of northeastern Arkansas and southeastern Missouri. Pigg and Hill (1974) doubt that *P. ouachitae* occurs in Oklahoma in spite of one early record of this species. Across the Missisippi the species is found in western Kentucky as far east as the lower Green River and up the Tennessee River as far as north-central Alabama. It is known from western Tennessee and certain eastern tributaries of the Mississippi from Bayou Pierre southward into Louisiana. It also occurs in eastern Gulf Coast streams, principally below the Fall Line, to the Escambia River in Alabama and Florida. It has long been confused with *P. uranidea,* an upland form of the Ozarks, and distribution records must be reexamined carefully.

Natural History. The saddleback darter is most commonly taken in small to large rivers in areas of moderate current over sand and gravel or gravel and rubble substrates. These conditions usually prevail toward the foot of a chute or riffle but also where snags and log jams create enough current to sweep away silt and finely divided organic material. As noted by Starnes (1977), *P. ouachitae* may achieve rather high population densities in undisturbed streams. The species, like its relative *P. shumardi,* tolerates the murky water which characterizes so much of the Mississippi River lowlands. Under the name *P. uranidea,* Pflieger (1975) notes that *P. ouachitae* and *P. shumardi* may be taken in the same collection in southeastern Missouri but that one species invariably is common and the other uncommon. He suggests that the two are probably competitive for similar environmental resources. Channelization and drainage projects in much of its range may be taking their toll on this species. Smith and Sisk (1969) and Webb and Sisk (1975) found *P. ouachitae* in only two western Kentucky streams, both scheduled for extensive channelization.

Thompson (1974) reports that *P. ouachitae* eats snails and limpets, as other *Imostoma* are known or suspected to do. There are no detailed life history studies on the species, however. Since maximum tubercle development occurs during February in specimens from the Pearl River, Collette (1965) surmises that this species (discussed under the name *P. uranidea*) is a late winter spawner. We have collected tuber-

culate but spent males from Bayou Pierre in mid-March, which is in keeping with Collette's view.

Abundance. Though range shrinkages and deletions seem to have occured, *P. ouachitae* remains abundant enough at many sites to be considered safe from human threat.

Name. The trivial name is taken from the Ouachita River, the type material having been collected from its tributary, the Saline River, at Benton, Arkansas.

Percina shumardi (Girard)   Plate 5
River Darter   Subgenus *Imostoma*

Description. A robust and large member of the subgenus *Imostoma,* 67.5 mm SL in our largest specimen but probably exceeding 70 mm SL in some individuals. It fits in *Imostoma* by virtue of having separate gill membranes, a narrow frenum, eyes closely set high on the head, scarcity of belly scalation, an elongated anal fin in males, and numerous breeding tubercles. It differs from its congeners in the number of dorsal saddles. There is a large pad of teeth in the upper jaw and several rows of small teeth in the lower jaw. Gill membranes are slightly connected to separate, even overlapping anteriorly in some cases.

Dorsum appears mottled. Additional cross-hatching in most cases creates a dusky appearance on most of body. There may be 5-9 rather indistinct saddles or a dorsal pattern without saddles. If dorsal saddles are present, only posterior ones appear sharply defined. Eight to 11 is normal number of vertically elongated lateral blotches, but there may be as many as 15. Posterior blotches are more rounded and tend to be partly fused. Small caudal spot may be partly joined with last lateral blotch.

Dense concentrations of melanophores are found in top of eye and often ventrally, as well. A narrow preorbital bar may join counterpart on snout. Suborbital bar is long and posteriorly directed at tip. Postorbital spot may continue across cheek and opercle as a bar. One or 2 faint diagonal lines may occur on cheek. Gill membranes and prepectoral area are lightly stippled; breast usually is pale.

Spines of first dorsal fin are clear and membranes stippled to produce a narrow faint marginal band, a submarginal clear band, and successively darker appearance basally; fin is darkest at base of first membrane and last 2 or 3 membranes. Soft dorsal rays are clear except for possible darkening near fin base; membranes are most heavily stippled basally and produce weak banding, if any. Pigment in caudal rays produces 3 or 4 faint wavy vertical bands. Both rays and membranes of elongated anal fin are virtually without pigment, as is pelvic fin. Pectoral fin appears virtually clear, though rays are slightly darkened basally.

Cheek scales are exposed or partially embedded. Opercle is well scaled; nape is scaled posteriorly but naked to various degrees near head. Breast varies from naked to partly scaled. Anterior portion of belly is naked in both sexes, and entire ventral midline is scaleless in females. A row of elongated and

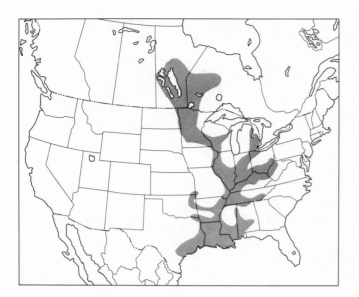

Distribution of *Percina shumardi*

somewhat enlarged belly scales is present in most males, though some either lose or do not produce such scales. Lateral line contains 52-58 (46-62) scales. Fin counts are: dorsal IX-XI, 12-16; anal II, 10-12; pectoral 13-15. Vertebrae number 38-40.

Dorsal and lateral markings in breeding males become better defined than in nonbreeding individuals, but bright coloration is absent. Anal fin is much elongated, reaching almost to base of caudal fin when pressed against body. Breeding tubercles may occur on distal portion of anal rays 3 and 4, on the 5 (sometimes more) ventral rays of caudal fin, and less commonly on ventral belly scales or along infraorbital and preoperculomandibular canals. Genital papilla is a short tapered tube. Breeding females are less darkened and have less expansive anal fins. Female genital papilla is an elongated tube.

Distribution. Present in the lower Mississippi River and quite common in the upper Mississippi. The species probably once occurred frequently in the preimpounded Ohio River, as well. It apparently does not invade the Missouri River basin. It occurs northward into the Hudson Bay drainage of central Manitoba as far as Lake Sipiwesk, thence east into western portions of Ontario. It is spottily distributed in the Ohio River basin, mostly in the lower, somewhat turbid reaches of major tributaries as far east as western Pennsylvania. Populations are known from fairly far up the Tennessee River system, for example, the lower Little Tennessee River. From the lower Mississippi River basin, river darters have penetrated westward into the lower White River, the Arkansas River basin of northeastern Oklahoma and southeastern Kansas, and the Ouachita-Red basins in Arkansas and Louisiana. Along the Gulf Coast, it is found eastward to the Mobile basin in Alabama and westward to the lower Guadalupe River in Texas.

Natural History. The river darter typically inhabits the deeper, lower ends of riffles in streams of moderate to great size. It is the most common darter in the Mississippi River channel. Substrate usually consists of gravel, rubble, or partially exposed bedrock. Only young specimens can be expected to enter water shallower than 1/2 m, and 1 m or more is best for capture of adults. Pflieger (1975) and Trautman (1957) stress the fact that the river darter does well in waters which are too turbid for most darter species. Because of its current and depth preference and its tolerance to murkiness, it is most often taken in conjunction with other species of *Percina* and seldom with *Etheostoma* or *Ammocrypta*. *P. caprodes*, *P. phoxocephala*, and *P. sciera* are frequent associates, but *P. copelandi*, *P. evides*, *P. maculata*, *P. ouachitae*, and others may also be taken with it.

Thomas (1970) found that *P. shumardi* remains the most common darter in the lower Kaskaskia River but no longer enters the middle portion of the stream, as it was known to early in this century. He found that most growth is achieved in the first year of life and that 2 or 2 1/2 years is the normal lifespan, although they can live 3 years, perhaps even 4. Breeding behavior has not been described, even in fragmentary fashion, but the time of breeding has been mentioned by several authors. Scott and Crossman (1973) suggest that river darters may spawn as late as June or July in Manitoba and adjacent Ontario. Cross (1967) found them apparently in spawning condition on April 10 in Kansas. Starnes (1977) believes *P. shumardi* spawns almost as early as its relative *P. tanasi* in the Little Tennessee; this suggests that February and March are prime spawning months, at least toward the southern part of this darter's range. Spawning at depths of 1/2 m or a little more in areas with strong current, scattered rubble, and associated clean gravel would seem to be typical. Migration of adults has been suggested by Trautman (1957), who collected Ohio specimens during spring in flooded fields adjacent to the Scioto River.

In the Kaskaskia River, Thomas (1970) found *P. shumardi* to eat primarily midge and caddisfly larvae. Starnes (1977) indicates that, like other *Imostoma*, it probably subsists on a diet heavy in snails where these are present.

While the river darter has not adapted to a diversity of habitats, staying closely confined to major streams and lakes at the northern extreme of its range, it nonetheless spans enormous climatic differences from Canada to the Gulf Coast. It would be extremely interesting to have additional information on its life history and breeding behavior.

Abundance. The species has fared better than virtually all other darters of the big rivers, probably because of its tolerance to turbidity. It is a species seldom obtained in large numbers, however, and may now be rare or absent in some parts of its range where formerly common.

Name. The trivial name was given in honor of the discoverer, George C. Shumard, surgeon and naturalist of the U.S. Pacific Railroad Survey.

Percina tanasi Etnier   Plate 5
Snail Darter   Subgenus *Imostoma*

Description. A large member of its subgenus reaching about 75 mm SL. Typical subgeneric characteristics include eyes closely set high on the head, belly largely naked, 4 dorsal saddles, bright breeding colors absent, and the anal fin of breeding males extremely elongated. Prominent saddles plus robust appearance distinguish *P. tanasi* from other *Imostoma* except *P. uranidea,* from which it differs in few respects other than having shorter, more rounded pectoral fins and usually 1 additional anal ray (12 versus 11).

Back is crossed by 4 dark saddles extending to about lateral line. Blotchiness along lateral line tends to form a midlateral band that becomes prominent only posterior to third saddle. Mottled continuations of saddles usually continue onto lower side. Belly is pale except for dark spots near anus, but ventral areas posterior to belly may be stippled.

Upper surface of head is uniformly dark while cheek and opercle are mottled. Suborbital bar is fairly broad and poorly defined; preorbital and postorbital bars are indistinct or absent. A narrow frenum may be present and numerous small teeth are noticeable. Gill membranes are separate to slightly joined. Ventral surface of head is pale but may be lightly stippled. Breast apparently becomes more stippled with age.

Spines of first dorsal fin are clear except near tips and again at midpoints. Additional stippling in membranes produces a weak marginal band as well as a darkened zone along base. Soft dorsal fin rays have 4 or 5 dark zones which may produce a weakly banded effect against clear membranes. Pigment in pelvic, anal, and caudal fins is alternately light and dark, but only caudal fin appears to be distinctly banded.

Cheek bears scales, usually embedded. Exposed scales are found on opercle and nape. Breast and prepectoral area vary from naked to scaled, apparently becoming more squamous with age. One or more scales lie between pelvic fins. Belly is naked in females, and is mostly so in males except for slightly enlarged midventral scales posteriorly. Lateral line contains 48-57 scales, 1 or 2 of which extend onto caudal fin. Fin counts are: dorsal X-XI (IX-XII), 14-16 (13-17); anal II, 11-12 (10-13); pectoral 13-15. Vertebrae usually number 40 (39-41).

Mature males are recognized by much elongated anal fin and are unusual in normally being less heavily pigmented than females. Male tuberculation is found on lower surfaces of inner 4 pelvic rays and on breast scales of some individuals. Tubercles also occur on anal fin rays and on several ventral caudal fin rays. Genital papilla of males is a small flattened flap with longitudinal creases; that of females is not described. Females may have more subtle hues than males, an unusual condition among darters.

Distribution. When originally described by Etnier (1976), the snail darter was known only from the lower 25 km of the Little Tennessee River and the Tennessee River channel for perhaps another 16 km. Persistence of this population is not likely due to the construction of Tellico Dam. But additional populations have been discovered by Etnier or personnel of the

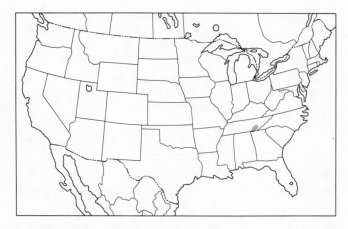

Distribution of *Percina tanasi*

Tennessee Valley Authority in Chickamauga Creek, Sequatchie River, and Sewee River (Norman, 1981). More populations may yet be discovered. In 1976 TVA biologists transferred over 200 snail darters to the Hiwassee River, where the species seems to be permanently established. We surmise that the original range of this species included most of the upper Tennessee River and adjacent parts of its major tributaries.

Natural History. We have never taken a specimen of the snail darter and base our information on the studies of Etnier (1976) and Starnes (1977). It occurs in rather deep water over sand and gravel shoals to depths of over 1 m. *Percina caprodes, P. evides, P. shumardi, Etheostoma blennioides, E. rufilineatum,* and *E. simoterum* are present at the type locality of the snail darter, but most are found in shallower areas.

Starnes (1977) has studied *P. tanasi* under TVA sponsorship. The species feeds actively in spring and winter, with snails constituting over half its food intake and caddisflies contributing additional volume. Population densities are low, ranging from 6 to 10 individuals per 100 sq m of shoal habitat. The dorsal saddles make the species hard to see and it often lies partly buried in sand, either to avoid possible predators or to conserve energy. Snail darters are early breeders, spawning from early February through March at temperatures of 12-13°C. Females produce about 600 eggs and spawn with several males over a period of 2 weeks. Larvae drift several kilometers downstream, and juveniles apparently migrate upstream during spring; they reach approximately 55 mm SL by autumn. Breeding occurs the following February or March, and usually these darters do not live much beyond 2 years. Drifting larval snail darters and migrating juveniles may be subject to considerable predation, but only the banded sculpin, *Cottus carolinae,* poses much threat to adults over riffles. Starnes includes much valuable additional information in his study.

The snail darter has been the subject of great controversy during the opposition to construction of Tellico Dam mounted by conservationists and others. Its status as an endangered species was used to oppose completion of the dam and many Americans became familiar with this darter through the news media.

Abundance. The snail darter is recognized as an endangered species by Deacon et al. (1979). Little suitable habitat remains in the upper Tennessee River basin due to extensive impoundment of streams, and its future looks precarious at best.

Name. *Tanasi* was an important Cherokee settlement on the Little Tennessee River. Corruption of that word gave rise to our name for the river and the state of Tennessee.

Percina uranidea (Jordan & Gilbert)   Plate 5
Stargazing Darter   Subgenus *Imostoma*

Description. A large member of its subgenus reaching about 65 mm SL. It is recognizable as an *Imostoma* by the presence of 4 dorsal saddles, eyes closely set high on the head, belly largely naked, absence of bright breeding colors, and a greatly elongated anal fin in breeding males. Its robust body and obvious saddles combine to distinguish it from other members of *Imostoma* except for *P. tanasi*, which has shorter, rounder pectoral fins and usually 1 more anal fin ray (12 versus 11).

Back is crossed by 4 dark saddles that extend downward to a series of 10 or 11 poorly defined lateral blotches. Lower side and ventral surface of caudal peduncle are flecked with small spots. Belly lacks markings. Head is heavily darkened between eyes, and pigment actually enters upper third of each eye. Cheek is stippled. Upper part of opercle is dark, and lower portion is pale but stippled. Short preorbital bar extends somewhat downward to corner of mouth. A weak frenum may be present; many small teeth are evident. Suborbital bar is fairly dark, long, and recurved posteriorly. A very short postorbital bar extends diagonally downward from eye. Chin, throat, and prepectoral area are lightly stippled. Breast lacks markings.

First dorsal fin spines are darkened at tips and contribute to a faint marginal band formed by stippling in membranes; membranes are also stippled to produce a second weak band near fin base. Membranes of soft dorsal fin are pale, and rays are alternately light and dark; 3-5 horizontal bands may be discernible. Caudal fin has 5-7 wavy vertical bands. Anal and pelvic fins are pale, usually devoid of pigmentation. Wavy vertical bands develop weakly in pectoral fin.

Cheek scales may be partly embedded; opercle and nape are well scaled. A few small scales may lie along midline of breast, and 1 or 2 greatly enlarged scales lie between pelvic fins. Belly is mostly naked in both sexes but supports a single midventral row of scales in males. Several scales in humeral region stick out from body. Lateral line contains 48-56 scales. Fin counts are: dorsal X-XI, 13-15; anal II, 10-11; pectoral 13-15. Vertebral counts need to be made for this species.

Breeding males do not become colorful but develop a greatly elongated anal fin. Tuberculation needs description but resembles that of *P. tanasi*. Male genital papilla is a short flattened tube, somewhat expanded and rounded at tip and longitudinally grooved. We have not seen breeding females.

P. uranidea and *P. ouachitae* have been confused in the literature and erroneously regarded as the same species. Both

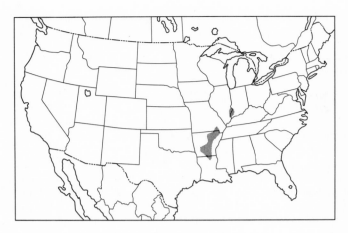

Distribution of *Percina uranidea*

occur in the Saline River in Arkansas and are seen to be quite different, the latter being far more delicate in appearance.

Distribution. Narrowly restricted to upland streams of the Ouachita River in Arkansas and Louisiana, eastern components of the White River of Arkansas and Missouri, and the St. Francis River of the same states. Old records from the lower Wabash apparently are valid, though *P. uranidea* probably is no longer found east of the Mississippi River.

Natural History. Little is known or reported on the stargazing darter. It occurs in large upland streams and strongly flowing riffles, and may be associated with aquatic vegetation. Thompson (1974) reports its diet to consist mainly of snails and limpets, which is similar to the food selection of *P. tanasi*. Indeed, the 2 forms seem virtually to be counterparts isolated east and west of the Mississippi Embayment. The range of *P. uranidea* differs in having been far less altered by construction of reservoirs.

Abundance. Although records of *P. uranidea* are few and scattered, it has received no recognition of rarity. Major changes in the watersheds where it now lives may initiate rapid deterioration of the situation, however. The species warrants careful monitoring.

Name. *Uranidea* means sky-looking and refers to placement of the eyes high on the head.

Percina burtoni Fowler   Plate 5
Blotchside Logperch   Subgenus *Percina*

Description. A large darter probably exceeding 120 mm SL but ordinarily less than 100 mm SL. The elongated snout, extending well beyond the upper jaw, marks it as a member of subgenus *Percina*. A series of oval midlateral blotches distinguish it from other species of the subgenus, all of which are vertically banded to some degree.

Back is crossed by 17 or more bands, most quite narrow.

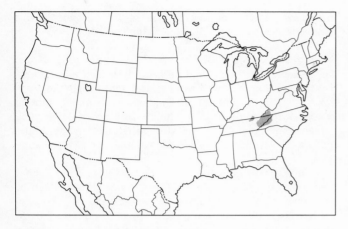

Distribution of *Percina burtoni*

One just anterior to spiny dorsal fin, another between dorsal fins, and a third just behind soft dorsal fin are more prominent and appear to be true saddles. Seven to 9 large lateral blotches are joined by a midlateral band. Lower side and belly are pale.

Membranes of spiny dorsal fin are clear; weak pigmentation in spines sometimes makes them stand out, particularly near base. Soft dorsal fin has 1 or 2 horizontal bands near base and indefinite spots toward margin. Three or 4 vertical bands occur in caudal fin. Except in breeding individuals, remaining fins are nearly devoid of markings.

Preorbital bar appears as a dusky band. Postorbital bar is absent from cheek, but opercle is crossed by a broad diffuse band. Suborbital bar varies from faint to fairly obvious. Chin, throat, and breast are pale.

Long considered a subspecies of *P. caprodes,* the blotchside logperch remains poorly known. Until a good series of specimens can be examined we presume that scalation, fin counts, and vertebral counts are close to those of *P. caprodes.*

Breeding males of *P. burtoni* are easily the most colorful members of subgenus *Percina*, as shown by color plate. Females do not attain bright coloration.

Distribution. Can be obtained regularly at two sites in the upper Tennessee River basin—Little River in Tennessee and Copper Creek in Virginia. Older records exist from elsewhere in the upper Tennessee basin and from the Little South Fork of the Cumberland River. The latter record may be in error.

Natural History. The blotchside logperch inhabits large creeks and upland rivers with strong currents. We caught the species over clean gravel in the lower portion of a strong riffle in Copper Creek at a depth of 1/2 m. Protection of the remaining good habitat occupied by this darter is imperative to its survival. Additional knowledge of its environmental requirements would also be valuable in assuring survival.

Abundance. One of the rarest and least known of all darters, *P. burtoni* is listed by Deacon et al. (1979) as being of special concern.

Name. This darter is named in honor of its first collector, E.M. Burton.

Percina caprodes (Rafinesque)
Logperch

Plate 5

Subgenus *Percina*

Description. A large darter often exceeding 100 mm SL and reaching at least 135 mm SL. The conical snout marks it as a member of subgenus *Percina*. It lacks the lateral blotches of *P. burtoni,* the intense suborbital bar of *P. rex,* and has a larger head than *P. macrolepida.*

Back is usually crossed by 16-22 narrow bands, at least 3 of which are dark and resemble dorsal saddles; they are on nape, between dorsal fins, and just behind soft dorsal fin. Bands continue down side in a general arrangement of short thin lines alternating with long thicker ones. Longer bands extend below lateral line and may end in somewhat darkened and expanded spots. Midlateral band is variably developed in different populations. Basicaudal spot is a bit larger and less intense than in other members of subgenus *Percina*.

Preorbital and suborbital bars are absent, or present as faint dusky bands. Posterior margin of eye is dark, as is upper part of opercle, but no true postorbital bar is present. Chin, throat, and breast are pale.

A submarginal pale zone lies beneath stippled margin of spiny dorsal fin. Fin membranes are variably pigmented but generally darkest at base. Dorsal spines are alternately light and dark but do not contrast enough to produce distinct bands. Soft dorsal fin rays are alternately light and dark, producing several bands that contrast with lightly stippled to pale membranes. Caudal fins are similarly pigmented to produce 3 or 4 wavy vertical bands. Little pigmentation develops in anal and pelvic fins, except basally in mature males. Pectoral fin varies from faintly banded to clear.

Cheek and opercle are scaled, though to a quite variable extent in different populations. Scalation of nape is one of the traits used in recognition of subspecies. Subspecies *carbonaria* and *fulvitaenia* have fully scaled napes. Anterior nape scales of subspecies *caprodes* usually are small and embedded, while nape of subspecies *semifasciata* is naked or has only a few embedded scales. Breast is naked in nominate subspecies except for 1 or more enlarged scales between pelvic fins. Scales on breast typify undescribed forms from eastern Gulf drainages. Midline of belly is naked in females, and covered by a row of enlarged scales in males, a few of which may be absent just behind pelvic fins. Lateral line is complete, with 71-92 (67-95) scales. Subspecies *semifasciata* usually has 70-80 scales in series; subspecies *caprodes* and *fulvitaenia* usually have 80-90; and subspecies *carbonaria* has 80-94. Fin counts are: dorsal XIV-XV (XII-XVII) 14-17; anal II, 10-11 (8-13); pectoral 13-15. Scott and Crossman (1973) list 40-42 as vertebral count for subspecies *semifasciata;* Stevenson (1971) indicates 42 for subspecies *carbonaria*; and Bailey and Gosline (1955) indicate 44-46 for subspecies *caprodes.*

Coloration of mature males is similar to that shown in color plate. Scott and Crossman (1973) state that specimens of subspecies *semifasciata* may be grayish green when taken from deep water. Breeding males of subspecies *carbonaria* and *fulvitaenia,* and of certain populations from eastern Gulf Coast drainages develop a yellow submarginal band in spiny

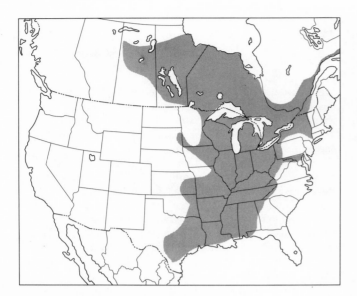

Distribution of *Percina caprodes*

dorsal fin. Breeding tubercles are not easily seen and are absent from many mature males; they may occur on enlarged belly scales and on adjacent scale rows of belly, as well as adjacent to anal fin insertion and posteriorly along ventral caudal peduncle. In subspecies *caprodes* genital papilla is a short flattened tube, knobbed at tip. Tuberculation and genital papillae are possible variables among subspecies.

Thompson (1978) recommended that *carbonaria* be recognized as a full species. Morris and Page (1981) do so in a paper also describing subspecies *fulvitaenia*. But *carbonaria* overlaps *P. caprodes* in virtually every regard other than presence of a yellow dorsal stripe, which also occurs in subspecies *fulvitaenia*. There is an apparent range gap between *carbonaria* and other logperch populations, but additional evidence seems warranted to erect it now as a full species. Thompson (1978) notes 4 variants of the logperch, perhaps independent species, in southeastern United States. Additional information is needed to clarify this taxonomic problem.

Distribution. Easily the most widely distributed of all darters. The nominate subspecies occupies the Ohio River basin and much of the upper St. Lawrence basin. It is native or introduced in some Atlantic drainages from the Potomac to the Hudson. Subspecies *semifasciata* is the northern form, extending from Iowa and Illinois northward to the Churchill River, James Bay, and St. Lawrence basin in Canada. Subspecies *fulvitaenia* occurs in the Ozark region and eastern Kansas, while the nominate subspecies reappears in southern Oklahoma, southern Arkansas, and northern Louisiana. Subspecies *carbonaria* may be absent from the Sabine and Trinity drainages of Texas and thus be isolated in the Brazos, Colorado, and Guadalupe systems within that state.

Bailey and Allum (1962) discuss stream capture and the occurrence of the logperch in South Dakota. Intergradation is clearly discussed in Morris and Page (1981). The logperch

may have been introduced by now into many parts of the United States in which it did not originally occur.

Natural History. The logperch exploits a variety of habitats. In Canada it may be found in large rivers and along sandy beaches of lakes, as well as at considerable depths in some lakes. It is fairly common in some reservoirs and is unusual among darters in this regard. The species is not found in small streams which lack chutes and strong riffles. Darter associates potentially include more species than those of any other darter.

Thomas (1970) reports on several aspects of life history and behavior. Reighard (1913) and Winn (1958b) describe spawning behavior of subspecies *semifasciata* in lakes. Females repeatedly enter an aggregation of males and burrow into sand with a mounted male, laying 10 to 20 eggs. Northern populations spawn in June, while Texas populations are winter spawners, essentially through by early March. Feeding studies by Turner (1921), Ewers and Boesel (1935), Dobie (1959), and other authors are not in strong agreement on principal food items. Mullan, Applegate, and Rainwater (1968) report on feeding habits in reservoirs on the White River. Keast and Webb (1966) observed logperch turning small stones with the snout while searching for food. Microcrustacea and aquatic insects constitute commonly cited food items in various studies.

Hubbs (1961) and Cooper (1978) have conducted studies on the range of temperatures required for embryonic development. Requirements for southern and northern stocks are amazingly similar, perhaps accounting partly for the great temporal spread observed for breeding. Parasites of the logperch are discussed by Hoffman (1967). Hubbs (1971) performed interspecific and intergeneric crosses with other darters, and various natural hybrids are not uncommon.

The logperch is known to many fishermen, especially those who use small flies. Ambitious logperch sometimes rise to the bait as might their larger relatives, the walleye and sauger. Undoubtedly many common names exist locally. We have heard the logperch called "jackfish," and in eastern Kentucky have even heard it referred to as the "prisoner perch" in reference to its stripes.

Abundance. The logperch remains one of the most common darters. Trautman (1957) has verified its disappearance from many Ohio streams in response to siltation, domestic pollution, industrial wastes, and other human activities. Drought in combination with feedlot pollution eliminated upper Neosho River populations (Cross and Braasch, 1968). The strong reinvasive abilities of the logperch in Illinois are noted by Larrimore and Smith (1963).

Name. *Caprodes,* indicating a resemblance to the pig, refers to the peculiar snout. The logperch was the first named of all darters. *Carbonaria* means coal-like; *fulvitaenia* refers to the reddish-yellow band; *semifasciata* means half-banded.

Percina macrolepida Stevenson
Bigscale Logperch

Plate 6

Subgenus *Percina*

Description. A rather small logperch reaching at least 85 mm SL. Recognizable as a species in subgenus *Percina* by the distinctive snout, it differs from its congeners by having a smaller head and somewhat larger body scales. The eye appears large relative to the small head. The species has narrower vertical bands on the body than *P. caprodes carbonaria,* with which it occurs.

Body markings consist primarily of 20 or more narrow vertical bars extending downward from dorsal midline, 5-8 of which are darker than remainder. Half or more of bars extend below midlateral area; last 1 or 2 meet on ventral midline of caudal peduncle. Remainder of body is pale.

Broad dark preorbital bar becomes a dull band as it meets counterpart on lip. Suborbital bar is faint or absent, though some pigment develops along margin of eye. There is merely a postorbital spot on cheek; opercle is dark. Chin, throat, and breast lack pigmentation.

Spiny dorsal fin may be slightly darkened along outer margin but lacks submarginal orange coloration; membranes are darkly stippled at base but become clear below margin. Two or 3 indistinct horizontal bands cross soft dorsal fin. Three to 5 similar vertical bands cross caudal fin. In nonbreeding individuals, anal, pelvic, and pectoral fins are clear to weakly pigmented.

Scales are well developed on cheek and opercle. Nape is completely scaled and a few scales extend onto head. Breast and prepectoral area bear some small and partly embedded scales. Belly in females is naked anteriorly and along midline to anus. Enlarged midventral scales of males may be absent just anterior to anus. Lateral line is complete or lacks last 1 or 2 pores; there are 79-86 (77-90) pored scales. Fin counts are: dorsal XIV (XIII-XV), 14 (12-15); anal II, 9 (7-10); pectoral usually 13. Vertebrae usually number 40.

Breeding males are not brightly colored but head and body are tinged with green and yellow, not shown in color plate. Dull yellow spots appear in spiny dorsal fin, which however lacks a submarginal yellow band; membranes are darkened. Banding in soft dorsal and caudal fins is better defined. Remaining fins and lower surfaces of entire body are somewhat dusky. Development of breeding tubercles has not been described. Male genital papilla is a horizontally grooved tube. We have not seen genital papilla of ripe females.

Distribution. Occurs in the Red River in Texas and Oklahoma and then southward and westward in Gulf Coast drainages from the Sabine to the Rio Grande, where its limits are not well known. Specimens are known from the Pecos River in New Mexico. It is uncommon in the Edwards Plateau, where sympatric with *P. caprodes carbonaria.* Its distribution is similar to the southern range of *Etheostoma spectabile pulchellum,* and both forms may have entered the region via ancient north-south drainages across the southern plains states.

Bait introductions in western America have spread *P. macrolepida* to the interior valleys of California, where it is

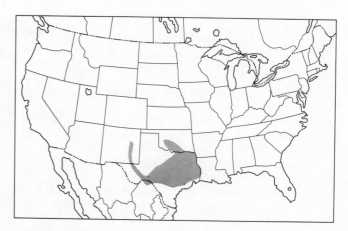

Distribution of *Percina macrolepida*

successful according to Moyle (1976). It would not be surprising to discover other such transplants.

Natural History. Bigscale logperch are most often taken in mainstem rivers with strong but nonturbulent currents. Murky waters and absence of turbulent riffles seem less of a deterrent than they are to *Percina caprodes.* In clear streams like those of the Edwards Plateau, *P. macrolepida* is absent or is the less common of the 2 species in cases of sympatry. The bigscale logperch is often found in impoundments and occasionally in small streams. Artificial crosses with other darters produce offspring of intermediate characteristics, but natural hybrids apparently are very uncommon (Stevenson, 1971).

Bigscale logperch produce rather few, small eggs. The largest number reported by Stevenson was 365 eggs from a very large female. Laboratory-reared hybrids between this logperch and *P. caprodes* had very low fecundity, producing a maximum of 84 eggs in any female. Additional natural history information is needed.

P. macrolepida has long been confused with *P. caprodes carbonaria,* the few specimens encountered being considered as variants of *P. caprodes.* Hubbs, Kuehne, and Ball (1953) noted that logperch from the Guadalupe River, all then assigned to *P. caprodes,* were variable and confusing.

Abundance. The abundance of the bigscale logperch cannot be accurately determined at this time, but the species does not seem to warrant special concern. It and other southwestern fishes may be more heavily impacted by water withdrawals, channel modifications, and pollution than species in larger eastern streams, but these factors are not working preferentially against the bigscale logperch.

Name. *Macrolepida,* big-scaled, refers to the larger scales of the lateral line in this species as compared with *Percina caprodes carbonaria.*

Percina rex (Jordan & Evermann)
Roanoke Logperch

Plate 6

Subgenus *Percina*

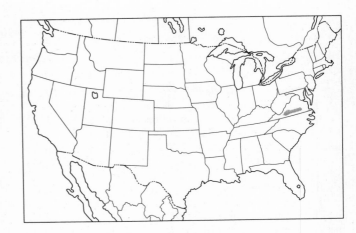

Distribution of *Percina rex*

Description. A large robust darter reaching 124 mm SL. The protracted snout marks this species as a member of subgenus *Percina*, within which it is uniquely endowed with a very bold suborbital bar. The head appears particularly narrow. The eyes seem to be set very high on the head.

Dorsum is crossed by 10-12 narrow dark saddles. From these there extend ventrally a like number of vertical bands which end below lateral line as expanded dark blotches. Additional narrow stripes, often interrupted, lie between principal vertical bands. A faint midlateral stripe is present at least on posterior half of body. Some of side bands occasionally extend onto otherwise pale belly and lower caudal peduncle.

Preorbital bar is faint to absent. Posteriorly recurved suborbital bar is one of the boldest seen in any darter. Postorbital bar appears to be replaced by 1 or sometimes 2 narrow bars that extend diagonally backward and upward across cheek. Chin, throat, and breast are pale.

Spiny dorsal fin is narrowly edged in black. Submarginal zone lacks dark pigment but is pale yellow in females and a brighter yellow or orange in males. Lower half of fin has clear spines except for darkening in first spine and considerable amounts of black in membranes. Darkening tends to produce continuous black slashes in males and interrupted diagonal marks in females. Dark pigment on and adjacent to rays of soft dorsal fin forms 2 or 3 irregular bands, much bolder in males than in females. Three or 4 similar bands are vertically set in caudal fin. Anal fin is a little darkened near base. Pelvic fin is clear or basally darkened in males. Expansive pectoral fin is striped to produce up to 5 vertical bands.

Cheek and opercle are scaled. Nape scales are small, those toward head often partly embedded. Embedded scales are found in dorsolateral patches adjacent to nape. Breast in males contains a prominent series of scales down middle; such scales are usually present but less prominent in females. Anterior portion of belly may be naked in both sexes. Posterior portion of belly is naked in females but has a midventral row of enlarged scales in males. Lateral line is complete and usually consists of 84-87 pored scales. Fin counts are: dorsal XIV-XVI, 14-16; anal II, 9-10; pectoral 14-15. Vertebrae number 44-46.

Breeding males become rather bright, as indicated in color plate, but do not develop as much fin or body coloration as the related *P. burtoni*. Besides orange submarginal stripe of spiny dorsal fin, bases of other fins tend to become pale yellow. Male genital papilla is a short longitudinally grooved tube. Small breeding tubercles may develop on belly scales adjacent to midline and on ventral scales of caudal peduncle. Breeding females develop a little yellow coloration in much the same manner as males. Genital papilla is a round tube, horizontally grooved, at least at tip.

Distribution. An endemic species confined to the montane and Piedmont portions of the Roanoke River system.

Natural History. The Roanoke logperch inhabits the larger creeks and rivers of the Roanoke basin, where it usually is associated with deeper portions of riffles. It may occur in clear and slightly turbid streams, but probably not those which are silted. In our limited experience this species seems to favor strong currents at the foot of riffles, where the water is 40-100 cm deep. The substrate in such areas usually is composed of rubble with intervening pockets of clean sand and gravel. Our May and early June collections did not contain gravid females, which makes us feel that spawning probably had already occurred. The most common darters taken with the Roanoke logperch were *Etheostoma podostemone* and *P. roanoka,* both of which favor shallower water and reduced current speed. *E. flabellare* also was rather common in gravelled areas not exposed to full current.

Robert E. Jenkins and Robert Ross supplied us information on collecting sites, and the latter accompanied us on a successful trip for *P. rex* in the South Fork of the Roanoke River. Jenkins and Freeman (1972) reported the distribution of this species in the downstream portion of Mason Creek, a Roanoke tributary. They found that adults and juveniles occurred in all available habitats, but that young were restricted to quiet water. Starnes (1977) states that Jenkins observed the Roanoke logperch to turn stones with its snout in search of food, much as *P. caprodes* does. Much remains to be known about this striking darter.

Abundance. Jenkins and Freeman (1972) were disturbed by the scarcity of *P. rex.* Deacon et al. (1979) list the species as threatened. Its extremely limited range, and physical disturbances within it, are matters of serious concern.

Name. *Rex* means king. Jordan and Evermann (in Jordan, 1889) caught at least 1 very large individual, perhaps the largest darter known at that time, near Roanoke, Virginia, and chose this as an appropriate epithet.

PLATE 1

Percina sciera, breeding male

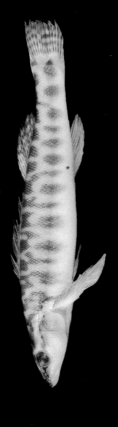

Percina nasuta, preserved adult

Percina oxyrhyncha, breeding male

Percina aurolineata, preserved adult

Percina lenticula, preserved adult

Percina nigrofasciata, adult male

PLATE 2

Percina gymnocephala, adult male

Percina macrocephala, young adult

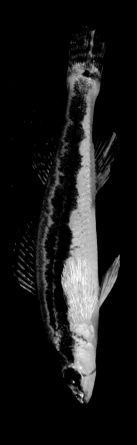

Percina maculata, adult male

Percina phoxocephala, breeding male

Percina squamata, preserved adult

Percina crassa, adult female

Percina roanoka, breeding male

Percina sp. (*Alvordius*), young adult

Percina evides, breeding male

Percina notogramma, adult male

Percina pantherina, preserved adult

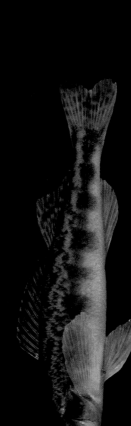

Percina peltata, adult male

PLATE 3

PLATE 4

Percina aurantiaca, breeding male

Percina copelandi, adult male

Percina antesella, preserved adult

Percina palmaris, breeding male

Percina cymatotaenia (Niangua R.), young adult

Percina cymatotaenia (Kentucky R.), adult male

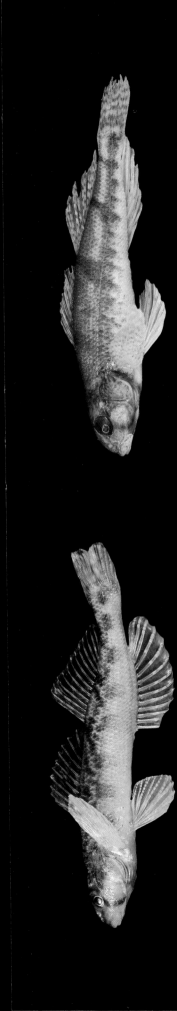

PLATE 6

Ammocrypta beani, preserved male

Percina macrolepida, young adult

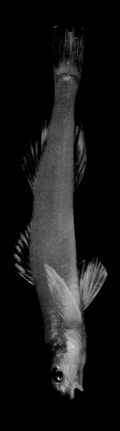

Ammocrypta bifascia, young adult

Percina rex, adult male

Ammocrypta clara, adult male

Ammocrypta asprella, adult male

PLATE 8

Etheostoma blennius, breeding male

Etheostoma euzonum, adult male

Etheostoma histrio, breeding male

Etheostoma cinereum, breeding male

Etheostoma b. blennioides, breeding male

Etheostoma blennioides newmanii, breeding male

Etheostoma inscriptum, breeding female

Etheostoma rupestre, adult male

Etheostoma kanawhae, breeding male

Etheostoma sellare, preserved adult

Etheostoma osburni, breeding male

Etheostoma swannanoa, breeding male

PLATE 9

PLATE 10

Etheostoma z. zonale, breeding male

Etheostoma zonale lynceum, breeding male

Etheostoma atripinne, breeding male

Etheostoma tetrazonum, breeding male

Etheostoma thalassinum, adult male

Etheostoma variatum, breeding male

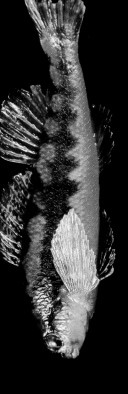

Etheostoma baileyi, breeding male

Etheostoma duryi, breeding male

Etheostoma barrenense, breeding male

Etheostoma etnieri, breeding male

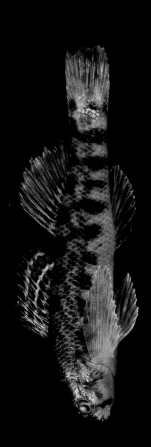

Etheostoma coosae, breeding male

Etheostoma rafinesquei, breeding male

PLATE 11

PLATE 12

"Gulfcoast snubnose darter" (*Ulocentra*), breeding male

"Black Warrior snubnose darter" (*Ulocentra*), breeding male

"Upland snubnose darter" (*Ulocentra*), breeding male

Etheostoma simoterum, breeding male

"Golden snubnose darter" (*Ulocentra*), breeding male

"Redbelly snubnose darter" (*Ulocentra*), breeding male

Etheostoma stigmaeum (Rockcastle R.), breeding male

Etheostoma longimanum, breeding male

Etheostoma nigrum, breeding male

"Tallapoosa R. snubnose darter" (*Ulocentra*), breeding male

Etheostoma jessiae, breeding male

Etheostoma stigmaeum (Mobile R.), breeding male

PLATE 13

PLATE 14

Etheostoma olmstedi, adult male

Etheostoma vitreum, adult male

Etheostoma perlongum, young adult

Etheostoma chlorosomum, adult female

Etheostoma podostemone, breeding male

Etheostoma acuticeps, adult male

Etheostoma aquali, adult male

Etheostoma chlorobranchium, adult male

Etheostoma bellum, breeding male

Etheostoma jordani, breeding male

Etheostoma camurum (Cumberland R.), breeding male

Etheostoma juliae, breeding male

PLATE 15

PLATE 16

Etheostoma microlepidum, breeding male

Etheostoma moorei, breeding male

Etheostoma rubrum, adult male

Etheostoma m. maculatum (Green R.), adult male

Etheostoma maculatum sanguifluum (Cumberland R.), adult male

Etheostoma maculatum vulneratum (Tennessee R.), breeding male

Etheostoma rufilineatum, breeding male

Etheostoma okaloosae, adult female

Etheostoma boschungi, breeding male

Etheostoma tippecanoe, breeding male

Etheostoma cragini, breeding male

Etheostoma edwini, adult male

PLATE 17

PLATE 18

Etheostoma australe, preserved adult

Etheostoma asprigene, breeding male

Etheostoma caeruleum, breeding male

Etheostoma pallididorsum, preserved male

Etheostoma punctulatum, breeding male

Etheostoma trisella, young female

Etheostoma fricksium, breeding male

Etheostoma grahami, breeding male

Etheostoma hopkinsi (Altamaha R.), adult male

Etheostoma collettei, breeding male

Etheostoma ditrema, breeding male

Etheostoma exile, adult male

PLATE 19

PLATE 20

Etheostoma nuchale, breeding male

Etheostoma parvipinne, breeding female

Etheostoma pottsi, adult male

Etheostoma lepidum, breeding male

Etheostoma luteovinctum, breeding male

Etheostoma mariae, adult male

PLATE 21

Etheostoma swaini, breeding male

Etheostoma w. whipplei, breeding male

Etheostoma whipplei artesiae, young male

Etheostoma radiosum, breeding male

Etheostoma s. spectabile, breeding male

Etheostoma spectabile squamosum, breeding male

PLATE 22

Etheostoma neopterum, adult male

Etheostoma obeyense, breeding male

Etheostoma olivaceum, breeding male

Etheostoma barbouri, breeding male

Etheostoma flabellare, breeding male

Etheostoma kennicotti, adult male

Etheostoma virgatum, breeding male

Etheostoma collis, breeding male

Etheostoma fusiforme, adult male

Etheostoma smithi, breeding male

Etheostoma squamiceps, breeding male

Etheostoma striatulum, breeding male

PLATE 23

PLATE 24

Etheostoma fonticola, breeding male

Etheostoma microperca, breeding male

Etheostoma proeliare, breeding male

Etheostoma gracile, breeding male

Etheostoma saludae, breeding male

Etheostoma serriferum, young adult

Ammocrypta
and Its Subgenera

Ammocrypta is the smallest genus of darters and in many respects is the most distinctive. We refer to them collectively as the sand darters, though some authorities would exclude the crystal darter. Morphologically the genus is intermediate between *Percina* and *Etheostoma*. It is easily separated from *Percina* because members lack the modified midventral scales found in males of *Percina*. The extreme slenderness of *Ammocrypta* clearly separates it from all members of *Etheostoma* except *E. chlorosomum*, *E. davisoni*, and *E. vitreum*, which are almost as slender. *E. vitreum* also is semitransparent, more so than the crystal darter but less so than other sand darters.

A partial generic characterization of *Ammocrypta* is: Body elongated and subcylindrical. Flesh glassy and nearly transparent in life, becoming white and opaque in preservation. Eyes closely set. Gill membranes narrowly joined to separate. One anal spine. Anal fin rays elongated. Breeding tubercles developed on pelvic, anal, and rarely caudal fins of males. Breeding colors absent, or present as delicate hues.

To varying degrees all species of *Ammocrypta* are associated with a sand substrate in which they may bury themselves, with only the eyes and top of head protruding (Linder, 1953). This behavior may afford protection from predators and, as noted by Williams (1975), it also saves swimming energy in what ecologists agree is a food-poor habitat that affords no other escape from currents. Extensive sand deposits characterize those streams of low to moderate gradient that support sand darters. *Ammocrypta* are seldom found in creeks where suitable sand beds are likely to be quite patchy.

The distribution of the genus reflects habitat requirements. Species are concentrated in the Mississippi Embayment and the Gulf Coast to its east and west. *A. asprella*, *A. clara*, and *A. pellucida* extend north and east of this region but still are found in streams of low to moderate gradient.

The recognized subgenera are *Crystallaria* with 1 species, *A. asprella*, and *Ammocrypta* with the remaining 6 species. The former is more generalized in terms of size, scalation, and body pattern and is considered to be a monotypic genus by some ichthyologists.

Distinctive traits of *Crystallaria* are: Frenum present. Most of body covered with small, rough scales. Vertebrae numbering 45-48. Lateral line scales numbering 83-100. Large size, sometimes exceeding 100 mm SL. Reproduction occurs during spring as with most darters.

Special characteristics of the subgenus *Ammocrypta* are: Body variably but incompletely scaled. Lateral line with 55-81 scales. Frenum absent (rarely present). Spiny and soft dorsal fins widely separated. Vertebrae numbering 38-45. Williams (1975) recognizes 2 species groups. The *beani* group (*A. beani*, *A. bifascia*, and *A. clara*) have an almost scaleless body, scaleless prepectoral area, few if any lateral blotches, usually 40 vertebrae, pelvic fins unpigmented, and well developed breeding tubercles on males. The *pellucida* group (*A. meridiana*, *A. pellucida*, and *A. vivax*) have a moderately well scaled body, embedded scales commonly in the prepectoral area, usually 42-43 vertebrae, lateral blotches variously developed, pelvic fin membranes pigmented in males, and poorly developed breeding tubercles in males. Some if not all members of the subgenus breed during summer.

Sand darters are difficult to collect or preserve, the result being a scarcity of information on their habits and perhaps imprecise knowledge of the range of some species. Such information is needed in hope of saving *A. asprella* and *A. pellucida*. Siltation appears to be the principal cause of decreases in numbers or local extirpations that have already occurred, but other factors such as pollutants, damming, and channelization may be regionally important.

The evolutionary relationships of *Ammocrypta* are somewhat obscure. Translucence and extreme slenderness are shared with a few members of *Etheostoma*, notably *E. chlorosomum* and *E. vitreum*. Williams (1975) points out the similarities of *Ammocrypta* to the subgenus *Imostoma* in *Percina* in both habit and appearance, and he favors the view that *Ammocrypta* may be derived from an *Imostoma*-like ancestral stock. Isozyme patterns obtained by Page and Whitt (1973a) from tissues of many darter species strengthen the view that *Ammocrypta* and *Etheostoma* are more closely related to each other than either is to *Percina*. Page (1981) states that *Ammocrypta* probably diverged from early *Etheostoma* stock.

The name *Ammocrypta* appropriately means sand-hidden, in reference to the burrowing habit of the sand darters. *Crystallaria* suggests the glassy appearance which characterizes *A. asprella* as well as its relatives.

Ammocrypta asprella (Jordan)   Plate 6
Crystal Darter   Subgenus *Crystallaria*

Description. The largest member of its genus, reaching perhaps 130 mm SL. It is placed in subgenus *Crystallaria* apart from other sand darters by virtue of higher lateral line scale counts, more complete scalation, presence of a frenum, bold dorsal pattern, and much greater size. Gill membranes are separate to slightly joined.

Back is crossed by 4 broad saddles, as bold as seen in any darter. Saddles are concave anteriorly and continue downward and forward on side to fuse with midlateral stripe, which usually is interrupted at several points. In young individuals body pattern is less developed. Lower side and belly lack pigmentation. Top of head is darkened. Broad preorbital bar extends to corner of mouth; upper lip is pigmented. Suborbital bar is not developed. Postorbital bar is short but may be continuous with a broader band across opercle. Opercular spine is well developed.

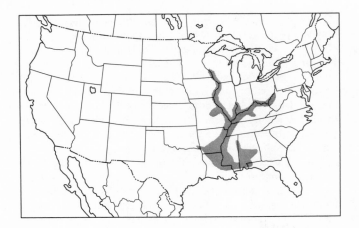

Distribution of *Ammocrypta asprella*

Spiny dorsal fin is nearly clear and lightly stippled along posterior margins of spines. Soft dorsal fin is similarly pigmented. Caudal fin is virtually clear except for darkening on margins of ventral rays. Anal, pelvic, and pectoral rays are essentially clear.

Cheek and opercle are scaled. Breast may bear embedded scales between pelvic fins or on adjacent prepectoral area. Nape and dorsolateral portion of head are scaled. Remainder of body has small exposed scales except on belly, which has scattered, partly embedded scales. Lateral line is complete, with 82-100 scales; scale counts are usually 82-85 in Mobile system, higher elsewhere. Fin counts are usually: dorsal XII-XIV, 13-15; anal I, 12-14. Vertebrae number 45-48.

Breeding coloration does not develop but both males and females in life have richer tones of brown or green than are seen in color plate. Breeding males develop large tubercles on anal spine and all but last 1-3 anal rays. Tubercles appear on at least first 3-5 pelvic fin rays. Male genital papilla is undescribed; that in females is a tapered, somewhat flattened tube.

Distribution. Occurs predominantly in major tributaries adjacent to the mainstem Mississippi River from southern Minnesota and western Wisconsin to southern Louisiana. In the Red River drainage it extends as far as the Little River in southeastern Oklahoma. Lowland streams of eastern Arkansas and southeastern Missouri may have good populations. The Gasconade River is the only tributary of the Missouri River with verified records, and these are rare. Formerly present in the mainstem Ohio or tributaries immediately adjacent to it as far upstream as Ohio and West Virginia, the crystal darter is now virtually absent there. The species also is found in the Mobile Bay basin and Perdido River from the lower Coosa westward, and is most common in the Tombigbee River.

Natural History. The crystal darter lives in moderate to large streams, most frequently in steady current over clean sand or gravel. Glenn Clemmer (Mississippi State University) has told us that evening collecting in slackening current at the foot of large riffles may produce success when day collecting at such sites has proved fruitless. Pflieger (1971) states that the crystal

darter in Missouri lives in large clear streams of low to moderate gradient and may be captured in open stretches over sand or fine gravel. Miller and Robison (1973) have observed it to burrow in sand, from which it attacks small prey.

Appearance of breeding tubercles in late autumn and winter indicates that spring is the likely breeding time. Life history and behavioral studies are badly needed for this unusual darter, but dependable access to adequate numbers has undoubtedly discouraged such an undertaking.

Percina ouachitae or *P. shumardi* may be collected with *A. asprella,* but its habitat is not consistently characteristic of these *Percina.*

Abundance. The crystal darter continues to lose ground in the battle for survival. Large streams are the repositories of silt and pollutants, and many have been dammed or are regularly dredged for navigation. Extensive areas of clean sand are becoming ever less common. This species will be lucky to persist in a few isolated streams. It is placed in a category of special concern by Deacon et al. (1979).

Name. *Asprella* is the diminutive of *Aspro,* meaning rough, in reference to scalation. Indirectly the name is associated with a small European member of the perch family, *Zingel asper.*

Ammocrypta beani Jordan   Plate 6
Naked Sand Darter   Subgenus *Ammocrypta*

Description. A small member of the subgenus reaching 53 mm SL and with SL 7-9 times maximum body depth. A member of the *beani* species group, it is distinguished from *A. bifascia* and *A. clara,* also with greatly reduced scalation, by the presence of a single median dark band in the spiny dorsal, soft dorsal, and anal fins of mature males. The posterior angle of the jaws extends as far back as the anterior rim of the eye. Gill membranes are slightly connected.

Dorsum bears a few scattered melanophores and there is a midlateral band along posterior half of body. Lateral scales, especially posteriorly, may have dark margins. A weak midventral line may extend from posterior end of anal fin to caudal fin base. Upper portion of opercle and sometimes cheek is lightly stippled; upper lip and snout are variably spotted. Body pigment is best seen in preserved specimens.

Pigmentation on fins is similar in both sexes but more intense in males. A median dark band in spiny dorsal fin is darkest anteriorly. A similar uniform median band in soft dorsal fin is more diffuse. A comparable vertical band in caudal fin may be poorly developed. A median anal fin band is comparable to that in soft dorsal fin. Pelvic fin lacks pigmentation; pectoral fin is lightly stippled along upper rays.

Most of body is devoid of scales. Lateral line scale row plus 1 row above and below extend length of body. Behind anal and soft dorsal fins additional rows appear, almost encircling caudal peduncle. Lateral line is bent downward near its terminus. There are 65-70 (57-77) scales with a slight average decrease from east to west across the species range. Fin counts

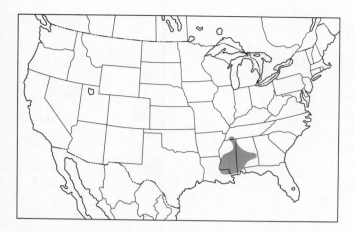

Distribution of *Ammocrypta beani*

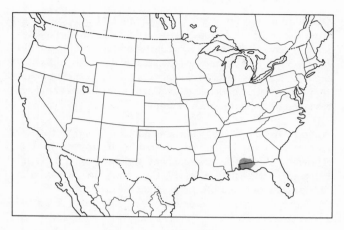

Distribution of *Ammocrypta bifascia*

are: dorsal IX-X (VII-XII), 10-11 (9-13); anal I, 9 -10 (8-11); pectoral usually 13. Vertebrae usually number 40 (39-42).

Life colors are completely described by Williams (1975). They consist of very delicate touches of yellow and green on body, blue or green highlights on head, and yellow or white on fins. These are almost immediately lost on preservation.

In males breeding tubercles are found on pelvic spine and rays, and at peak development on anal spine and rays.

Distribution. Occurs throughout the Mobile basin below the Fall Line, then westward in coastal drainages to the Mississippi River and its eastern tributaries as far north as the Black River in central Mississippi. An isolated population occurs in the Hatchie River in western Tennessee, a fact which suggests stream capture between it and the Tombigbee River.

Natural History. The naked sand darter usually lives on shifting sand bottoms at depths of 1 m or less in clean streams of moderate to large size and occasionally in creeks.

Gravid females may be found from early June through August, and contain fewer than 75 mature ova (Williams, 1975). This is a low reproductive potential for darters, as well as a late breeding season. Additional behavioral and life history data are needed.

Darter associates are *Ammocrypta vivax* and *A. meridiana* on occasion, as well as *Percina nigrofasciata* and *P. ouachitae. Notropis longirostris, Ericymba buccata,* and *Hybopsis aestivalis* are minnows often found within the habitat of *A. beani* and other sand darters along the Gulf Coast.

Abundance. The naked sand darter is widely enough distributed to be in little danger of extirpation. But channelization of coastal drainages has led to faunal decreases generally, as at the type locality, the Notalbany River, where we found few fish of any sort and no *A. beani.*

Name. Named in honor of T.H. Bean, its discoverer.

Ammocrypta bifascia Williams   Plate 6
Florida Sand Darter   Subgenus *Ammocrypta*

Description. The largest species of its subgenus, reaching 64 mm SL and with SL 8-10 times maximum body depth. A member of the *beani* species group by virtue of greatly reduced scalation, it differs from all other sand darters by having mature males with marginal as well as median dark bands in the spiny dorsal, soft dorsal, and anal fins. The posterior angle of the jaws extends well behind the anterior margin of the eye. Gill membranes are slightly connected.

Dorsum bears a few scattered melanophores, and there is a midlateral band on posterior half of body. Lateral scales, especially posteriorly, may have dark margins. Upper opercle often bears a dusky spot, and additional darkening occurs on upper cheek, tip of snout, and above angle of jaw. These markings are best seen in preserved specimens and are best developed in males.

Spiny dorsal fin, soft dorsal fin, and anal fin in males have both median and marginal dark bands; median band of spiny dorsal fin is the most pronounced. Darkening at margins of caudal fin rays produces weak median and marginal bands. Pelvic and pectoral fins are clear. Females have little of the fin pigmentation of males.

Most of body is devoid of scales. Lateral line scale row plus at least 1 row above and below extend length of body. Behind anal and soft dorsal fins additional rows appear, almost encircling caudal peduncle. Lateral line is bent downward near its terminus. Lateral line contains 63-74 scales and is deflected downward terminally. Fin counts are: dorsal IX-X (VII-XII), 11 (9-13); anal I, 9-10 (8-12); pectoral usually 13. Vertebrae number 40 (39-41).

Williams (1975) describes life colors completely. These are dominated by soft hues of yellow and orange on body and head, with additional bluish green on head. Some fins may also be tinged with yellow.

Breeding tubercles occur in males on pelvic spine and rays and on anal rays but seldom on anal spine.

Distribution. Occurs in coastal Alabama and western Florida from the Perdido drainage eastward to the lower Apalachicola system. It is the only sand darter within that region. Difficulty of capture perhaps is indicated by its recent addition to the Apalachicola basin by Starnes and Starnes (1979b) from a frequently visited collecting site. Alternatively, this could represent an introduction with bait minnows.

Natural History. The Florida sand darter normally is found in moderate to strong current, at depths of from .5 to 1 m. Spawning occurs between late May and July, apparently several weeks earlier than *A. beani.* Egg counts do not exceed 75. Other behavioral and life history data are needed.

Darter associates include *Etheostoma davisoni, E. edwini, E. okaloosae, E. swaini, Percina nigrofasciata,* and *P. caprodes* (perhaps a separate species).

Abundance. Though geographically restricted, this species seems not threatened at present.

Name. *Bifascia* refers to the double bands on median fins, which uniquely characterize this species.

Ammocrypta clara Jordan & Meek   Plate 6
Western Sand Darter   Subgenus *Ammocrypta*

Description. A moderate sized member of its subgenus reaching 59 mm SL and with SL 6-8 times maximum body depth. A member of the *beani* species group by virtue of greatly reduced scalation, it differs from *A. beani* and *A. bifascia* in the absence of fin banding in males and in the presence of an opercular spine in all specimens. Gill membranes are slightly joined. The posterior angle of the jaws usually does not reach as far as the anterior rim of the eye.

Body pigmentation is more distinct in preserved specimens than in life. Twelve to 16 small blotches are rather evenly spaced along dorsal midline, though some individuals develop only a dusky stripe. Nine to 13 horizontally elongated lateral blotches are connected by a stripe, which is more prominent in males than in females. A row of melanophores extends from end of anal fin to caudal fin base. Most body scales and the few opercular and cheek scales are edged in black. Dusky pigment on head extends onto snout, upper cheek, and upper opercle.

Fin pigmentation is sparse, confined to margins of spines or rays, and most pronounced in soft dorsal fin.

Lateral line scale row plus 1 row above and below extend length of body. Behind anal and soft dorsal fins additional rows appear, sometimes completely encircling caudal peduncle. Nape and back may have a few scales, usually partly embedded. Cheek and opercle vary but usually are partly scaled. Lateral line has 68-77 (63-84) scales and is deflected downward posteriorly. Fin counts are: dorsal XI (IX-XIII), 11 (9-13); anal I, 9 (8-11); pectoral 13-14 (12-15). Vertebrae number 39-40 (38-42).

Coloration in life is described by Williams (1975). Body is tinged with yellow dorsally, becoming colorless ventrally.

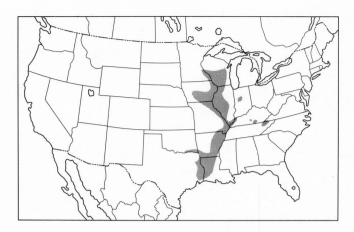

Distribution of *Ammocrypta clara*

Upper half of head is slightly yellow, and cheek and opercle are greenish yellow.

Evenly spaced breeding tubercles develop on males from late May through July, appearing first on anal and pelvic spines and rays and finally on lowermost caudal fin rays.

Distribution. Known from the Neches, Sabine, and lower Red River drainages of Texas and Oklahoma northeastward in many of the tributaries entering the Mississippi River from the west. Its presence has not been verified for the Arkansas, Missouri, or Minnesota river basins. It has occasionally been taken in the upper Mississippi channel from St. Louis north to St. Anthony Falls in Minnesota, and lives in several eastern tributaries of the upper Mississippi. Becker (1965) found it in a tributary of Green Bay in the Great Lakes drainage, where it arrived by passage through the Fox-Wisconsin River canal or alternatively by local post-Pleistocene stream course changes, as suggested for mollusks by Goodrich and Van der Schalie (1939). It has been taken in upper sections of the Wabash, Cumberland, and Green rivers but now is apparently absent there. Starnes et al. (1977) have taken this species in the Powell River, a headwater component of the Tennessee River system.

Natural History. The western sand darter usually inhabits large streams and is most common in slight to moderate current over a sandy bottom, though also known from areas of gravel or silt. Pflieger (1971) took it from drainage canals in southeast Missouri. It can be netted from waters to depths of 1.5 m.

Southern populations may coexist with *Ammocrypta vivax, Percina ouachitae,* and minnows such as *Hybopsis aestivalis* and *Notropis sabinae.* Starrett (1950) suggests July and August as the breeding months in Iowa. Southern populations probably breed a month earlier. More life history information is needed.

Abundance. This darter remains common in certain Wisconsin localities according to George Becker, who supplied us with live specimens. Smith (1979) reports it as threatened in Illinois. Most records for the Ohio River basin are quite old.

There is an apparent trend toward decreasing abundance, and the western sand darter may become endangered in the future.

Name. *Clara,* clear, is appropriate for this species, which is nearly transparent in life.

Ammocrypta meridiana Williams Plate 7
Southern Sand Darter   Subgenus *Ammocrypta*

Description. A moderate sized member of its subgenus reaching 58 mm SL and with SL 7-9 times maximum body depth. A member of the *pellucida* species group because of extensive body scalation, it is readily distinguishable from *A. vivax,* which has bolder lateral blotches and some pigmentation in the dorsal fins. It is narrowly distinguishable from *A. pellucida,* which usually has 4-7 scale rows below the lateral line series on the caudal peduncle, versus 8-9 in *A. meridiana.* Gill membranes are slightly connected. A narrow frenum is sometimes present.

Dorsum bears 10-15 small irregular blotches which may vary in intensity or may be split into paired spots. Scattered stippling may give the back a slightly dusky appearance. Eight to 13 small lateral blotches vary in size and intensity, posterior ones often being connected by a faint stripe. Body scales are edged in black. Top of head may have a dark median blotch. Preorbital bar is represented by a dark blotch adjacent to upper lip, which usually is darkened. A postorbital spot is represented by a dusky area between cheek and opercle.

All fins appear clear, though the margins of spines and rays are slightly pigmented.

Cheek and opercle are scaled, nape is partially scaled, and prepectoral area may have a few scales. Belly is naked; rest of body bears small scales. Lateral line has 66-75 (63-79) scales. Fin counts are: dorsal IX-XI (VII-XII), 10 (9-11); anal I, 8-9 (7-10); pectoral 14 (12-15). Vertebrae number 42 (41-43).

Breeding tubercles in males are confined to outer 3 pelvic rays, but often fail to develop. Pelvic fin may darken considerably.

Life colors are described in detail by Williams (1975). The body has tinges of yellow and orange, becoming fainter ventrally. Pale green may occur along sides. Head and fins are tinged with yellow or orange. Cheek and opercle are faintly bluish green.

Distribution. Restricted to the Mobile basin. This species occurs throughout the Alabama and Tombigbee rivers and in the Coastal Plain sections of the Warrior, Cahaba, and Tallapoosa drainages. It is a recently named addition to the surprisingly long list of fishes and mollusks which are endemic to the Mobile basin.

Natural History. The southern sand darter occurs over clean sandy bottoms in moderate current at depths from .1 to just over 1.5 m. Spawning probably takes place between early June and late July.

In smaller streams it occurs with *A. beani,* and in rivers

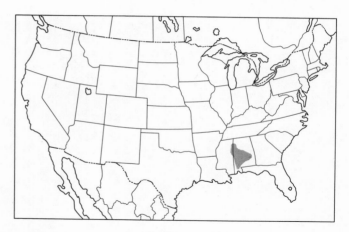

Distribution of *Ammocrypta meridiana*

may be associated with *Percina ouachitae.* The minnows *Ericymba buccata, Hybopsis aestivalis,* and *Notropis longirostris* (or a related, unnamed form) are commonly captured with *A. meridiana.* More detailed life history information is needed.

Abundance. With its widespread occurrence in the Mobile basin there is little reason to be pessimistic about this darter. We hope it will be monitored, however, and that environmental excesses within its range will be minimized.

Name. *Meridiana* is a modification of *meridionalis,* meaning southern. The name emphasizes the relationship of this species to its northern counterpart, *A. pellucida.*

Ammocrypta pellucida (Putnam) Plate 7
Eastern Sand Darter   Subgenus *Ammocrypta*

Description. A small member of its subgenus reaching about 51 mm SL and with SL usually 8-10 times maximum body depth. A member of the *pellucida* species group, it is distinguished from *A. meridiana* by having 4-7 scale rows below the lateral line series on the caudal peduncle, versus 8-9 in the latter species. It lacks the bolder body markings and dorsal fin pigmentation of *A. vivax.* Gill membranes are slightly joined.

Back is marked by 11-19 blotches of various sizes, some often subdivided, producing a variety of patterns. Light stippling on back may produce a dusky effect. Side supports 8-13 horizontally elongated blotches which may be connected by a faint band posteriorly. On upper half of body, scales may be darkly edged. Top of head may have a dusky blotch. Upper lip is dusky, and preorbital bar is obvious only adjacent to lip. Upper cheek and opercle may be dusky.

All fins appear to be clear, though the margins of spines and rays are slightly darkened.

Cheek and opercle vary from well to weakly scaled; nape is usually partially scaled. Belly is naked, and dorsal and ventral midlines of caudal peduncle vary from scaled to naked. Lat-

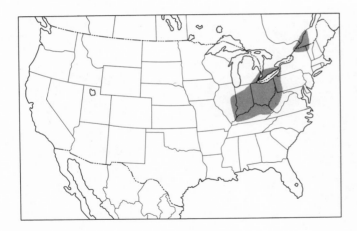

Distribution of *Ammocrypta pellucida*

eral line contains 69-75 (65-84) scales. Fin counts are: dorsal IX-XI (VII-XII), 10-11 (8-12); anal I, 8-9 (7-11); pectoral 14-15 (12-16). Vertebrae number 43 (42-45).

Breeding tubercles in males develop only as small protuberances on ventral surface of pelvic fin base, and may be absent in some individuals. Pelvic fins are darkened basally.

Trautman (1957) describes coloration. In life, upper half of transparent body and upper half of head are faint yellow. Ventrally, head lacks coloration and body is without coloration or has a white or silver cast. Greenish blotches are seen along dorsal midline and sides. A faint yellow lateral band may be present. Fin membranes are clear or show a yellow tinge. Breeding males are more yellowish than other adults. Juveniles are less yellowish and more silvery than adults.

Distribution. *Ammocrypta pellucida* was described before *A. clara* and *A. vivax,* and these latter 2 have at various times been confused with it or treated as subspecies of it. Williams (1975) examined early collections which still exist and reevaluated older citations in an attempt to clarify the patterns of distribution of the 3 species. *A. pellucida* apparently is found only in the Ohio and St. Lawrence river basins. In the Ohio system it has been reported from the mouth of the Cumberland River upstream to the Allegheny and Monongahela, excluding their upland tributaries. Likewise the Kanawha and Big Sandy rivers have never yielded the species except in their lowest reaches. The species apparently entered the Great Lakes system via the late Pleistocene Maumee-Wabash connection and spread to local drainages of Lake Erie and Lake St. Clair and to the southernmost tip of Lake Huron. It is absent from the northeastern corner of Lake Erie but reappears in extreme upstate New York, Vermont, and the vicinity of Montreal.

Natural History. The eastern sand darter inhabits a variety of waters from creeks to large rivers and has even been reported once from Lake Erie trawl hauls (Scott and Crossman, 1973). It is most often found in larger streams over clean sand and in moderate current, although it has been reported over substrates ranging from silt to gravel. In Kentucky streams we have found eastern sand darters at depths of 1/2 m or less in the clean sand accumulated just below and beside riffles. Forbes and Richardson (1920) and Turner (1921) report that midge larvae comprise the bulk of the diet. Spawning occurs in June and July in the Ohio basin and 2-3 weeks later in the St. Lawrence populations. Bangham and Hunter (1939) found several species of trematode parasites of *A. pellucida.*

Many species of darters may live in riffles adjacent to suitable habitat for the eastern sand darter without being directly associated with it. Minnows, such as *Notropis stramineus,* are likely to occupy the same habitat. *Ammocrypta clara* may occur with it in the Green River basin but neither is common in the region of overlap.

Abundance. All indications are that the eastern sand darter is a steadily declining species. Siltation caused by a variety of human activities has reduced its numbers and probably eradicated it from much of the range outlined above. We have seen a single old collection taken from Quicksand Creek (where it apparently no longer exists) in the upper Kentucky drainage which far outnumbered all the specimens we have ever caught. Scott and Crossman (1973) state that recent collections in Canada are not common and that much potential habitat has been industrialized. Our specimens used for photographs were taken from a site on the Licking River now lost to a reservoir. The species is listed by Deacon et al. (1979) as threatened.

Name. *Pellucida* means transparent.

Ammocrypta vivax Hay
Scaly Sand Darter

Plate 7
Subgenus *Ammocrypta*

Description. A moderately large member of its subgenus reaching 61 mm SL and with SL 7-9 times maximum body depth. A member of the *pellucida* species group, it differs from both *A. meridiana* and *A. pellucida* in its bolder lateral markings and spots in the dorsal fins. Gill membranes are separate to slightly joined.

Back is variously marked by 10-15 blotches which may be separated to form paired spots. Some of these may extend downward and diagonally backward to form reticulations with several of the 9-16 lateral blotches. The latter vary in size and shape but usually are vertically elongated. Most scales of body, cheek, and opercle are darkly edged. Head is weakly pigmented, there being dusky areas on and above upper lip and on opercle.

Spiny dorsal fin is more intensely marked in males than in females and is characterized by a narrow marginal band and a wider submarginal band, both of which tend to be broken into spots on membranes. Bands occasionally merge into a single ill-defined broad band. In both sexes soft dorsal fin exhibits marginal and submarginal pigmentation which is concentrated in rays and appears to form 2 bands. Caudal fin is similar to soft dorsal except that marginal band may be weak or

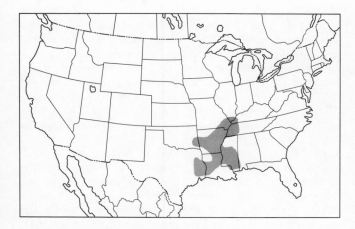

Distribution of *Ammocrypta vivax*

absent. Anal fin bears some pigmentation along edges of rays and often scattered melanophores in membranes. Upper rays of pectoral fin are lightly pigmented. Pelvic fin in females is unmarked but that in males is pigmented basally on both rays and membranes. In small and juvenile individuals, characteristic dorsal fin bands may be weakly developed or absent.

Body is well scaled except on belly, which remains naked near midline. Cheek and opercle are scaled; nape is partially scaled and prepectoral area may be weakly scaled. Lateral line contains 64-72 (58-79) scales. Fin counts are: dorsal X-XII (VIII-XIV), 10-11 (9-12); anal I, 8-9 (7-10); pectoral 14-15 (13-17). Vertebrae number 42 (41-43).

Breeding tubercles in males appear on spines and rays of both pelvic and anal fins, and are best developed on ventral surface of pelvic fin rays.

Williams (1975) describes colors in life. Body hues are dominated by yellow and orange; head is similarly colored and tinges of green appear on cheek and opercle.

Distribution. Occurs in a number of rivers in the Mississippi Embayment and in the Coastal Plain portions of Gulf drainages as far west as the San Jacinto River in Texas and as far east as the streams entering Pascagoula Bay in Mississippi. It enters southeastern Oklahoma via both the Red and Arkansas rivers and occurs outside the Coastal Plain both here and at a few Arkansas localities. The northern limit is the St. Francis and Little River system of southeastern Missouri. The lower Tennessee, Hatchie, Yazoo, Black, and Bayou Pierre drainages are eastern tributaries of the Mississippi River which harbor the species.

Natural History. The scaly sand darter is an inhabitant of creeks and rivers of various size, where it most often occurs in moderate current over sandy substrate. In Missouri and Arkansas it has been caught in sloughs and drainage ditches, where silt, gravel, and hard clay bottom predominates.

Tuberculate males examined by Williams (1975) were collected between mid-April and mid-August, which implies that the height of spawning is probably June and July. A comprehensive life history study of this species is much needed.

The scaly sand darter has been taken in association with *A. clara,* mostly to the west of the Mississippi River, and with *A. beani* to the east. It sometimes is captured with *Etheostoma chlorosomum, E. asprigene, E. swaini, Percina ouachitae, P. sciera,* or *P. shumardi.*

Abundance. While it is unlikely to be thriving, this species is not in an endangered status. But serious depletions may be occurring at the margins of the range, and its status should continue to be monitored.

Name. *Vivax* means vigorous or lively.

Etheostoma
and Its Subgenera

Etheostoma is the largest and most diverse genus of darters, constituting 94 species as treated here. We include some information on 8 probably valid unnamed snubnose darters in the subgenus *Ulocentra* because some or all will undoubtedly be named soon. Some additional new species can be anticipated. *Etheostoma stigmaeum* seems to be a complex with 2 or 3 forms awaiting either description or redescription based on an older name in the literature. At least one relative of *Etheostoma flabellare* is unnamed in the Tennessee River basin, and the fantail darter itself may be a species complex, particularly on the southern Atlantic slope. Some forms considered here as subspecies, particularly *E. whipplei artesiae* and *E. zonale lynceum,* have enjoyed specific status in the past and may again be found to warrant such. One or more unnamed members of the genus may live in Mexico, an area in need of further study. Discovery of an additional species in subgenus *Nothonotus* is not unlikely, and the variability in *E. squamiceps* of subgenus *Catonotus* needs clarification. Allowing for such changes and the discovery of a few more species, it is probable that the genus may contain 120 species maximally. The purely taxonomic phase of darter study is certainly nearing its end, so that future research will focus more strongly on population dynamics, physiology, and other experimental approaches for which the group is suited. The final taxonomic decisions and work on phylogeny will be greatly aided by electrophoretic studies such as those of Page and Whitt (1973a,b) and karyological investigations like that of Danzmann (1979).

Some species of *Etheostoma* share characteristics with *Ammocrypta*, but only *E. vitreum* approaches both the slenderness and the translucence of the latter, and no *Etheostoma* is as finely scaled. Males in *Percina* have either a midventral row of enlarged toothed scales, or absence of scales on the midline of the belly, or at least toothed scales between the pelvic fins. Some species of *Etheostoma* lack scales on the anterior portion of the belly, but almost always have normal scalation posteriorly and always lack toothed scales between the pelvic fins. The top of the head is a little arched, not as flat as in *Percina.* Most members of *Etheostoma* are slightly to much smaller than *Percina,* but a few reach large size (127 mm SL in *E. blennioides*).

Members of *Etheostoma* exploit a large variety of habitats, ranging from poorly oxygenated swamps to turbulent, well aerated streams. They often are abundant in streams smaller than those invaded by the other 2 darter genera. What seem to be secondary adaptations have carried various *Etheostoma* from streams into lakes, springs, and quiet pools. Neither *Percina* nor *Ammocrypta* occupies a major habitat type to the total exclusion of *Etheostoma.*

The diversity of habitats utilized by *Etheostoma* is paralleled by morphological diversity within the genus. For most of the taxonomic history of the group a new species was as often as not put in a new genus, as well. The problems of finding consistent differences among numerous genera became virtually impossible as the discovery of new species continued. Without explanation, Bailey and Gosline (1955) lumped all darters into the presently used 3 genera and utilized available names to group assemblages into phylogenetically arranged subgenera as seemed appropriate to them. Some ichthyologists mentioned the lack of complete subgeneric characterization, but all biologists quickly adopted this convenient scheme, which has survived remarkably intact. We follow closely the subgenera of *Etheostoma* presented by Collette and Banarescu (1977) but accept the sequence of Page (1981) and some of the species shifts he recommends.

Subgenus *Psychromaster* contains the single spring-dwelling species *E. tuscumbia,* which is unique in the heavy extent of scalation on the head and gill membranes, as well as the presence of 1 thick anal fin spine.

Subgenus *Litocara* contains 2 species with apparent relict distribution patterns in the Ozark and Cumberland plateaus. Though formerly placed in subgenus *Oligocephalus,* they are quite unusual in having a high number of anal fin rays (9-12), many lateral line scales (52-82), an elongated head, and a body shape closer to that of *Percina* than those seen in any other members of *Etheostoma.* Adult males are larger than female counterparts.

Subgenus *Allohistium* also is a generalized form consisting of a species endemic to the Cumberland and Tennessee river basins. Its distinguishing traits are a sloping head, rather long snout, papillose lips, and an elongated soft dorsal fin, best developed in males.

Subgenus *Etheostoma* is an assemblage of 14 species characterized by a combination of features that includes: eyes set high on a broad head with short rounded snout, rather heavy lips, and usually a well developed frenum; gill membranes broadly joined; large rounded pectoral fins; supratemporal and infraorbital sensory canals complete; first anal fin spine thick and stiff; body coloration of males predominantly green and spiny dorsal fin usually having a submarginal red band; genital papilla of females a long rounded tube and that of males a short, often flattened tube. Males are larger than females in several species.

Three species groups within subgenus *Etheostoma* were recognized by Richards (1966). A *variatum* group, loosely referred to as saddled darters, consists of *E. variatum, E. kanawhae, E. osburni, E. euzonum,* and *E. tetrazonum.* They have 4-6 prominent dorsal saddles and breeding tubercles in both sexes. All have restricted ranges in the upper Ohio River basin or streams of the Ozark region. *E. blennius* and *E. sellare* have prominent saddles but lack breeding tubercles. Their ranges fall outside that of the saddled darters and they may best be viewed as relatives. A *thalassinum* group includes *E. thalassinum, E. inscriptum,* and *E. swannanoa,* all of which have saddles reduced to squarish blotches and breeding tubercles only in males. They are confined to the upper Tennessee River basin and Atlantic drainages immediately to the east and southeast. The remaining species are placed in a *blenni-*

oides group including *E. blennioides, E. histrio, E. rupestre,* and *E. zonale*. All have reduced frenum size and breeding tubercles few (as in *E. blennioides*) or absent. Reduction of head size and gill support rays from 6 to 5 in *E. zonale* make this species intermediate between subgenera *Etheostoma* and *Ulocentra*. Whereas *E. rupestre* is restricted to the Mobile system, each of the others is more widely distributed both east and west of the Mississippi River.

Members of subgenus *Etheostoma* occur in streams varying from large creeks to moderate sized rivers. They are most common in riffles of moderate strength. Some species are fairly common in shallow pools of slow but steady flow lacking great amounts of silt. Spawning apparently occurs in gravel or on aquatic plants and algae.

Subgenus *Ulocentra* consists of 8 named species and about 8 unnamed forms all of which are confined to southern tributaries of the Ohio River, eastern tributaries of the lower Mississippi River, and eastern Gulf coast drainages. Basic characteristics are: short snout abruptly rounded or blunt and overhanging a small mouth; frenum absent or sometimes present as a narrow bridge; cheek and nape slightly to markedly protuberant; eye set high on head; gill membranes broadly joined and supported by 5 rays (6 in *E. coosae*); supratemporal and infraorbital sensory canals complete; pectoral fins long, often expansive; usually 8-9 small squarish dorsal saddles; usually 8-10 lateral blotches, sometimes fused into a band; breeding males colorful in all but 1 unnamed form; genital papilla of males a small rouded tube and that of females a longer narrow tube; and spawning position in some species known to be vertical, with a few eggs deposited at a time. Species groups are not recognized. The subgenus was completely diagnosed by Bouchard (1977). Species tend to be quite restricted geographically. They are common in clear riffles of moderate strength in streams varying from large creeks to medium sized rivers.

Subgenus *Doration* consists of 2 species which superficially resemble subgenus *Boleosoma*. Distinguishing characteristics are: lateral line incomplete; gill membranes narrowly to moderately joined; breeding males with bright blue or green on body and a blue marginal and red or orange submarginal band in the spiny dorsal fin; and eggs apparently laid in sand or gravel without specialized spawning position. *Etheostoma jessiae* is restricted to the Tennessee and Cumberland river basins, but *E. stigmaeum* as now recognized occurs in the eastern Gulf coast drainages, southern tributaries of the lower Ohio River, and streams in and near the Ozark uplands. Howell (in Lee et al., 1980) resurrects the name *E. meadiae* for a form in the upper Tennessee basin; when fully described, this and other variants of *E. stigmaeum* may increase the size of subgenus *Doration* considerably. Members are usually found in shallow riffles of streams varying from large creeks to medium sized rivers. They avoid the strongest currents and may occupy pools with clean substrate and steady current.

Subgenus *Boleosoma* contains 5 species (Cole, 1967) and is characterized by: lateral line complete or nearly so; snout blunt to slightly pointed; frenum absent; 1 or 2 short thin flexible anal fin spines with little difference in thickness when both are present; usually 6 small squarish dorsal saddles; female genital papilla rather short and bilobed and that of males short and conical; no breeding tubercles; breeding males darker on the body or with dark blue and sometimes deep orange on body; and spawning position, when known, inverted beneath rocks or other objects. Members occupy an array of habitats including pools and riffles of streams ranging from very small to moderately large, slightly brackish water in one case, and a lake in another. Only *E. nigrum* occurs outside the Atlantic coastal streams, but it enters that region. Cole (1971) considers the former to be an independent line within the subgenus, *E. olmstedi* to be another, and the remaining 3 species to be a line closer to *E. olmstedi* than to *E. nigrum*. Both *E. longimanum* and *E. podostemone* appear to us to have considerable resemblance to subgenus *Ulocentra*.

By present reasoning (Winn and Picciolo, 1960; Collette, 1965; Jenkins, 1971) subgenus *Ioa* is similar to subgenus *Boleosoma* but differs as follows: body very slender (maximum body depth about one-seventh of SL); flesh almost transparent in life; breeding tubercles on pectoral and pelvic fins in both sexes; genital papilla surrounded with fleshy villi in both sexes. Spawning by swarms of males and females has been observed. Similarity of the sole species in *Ioa* to *Ammocrypta* may result from convergence, since both occupy areas of clean washed sand.

Subgenus *Vaillantia* is diagnosed by Cole (1967) and differs from *Boleosoma* in 3 ways: lateral line incomplete, sometimes fewer than half the scales pored; females with a rugose heart-shaped genital papilla; and breeding males with tubercles on anal and pelvic fin rays. Both members are characteristic of small to fairly large streams with sluggish flow and are confined to the Gulf Coast or the main axis of the Mississippi River basin. *Etheostoma davisoni* was treated as a member of subgenus *Doration* by Bailey and Gosline (1955).

Subgenus *Nothonotus* is a rather homogeneous assemblage of 13 species diagnosed by Bailey (1959) and Zorach (1972). It is partially characterized by: small to moderate size with compressed sides, deep caudal peduncle, and robust appearance; snout sharp to somewhat rounded, the upper jaw usually protruding a little, and frenum well developed; eyes closely set; gill membranes separate to narrowly connected; pelvic fins closely set; lateral line complete or nearly so (incomplete in *E. tippecanoe*); small scales extending at least a short distance onto the caudal fin; some males with red spots on the sides; most species with thin horizontal dark bands on the posterior portion of the body; supratemporal and infraorbital sensory canals complete; fins in males having some bright colors and those in females usually having fine spots; female genital papilla a short tube, rounded or flattened, male papilla a small tube; no breeding tubercles; and adult males usually larger than female counterparts. *Etheostoma juliae* was noted as similar to *Nothonotus* by Zorach and was transferred from *Oligocephalus* by Page (1981).

Females of *Nothonotus* may be quite similar; where several species occur in the same area, mature males are the best means of positive identification. Adults of all species occur in deeper portions of riffles, abandoning these during extreme drought and cold. Two or 3 species enter fairly small creeks as well as larger streams, while the rest occur in large creeks and rivers up to considerable size. Three wide-ranging species of the Ohio River basin have spotty distributions and no longer occur in many places where historically recorded. The Tennessee, Cumberland, and Green rivers with 6 endemic species collectively are the center of abundance for the subgenus. Only 4 species occur outside the Ohio basin, 2 to the south and 2 west of the Mississippi. No members occur above Cumberland Falls or in the upper Kanawha River. For such strong swimmers it seems strange that none have invaded the Great Lakes drainage or the upper Mississippi basin. In spite of morphological similarity there is a sharp dichotomy in breeding patterns in *Nothonotus*, 2 or more species burying eggs in gravel and 1 or more species laying eggs on the underside of rocks in similar fashion to subgenus *Catonotus*.

Subgenus *Villora* is characterized by Collette and Yerger (1962) and contains 2 species of rather dubious affinity but each with similarity to subgenus *Oligocephalus*. Distinctions from the latter subgenus are: lateral line slightly to distinctly arched anteriorly; pelvic fins closely set; and genital papilla of females a short tube grooved at the tip. Both species inhabit riffles or pools with some flow in small to medium sized streams of the extreme southeastern United States. Both apparently lay eggs on aquatic plants.

Subgenus *Ozarka* was erected by Williams and Robison (1980) to accommodate the assemblage of stippled darters formerly in subgenus *Oligocephalus*, plus *E. trisella*, previously in subgenus *Psychromaster*. Blair (1964) and Wall and Williams (1974) discuss the closeness of the stippled darters. *Etheostoma trisella* fits marginally in the subgenus on the basis of morphology but well on the basis of habitat preference and aspects of breeding behavior. Characteristics of *Ozarka* are: gill membranes separate to slightly joined; caudal peduncle deep; humeral mark distinct or at least present; suborbital bar well developed; 3-9 dorsal saddles distinct in most individuals; sides stippled or blotchy in most individuals; breeding males with a narrow dark marginal band, a red or orange submarginal band, and a dark basal band in the spiny dorsal fin, and with a horizontal orange band on the lower side (*E. trisella* with little breeding coloration); genital papilla of males a short flat triangular tube and that of females longer and tubular. All inhabit small streams or the protected shoreline of larger streams and most are known to breed in shallow water, often in seepages with water present only in early spring. Three of the species occur in the Ozark uplands, 1 in the middle Tennessee River basin, and 1 in the upper Coosa River basin.

Subgenus *Austroperca* was proposed by Hubbs (1936) for the single species *E. australe*, which differs from members of *Oligocephalus* only in having a single thick and rather long anal fin spine. The spine appears to us to be a fusion of the 2 spines typical of most darters. This species is a riffle inhabitant of Mexican streams of rather small to moderate size.

Subgenus *Oligocephalus* is the largest and most heterogeneous group in *Etheostoma*. Shared traits include: a broad or rather broad frenum; separate to moderately connected gill membranes; naked or virtually naked head and anterior nape; head of rather small size compared with body diameter; and males usually with a submarginal red band in the spiny dorsal fin. Collette (1965) discusses 2 tuberculate and 1 nontuberculate group. The *radiosum* group has up to 3 rows of rounded tubercles along the belly and around the anal fin continuing to the caudal peduncle. The pattern occurs in *E. radiosum, E.*

whipplei, E. caeruleum, and *E. collettei.* Relationships within the assemblage are not clear. A *spectabile* group has tubercles at least on the anal fin and sometimes on the pelvic and pectoral fins and ventral scales, as well. This group includes *E. spectabile, E. luteovinctum, E. hopkinsi, E. fricksium,* and *E. parvipinne,* the latter having so few tubercles as to be transitional to the nontuberculate group. Among the nontuberculate species, *E. asprigene, E. swaini, E. ditrema,* and *E. nuchale* seem closely related. The remainder, *E. exile, E. mariae, E. lepidum, E. grahami,* and *E. pottsi,* do not seem very closely related. *E. exile* has a slightly arched lateral line and appears transitional to subgenus *Hololepis*.

Oligocephalus darters usually inhabit riffles of streams varying from small creeks to moderate sized rivers and favor areas of steady but not highly turbulent flow. But some are found in springs, others in murky sluggish streams, 1 in weedy lakes as well as streams, and 1 in rivulets and seepages.

Subgenus *Catonotus* is a distinctive group of 10 species diagnosed by Kuehne and Small (1971) with modifications by Braasch and Page (1979). Some important traits are: lateral line incomplete; frenum present; snout somewhat to quite pointed; spiny dorsal fin low and provided with thickened tips in some species; pelvic fins closely set; breeding tubercles absent; male genital papilla a triangular flap and that of females a grooved circular pad; spawning position inverted with eggs laid on the underside of rocks. Collette (1965) recognized 2 groups based on the presence or absence of spiny dorsal fin knobs. Species with knobs on the dorsal fin darken during breeding season but do not become colorful. Page (1975b) subdivided these on the basis of the shape of the terminal knobs. *Etheostoma flabellare* and *E. kennicotti* (with possible additional species unnamed) have rounded terminal knobs. *E. squamiceps, E. olivaceum,* and *E. neopterum* have smaller pointed knobs. The remaining species have little or no development of knobs, become bright during breeding, and constitute a *virgatum* group, commonly called barcheeked darters. *Catonotus* has loose similarity to *Oligocephalus* and in terms of breeding behavior a close similarity to some members of *Nothonotus*. The barcheeked species reside only in the Green, Cumberland, and Tennessee basins. Of the remaining species, only *E. flabellare* has an extensive range outside those river basins. It also is the only member of *Catonotus* to occur in riffles of small to large streams, though *E. kennicotti* and *E. squamiceps* enter slower riffles frequently. Barcheeked darters reside in pools of small streams during most of the year but may enter riffles in spring, presumably to spawn.

Subgenus *Hololepis* constitutes a group of 6 similar species sometimes referred to as swamp darters. Collette (1962) clarified the group taxonomy and diagnosed the subgenus, as well. Members have: a highly arched incomplete lateral line with pored scales ending beneath one of the dorsal fins; slender appearance created by a small head, narrow pectoral fins, somewhat cylindrical shape, and constricted caudal peduncle; first anal fin spine somewhat shorter and thicker than the second; males without breeding colors except in 2 species; breeding tubercles in males present on anal and pelvic fins and in 2 forms on the chin; male genital papilla a small tube and that of females an elongated tube (except in *E. serriferum*); and males usually smaller than females of the same age. Neotenic traits are displayed in the subgenus, culminating in *E. collis,* which consistently has only 1 anal fin spine. The subgenus shows some similarity to *Oligocephalus* and marked similarity to subgenus *Microperca.* Members utilize shallow sluggish streams and, with the exception of *E. collis* and *E. saludae,* also tend to enter oxbows, lowland ponds, and swamps. Their distributions include 3 species confined to the Atlantic slope only, 1 species of the Atlantic and Gulf coastal regions, and 2 species of the Mobile drainage and lower Mississippi basin.

Subgenus *Microperca* includes 3 similar species sometimes referred to as the least darters, which have been treated monographically by Burr (1978). Principal traits are: small darters never reaching 40 mm SL; adult females larger than male counterparts; 5 rather than 6 rays supporting each gill membrane; lateral line incomplete with 0-9 pored scales; pelvic fin of males highly specialized and forming a cuplike structure with its counterpart; males with a submarginal red band or dots in the spiny dorsal fin and sometimes additional pigment on caudal and anal fins; male breeding tubercles on the ventral surface of pelvic fin and lateral surfaces of anal fin; male genital papilla a small tube; and that of females an elongated tube, sometimes flattened and variably grooved. The subgenus is most similar to *Hololepis.* Members live in weedy lakes, ponds, backwaters, pools in sluggish streams, or weedy spring-fed streams. Their distribution lies on each side of a line from the Great Lakes south through the Mississippi basin. *Etheostoma fonticola* is closely related to and perhaps derived from *E. proeliare. Microperca* shows the greatest degree of neotenic specialization of all darter subgenera.

There is an element of subjectivity in placing species of *Etheostoma* in subgenera and there certainly is such in our arrangement. The subgenera may best be thought of as aids to the understanding of species relationships and a convenient mechanism for organizing information. To a remarkable degree the habitat preferences and breeding behavior as well as morphology of subgeneric partners show strong similarities.

Etheostoma tuscumbia Gilbert & Swain   Plate 7
Tuscumbia Darter   Subgenus *Psychromaster*

Description. A small darter reaching 43 mm SL in our largest specimen. The only species in subgenus *Psychromaster,* it is characterized by very heavy head scalation, incomplete lateral line, and single anal spine. The snout is short, the mouth small, and the frenum well developed. Gill membranes are separate. The opercular spine is partly hidden by scales. Infraorbital canal is complete; supratemporal canal is usually interrupted.

Back bears 5-7 squarish saddles but only the first and the last 2 are always strongly developed. Many individuals have 8 or 9 small midlateral blotches but others fail to develop some or all of these. A vertically elongated basicaudal bar is also variably developed. Upper side is stippled and posterior half of body is stippled ventrally. Belly is clear.

Preorbital bar is distinct but suborbital bar may be weak, sometimes only a number of spots on cheek. Postorbital bar

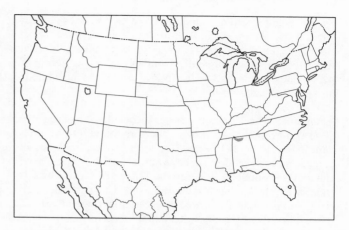

Distribution of *Etheostoma tuscumbia*

appears as a dark streak or merely a dark spot. Chin, throat, and breast vary from unpigmented to stippled.

First spine of spiny dorsal fin is very short. Dark spots found on both membranes and spines fail to produce a sharp pattern. Membranes of soft dorsal fin are clear, and rays are pigmented to produce banding. Vertical bands are similarly produced in caudal fin. Anal and pelvic fins are pale; pectoral fin rays are stippled. Both pelvic and pectoral fins are short and stubby.

This is perhaps the most squamous of all darters, and most scales are strongly ctenoid. Cheek and opercle are fully scaled; head is scaled forward to margin of eye. Nape is covered with small scales. Scales cover breast and extend forward to gill membranes and laterally onto prepectoral area. Belly is fully scaled.

Lateral line is incomplete, with 17-27 pored and 18-29 unpored scales. Full lateral series consists of 43-52 scales, which appear somewhat smaller than other body scales. Fin counts are: dorsal IX-XI, 11-14; anal I, 7-8; pectoral usually 11-12. Vertebrae number 35-37.

Breeding males may show more coloration than the specimen in color plate, which was captured in June. Genital papilla in males is a long tapered tube; that in females is shorter and terminally bilobed. Female coloration is similar to but less well developed than that of males.

Distribution. Known from a few limestone springs restricted to the great southern bend of the Tennessee River in northern Alabama. This darter's presence in the adjacent limestone region of Mississippi is not verified, and it probably has been extirpated in Tennessee since construction of Pickwick Reservoir.

Natural History. According to Armstrong and Williams (1971), the Tuscumbia darter lives among mats of aquatic vegetation, such as *Nasturtium* and *Myriophyllum.* It was under exactly such conditions that our specimens were secured near Huntsville, Alabama. This species seems never to have been captured in brooks or in springs of feeble or intermittent flow. The above authors found the Tuscumbia darter in only 6 of 67 springs visited in the bend of the Tennessee River. Many of these sites have become inundated by reservoirs or have themselves been dammed, walled, or otherwise altered. Koch (1978) found Tuscumbia darters to feed maximally from April to June and minimally from December to February. Amphipods, snails, and midge fly larvae were the most important food sources.

Abundance. The Tuscumbia darter is considered by Deacon et al. (1979) as threatened. Early collectors found it to be abundant in the stream below the great spring at Tuscumbia, Alabama, and at several other large springs of the region, especially those issuing directly into the Tennessee River. The Tuscumbia spring has been dammed, walled in part with concrete, and periodically cleared of vegetation in recent years. It is used directly as the city water supply. Worrisome to us was not only the total absence of Tuscumbia darters in the spring-fed stream where we collected in 1969, but also the virtual absence of fish of any type. Poisoning of the spring from pesticides used on local cotton crops may explain this. Ramsey (1976) states that 3 specimens were caught from the spring after intensive collecting in 1976. Well over 200 were taken in 1963, and Ramsey indicates that frequent removal of aquatic vegetation may be responsible for the drastic decrease.

Name. *Tuscumbia* is taken from the great spring, itself named for the Indian chief Tuscumbia.

Etheostoma nianguae Gilbert & Meek   Plate 7
Niangua Darter   Subgenus *Litocara*

Description. A rather large darter perhaps reaching 100 mm SL. The slender but powerful body, long pointed snout, large mouth, and virtually scaleless head place it in subgenus *Litocara*. It is finer scaled than *E. sagitta* and is unlikely to be confused with any other darter. The snout slightly overlaps the mouth; the frenum is well developed. Gill membranes are separate to slightly connected; branchiostegal rays are sometimes 7 instead of the typical 6. Infraorbital canal is complete but supratemporal canal is sometimes narrowly interrupted.

Back is crossed by 7 or 8 dark saddles, several of which may fuse with 1 of the 8-10 lateral blotches. Blotches may be oval with pale centers or may open into V- or U-shaped markings. Belly is pale. Two distinct basicaudal spots sometimes fuse into a vertical bar.

Preorbital bar does not meet counterpart on snout; postorbital bar may extend as far as opercle. Lower cheek and opercle are pale, as are chin, throat, and breast.

Vertical dashes in membranes constitute pattern in spiny dorsal fin. Similar markings in soft dorsal fin produce several diagonal bands. Caudal fin has such bands vertically set. Anal, pelvic, and pectoral fins have little or no pigmentation.

Cheek has a few embedded scales; opercle, nape, and breast are naked. Belly is fully scaled. Lateral line is nearly complete but may lack pores on last 2-7 scales. Series consists of 73-82 scales. Fin counts are: dorsal X-XII, 13-14; anal II (rarely I), 10-12; pectoral 14-16. Vertebrae usually number 40.

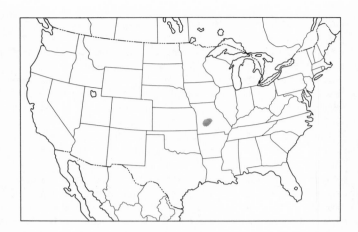

Distribution of *Etheostoma nianguae*

Breeding males become brightly colored, more so than shown in color plate. Unusual conical breeding tubercles occur on several ventral scale rows from pelvic fin base to caudal peduncle. Though not observed by us, genital papilla may be of the type described for *E. sagitta*. Breeding females become olivaceous with a red to orange marginal band in spiny dorsal fin and often golden flecks in soft dorsal fin. We have not seen genital papilla of a breeding female. Even very small individuals of *E. nianguae* are recognized by distinctive lateral marks.

Distribution. Restricted to several southern tributaries of the Osage River in Missouri. Recorded only once in the Sac River and rarely from the Niangua and Little Niangua basins, the species is now found regularly only in Big Tavern Creek and the Maries River.

Natural History. The Niangua darter is a very uncommon fish inhabiting small to medium-sized streams with permanent flow. It may occur in the deeper portions of riffles or in pools, particularly where aquatic vegetation near the edges provides some protection.

Collette (1965) found breeding tubercles well developed on a specimen captured in March. Pflieger (1975) observed males to establish territories in swift gravelly riffles and to breed in early April. A female entering a territory is followed by the male, who performs a head-bobbing courtship. The female burrows into gravel with only her head and tail exposed as the male is positioned over her releasing sperm. Eggs remain unattended as the female repeats spawning with the same or other males. Individuals do not seem to become mature until their second year.

Abundance. Pflieger (1971, 1975) has observed this fish more than anyone else. He feels that it has held its own fairly well since the 1940s and may never have been a common species. Because of its confinement to so few sites, the Niangua darter is listed by Deacon et al. (1979) as threatened. We agree that its situation is precarious.

Name. *Nianguae* is taken from the Niangua River, the type locality.

Etheostoma sagitta (Jordan & Swain)   Plate 7
Arrow Darter   Subgenus *Litocara*

Description. A rather large darter, 85 mm SL in our largest specimen and perhaps exceeding 90 mm SL. The strong slender body, elongated snout, large mouth, and virtually scaleless head place it in subgenus *Litocara*. It is coarser scaled than *E. nianguae* and unlikely to be confused with any other darter. The snout slightly overhangs the mouth; the frenum is well developed. Gill membranes are slightly connected; sometimes there are 7 branchiostegal membranes instead of 6. Infraorbital canal is complete but supratemporal canal may be narrowly interrupted.

Back is crossed by 5-7 weak dorsal saddles, some of which may fuse with the 8-11 vertical lateral blotches. Anterior blotches tend to be oval with pale centers. Posteriorly blotches extend ventrally almost to midline and may resemble the letters N, W, or V. A dark vertical bar occurs at base of tail, sometimes separated into 2 distinct spots. Belly is pale.

Preorbital bar meets or nearly meets counterpart on snout; postorbital bar is narrow but distinct. Chin, throat, and breast are pale to lightly stippled.

In females, spiny dorsal fin is marked with dark vertical streaks in membranes, but males have a broad horizontal stripe through middle of fin and another band on plunging posterior margin of fin. Similar markings in membranes of soft dorsal fin in females produce diagonal bands; soft dorsal in males is more uniformly dusky. Vertical wavy bands, boldest at fin base, occur on caudal fin. Anal, pelvic, and pectoral fins in females are clear, but in males are dusky or stippled with melanophores.

Cheek, opercle, and breast are scaleless. Small embedded scales are restricted to posterior part of nape. Belly is fully scaled. Subspecies *E. s. sagitta* has 55-69 scales in lateral series, fewer than 8 of them unpored. Subspecies *E. s. spilotum* has 52-61 scales in lateral series, the last 4-23 unpored. Fin counts for both subspecies are: dorsal IX-XI, 12-15; anal II (rarely I), 9-12; pectoral 14-16. Vertebrae number 39-40.

As seen in color plate, breeding males are gaudily colored. Unusual conical breeding tubercles develop on 3 or 4 ventral scale rows from midbelly to anus and on 2 midventral rows from anal fin to caudal peduncle. Some breeding males develop less tuberculation. Genital papilla is flattened and triangular, sometimes with a few dark spots. Adult females are more dusky and mottled than males, lacking their well defined body pattern. Body of breeding females becomes olivaceous, and spiny dorsal fin margin is dull red. Tinges of yellow appear in soft dorsal and caudal fins. Genital papilla arises from a distended cloacal pad and is a long posteriorly recurved tube.

The 2 subspecies of *E. sagitta* are essentially separable on the basis of lateral scale counts, 90% of *E. s. sagitta* having 60 or more and 90% of *E. s. spilotum* having 59 or fewer.

Distribution. *Etheostoma s. sagitta* occupies the Cumberland River basin above the falls and a few streams below. *E. s. spilotum* occurs in the upper Kentucky River system as far downstream as the Red River. Kuehne and Bailey (1961) reduced

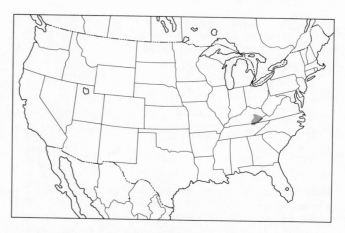

Distribution of *Etheostoma sagitta*

the latter to subspecific status and demonstrated its probable transfer to the Kentucky basin via a quite recent stream capture.

Natural History. The size of the arrow darter belies the fact that it is common only in intermittent first- and second-order creeks and is quite uncommon in larger streams. Most of the year it lives in shallow pools, preferring protective stones close to the bank, or ledges and recesses at the stream margin. We have noted that the species feeds on aquatic insects and that large individuals frequently capture tiny crayfish in late May and early June. Darter associates in the Cumberland basin include primarily *E. kennicotti* and *E. caeruleum*. In the Kentucky basin *E. flabellare*, *E. nigrum*, and *E. caeruleum* are the common headwater associates. But the arrow darter enters first-order streams in which the only other fish is the creek chub; we know of no other darter besides *E. parvipinne* which is so invasive of this precarious habitat.

Males establish territories over riffles in March, April, and May, where they are quite conspicuous in water 5-15 cm deep. Females gather in pools just above the male territory and presumably drift downstream in a manner similar to that described by Pflieger (1975) for *E. nianguae*. By mid-June some young already exceed 20 mm SL. As riffles dry up, all arrow darters move into pools and tend to remain there even when summer and autumn rains restore stream flow. Based on size classes, it seems that arrow darters live 3 years, though it is primarily males which reach the largest size.

Abundance. The arrow darter lives within one of the most intensively mined areas in America, both deep and surface coal mines occurring within the region. Resulting siltation has extirpated the fish from many streams and reduced its abundance elsewhere. It tolerates such disturbed conditions to a degree, has demonstrated some invasive qualities, and thrives in a few protected enclaves. The species should survive the period of intense mining, but its status, especially that of the scattered Cumberland River populations, should be watched carefully.

Name. *Sagitta* means arrow and calls attention to the long and slender appearance of this darter. *Spilotum* means spotted and probably refers to the lateral blotches with clear centers seen in many individuals.

Etheostoma cinereum Storer   Plate 8
Ashy Darter   Subgenus *Allohistium*

Description. A moderately large darter reaching 83 mm SL in our largest specimen. It is distinguished from all other *Etheostoma* by a combination of long snout, papillose lips, gill membranes separate, interorbital space narrow and concave, and soft dorsal fin greatly elongated in breeding males. Infraorbital and supratemporal canals are complete. The mouth is subterminal, rather large. Several teeth of unusual size for darters are found on the upper jaw.

A middorsal stripe usually extends length of nape. About 7 dorsal saddles may be present, the first, third, and fifth being most prominent. Side bears 11 or 12 dark blotches. Spots on upper side are arranged in 4 wavy bands which tend to fuse into a continuous band anteriorly. Lower side and belly are abruptly paler, except for a faint diagonal extension of each lateral blotch.

Broad preorbital bar meets counterpart on snout, and prominent postorbital bar crosses cheek and opercle. Ventral portions of head are pale or lightly stippled.

Spines of first dorsal fin are clear; membranes are darkly spotted to produce a basal stripe and several irregular stripes toward dark-edged fin margin. Soft dorsal fin is somewhat enlarged in females and sail-like in mature males. Dorsal rays are clear; membranes are spotted near base and vertically streaked toward fin margin. Caudal fin membranes are clear and rays are darkened in some individuals to produce weak vertical bands. Small scales cover as much as basal third of caudal fin. Anal, pelvic, and pectoral fins are clear or nearly so.

Cheek scales are small and not prominent; opercle is heavily scaled. Nape and breast are naked; belly is completely scaled. Lateral line is complete, with 55-61 scales. Fin counts are: dorsal XI-XIII, 11-13; anal II, 7-9; pectoral 14-15. Vertebrae number 42.

The general pattern is intensified in breeding males; diagonal bands are distinct, soft dorsal fin is greatly elongated, and coloration is striking, as seen in color plate. Genital papilla is a short round tube. Breeding females may develop tinges of orange but are not brightly colored. Genital papilla is a short tapered tube with scattered spots near tip.

Distribution. Although described from Florence, Alabama, the ashy darter has not again been reported from that state. It occurs quite sporadically in the upper Tennessee River basin in Virginia, Tennessee, and Georgia, and in the Buffalo and Duck rivers of the lower Tennessee River system. It also occurs sporadically in the Cumberland basin from the Rockcastle River downstream.

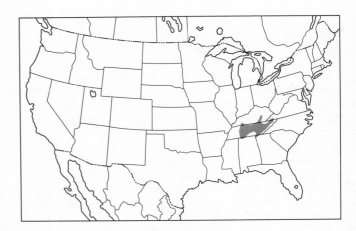

Distribution of *Etheostoma cinereum*

Natural History. The ashy darter inhabits large streams where it is caught typically in shallow water with little current. We have taken it most often over clean gravel and rubble just above or below riffles, particularly in or near stands of water willow, *Justicea*. Good conditions usually occur near the entrance of small tributary streams. Since the specimen used in our color plate came from a moderate sized tributary, it is possible that they enter such streams to spawn. This species does not seem to achieve high population density, 1 or 2 individuals taken from a site denoting good collecting. Few darters are in direct association with the ashy darter, but adjacent riffles are likely to yield the typical river forms of the region.

We find no reference to the ecology of the ashy darter. Life history information might explain the scarcity of this species and help in possible management decisions to assure its survival.

Abundance. Disappearance of the ashy darter from large portions of the Tennessee River basin probably is the result of the construction of dams. It persists in a few free-flowing streams with suitable riffles. Dams and, to a greater degree, siltation are the principal threats in the Cumberland River basin. Persistence in a few widely scattered localities allows guarded optimism for its survival. Though having shown many students this fish before release, we have retained few specimens. Deacon et al. (1979) listed this as a species of special concern.

Name. *Cinereum* means ashy gray, which is typical of preserved specimens but not of the living animal.

Etheostoma blennioides Rafinesque   Plate 8
Greenside Darter   Subgenus *Etheostoma*

Description. A robust species probably larger than any other *Etheostoma* at a maximum size of 127 mm SL. Marked as a member of subgenus *Etheostoma* by broadly connected gill membranes, expansive pectoral fins, frenum, complete lateral line, complete infraorbital and supratemporal canals, and 6 branchiostegal rays, it differs from its closest relatives in the unique fleshy union of the upper jaw with the preorbital portion of the head, and in most populations by a terminal nipple on the snout. Branchiostegal rays are 6-6, sometimes 6-7, rarely 7-7.

Usually 7 (5-8) saddles of varying intensity are formed on back, not extending far down side. Usually 7-8 (6-10) lateral blotches are developed, the first 2 ovoid, the remainder more vertically elongated, often in the shape of letters V or W. Upper side is flecked with large dark spots, reddish brown in life. Lower side is clear to slightly dusky; belly is clear. A small humeral spot is partly hidden by pectoral fin.

A diffuse preorbital bar extends downward to meet counterpart on snout. Narrow suborbital bar is directed slightly forward. Cheek is often quite full and protuberant. A postorbital spot is matched by another on opercle. Chin and throat are pale; breast may be dusky.

Spiny dorsal fin is variably pigmented, most often with a basal dark band. A rather distinct median band and faint marginal band occur in some males, but tend to be indistinct in females. Pigmentation on margins of rays in soft dorsal fin may produce banding in males but usually not in females. Membranes of soft dorsal are most heavily stippled near base, becoming progressively less so toward margin. Darkening in caudal fin rays produces 3 or 4 wavy vertical bands. Anal and pelvic fins are lightly stippled basally. Large pectoral fins have darkened rays producing a series of vertical bands.

Opercle is scaled; cheek has embedded scales or is naked. Nape often is naked anteriorly but has embedded or exposed scales near spiny dorsal fin. Breast is naked. Anterior portion of belly is variably scaled to naked. Complete lateral line consists of 50-86 scales; rather consistent differences characterize the 4 subspecies: usual counts are 53-60 in *E. b. gutselli*, 53-68 in *E. b. pholidotum*, 58-72 in *E. b. blennioides,* and 63-84 in *E. b. newmanii*. Miller (1968) presents additional differences among the subspecies. Fin counts are: dorsal XII-XIV (XI-XVI), 12-14 (11-16); anal II, 7-9 (6-10); pectoral rays number 14-16 (13-17). Vertebrae number 40-42 in *pholidotum,* 42-44 in *gutselli* and *newmanii,* and probably 42-44 in subspecies *blennioides.*

Breeding males are handsomely colored, as seen in color illustrations. At its height, green on body may entirely hide dark pattern beneath. Pelvic spine is covered with spongy white tissue and often becomes bent. Male genital papilla is a short tapered, somewhat flattened tube. Breeding tubercles consist of flat pads from posterior midline of belly to caudal peduncle. Many breeding males lack tubercles. Mature females become yellowish green, spots on upper side are reddish brown, and base of spiny dorsal fin is dull orange to yellow. Genital papilla is a short rounded tube.

Distribution. Distribution of the greenside darter is more thoroughly understood than that of any other darter with a large range. As greater amounts of information become available on hydrological changes during and since the Pleistocene a more complete picture will emerge for other species as well.

Subspecies *gutselli* is the most restricted form, displaying what appears to be a relict distribution in the Little Tennessee system from the Cheoah River upstream and in a few head-

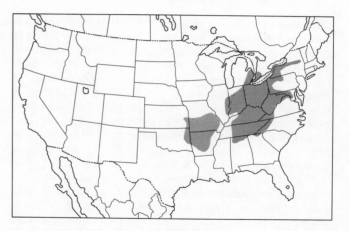

Distribution of *Etheostoma blennioides*

water tributaries of the adjacent Pigeon River. Greenside darters in most, if not all, of the Hiwassee River basin are intergrades between *gutselli* and *newmanii*. At present confined to cool high-gradient streams, *gutselli* may have enjoyed much greater distribution during 1 or more glacial advances. Superior cold tolerance has never been experimentally verified for *gutselli,* however.

A Tennessee River race of *newmanii* is widely distributed in the upper and middle Tennessee River system but is absent in some of the sluggish western tributaries of the lower basin. A Cumberland River race of *newmanii* occupies the entire Cumberland River system, including that portion above the falls. Upper Cumberland basin specimens, however, particularly upstream from the Big South Fork, have more lateral blotches, lower scale counts, and other characteristics attributable to an infusion of genes from subspecies *blennioides.* Miller (1968) believes that the gene exchange occurred during a well documented stream piracy of a Cumberland tributary by a branch of the Kentucky River (Kuehne and Bailey, 1961). Specimens from the Green River basin display many *newmanii* traits and are interpreted by Miller to be intergrades between this subspecies and *blennioides.*

Greenside darters are fairly widespread west of the Mississippi River. Miller assigns those of the St. Francis, Current, Black, and upper White rivers of Missouri and Arkansas to the Cumberland race of *newmanii*. Also included here are specimens from the Whitewater River, formerly a headwater unit of the St. Francis River but now diverted eastward to the Mississippi River as part of an agricultural drainage scheme. Populations from the Little Red, Arkansas, Ouachita, and Saline rivers are assigned to an Arkansas race of *newmanii*. It not only occurs in Arkansas but extends into extreme eastern Oklahoma, and, via the Spring and Elk rivers, into southwestern Missouri and the southeastern tip of Kansas.

Not all western greenside darters are *newmanii*. Cross (1967) notes that those which just enter Kansas in the Little Osage and Marmaton rivers are certainly different from those encountered in the adjacent Spring River system, which are clearly referable to *newmanii*. Miller recognizes the subspecies *pholidotum* to include this western stock, which occurs from Osage River tributaries of extreme eastern Kansas eastward through other streams entering the Missouri River from the south and thence southward in the Meramec River and tiny streams which enter the Mississippi River from the west to, but not including, the Whitewater River. Miller considers the Gasconade River populations to be intergrades between the Missouri race of *pholitodum* and the Cumberland race of *newmanii,* but has found no direct evidence for stream capture. Pflieger (1971) mentions a large subterranean piracy involving Roubidoux Creek in Texas and Pulaski counties of Missouri. Other similar captures in that karst region could have infused *newmanii* stock into the Gasconade.

An eastern form of *pholidotum,* the Wabash-Great Lakes race, occurs through most of the Wabash basin of eastern Illinois and Indiana, across the Maumee drainage of Ohio and Michigan, and then northward just into Ontario and eastward along the southern shores of Lake Erie and Lake Ontario to New York. Previously most ichthyologists had considered these to be *Etheostoma b. blennioides.* Trautman (1957) obviously saw the difference in Ohio, recognizing a "prairie type" in the Maumee and Wabash basins east to the Sandusky and an "Allegheny type" elsewhere in the state. There are also a number of Michigan records of *pholidotum* from streams tributary to Lake Erie, the Detroit River, and Lake St. Clair. An isolated record from the Saginaw River and one each from headwaters of the Grand and St. Joseph rivers (Hubbs and Lagler, 1949) indicate that greenside darters entered additional drainages after the last glaciation but apparently have disappeared since human settlement. In Canada the greenside darter has been recorded only from Lake St. Clair and its tributary streams, the Thames and Avon rivers (Scott and Crossman, 1973). Many of the short southern tributaries of Lake Erie from Ohio to New York contain *pholidotum.* The subspecies also is known from southern tributaries of Lake Ontario, the Genesee (only below the falls), Seneca, and Mohawk rivers, all in New York. Hough (1963) has shown that during the lowest Lake Warren-Lake Grasmere stage through the Algonquin stages of Great Lakes development there was an eastward proglacial drainage into the Mohawk-Hudson system. Miller believes that this was the time when *pholidotum* obtained its isolated eastern footholds. That it has never spread more extensively through the Hudson River basin remains a puzzling fact. Another peculiarity is the distributional gap between eastern *pholidotum* and the Missouri race from which it seems to be derived. Although greenside darters do not now occur in lowland streams of southern Illinois or southwestern Indiana, Miller believes that western *pholidotum* must have moved across this barrier and up the Wabash arm of the old Ohio River, perhaps when the Cache River outlet existed. Several minnows and darters, including *Etheostoma histrio,* occur in the Wabash drainage but are not now known from its lower reaches.

Subspecies *blennioides* occurs widely throughout the entire Ohio River basin above the falls at Louisville. It is undoubtedly the form associated with the upper portion of the old Teays River and has established its distribution in response to the drainage changes that have produced the present configuration of the upper Ohio River basin. *E. b. blennioides* also has moved down the Ohio to become the sole form of greenside darter in the Salt River and apparently to intergrade with *newmanii* throughout the Green River system. This situation is the only readily apparent example of ongoing displacement of one subspecies of greenside darter by another. In the upper Ohio basin *blennioides* has spread into most of the headwater tributaries of the Allegheny and Monongahela basins and by stream capture into the Potomac River basin (Schwartz, 1965b).

As noted previously, Miller assigned greenside darters of the lower Genesee River to *pholidotum,* but those from above the falls he found to be subspecies *blennioides.* He attributed this to the fact that a small proglacial lake, Belfast-Filmore, drained for a short time through a valley at Cuba, New York, into the Allegheny, thus allowing the subspecies to gain entrance. Subsequent glacial retreat and lake drainage established the Belfast-Filmore area as part of the upper Genesee River. Denoncourt, Potter, and Stauffer (1977) have taken *blennioides* in Susquehanna tributaries just across the divide from the head of the Allegheny River in Pennsylvania. Whether by stream capture or by human introduction, the greenside darter has joined the fauna of the Susquehanna basin.

Miller's examination of morphological data indicated to him that *blennioides* took its origin in the Tennessee race of *newmanii.* Ross and Carico (1963) show that New River, the original headwaters of the old Teays system, captured a portion of the Holston River system away from the Tennessee basin at Burkes Garden, Virginia. They also discuss an opposite piracy of the New River basin by a tributary of the Holston at Sugar Grove, Virginia. These could be the very piracies involved in the transfer of greenside darters into the upper Ohio basin.

The invasiveness of many darters is obvious but we have only a few examples of how rapidly dispersal has been accomplished. The rush of several species across the Wabash-Maumee glacial connection is the most dramatic example, and has been responsible for postglacial reestablishment of several darters in the lower Great Lakes and southeastern Canada. In the case of no other single species, however, do we have distributional information to compare to that of the greenside darter. The painstaking taxonomic work of Miller, coupled with the studies of other biologists and of Pleistocene geologists, has produced the evidence summarized here.

Natural History. *Etheostoma blennioides* is widely distributed in a variety of habitats but most often is seen in medium-sized to large creeks and small rivers supplied with gravel- or rubble-strewn riffles. The filamentous algae *Cladophora* and the aquatic moss *Fontinalis* attract these darters. When relatively free of silt, shallow bedrock pools with steady current are another favorite habitat. Greenside darters do not enter tiny creeks, and when present in rivers are relegated to the margins and heads of riffles. Trautman (1957) noted their former occurrence around the islands of western Lake Erie and in the preimpounded Ohio River. Greenside darters may still be seen along the sandy beaches of Lake St. Clair. We have taken them commonly in eastern Kentucky over shale or sandstone bedrock and also in rubble-strewn riffles that support little or no filamentous algal growth at any season, so it is apparent that the species tolerates a great range of conditions.

The rainbow darter, *Etheostoma caeruleum,* is perhaps the most frequent associate of the greenside darter in much of the latter's range, but one is likely to encounter greensides with almost the entire regional assemblage of darters because of its wide selection of habitats.

Lachner, Westlake, and Handwerk (1950) studied darters inhabiting an upper Allegheny River tributary. *E. blennioides, E. variatum,* and *E. zonale* were the most abundant species, collectively reaching a density that approached one fish per square meter over a suitable riffle. Greenside darters grew rapidly for the first two years of life but much more slowly thereafter. Growth rate for males exceeded that for females in each age class. Males exceeded females in number on riffles. Many individuals were found to survive into their fourth year and one into his fifth. Spawning was concentrated in May in Pennsylvania. We have seen males and females spawning in algal beds of *Cladophora* from early to late April in Kentucky. Wolfe, Bauer, and Branson (1978) indicate that females outnumber males in the first year but that by completion of the second year males are relatively more numerous and distinctly larger than females of similar age.

Abundance. Although there are many streams from which the greenside darter has been extirpated or in which its numbers are greatly reduced, it remains one of the most abundant and widespread forms in the Ohio River basin and to a lesser extent in the Ozarks.

Name. The species was named *blennioides,* blenny like, by Rafinesque (1819) in remembrance of its similarity to the Mediterranean blennies familiar to his early years. Newman and J.S. Gutsell were early fish collectors. *Pholidotum,* scaled, refers to the fully scaled belly.

Etheostoma blennius Gilbert & Swain   Plate 8
Blenny Darter   Subgenus *Etheostoma*

Description. A robust but moderate-sized darter reaching 69 mm SL but seldom exceeding 60 mm SL. It has typical subgeneric traits of broadly connected gill membranes, expansive pectoral fins, frenum, complete lateral line, complete infraorbital and supratemporal canals, and 6 branchiostegal rays. It is unique within its subgenus in the coupling of 4 prominent saddles with a nearly vertical anterior profile. The frenum is narrow. Cheek and opercle are protuberant.

Back is crossed by 4 dark saddles, the first most prominent and each succeeding 1 less so. Upper side may have scattered spots, arranged in thin vertical strips in some specimens. A dull midlateral band of 7-9 partly fused blotches extends from second saddle to fourth. Irregular ventral extensions and small spots constitute pigmentation of lower side. Belly is pale. Most individuals have a distinct prepectoral spot.

Upper half of opercle is dark, contrasting with lower opercle and cheek. Suborbital bar varies from weak to distinct. Chin, throat, and breast are stippled in males; breast is pale in females.

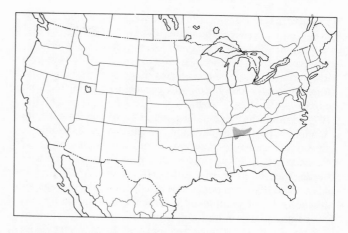

Distribution of *Etheostoma blennius*

Spiny dorsal fin in males is narrowly edged in black, while that in females may lack such darkening. Spines are alternately light and dark in females but lack pigment in males. In both sexes last membrane lying just above second saddle is blackened. Rays of soft dorsal fin are clear in both sexes; membranes are clear in females, lightly stippled in males. Caudal fin rays in both sexes are alternately light and dark but do not appear distinctly banded. Anal, pelvic, and pectoral fins may have a little pigmentation in rays and be lightly stippled in males, but are pale in females.

Cheek, opercle, and breast are usually devoid of scales, but nape and belly are scaled. Lateral line consists of 40-51 scales. Small scales extend slightly onto caudal fin. Fin counts are: dorsal XI-XII (X-XIII), 11-13; anal II, 7-9; pectoral usually 16. Vertebrae number 40-41.

As seen in color plate, breeding males are handsomely colored. Head usually is very dark, often nearly black, and fins are better pigmented. Breeding tubercles occur as slightly elevated pads on scales immediately before and beside short flattened wedge-shaped genital papilla. Additional tubercles continue posteriorly a short distance on either side of anal fin base. Collette (1965) and Richards (1966) reported no tubercles for this species. Body of females may be infused with a little yellow but is not showy. Genital papilla is much thickened and somewhat flattened near its base and at least as long as first anal spine.

Distribution. Narrowly restricted to the middle and lower Tennessee River basin in Tennessee and Alabama from the Sequatchie River downstream to the Duck River and White Oak Creek. Burr (1979) has shown that 2 quite distinct subspecies exist, the type subspecies from Shoal Creek, Alabama, downstream, and his subspecies *E. b. sequatchiense* in the Sequatchie River of Tennessee. He identified specimens from the intervening area, almost exclusively restricted to the Elk River, as intergrades. The 2 subspecies are almost always separable on the basis of lateral line scales, 40-44 in *sequatchiense* and 42-51 in *blennius.*

Natural History. We encountered a good breeding series of *Etheostoma blennius* only in a large tributary of Shoal Creek in southern Tennessee, where it, *E. caeruleum, E. duryi,* and *E. rufilineatum* were abundant. Other darters also present were *E. flabellare, E. jessiae,* and *E. simoterum.* Blenny darters were taken at depths of 10-20 cm from a riffle with swift flow and a substrate of coarse gravel and scattered embedded stones. Breeding coloration was excellent in males but some females were already spent, the date being April 21. Burr (1979) reports that several large series of specimens have now been taken, particularly in night collecting over riffles. He obtained specimens from rivers and creeks but found the species most commonly in streams of intermediate size. He set the breeding season between mid-March and mid-April. Individuals apparently were not found to exceed 3 years in age and most were 1 or 2 years old. Chironomids and immature mayflies comprised the main food items in stomachs he examined.

Thompson (1973) suggested that the blenny darter is closest to the *thalassinum* group of subgenus *Etheostoma,* and Burr agrees, based on a comparison with *E. swannanoa.* More information, particularly on the life history of the blenny darter, is now needed.

Abundance. Although the species is not so uncommon as previously thought, range gaps may be partly the result of altered habitat, especially in Alabama, where the blenny darter is poorly represented. The major trunk reservoirs in the Tennessee valley and proposed or authorized ones on major tributaries have or will have an adverse impact on the species.

Name. The authors of this species were, like Rafinesque with *E. blennioides,* impressed with the resemblance of this darter to the marine blennies. *Sequatchiense* refers to the Sequatchie River.

Etheostoma euzonum (Hubbs & Black)   Plate 8
Arkansas Saddled Darter   Subgenus *Etheostoma*

Description. A fairly large darter, 81 mm SL in our largest specimen but perhaps reaching 90 mm SL. Broadly connected gill membranes, expansive pectoral fins, frenum, complete lateral line, complete infraorbital and supratemporal canals, and 6 branchiostegal rays identify it as a member of subgenus *Etheostoma.* Of the members of the subgenus with 4 prominent saddles, *E. euzonum* is unique in the gradually sloping head profile and long snout. The frenum is broad. Teeth of the upper jaw are prominent. Viewed from the front, the head appears almost triangular. Gill membranes are not always so broadly connected as is typical for this subgenus.

Four dorsal saddles stand out boldly against rather pale back and lightly stippled upper side, and reach to just below lateral line. Small blotches often occur on upper side between first pair of saddles, and lateral blotches may lie between or beneath the last 3 saddles. Caudal spot is large but not heavily blackened. Many individuals display a small humeral spot. Belly is pale.

Opercle is darker than pale, lightly-stippled cheek. Opercular spine is quite distinct. Preorbital bar does not quite meet

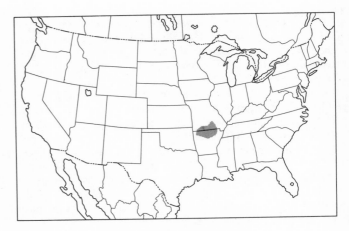

Distribution of *Etheostoma euzonum*

counterpart on lip. Suborbital bar is short and indistinct; postorbital spot is small. Chin and throat are stippled in both sexes but only males have a slightly darkened breast.

A narrow submarginal band is prominent in spiny dorsal fin, and a dull basal band completes fin pattern. Weak horizontal bands run through soft dorsal fin, only basal 1 being very distinct. Fin is edged with a narrow dusky band. Caudal fin membranes are clear; 4-6 wavy vertical bands are produced by dark pigment in and adjacent to rays. Anal and pelvic fins are clear in females, dusky in males. Pelvic fins are rather long and pointed. Pectoral fins are clear to stippled and have weak vertical bands produced by darkening in rays.

Cheek is usually naked but may have a few exposed scales. Opercle and nape are well scaled; head is scaled adjacent to nape. Prepectoral area is naked; breast is heavily scaled and belly is fully scaled. Lateral line contains 57-73 scales. A few small scales occur at base of caudal fin. Fin counts are: dorsal XII-XV, 13-15; anal II, 9-11; pectoral usually 15. Vertebrae number 41-42.

Breeding males may be more handsomely colored than our specimen, photographed in early June and somewhat faded. Genital papilla is a short wedge-shaped tube. Breeding tubercles are located on breast scales, a transverse band of scales anterior to genital papilla, a narrow band of scales on either side of anal fin, and a wider band along ventral midline of caudal peduncle. Breeding females have a dull yellow submarginal band in spiny dorsal fin and a tinge of yellow on body. Genital papilla is a rounded tube. Breeding tubercles are less prominent than in males and narrowly confined to ventral midline.

Hubbs and Black (1940) recognized 2 subspecies, *E. e. euzonum* and *E. e. erizonum,* and reported intergrades between them. Differences are mainly confined to the degree of cheek and breast scalation and slight color or pattern differences. Pflieger (1971) adds information on the subspecies.

Distribution. An endemic of the White River drainage in Arkansas and Missouri. Subspecies *erizonum* occurs in the Current River, and subspecies *euzonum* elsewhere. Intergrades or possible intergrades occur in the White River at Batesville, Arkansas, the lower Black River, and the Spring River.

Natural History. The Arkansas saddled darter is a common inhabitant of clear streams of moderate to large size, where it occupies gravel- and rubble-strewn riffles with depths of 10-50 cm. Unlike its relative on the northern slopes of the Ozarks, *E. tetrazonum,* it often enters creeks, where we have taken it in runs and narrow chutes. It is frequently captured with *E. caeruleum, E. zonale, E. blennioides, E. flabellare,* and *E. stigmaeum.*

The life history and ecology of this species await study. It is the most distinct of the saddled darters in the Mississippi basin, and may be the longest isolated member, since it has given rise to recognizable subspecies.

Abundance. Although this species is restricted in distribution, Robison (1974a) does not indicate it to be of special concern in Arkansas. It is well established in a variety of habitats and hopefully safe from extirpation.

Name. *Euzonum* means well banded; the subspecific name *erizonum* means intensively banded.

Etheostoma histrio Jordan & Gilbert   Plate 8
Harlequin Darter   Subgenus *Etheostoma*

Description. A moderate-sized darter rarely exceeding 60 mm SL. It is recognized as a member of subgenus *Etheostoma* by broadly connected gill membranes, expansive pectoral fins, complete lateral line, complete infraorbital and supratemporal canals, and 6 branchiostegal rays. It is unique in the subgenus in the speckled appearance of the head and fins. It has a narrow frenum or may lack the frenum, an unusual condition for the subgenus.

Six or 7 small dorsal saddles are well developed in most specimens. Nine to 11 vertically elongated lateral blotches may touch or fuse with dorsal saddles. On caudal peduncle lateral blotches most closely resemble vertical bands. Lower side is irregularly spotted and belly may also have a few spots. A small dark humeral bar is present and 2 large diffuse basicaudal spots extend onto fin base.

Irregularly shaped dark spots are scattered across otherwise pale cheek, opercle, and prepectoral area. Broad dark preorbital bands cover all but middle portion of snout and upper lip. Suborbital band may be missing or may be present as 1 of dark facial marks. Presence of a postorbital bar also is dependent on appropriate placement of facial spots. Two to 5 spots on chin, 3 or more diffuse spots on gill membranes, several weak spots on lightly stippled breast, and a vertical slash in front of each pectoral fin complete anterior markings.

A broad diffuse submarginal band and a narrow basal band occur in spiny dorsal fin. Remaining clear regions have a few dark spots on rays and adjacent membranes. Anterior 1 or 2 membranes are rather uniformly darkened. Soft dorsal fin has 2 bands formed by darkening in and adjacent to rays. Similarly, 2-4 vertical bands occur in caudal fin, and 2 or 3 such bands develop in anal and pelvic fins. Up to 5 vertical bands of similar origin occur in pectoral fin.

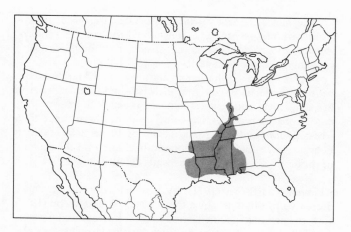

Distribution of *Etheostoma histrio*

Head scalation is quite variable. Cheek is naked or has several embedded scales dorsally. Opercle varies from moderately scaled to naked. Breast and anterior portion of belly are naked. Anterior nape scales are small and often embedded. Lateral line is complete or nearly so, and consists of 45-58 scales. Fin counts are: dorsal IX-XI, 12-13 (11-14); anal II, 7 (6-8); pectoral 14-15 (13-16). Vertebrae number 37-38.

Breeding males are brightly colored and intensely marked, as seen in color plate. Breeding tubercles are absent. Genital papilla is a small triangular flap. Females develop some green and dull yellow on body and fins. Body and fin markings may be bolder than those of males. Genital papilla is a short thick tube crenulate at tip. This may be the sauciest looking darter of all.

Distribution. Tsai (1968a) clarified the distribution of the harlequin darter. With a few notable exceptions it occurs in lowland portions of the Mississippi River basin. In the Red River basin it extends as far west as northeastern Texas and southeastern Oklahoma. Along the western Gulf Coast it extends only to the Neches River in Texas, but east of the Mississippi below the Fall Line it extends into the Escambia River of western Florida. Harlequin darters occur well above the Fall Line in the Arkansas River system, being found upstream to the Poteau River in Oklahoma. They also enter the lower Ohio River basin and occur above the Fall Line in the Embarras River, an Illinois tributary of the Wabash, and eastward to the lower Green River basin in Kentucky.

Natural History. The harlequin darter is a widespread but spottily distributed inhabitant of creeks and medium-sized rivers, and is found in 2 distinct habitats. Above the Fall Line it has been captured most frequently in riffles with coarse gravel substrate (P.W. Smith, 1979). In lowland streams, however, it often lives over sand among brush and detritus where log jams have created strong midstream currents. This microhabitat preference is reported in detail by Hubbs and Pigg (1972) for eastern Texas, and again by Sisk and Webb (1976) for western Kentucky. We have seined under these conditions and appreciate the difficulty, and sometimes danger, of collecting from log jams.

The most frequent lowland associates are those *Ammocrypta* within its range, *Etheostoma asprigene, E. chlorosomum, E. zonale, Percina nigrofasciata, P. ouachitae,* and probably several other species.

We collected the harlequin darter in mid-March over a bedrock riffle in Bayou Pierre, Mississippi. Males were in breeding color and females apparently ready to spawn. This date probably precedes spawning in its northern range by 6 weeks. Hubbs and Pigg found Texas specimens to be gravid in February. We find no additional information on the ecology of the harlequin darter, which awaits detailed study.

Abundance. Pflieger (1971) says that harlequin darters have decreased in Missouri since the 1940s. Sisk and Webb (1976) view the pending channelization of Obion Creek and perhaps other streams of western Kentucky with alarm because the harlequin darter is already so restricted in that state. Miller (1972) lists the species as rare and endangered in Illinois, Kentucky, and Missouri. The Illinois population mentioned by Smith (1979) is in a precarious situation. Southern populations may be faring much better. This species should be watched closely, since it is rare and perhaps endangered at the margins of its range.

Name. *Histrio* is the latinized term for harlequin. The masked face, shaven head, and particolored tights of the harlequin of Italian comedy can easily be conjured by the appearance of this saucy little fish.

Etheostoma inscriptum (Jordan & Brayton)   Plate 9
Turquoise Darter   Subgenus *Etheostoma*

Description. A moderate-sized darter reaching 66 mm SL, but usually less than 60 mm SL. Broadly connected gill membranes, expansive pectoral fins, frenum, complete lateral line, complete infraorbital and supratemporal canals, and 6 branchiostegal rays mark it as a member of subgenus *Etheostoma.* It is similar to *E. swannanoa,* which tends to have more clearly defined and more vertically elongated lateral blotches. It is even more similar to *E. thalassinum,* which almost always has 7 dorsal blotches rather than 6 or 5, as in *E. inscriptum.* The frenum is narrow to moderately broad. Gill membranes may be moderately rather than broadly connected.

Six, occasionally 5, dorsal saddles are usually distinct but may contrast poorly with spaces between. Upper side is mottled. Seven or 8 lateral blotches are located mostly ventral to lateral line. A small spot often develops on each lateral scale to produce a dotted horizontal pattern. Belly and ventral caudal peduncle lack pigmentation. A basicaudal spot may be split into dorsal and ventral elements. There is a small humeral spot.

Cheek is rather pale, opercle somewhat darker. Diffuse preorbital bar does not meet counterpart on snout. Broad diffuse suborbital bar is directed slightly posteriorly. A distinct postorbital spot is matched by another on opercle, and there is a vertical slash on prepectoral area. Chin and throat are stip-

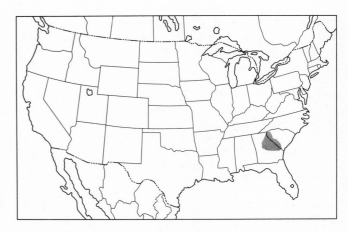

Distribution of *Etheostoma inscriptum*

pled or sometimes spotted. Breast is spotted, a central spot often being triangular.

First and last membranes of spiny dorsal fin are dark; the rest are dark only basally and along fin margin in some specimens. Membranes of soft dorsal fin may be darkened toward base or may support 3 horizontal bands. Caudal fin has 3 wavy vertical bands. Anal and pelvic fins are usually clear in females and rather dusky near anal base and pelvic margins in males. Pectoral rays are alternately light and dark but are not noticeably banded.

Cheek, opercle, and breast are naked. Nape is scaled; anterior scales are sometimes embedded. Anterior belly scales also may be partly embedded. Lateral line consists of 44-53 (39-61) scales. Fin counts are: dorsal IX-XI (VIII-XII), 10-12 (9-13); anal II, 7-9 (6-10); pectoral 14-15 (13-16). Vertebrae number 38-39.

Breeding males may become more colorful than specimen shown in color plate, taken in late May. Breeding tubercles occur as white pads just anterior to genital papilla and along ventral midline of caudal peduncle. Genital papilla is a very small tube, scarcely protruding from cloaca. Breeding females appear rather robust and develop some green on body and a dull red submarginal band in spiny dorsal fin. They lack breeding tubercles. Genital papilla is a moderately long tube, grooved at tip.

Richards (1966) found only slight differences between Altamaha and Savannah River populations. Our Savannah River specimens are more robust, while the Altamaha specimens have more evident horizontal bands.

Distribution. Occurs above the Fall Line in both the Oconee and Ocmulgee arms of the Altamaha River basin. It is found in the Savannah basin above the Fall Line and rarely below it. The species has also been recorded from the upper Ogeechee and Edisto rivers.

Natural History. The turquoise darter typically inhabits riffles of large creeks and small rivers. In much of its range such conditions occur sporadically, accounting for its spotty distribution. We have caught it at depths of 5-15 cm in bedrock runs, where it is usually found near large stones. Where gravel and stony riffles are present it lives in moderately swift spots at depths of 10-30 cm. Darter associates may include *Etheostoma hopkinsi, E. olmstedi, E. fusiforme, E. serriferum, E. fricksium,* and *Percina nigrofasciata,* but it is unusual to take this species with more than 1 or 2 other kinds of darters.

Females still had large yolky eggs when captured near Athens, Georgia, in mid-May, but Savannah River specimens were approaching maturity toward the end of March. We surmise that these dates fully span the breeding season of this species. Additional life history information is needed.

Abundance. A careful eye should be kept on this darter because destruction of additional habitat could lead to its decline.

Name. *Inscriptum* means written on and presumably refers to the horizontal lines found on the body of mature males.

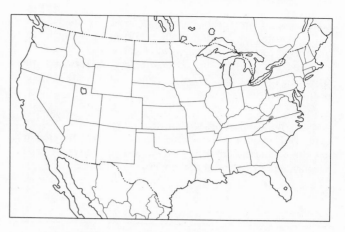

Distribution of *Etheostoma kanawhae*

Etheostoma kanawhae (Raney) Plate 9
Kanawha Darter Subgenus *Etheostoma*

Description. A moderate sized darter reaching somewhat over 70 mm SL. Broadly connected gill membranes, expansive pectoral fins, frenum, complete lateral line, complete infraorbital and supratemporal canals, and 6 branchiostegal rays identify it as a member of subgenus *Etheostoma*. One of the saddled darters by virtue of 5 or 6 prominent dorsal saddles, it is quite similar to *E. variatum* but usually has 1 more saddle, a blunter snout, more broadly connected gill membranes, and fewer breast and opercular scales. It differs from *E. osburni* both in the presence of an extra saddle and in having fewer scales in the lateral line. The frenum is well developed.

Five or more often 6 dark saddles do not extend far down side. Nine to 11 lateral blotches are variable in shape, size, and intensity; on anterior half of body they tend to connect with small irregular spots and blotches on upper side. Lateral blotches on posterior half of body are usually vertical bands, the last occurring at junction of and extending a bit onto caudal fin. Lower side is somewhat spotted but belly is clear or lightly stippled. A narrow humeral bar is present. A caudal spot may be separate from or fused with last vertical band.

A short preorbital bar is distinct in some individuals but is lost in darkly pigmented snout of others. A broad suborbital bar is diffuse in males, more distinct in females. A partial ring of pigment behind eye is the only indication of a postorbital bar. Darker opercle may bear a small spot at eye level. In females chin often is lightly stippled; throat and breast are immaculate. In males only breast is stippled.

Separate dark spots form a basal band in spiny dorsal fin. A median dark band fades toward fin margin. Soft dorsal fin of males is narrowly edged in black and is heavily stippled near base of each membrane. In females most pigment occurs on or adjacent to rays. Pigment in caudal fin is distributed along edges of rays, tending to form more distinct vertical bands in females than in males. Anal and pelvic fins of females are almost clear while those of males are moderately stippled. Vertical banding is more apparent in pectoral fins of

females than of males. Females usually have a better defined prepectoral spot than males.

Cheek and opercle are naked or latter may bear 1 or 2 small embedded scales. Scales on nape may be small and embedded anteriorly. Breast scales, if present, occur between pelvic fins. Belly is fully scaled. Lateral line has 52-57 (48-57) scales. Fin counts are: dorsal XII-XIII (XI-XIV), 12-13; anal II, 8-9; pectoral 15-16. Vertebrae number 41-42.

Breeding males are rather gaudy, as seen in color plate. Breeding tubercles occur on several ventral scale rows of belly and in a narrower band to end of caudal peduncle. Genital papilla is a tiny tube. Females may have a little yellow on body and a dull red marginal band on spiny dorsal. Genital papilla is a rounded tube of moderate length. Breeding tubercles occupy fewer scale rows than in males.

Distribution. An endemic of the New River basin, that is, the Kanawha River system above the falls in Virginia and North Carolina. It is apparently absent in the New River basin in West Virginia, perhaps replaced by *E. osburni.*

Natural History. The Kanawha darter is an inhabitant of medium to large streams. It is taken most commonly over substrates composed of gravel and small rubble at depths of 10-40 cm. Its most frequent darter associates are *Etheostoma flabellare, E. blennioides,* and *Percina gymnocephala.*

Raney's (1941) type material taken from New River at Crumpler, North Carolina, on April 1, 1940, included males in nuptial coloration and gravid females, suggesting to him that the breeding season was imminent. Collette (1965) observed breeding tubercles on males and females taken as late as June 8. We encountered a dense breeding assemblage in about 10 cm of water over swift riffles in West Fork, Little River, on May 15, 1969.

Several streams from which the Kanawha darter has been reported are lower gradient components of the New River basin. In swifter montane streams the species seems to be rare or is replaced by *E. osburni.* Ross (1959) reported both *E. kanawhae* and *E. osburni* in the Little River, but from different localities. Ross helped us obtain our best specimens.

Life history data are badly needed for this darter.

Abundance. Common in only a few localities, the Kanawha darter is listed by Deacon et al. (1979) as threatened. Rotenone used to treat bean crops adjacent to New River at the type locality has had an adverse effect on this and other fishes. In 1969 we caught only 2 females at this site in spite of prolonged seining.

Name. This species was named for the parent stream of capture, the Kanawha, known above its falls as New River. These are the ultimate headwaters of the ancient Teays River, the preglacial predecessor of the modern Ohio River.

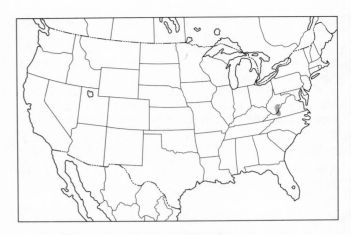

Distribution of *Etheostoma osburni*

Etheostoma osburni (Hubbs & Trautman)   Plate 9
Finescale Saddled Darter   Subgenus *Etheostoma*

Description. A rather large darter reaching 86 mm SL. Expansive pectoral fins, a frenum, complete lateral line, complete infraorbital and supratemporal canals, and 6 branchiostegal rays mark this as a member of subgenus *Etheostoma*. Among the saddled darters only *E. euzonum* has as many scales in the lateral line, and that species does not have vertical bands on the sides, as has *E. osburni*. The gill membranes are less broadly connected than in most species of the subgenus. The frenum is well developed.

Five or rarely 6 dorsal saddles are present, the first extending down to lateral line and the rest closely confined to dorsum. Usually 11 (10-12) vertically elongated lateral blotches are present, anterior ones extending little beneath lateral line and posterior ones extending as vertical bands well toward ventral midline of body. Last band is found partially on body and partially on caudal fin. A dusky appearance is created by dark spots on most scales of body as far ventrally as belly, which is clear to lightly stippled. Scales of humeral region are somewhat enlarged but not marked with a bar.

Cheek and opercle are protuberant, the latter distinctly darker than the former. A short broad diffuse preorbital bar often does not reach lips. Suborbital bar is distinct and bent posteriorly. Postorbital spot may be arc-shaped. Stippling on chin of some individuals is the only ventral pigmentation.

Membranes of spiny dorsal fin are stippled except along clear margin. Spines are clear. In males stippling is denser except for clear windows at base of each membrane. Soft dorsal fin has a dark margin and in females an additional 3 or 4 longitudinal bands. In males there is a clear submarginal zone, stippling then becoming steadily denser toward fin base. Vertical banding in caudal fin is moderately developed in females, poorly developed in males. Anal and pelvic fins of males are clear or virtually so, while those of females are lightly stippled or banded. Broad diffuse bands occur in pectoral fins of both sexes.

Cheek is naked; opercle is naked or has 1-3 embedded scales. Scales on nape are small; those toward head are partially embedded. Breast varies from naked to having a few embedded scales between pelvic fins. Lateral line contains 59-70 scales, usually fewer than 67. Tiny scales extend onto caudal fin base. Fin counts are: dorsal XI-XII (X-XIII), 13-14 (12-16); anal II, 9-10 (8-11); pectoral usually 15. Vertebrae number 41-43.

As seen in color plate, breeding males are among the showiest of darters. These colors also persist longer than in almost any other darter. Genital papilla is a short flattened tube. Breeding tubercles may develop on several scale rows anterior to genital papilla and along base of anal fin and caudal peduncle. Breeding females are dull compared to males but still develop much of the same general pattern. Genital papilla is a fairly long rounded tube. Tubercles of reduced size are distributed as in males.

Distribution. Restricted to the New River in West Virginia and Virginia, not extending to the headwaters in North Carolina.

Natural History. The finescale saddled darter is poorly known but seems to prefer cool rocky montane streams of good clarity and turbulent flow. Our specimens came from a heavily stocked trout stream which also supported sculpins, longnose dace, and stonerollers. Riffles were 10-20 cm deep and composed mostly of rubble. Pools were scoured in bedrock to depths of 2 m and often contained boulders as well as rubble. Specimens were captured from the foot of riffles with coarse substrate that included small boulders. Individuals were seen to move beneath boulders in pools to a depth of 1 m. The only darter associate was *Etheostoma flabellare*. Extensive collecting might reveal other darter associates, such as *E. blennioides*, *E. kanawhae*, *Percina roanoka*, and *P. oxyrhyncha*.

This species survives nicely in turbulent streams of steep gradient where massive stocking of trout has come into vogue. The impact of such plantings on *E. osburni* and other native fishes deserves serious attention because of potential depletion of food supply or direct predation.

In spite of the persistence of bright colors well into summer, our specimens taken in June seemed to be past breeding condition.

The life history of the finescale saddled darter needs investigation to reveal spawning site and season, life span, food supply, population density, and other information valuable in judging its status.

By way of comment, this was the species that caused us the greatest amount of effort in capture. It was finally taken and photographed only after a special 24-hour nonstop trip with Jim Barbour to a spot revealed by Raymond Bouchard. Ironically, we had collected nearby on several occasions without success.

Abundance. The loss of suitable habitat within its restricted range has caused *E. osburni* to be listed by Deacon et al. (1979) as threatened.

Name. Hubbs and Trautman (1932) named this darter for Raymond C. Osburn of Ohio State University, an ichthyologist of note.

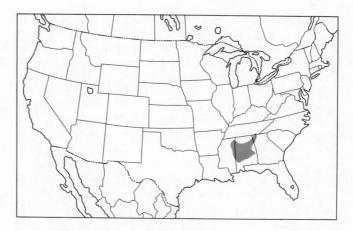

Distribution of *Etheostoma rupestre*

Etheostoma rupestre Gilbert & Swain   Plate 9
Rock Darter   Subgenus *Etheostoma*

Description. A moderate sized darter reaching 70 mm SL but seldom more than 60 mm SL. Broadly joined gill membranes, expansive pectoral fins, frenum, complete lateral line, complete infraorbital and supratemporal canals, and 6 branchiostegal rays mark this as a member of subgenus *Etheostoma*. In lateral markings it is similar to *E. blennioides* but has a suborbital bar lacking in the latter. It resembles *E. histrio* in some regards but lacks the prominent spots on the cheeks and ventral fins. Gill membranes are rather broadly joined, the margin forming a shallow V.

Back is crossed by 6 squarish saddles, each darkest at midline and fading ventrally. Scattered spots, often vertically elongated, occur on back and upper side. Usually 7 (6-9) irregularly shaped blotches occur on side, occasionally resembling letters V or W. In males these may be partially obscured by dull vertical bands which on caudal peduncle extend almost to ventral midline. Scattered small spots are the only other ventral pigmentation. A divided basicaudal spot varies from fairly distinct to obscure. A small humeral bar and diffuse prepectoral spot are also present.

Preorbital bar does not quite meet counterpart on lip. Cheek and opercle are rather pale but finely stippled and often have 1 or 2 faint spots. Suborbital bar is long and fairly distinct. A postorbital spot and another matching it on opercle are distinct. Chin, throat, and breast are lightly stippled.

Dark pigment appears at base of each membrane in spiny dorsal fin. Remainder of membranes are lightly stippled except for dark outer band. Spines lack pigmentation. Membranes of soft dorsal fin are dark basally; there may be 2 or 3 additional indistinct bands, or membranes may be rather uniformly stippled. Rays are clear. Caudal membranes are darkened to produce several vertical bands, somewhat obscured in mature males by additional darkening. Anal and pelvic fins are stippled in males, virtually clear in females. Pelvic fins are rather long and pointed. Pigment in both rays and membranes of pectoral fins produces numerous vertical bands.

Breast and cheek are scaleless; opercle has a few scales, often partially embedded. Belly typically is naked for some distance posterior to pelvic fins, occasionally almost entirely naked. Tsai (1968c) recognized an Alabama River race of *E. rupestre* in which nape is almost always completely scaled, and a Tombigbee River race in which nape almost always lacks many scales. Complete lateral line contains 46-57 scales in Tombigbee race and 51-65 scales in Alabama race. Fin counts are: dorsal XI-XII (X-XIII), 11-12 (9-13); anal II, 7 (5-8); pectoral 14. Vertebrae number 36-40 (mode is 38 in Tombigbee race, 39 in Alabama race).

Breeding males are not brilliantly colored but may exceed brightness shown in color plate. Breeding tubercles are absent. Genital papilla is a short flattened tube. Breeding females may develop touches of green and yellow. Genital papilla is a fairly long tube, somewhat flattened, posteriorly bent, and terminally pointed.

Distribution. Widely, if somewhat sporadically, distributed in each of the major arms of the Mobile River system, both above and below the Fall Line in Mississippi, Alabama, Georgia, and Tennessee. Large numbers occur at several localities just below the Fall Line but dense populations are characteristic of few places in the Piedmont region. The Alabama River drainage, including the Cahaba, Coosa, and Tallapoosa rivers, is inhabited by the somewhat variable Alabama River race. Most of the Tombigbee River drainage, including the Tombigbee and Black Warrior rivers, is occupied by the uniformly appearing Tombigbee River race. But that part of the Black Warrior lying above the Fall Line has rock darters only in the Sipsey Fork, and these are assignable to the Alabama River race, being most similar to the Cahaba River population. North River, which enters the Black Warrior just below the Fall Line, is inhabited by a population that Tsai (1968c) considers to be intergrades. He suggests that stream capture may explain the transfer of Alabama River stock into the Black Warrior. There is a parallel situation with *Etheostoma jordani*, which is widely distributed in the Alabama River system but also occurs above the Fall Line in the Black Warrior basin.

Natural History. The rock darter typically inhabits streams of medium to fairly large size and is not characteristic of tiny streams. Riffles underlain by coarse gravel or rubble and subjected to steady or rather strong current are most suitable. *Etheostoma jordani* and *Percina nigrofasciata* were the most common darter associates we saw in the Conasauga River, but almost any darters frequenting large streams of the Mobile River system could occur with the rock darter. A life history study of this darter would be a welcome scientific contribution.

Abundance. A species so widely distributed within the Mobile River system might be thought of as immune to extirpation, and indeed the rock darter is not in imminent danger. But reservoirs built above the Fall Line in the Coosa and Tallapoosa rivers may have further decreased the abundance of the species in those basins and certainly have fragmented the distribution pattern. The Sipsey Fork population is isolated above a reservoir, and the North River population is similarly threatened. A North River area we visited had been affected by cotton spraying and did not yield this or other darters. The Tennessee-Tombigbee Canal will further fragment and isolate populations in that basin. Rapid expansion of metropolitan Birmingham poses a threat to the upper Cahaba River. Big Sandy Creek south of Tuscaloosa was virtually wiped out by rupture of a diesel oil pipeline a few days before our appearance to capture *E. rupestre*. Such events pose a serious threat to any species with restricted chances for reinvasion and recolonization.

Name. *Rupestre* refers to living among the rocks, an appropriate epithet that has also supplied the common name.

Etheostoma sellare (Radcliffe & Welsh)   Plate 9
Maryland Darter   Subgenus *Etheostoma*

Description. A moderate sized darter reaching 70 mm SL. Expansive pectoral fins, frenum, complete lateral line, complete infraorbital and supratemporal canals, and 6 branchiostegal rays mark this as a member of subgenus *Etheostoma*. It is quite aberrant, however, in that gill membranes are only slightly joined. Some pores of the infraorbital canal emerge through scales on the quite protuberant cheek. Though possessing the markings of a saddled darter, *E. sellare* differs in squamation, elongated head shape, female genital papilla, and belly scalation. Its relationships may eventually prove to be with another subgenus or may warrant unique subgeneric status.

Irregularly shaped spots lie between 4 bold dorsal saddles which usually extend to lateral line. Atypically a saddle lacks the extension on one or both sides, or is missing entirely. Six to 8 lateral blotches occur just below lateral line; several are attached to and appear as ventral extensions of a saddle. Upper and lower side have irregularly shaped spots. Belly is clear. Humeral bar is fused with first dorsal saddle.

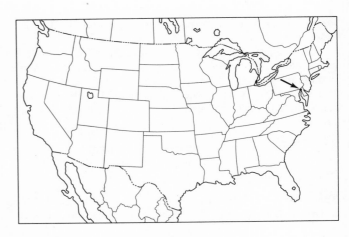

Distribution of *Etheostoma sellare*

A broad horizontal preorbital bar extends onto lips. Cheek is spotted and has a strong suborbital bar. Postorbital bar is reduced to a weak spot. Spotted opercle has dark vertical bands at anterior and posterior margins. Prepectoral area is stippled. Chin has a median cluster of spots and breast has several scattered spots.

Darkening of spines produces a narrow submarginal band in first dorsal fin, augmented by darkening in last membrane. A second distinct band near fin base ends at about sixth spine. Rays of soft dorsal fin are darkened to produce several weak diagonal bands. Caudal fin rays are similarly darkened, producing about 4 vertical bands. Anal fin is rather small; spines and rays are blotchy, membranes are clear. Pelvic fin is clear to weakly spotted. Pectoral fin is especially long; numerous vertical bands are produced by darkening in rays.

Cheek and opercle are heavily scaled; a patch of scales occurs on head near nape, which by contrast is naked along dorsal midline. Prepectoral area, breast, and anterior part of belly are naked, scales may be missing on midline almost to anus. Lateral line consists of 43-48 (43-53) scales. Small body scales may encroach on caudal fin. Fin counts are: dorsal IX-X (VII-XII), 11-13; anal II, 8-10; pectoral 13-15. Bailey and Gosline (1955) report 40 vertebrae and Knapp (1976) reports the range as 39-41.

Breeding males develop some coloration not seen in the preserved specimen shown in color plate. Knapp furnishes a color description indicating that dorsal surfaces are yellow or olivaceous, dorsal saddles reddish brown, and lower body white with a golden cast in some cases. White tips of dorsal spines and rays, anal and pelvic rays, and lower pectoral rays contrast with brown and yellow bands in fins. A yellowish orange blotch at base of each pelvic fin and similar prepectoral blotches are the only intense coloration. Genital papilla is a short pad in both sexes.

Distribution. This was once the poorest known of all darters. No specimens were taken from the time of the description of 2 juveniles by Radcliffe and Welsh (1913) until its rediscovery by Knapp et al. (1963). Deer Creek in Harford County, Maryland, supports the only known breeding population, and strays occur in Gasheys Run downstream. No specimens have been taken from Swan Creek since the original types in 1913. Whether additional populations were present before urbanization and industrialization of the lower Susquehanna River basin and the small streams at the head of Chesapeake Bay is a matter of conjecture.

Natural History. The Maryland darter occurs in the first major riffle above tidewater in Deer Creek but has not been taken in upstream riffles. Its only darter associate is *Etheostoma olmstedi.* Individuals, particularly young and juveniles, use adjacent pools to avoid strong currents. Knapp believes that the small specimens taken sporadically in tiny Gasheys Run have strayed downstream from Deer Creek and do not represent a self-sustaining population. Other nearby streams are badly silted and tend to support algal species which characterize overenrichment. A saltwater barrier exists down the bay, and Conowingo Dam lies just upstream from the mouth of Deer Creek.

Abundance. Federal agencies and those of Maryland were investigating ways of saving this species even before it was placed on the endangered list by Deacon et al. (1979). Possible sewage pollution from a town near the head of Deer Creek has become another problem. Artificial propagation and stocking of the Maryland darter are justifiable, since otherwise it is only a matter of time before some chance pollution event wipes out the species.

Name. *Sellare* means saddled.

Etheostoma swannanoa Jordan & Evermann   Plate 9
Swannanoa Darter   Subgenus *Etheostoma*

Description. A moderate sized darter reaching 75 mm SL. Broadly joined gill membranes, expansive pectoral fins, frenum, complete lateral line, complete infraorbital and supratemporal canals, and 6 branchiostegal rays identify it as a member of subgenus *Etheostoma*. It is similar to *E. inscriptum,* which has more green on the body , and to *E. thalassinum,* which has 7 rather than 6 dorsal saddles.

The first of 6 squarish dorsal saddles is the most prominent; the second and sometimes others may be poorly developed. Scale margins on upper body are lightly stippled, often creating a cross-hatched pattern under nape and spiny dorsal fin. Scattered spots occur on much of body. In males, the center of scales on lower side may be stippled to create horizontal bands. Usually 9 midlateral blotches are developed, those toward head vertically elongated and those toward tail ovoid. Belly is pale. A small, well defined humeral bar may be hidden behind pectoral fin. Basicaudal spot is large, extending onto caudal fin, and often contrasting with cream colored areas above and below.

Cheek and opercle are dark above, pale but stippled below. Preorbital bar, suborbital bar, and postorbital spot are diffuse. Chin, throat, and breast are lightly stippled, the breast more heavily so in males.

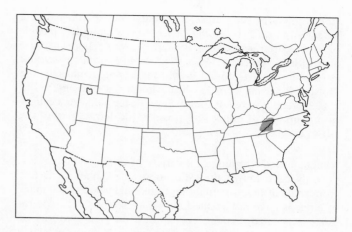

Distribution of *Etheostoma swannanoa*

Spiny dorsal fin has a thin dark marginal band. Beneath a clear submarginal zone, membranes become consistently darker toward fin base. Rays and adjacent portions of membranes of soft dorsal fin lack pigment, but center portion of each membrane is darkened, most intensely at base. Three or more vertical bands in caudal fin are produced by darkening of membranes. Anal and pelvic fin membranes in females are clear, while those in males are stippled. Pectoral fin is weakly banded in both sexes.

Cheek, opercle, breast, and prepectoral area are scaleless. Nape is well scaled toward dorsal fin, but scales toward head are embedded or partly so. Belly is scaled except for a small area adjacent to pelvic fins. Complete lateral line contains 48-58 (46-62) scales. Fin counts are: dorsal XI-XII (X-XIII), 12-13 (11-14); anal II, 8-9 (7-9); pectoral 15-16 (14-17). Vertebrae number 40-43.

Breeding males are handsomely but not intensely colored, as seen in color plate. Breeding tubercles in form of flattened pads occur on belly scales just anterior to anal fin and on ventral caudal peduncle. Genital papilla is a short tapered tube. Females retain a reddish tinge in spiny dorsal fin and develop yellow pectoral fins, but otherwise lack coloration. Genital papilla is a posteriorly directed tube of considerable length, often bearing some melanophores on lateral margins.

Richards (1966) found headwater populations in the French Broad River to have larger and fewer body scales than those elsewhere in the river. Otherwise he noted little geographic variability.

Distribution. An endemic species of the upper Tennessee River system. It occurs sporadically in the Little River of Tennessee and in some tributaries of the French Broad River in Tennessee and North Carolina. Specimens have been taken from the Nolichucky, Watauga, Holston, and Clinch rivers, but in recent years the species may have disappeared from one or more of these.

Natural History. The Swannanoa darter inhabits cool upland and montane streams of medium to large size. The swift riffles occupied by the species are usually characterized by rubble and even boulders. No other species in subgenus *Etheo-*

stoma tolerates such austere habitat. Our specimens were taken only with *Etheostoma chlorobranchium* and *E. blennioides* as darter associates. Richards (1966) reports capture also with *E. flabellare, E. rufilineatum, E. simoterum,* and *Percina evides.* He found gravid males and females in the Holston River on April 2, when water was a cold and turbid 8°C. Nest sites were not found. Several ripe pairs were caught over a mixture of rubble and gravel at the deepest part of the riffle (25-38 cm).

Abundance. Unfortunately a variety of mining activities apparently have caused the extirpation of Swannanoa darters from some of their original range, and many additional miles of streams have disappeared beneath reservoirs. The species exists in isolated remnant populations, the great majority of which are in the French Broad River basin. Though not yet reduced to rare and endangered status, the Swannanoa darter may not be able to survive much additional habitat destruction.

Name. Some of the type material of this darter was taken in the South Fork of the Swannanoa River at Black Mountain, North Carolina, and that particularly beautiful word was chosen for the trivial name.

Etheostoma tetrazonum (Hubbs & Black)   Plate 10
Missouri Saddled Darter   Subgenus *Etheostoma*

Description. A robust, moderately large darter reaching a maximum of about 80 mm SL. Broadly joined gill membranes, expansive pectoral fins, frenum, complete lateral line, complete infraorbital and supratemporal canals, and 6 branchiostegal rays place it in the subgenus *Etheostoma*. It differs from several of its fellow saddled darters in having 4 distinct saddles. From *E. sellare* it differs in lacking heavily scaled cheeks, from *E. euzonum* in having a rounded rather than pointed snout, but from *E. variatum* only in having a greater degree of scalation on cheek and breast, plus other small differences, such as fewer lateral line scales. The 2 forms may be so similar as to constitute mere subspecies, yet they are widely separated geographically, and traditionally have been treated as distinct species.

Four prominent saddles extend to or almost to lateral line. Patterns are variable, immature individuals having 9-11 ovoid lateral blotches, females having additional small irregular spots that join lateral blotches, and males having the last 5-7 blotches vertically expanded into distinct bands that extend almost to ventral midline. Mature females may show such banding to a lesser extent. All specimens have lightly cross-hatched upper sides, pale lower sides, and unpigmented bellies. Humeral area is dark, sometimes forming a large spot. A basicaudal spot is usually present.

Cheek is lightly stippled and pale compared to opercle. Diffuse preorbital bar extends to lip. There is a wide indistinct suborbital bar and sometimes a faint postorbital spot. Chin,

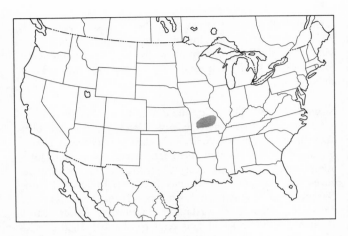

Distribution of *Etheostoma tetrazonum*

throat, and breast are clear to lightly stippled in females, more heavily stippled in males.

Little pigment occurs in dorsal fin spines but membranes are dark basally, forming a distinct band. A similar broader median band becomes less intense toward its outer margin. Soft dorsal fin in females has alternately light and dark rays and lightly stippled membranes except for a narrow marginal band. Dorsal rays are clear in males but membranes are darkened, particularly along blackened fin margin. Vertical banding is produced in caudal fin in females by alternately light and dark rays; this banding is less pronounced in males. Anal and pelvic fin in females is clear to lightly stippled; that in males are more dusky. Pectoral fin in males is more dusky but less distinctly banded than that in females.

Cheek is naked; opercle bears a patch of scales. Nape is scaled, and 1-3 scales are exposed on dorsolateral part of head anterior to nape. Posterior part of breast is scaled, and a few embedded scales may be found anteriorly. Belly is well scaled. Complete lateral line consists of 48-54 (46-57) scales. Fin counts are: dorsal XI-XIII, 12-14; anal II, 9-11; pectoral 14-16. Vertebrae number 39-42.

Breeding males are gaudily colored, often with even more orange on belly than is seen in color plate. Breeding tubercles occur on belly just anterior to genital papilla, on either side of anal fin base, and on ventral scales of caudal peduncle. Genital papilla is a short flattened tube. Females develop few of the bright colors of males. Yellow and blue may appear faintly in spiny dorsal, and yellow spots in soft dorsal, caudal, and pectoral fins complete coloration. Weakly developed breeding tubercles appear on belly. Genital papilla is a round elongated tube.

Distribution. Restricted to northward flowing Ozark streams from the Sac River of the Osage system eastward to the Meramec River. The species also occurs in the Moreau River. This distributional pattern has an interesting relationship with that of *Etheostoma variatum,* which is found in that portion of the Ohio River basin which was part of the ancient Teays system. Since neither the variegate darter nor the Missouri saddled darter is found in the Tennessee, Cumberland, or Wabash drainages, ancestral stock may have ranged across the preglacial Teays, which entered the upper Mississippi River about where the present Illinois River does. If this is the case, separation of the two stocks probably occurred at the time of the Kansan ice advance. Alternatively, these saddled darters may have existed more recently in southern Illinois and western Kentucky and have disappeared in response to geologically recent changes, thus leaving the distributional gap we now see.

Natural History. The Missouri saddled darter is abundant in clear, medium sized to large Ozark streams but is unlikely to be encountered in small streams. Strongly flowing deep riffles with clean gravel and rubble substrate are its favored habitat. Common darter associates include *Etheostoma blennioides, E. caeruleum, E. flabellare, E. spectabile, E. zonale, Percina phoxocephala,* and perhaps others.

Pflieger (1975) indicates that little is known of the habits of the Missouri saddled darter other than his observations that it spawns in late April and May and probably feeds on insect larvae of the riffles. Our specimens from the Niangua River taken in late May included two mature females that did not contain yolky eggs, and other females that still did. This spawning period coincides almost exactly with that of the variegate darter, reported in detail by May (1969). Life history studies on the Missouri saddled darter, coupled with biochemical analyses, might resolve the present quandary over validity of *E. tetrazonum* as a full species.

Abundance. It is fortunate that such a sharply delimited endemic as the Missouri saddled darter remains locally abundant. Still, the conversion of the Osage system into slackwater impoundments has eradicated much suitable habitat and has fragmented the western range of the species. Lavish stocking of trout at Bennett Springs State Park may be reducing the abundance of this and other native fishes in the adjacent Niangua River.

Name. *Tetrazonum* means four bands and refers to the prominent dorsal saddles.

Etheostoma thalassinum Jordan & Brayton Plate 10
Seagreen Darter   Subgenus *Etheostoma*

Description. A moderate sized darter reaching a maximum size of 65 mm SL. Broadly joined gill membranes, expansive pectoral fins, frenum, complete lateral line, complete infraorbital and supratemporal canals, and 6 branchiostegal rays place it in subgenus *Etheostoma*. It is similar to *E. inscriptum* and *E. swannanoa,* which have only 6 dorsal saddles.

Back is marked by 7 squarish saddles, or only 6 in some individuals. Upper side is rather dark, often appearing blotchy or with zigzag marks or rows of horizontal spots. Side bears 8 blotches, those on posterior half of body extending far downward. Belly and lower caudal peduncle lack pigmentation. There is a small humeral spot, and prepectoral area is stippled. A diffuse basicaudal spot is often bifurcate.

A broad diffuse preorbital bar extends onto lip. Cheek is

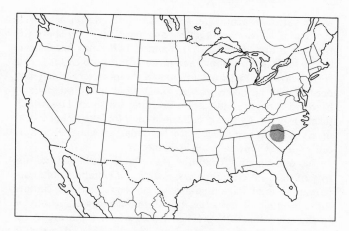

Distribution of *Etheostoma thalassinum*

pale and crossed by a distinct suborbital bar, somewhat posteriorly recurved. There is a postorbital spot. Chin, throat, and breast are stippled.

Spiny dorsal fin has a narrow submarginal dark band, most intense in first and last membranes. Additional darkening may occur in a portion of each membrane adjacent to a spine, giving a striped effect. Membranes of soft dorsal fin are darkly stippled near base and become less so toward margin. Rays are alternately light and dark, producing weak banding in some cases. Darkening in caudal rays and adjacent membranes creates a number of horizontal stripes, more sharply defined in females than in males. Anal and pelvic fins are virtually clear in females, variably darkened in males. Pectoral fins are horizontally streaked like caudal fin.

Cheek, opercle, breast, and prepectoral area are naked. Nape is variable but most often scaled except for anterior part, in which scales are embedded or absent. Belly usually lacks a few scales just behind pelvic fins. Lateral line is complete consisting of 39-45 (38-50) scales. Fin counts are: dorsal IX-XI (VIII-XI), 10-13; anal II, 8-9 (6-10); pectoral usually 14 or 15. Vertebrae number 39-40.

Breeding males are handsomely if not brilliantly colored. Breeding tubercles are on midventral scales just anterior to anus and on ventral midline of caudal peduncle. Genital papilla is a short triangular flap. Breeding females are tinged with green and may develop a dull red band in spiny dorsal fin. Fin and body markings stand out sharply. Genital papilla is a long slender tube.

Distribution. Occurs above and for a short distance below the Fall Line in the Santee River basin of North Carolina and South Carolina. Richards (1966) found that lateral line scale counts and certain other meristic data are somewhat higher in Congaree River than in Wateree River populations, but did not suggest subspecific recognition.

Natural History. The turquoise darter is found in riffles of large creeks and rivers, usually among debris and associated obstacles or gravel and rubble when available. It is widely adapted in terms of water clarity and temperature, occurring in headwater streams stocked with trout and lowland streams where various warm-water fishes thrive. Its darter associates are few. *Etheostoma flabellare* and *Percina crassa* share riffles with it above the Fall Line, and *E. collis* may occur nearby. *E. saludae* from above and *E. serriferum* and *E. fusiforme* from below the Fall Line are other swamp darters which may occasionally be taken with *E. thalassinum*. The presence of breeding tubercles indicates a breeding season of late March through April. Our only collection of colorful specimens was taken in an upland creek in the latter part of May, when only one male still showed much brilliance.

No additional information is available on the natural history of this interesting species. Scarcity of suitable habitat apparently limits its abundance or at least ease of capture through much of its range. In extreme headwaters it may be further threatened by stocked trout, which often are introduced in numbers beyond the carrying capacity of receiving streams.

Abundance. The turquoise darter is not threatened with extirpation but is common only locally.

Name. *Thalassinum* refers to the sea and indirectly implies green.

Etheostoma variatum Kirtland

Variegate Darter

Plate 10

Subgenus *Etheostoma*

Description. A rather large and robust darter, reaching 82 mm SL in our largest specimen. Broadly connected gill membranes, expansive pectoral fins, frenum, complete lateral line, complete infraorbital and supratemporal canals, and 6 branchiostegal rays place it in subgenus *Etheostoma*. It differs from several of its fellow saddled darters in having 4 distinct saddles. From *E. sellare* it differs in lacking heavily scaled cheeks, from *E. euzonum* in having a blunter snout, and from *E. tetrazonum* in minor respects only. The latter species has a greater degree of cheek and breast scalation and somewhat fewer lateral line scales, but many individuals are difficult to assign to one or the other category. The account on *E. tetrazonum* gives additional information on the problem.

The 4 dorsal saddles extend to or almost to lateral line. In a few cases additional darkening on back produces weak suggestions of saddles beneath 1 or both dorsal fins. Males usually have 6 vertical bands on side, the last 3 generally fusing with counterparts ventrally. Anteriorly body is mottled, with a suggestion of 4 or 5 lateral blotches. In females entire side is mottled and vertical bands are imperfectly formed, if at all. Ventral surfaces are pale in both sexes, finely spotted in males.

Cheek is pale with a diffuse wedge-shaped suborbital bar. A broad diffuse preorbital bar extends to or onto lip. A postorbital spot is rarely present. Chin, throat, and breast are stippled in males but only lightly so in some females.

Spiny dorsal fin has a narrow dark submarginal band, a broader, more diffuse median band, and a patch of dark pigment at base of each membrane. Banding is strongest in males. In females soft dorsal fin supports 4 or 5 thin bands

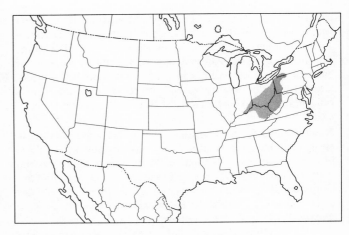

Distribution of *Etheostoma variatum*

formed by darkening in membranes. In larger males these bands become obscured by increased stippling throughout membranes. Four or 5 vertical bands formed by darkening of rays appear in caudal fin, which becomes more generally darkened in large males. Anal and pelvic fins are clear in females, dusky in males. Pelvic spines are especially thick in both sexes. Darkening in rays produces 5 or 6 vertical bands in pectoral fins, less distinct in males than in females.

Cheek is naked, and opercle is naked or may have a patch of embedded scales. One to 3 exposed scales occur on dorsolateral portion of head. Nape and belly are fully scaled. Prepectoral area is naked but breast has scales between pelvic fins and sometimes a bit anterior to that. Two to 4 rows of small scales extend onto caudal fin. Lateral line is complete or nearly so, with 50-58 (48-60) scales. Fin counts are: dorsal XII-XIII (IX-XIV), 13-14 (12-16); anal II, 9-10; pectoral 14-16. Vertebrae number 40-41.

Breeding males are brightly colored, as seen in color plate. Breeding tubercles appear in a wide patch just anterior to anus and continue to caudal fin base. Tubercles persist much of the year rather than only during the breeding season, as in many darters. Genital papilla is a short tube. Body and fin markings are prominent in breeding females. Blue and dull red or yellow appear in spiny dorsal fin, and tinges of yellow show up in other fins; body is olive green. Genital papilla is a long round tube. Tubercles appear shortly before spawning in a patch on belly just anterior to anus.

Distribution. Virtually confined to the Ohio River basin above the falls. The species' downstream limits are reached in the Whitewater and Blue rivers of southeastern Indiana and the Kentucky River. Upstream it can be expected to occur in most of the major tributaries of the Ohio to the headwaters of the Allegheny and Monongahela rivers. It does not occur in the Kanawha River basin above the falls, an area occupied by two other saddled darters, *E. kanawhae* and *E. osburni*. Because we have encountered it abundantly only in streams which are relatively free of silt, we suspect that the rarity or absence of variegate darters in some Appalachian rivers is environmentally induced by mining, farming, and other human activities.

Natural History. The variegate darter is most often found in rivers and their larger tributaries. It never enters creeks as small as those still occupied by its relative the greenside darter (*Etheostoma blennioides*), let alone those even smaller streams frequented by *E. caeruleum, E. flabellare,* and *E. nigrum.* To the extent that these species do enter rivers, they occur with *E. variatum.* Its more common associates also include *Percina maculata* and *P. oxyrhyncha.* In Kentucky we have found that the optimum habitat for variegate darters and that for *E. zonale* are the same, but we find the latter persisting in partly silted rivers that no longer sustain the former.

Most big-river darters have been suspected of completing sizable migrations during the year. In a comprehensive study of *E. variatum,* May (1969) confirmed Trautman's (1957) suspicion that this species moves seasonally. According to May, greatly reduced flow in Big Darby Creek, Ohio, crowds these darters and seems to initiate a downstream displacement at least as far as the deep pools immediately below each spawning and feeding riffle. He found some fin-clipped individuals which had moved as far as 5 km when recaptured in December, but about 40% of his marked population remained on their riffle at least until water temperatures of 2°C caused their displacement to pools downstream. Funk (1955) demonstrated the same phenomenon of a mobile and a sedentary component in populations of larger stream fishes in Missouri. The situation is analogous to that of small mammals which wander when they are unable to establish territories. May observed the spring reinvasion of riffles starting with a pronounced rise in water levels after a late February rain. Mature males took up residence behind rubble and boulders near riffles, while females remained near the foot of riffles. Apparently small territories are defended against intruders which approach closer than 25 cm and thereby elicit the erection of dorsal fins, brightening of the horizontal red band on the belly, outthrusting of the pectoral fin, and sometimes body contortions. Combatants appear to nip at each other's fins without actually doing damage, but one male eventually retreats. May found *E. caeruleum* males to be quickly intimidated into retreat from the territory of a variegate darter. In the pursuit of a female, 2 males with previously established hierarchy often would reinitiate combat.

May found male variegate darters to be ripe by mid-March at water temperatures not in excess of 5°C, and the majority of females to be delayed a month until water temperatures reached about 10°C. In the stream ripe females apparently move into the heads of riffles between April 17 and May 10 in Ohio, to join males and spawn in clean sand between boulders or in their lea. May observed details of spawning in laboratory tanks, where a ripe female would dart through open areas, ascend to the surface, and sink back to the bottom. Males followed, sometimes engaging in ritualistic fights. The female selected a spawning site and buried her head in the sand. The attending male would mount her as she settled down horizontally, his head over hers but the posterior half of his body beside and parallel to hers. The pair would quiver for about 30 seconds and remain quiet for 1-3 minutes thereafter. The female would resume her original darting, in one case spawning 4 times in 2½ hours. Fertilized egg masses numbered 20-70. Each female contained from 700 to 1,000 ripe eggs but it was unclear whether or not she laid the full complement. The reproductive behavior of the variegate darter is generalized for genus *Etheostoma* in that females choose suitable substrate in which to spawn and lead males to the site. Presumably optimal success is accorded those males whose territory contains substrate particularly attractive to ripe females.

May had remarkable success in rearing tank-spawned eggs, obtaining 90% hatch 13-14 days after spawning. During a 2-week postlarval stage the small darters swam freely in the water column and fed voraciously on brine shrimp supplied to them. By 6 weeks after hatching, young fish were considered juveniles and had initiated the benthic habits to follow them throughout life.

Lachner, Westlake, and Handwerk (1950) found the variegate darter to grow rapidly for 2 years and slowly thereafter, reaching ages of 3-4 years. Additional information on food habits and population dynamics is needed.

Abundance. We have observed the variegate darter to be common at fewer spots in the Licking and Kentucky rivers in recent years than in the period of 1958-1964. Trautman (1957) found the species common in the lower end of the Miami, Little Miami, and Scioto rivers, in the upper Muskingum, and in short tributaries of the Ohio River in the extreme eastern part of Ohio. Absent from the Ohio itself since 1920, these darters must have been common previously, according to Trautman, especially at higher gradients. He found them to be rare on riffles that were partially silted or contained detectable coal wastes. Though not rare and endangered, this species has disappeared from much of its former habitat and is often present elsewhere in reduced numbers.

Name. *Variatum,* meaning variegated, agrees closely with the common name. This darter has been called the "variegated" in various older publications, a name that sounds less stilted than the officially accepted common name, variegate darter.

Etheostoma zonale (Cope)   Plate 10
Banded Darter   Subgenus *Etheostoma*

Description. A moderate sized darter reaching 62 mm SL. Broadly joined gill membranes, rather expansive pectoral fins, frenum, complete lateral line, and complete infraorbital and supratemporal canals associate it with subgenus *Etheostoma,* but it approaches the characteristics of subgenus *Ulocentra* in having a small head and in often having the branchiostegal rays reduced from 6 to 5. Decreased head size combined with the presence of 6-8 squarish dorsal saddles distinguishes *E. zonale* from other members of subgenus *Etheostoma.* Variability is too great to discuss completely; the reader is referred to Tsai and Raney (1974) for analysis of geographic variation.

Back is usually crossed by 6 squarish saddles, sometimes 7 or 8. Six to 13, but usually 9-11, vertical bands are fairly equally spaced along side. Anterior bands are narrow and do not extend far ventrally, but those on caudal peduncle are broader and may continue almost to ventral midline. A mid-lateral stripe connects anterior bands but may become discontinuous toward tail. Spots on upper side sometimes coalesce into a poorly defined thin band. Lower side and belly are almost without pattern. A small humeral spot may be partly hidden by pectoral fin. Four tiny caudal spots, vertically arranged, are seen in a few cases but deletions and fusions occur, so that a single midcaudal spot is most common.

A distinct preorbital bar extends onto lip, while a diffuse suborbital bar continues downward and slightly backward across cheek. Postorbital marks consist of a diagonal line on cheek and often an opercular spot posteriorly. Chin is finely stippled and additional spots may occur on throat and breast.

A submarginal dark band extends the length of spiny dorsal fin. Dark pigment also develops at base of each membrane, extending farther upward in males. Remainder of fin varies from clear to lightly stippled. Membranes of soft dorsal fin are rather clear except for stippling near base and beneath margin. There may be some darkening adjacent to fin rays, sometimes producing small blotches in females. Caudal fin membranes are clear, but darkening of rays produces several ill-defined vertical bands. Anal fin rays are blotchy; membranes are clear to lightly stippled. Pelvic fin is unusually narrow, with 2 or 3 vague bands caused by darkening of rays. Pigment in pectoral fin rays produces poorly defined vertical bands.

Scalation is extremely variable. Opercle and nape are scaled. West of the Mississippi River, individuals usually have partly to completely scaled cheeks, but naked cheeks are not uncommon in some eastern populations. Likewise, breast and belly are well scaled except for a reduction in eastern populations. There are 36-63 scales in lateral series; a few individuals lack pores on last few scales. Highest counts occur in the Ozarks and upper reaches of the Tennessee River basin. By far the lowest counts occur in *E. zonale lynceum* from the Gulf Coast. Fin counts are: dorsal X-XI (VII-XIII), 11-12 (9-13); anal II, 7-8 (6-9); pectoral 14-15 (10-16). Vertebrae number 38-40 (37-42).

Breeding males become quite colorful, as shown in color photographs. Genital papilla is a triangular flap. Breeding tubercles are absent. Breeding females are dark, with green and yellow hues commonly found on body. Dull red spots usually appear along base of spiny dorsal fin; anal fin may become green. Genital papilla is a thick tube of moderate length lacking a basal pad. Young individuals are poorly marked and may be confused in the field with a number of species, including *E. caeruleum, E. spectabile,* and various species of subgenus *Ulocentra.*

Tsai and Raney (1974) indicate that they could have recognized 7 subspecies of the banded darter at the 90% level of separation. They thought that such a decision would obscure relationships and chose instead to recognize only *E. z. zonale,* with 7 different races, and *E. z. lynceum,* with 3 quite similar races. The latter subspecies has 38-44 (36-47) lateral lines scales, whereas the nominate subspecies has 43-63 (39-63) lateral line scales. We have noticed that the vertical bands are much broader and more distinctly separated in *lynceum* than in *zonale* and suggest that the former is eligible for full species recognition.

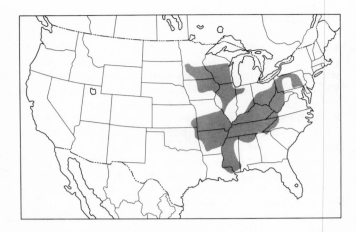

Distribution of *Etheostoma zonale*

Distribution. Within the Mississippi River system subspecies *zonale* occurs from the Verdigris River in Kansas eastward to the upper Allegheny River basin in New York and from the Minnesota River south to the Fall Line, both east and west of the mainstream Mississippi. The subspecies is absent from the upper Kanawha River and the Cumberland River above the falls. *E. z. lynceum* occurs in Mississippi River tributaries from Tennessee southward to Louisiana and in adjacent Gulf Coast drainages eastward to the Pascagoula basin in Mississippi and Alabama. The banded darter has entered western tributaries of Lake Michigan but apparently has not spread farther in the St. Lawrence basin. It also has been caught in the upper Savannah River basin in Georgia, presumably an introduction. Specimens have been captured throughout much of the Susquehanna River (Denoncourt and Stauffer, 1976) and are like individuals from the upper Ohio River basin. Kneib (1972) seems correct in saying that these were probably bait releases.

Natural History. *Etheostoma zonale zonale* typically lives in rivers and large creeks of moderate gradient. Trautman (1957) indicates that it enters smaller streams in Ohio, but we have only taken it in stream units of fourth order or larger. Substrates of coarse gravel to rubble are preferred. The species is best sought at depths exceeding 25 cm, ordinarily at or adjacent to midchannel, except along the margins of extremely swift riffles. Characteristic darter associates in the Ohio River basin include *E. blennioides, E. caeruleum, E. flabellare, E. variatum,* and members of subgenus *Nothonotus. Percina caprodes, P. copelandi, P. evides, P. phoxocephala,* and *P. sciera* are potential associates. In the Ozarks we have caught banded darters with *E. blennioides, E. euzonum, E. juliae,* and *E. tetrazonum.* It undoubtedly occurs commonly with additional species.

Subspecies *lynceum* lives in quite different habitat for the most part, because bedrock riffles are so rare within the Gulf Coastal Plain. Swift runs are created by fallen timber, allowing the development of clean sand and gravel bars often with associated aquatic plants. Under these conditions we have taken banded darters with *E. swaini* and *P. nigrofasciata.* Bedrock riffles such as those of Bayou Pierre in Mississippi are the rare exception in lowlands; at this spot we found banded darters in the strongest and deepest runs in association with *E. histrio, E. rubrum, P. ouachitae,* and *P. sciera.*

Various biologists have established the fact that *E. zonale* spawns in April, May, or even June. Several investigators— Blair (1959) in Oklahoma, Lachner, Westlake, and Handwerk (1950) in Pennsylvania, and Trautman (1957) in Ohio—have verified the close association of the banded darter with *E. blennioides,* particularly where filamentous algae and aquatic mosses abound. Since *E. blennioides* uses these areas for spawning, there is a possibility that the banded darter also does. Lachner, Westlake, and Handwerk found males to outnumber females in all age classes and to outgrow them, and 3-4 years to be the normal life expectancy. Unfortunately the life habits of the form *lynceum* are all but unknown.

Abundance. The banded darter remains common throughout much of its range and is in no particular danger, although populations on the margin of its range, particularly to the west, may be in jeopardy. The actual abundance of lowland populations is not well enough known to preclude their endangerment from large-scale dredging or other stream alterations. Beckham (1977) has voiced concern for protection of the Escatawpa River in which the southern banded darter reaches its eastern limit. The stream has been considered for a massive impoundment, unfortunately.

Name. *Zonale* means banded. *Lynceum* means lynxlike or sharp-sighted.

Etheostoma atripinne (Jordan)   Plate 10
Cumberland Snubnose Darter   Subgenus *Ulocentra*

Description. A robust moderate sized darter reaching a maximum length of about 60 mm SL. It is recognized as a member of subgenus *Ulocentra* by the combination of a blunt snout, small mouth, broadly joined gill membranes, 5 branchiostegal rays, fully scaled belly, nape distinctly humped, and 8 or 9 squarish dorsal saddles. It is distinguished from the majority of species in the subgenus by the presence of a frenum but is readily separable from *E. simoterum* only by the position of the 2 anterior dorsal saddles.

First 2 dorsal saddles lie anterior to first dorsal fin spine but may be partially fused. Fifth saddle is the most prominent of the 9. Nine or 10 vertically elongated blotches connected by a thin midlateral stripe constitute principal side markings. Tiny spots on upper side often occur in clusters. Ventral surfaces are clear to lightly stippled.

A marginal to submarginal dark band in spiny dorsal fin is produced by stippling in membranes, which elsewhere are almost clear. Spines are alternately light and dark but do not produce distinct banding. Membranes of soft dorsal fin are stippled and rays are less contrastingly light and dark than dorsal spines. Pigment in and adjacent to caudal rays creates weak vertical bands. Anal and pelvic fins are virtually clear; pectoral rays and membranes may be clear or lightly stippled.

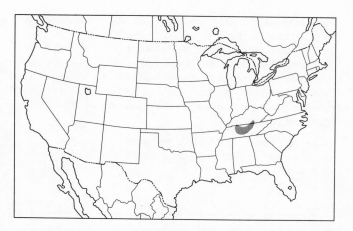

Distribution of *Etheostoma atripinne*

Opercle is scaled; cheek scales may be partially embedded or restricted to posterior half. Nape is partly to fully scaled. Prepectoral area is scaled but breast usually is naked. Lateral line is complete, consisting of 50-60 scales. Fin counts are: dorsal IX-XIII, 9-12; anal II, 6-8; pectoral usually 14. Vertebrae number 38-40.

Brightly colored breeding males develop fin patterns not seen in other specimens. Females may develop bold body pattern when sexually mature and display yellow tones on body. Female genital papilla is a short round tube thicker and longer than that of males. Juveniles are poorly marked and show little difference in appearance from *E. simoterum* and *E. etnieri. E. atripinne* and *E. simoterum* may be the same species, as noted by Etnier in Lee et al. (1980).

Distribution. Narrowly confined to the middle Cumberland River basin, where it occurs from Wolf River in Tennessee and Fishing Creek in Kentucky westward to the Harpeth River in Tennessee and the Red River in Kentucky and Tennessee. It is absent from much of Caney Fork.

Natural History. The Cumberland snubnose darter is an abundant inhabitant of clear shallow streams with rock or gravel substrates. In large rivers it is confined to gravelly margins of riffles. The species is absent from or occurs in much reduced numbers in murky water or where stream gravels are impacted in silt.

This darter presumably spawns in a vertical position like the 2 forms of subgenus *Ulocentra* observed by Winn (1958a). We encountered a breeding group in a tributary of the East Fork of Stones River on April 4, 1969. Breeding males and ripe females were caught along the steep bank against a stump and its roots, which broke the force of the adjacent turbulent riffle. It seemed quite doubtful that they were moving into the riffle to spawn, because we could catch no fish in the strong surge. More likely the fish were spawning against the rocky vertical bank or the tree roots themselves. A life history of the handsome fish would constitute a welcome addition to the knowledge of darters. Common or likely associates are *E. kennicotti, E. obeyense, E. virgatum, E. blennioides, E. stigmaeum,* and *E. caeruleum.*

Abundance. The Cumberland snubnose darter is in no danger of extermination because it is well established in so many small streams. But much of the limestone portion of the middle Cumberland River basin has fallen victim to poor land management. Overgrazing and poor timber management have all but allowed the disappearance of soil on many hillsides. Such conditions are bound to have a deleterious effect on all aquatic organisms.

Name. *Atripinne* means black fin, probably in reference to the dark pattern which persists in the dorsal fins of preserved adult males.

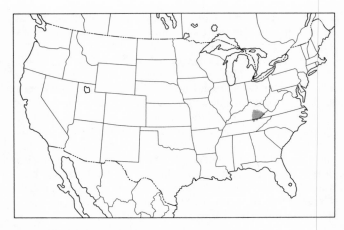

Distribution of *Etheostoma baileyi*

Etheostoma baileyi Page & Burr   Plate 11
Emerald Darter   Subgenus *Ulocentra*

Description. A moderate sized darter reaching 45 mm SL in our largest specimen. It is rather small and delicate for a member of subgenus *Ulocentra,* in which it is placed by having a blunt snout, small mouth, gill membranes broadly joined, 5 branchiostegal rays, scaled belly, humped nape, and 8 or 9 squarish dorsal saddles. A narrow frenum is present. A few individuals have 6 rather than 5 branchiostegal rays.

None of dorsal saddles is particularly intense; posterior ones tend to be small and poorly defined. Eight or 9 lateral blotches are evenly distributed. Upper side is stippled or marked with small spots, while lower side and belly are virtually devoid of pigment.

Diffuse preorbital bar fails to meet counterpart on lip. Suborbital bar is long but lacks intensity. Postorbital spots may be present and a dark band may extend upward and backward from eye.

Pigment in membranes of spiny dorsal fin produces 2 or 3 vague horizontal bands. Conversely, pigment in rays of soft dorsal fin produces 2 or 3 faint bands. Caudal fin is weakly pigmented but not patterned. Remaining fins are almost devoid of pigment. First few anal rays are particularly short.

Cheek and opercle are scaled, though cheek scales are sometimes hard to see. Posterior part of nape is scaled but scales may be embedded or absent nearer head. Prepectoral area may be scaled but breast is naked. Lateral line consists of 46-53 scales, the last 3 or 4 sometimes unpored. Fin counts are: dorsal X-XI (IX-XII), 10-11 (9-12); anal II, 7 (6-8); pectoral usually 14. Vertebral counts have not been made.

Bright coloration of breeding males, dominated by green, is well shown in color plate. Genital papilla is a short round tube. Breeding females may become darker and develop a yellow or green cast to body. Submarginal band of spiny dorsal fin may become reddish brown. Genital papilla, longer and thicker than that of male, is posteriorly bent near tip.

Distribution. Closely associated with the Cumberland Plateau. This is one of the few darters to occur above Cumberland Falls, and is found below them in the Laurel and Rockcastle rivers as well as a few eastern tributaries of the Big South Fork in Tennessee. It occurs in the upper Kentucky River basin as far downstream as Red River. This species and *Etheostoma sagitta* are the only endemic fishes restricted to the upper Cumberland and the Kentucky River. The situation was apparently explained by Kuehne and Bailey (1961), who found a quite recent stream capture of a Cumberland headwater creek by the headwaters of the South Fork of the Kentucky. A subspecies of the johnny darter, *E. nigrum susanae,* and *E. kennicotti* could also have been transferred to new habitat, but if they were, the former was genetically swamped by the nominate subspecies and the latter proved unsuccessful.

Natural History. The emerald darter is locally common within its range and occasionally is the most abundant darter in moderate sized streams with riffles containing gravel or rubble. In rivers it persists in the shallow, less swift portions of riffles. It is most often associated with *Etheostoma caeruleum, E. blennioides, E. flabellare,* and *E. nigrum.*

May is the month of maximum coloration for males and presumably is the peak spawning month. Spawning behavior has not been reported but may resemble that of *E. barrenense* and *E. rafinesquei* observed by Winn (1958a).

As the only *Ulocentra* to enter the upper Ohio River basin, this little darter should evoke the interest of ichthyologists. If the stream capture that allowed it to enter the Kentucky River can be accurately dated, this species would be useful to measure rates of morphological change in darters.

Abundance. Although the range of this species almost coincides with that of intense stripmining of coal, the emerald darter persists at a number of locations and seems to survive a degree of siltation. Deacon et al. (1979) indicate it to be threatened in Tennessee, but such status is unwarranted in Kentucky.

Name. Named for Reeve M. Bailey, who as curator of fishes at the University of Michigan Museum of Zoology contributed to many aspects of systematic ichthyology. Page and Burr (1982) assign the common name emerald darter to agree with the unofficial descriptive name used in several scientific papers that noted the unusual male coloration.

Etheostoma barrenense Burr & Page   Plate 11
Splendid Darter   Subgenus *Ulocentra*

Description. A moderate sized robust darter, 51.2 mm SL in our largest specimen, with characteristics typical of subgenus *Ulocentra*. The frenum is well developed and gill membranes are broadly connected.

The 8 or 9 dorsal saddles vary in intensity. The first and fourth are usually darkest, while those beneath spiny dorsal fin may be difficult to see. Many scales on upper side are darkened, producing small faint blotches. Eight or 9 lateral blotches occur; the 1 beneath gap between dorsal fins is ordinarily the largest and darkest. Lateral line is somewhat arched anteriorly, appearing as a light streak. Tiny blotches on lower side are rather faint except on some females.

Preorbital bar dissipates into stippling on snout. Suborbital bar is poorly defined but postorbital spot is distinct. Stippling on upper cheek may form a reticulate pattern. Many individuals display a distinct prepectoral spot.

A diagonally-set dark band at origin of spiny dorsal fin descends to base and disappears before end of fin. One or 2 median bands and a marginal band also are present. Soft dorsal fin has a dark basal band and scattered dark spots elsewhere. Caudal fin is vertically banded. Anal and pelvic fins are clear and pectoral is lightly stippled.

Nape and opercle are well scaled; cheek scales are small, often partly embedded. Prepectoral area is variably scaled; breast is naked. Lateral line is complete, consisting of 41-50 scales; small scales often extend onto caudal fin. Fin counts usually are: dorsal X-XI, 11-12: anal II, 7-8; pectoral 14. Vertebral number is unknown.

Breeding males may become even more gaudily colored than that in color plate, being one of the showiest species in *Ulocentra*. Genital papilla is a short round tube. Body pattern of breeding females is usually very distinct but color is virtually limited to a little red on spiny dorsal fin. Genital papilla also is a short round tube in the few mature females we have seen.

Distribution. Found in the Barren River arm of the Green River system in Kentucky and Tennessee.

Natural History. This species is locally abundant in clear streams of small to medium size where gravel riffles occur. In large streams it is confined to riffle margins. It can be taken with a number of other darters, particularly *Etheostoma caeruleum*.

The specimen used for our illustration came from Trammel Fork Creek near Scottsville, Kentucky. The stream contained several kinds of darters and numerous specimens of the hellbender, *Cryptobranchus alleganiensis*. Such fine conditions prevail in all too few places.

Breeding behavior is known in some detail. Winn (1958a) found that by mid-April males are holding widely scattered territories in pools at depths of 30 cm or less. At shallow depths these territories are often interspersed with those of *E. flabellare*. In numerous head-to-tail displays the smaller male

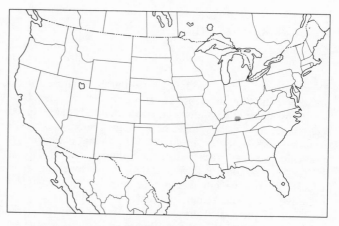

Distribution of *Etheostoma barrenense*

involved is usually the one to give ground and presumably tends to be relegated to raceways and shallow pool margins or is eliminated from the breeding population altogether. Females appear to be attracted by male displays to spawning sites on slanting rocks. With dorsal spines depressed the female moves up the rock surface, laying several eggs singly. Actual spawning movements seem to be initiated by the male's mounting the female, both partners maintaining balance against the rock with their pectoral fins. Most dominant males are 3 years old and the majority of spawning females are 2. Survival past 3 years is unlikely for either sex. A 2-year-old female will contain about 800 eggs; a 3-year-old female will be less fecund. Spawning activity is completed by mid-May. Winn's aquarium observations showed that a dominant male attracts females singly to its nest. A less dominant male occasionally spawns successfully with an unoccupied female. Failure by any male to continue guarding his clutch of eggs may result in predation by other darters in the aquarium. The dispersed pattern of nests in nature probably reduces such cannibalism. Aquarium spawning commenced as water temperature exceeded 20°C.

Winn's observations probably explain why we have often encountered breeding males of most *Ulocentra* species against clean banks where vertically or diagonally set rocks are swept clear of debris by a moderate current. Some species of *Ulocentra*, however, seem most active in areas of mixed gravel and rubble when breeding.

Abundance. Although dispersal through the Barren River basin is prevented by a reservoir, and local habitat destruction has occurred, this species is in no present danger of extermination.

Name. Named for the river basin in which it occurs. Page and Burr (1982) accepted the unofficial name splendid darter used by R.M. Bailey and others in referring to this species.

Etheostoma coosae (Fowler)   Plate 11
Coosa Darter   Subgenus *Ulocentra*

Description. A robust moderate sized darter reaching a maximum length of about 60 mm SL. It is placed in subgenus *Ulocentra* by virtue of a blunt snout, small mouth, broadly joined gill membranes, fully scaled belly, humped nape, and 8 or 9 squarish dorsal saddles. It is unusual in having the normal 6 branchiostegal rays rather than the 5 that characterize other *Ulocentra*. The snout is less blunt than that of most species in *Ulocentra* and the gill membranes may be somewhat less broadly joined. The frenum is absent.

None of the 8 or 9 dorsal saddles is exceptionally dark, and those beneath spiny dorsal fin are rather pale. A diffuse midlateral band is overlain by 9 or 10 blotches, the anterior ones rounded and those toward tail vertically elongated. Isolated spots and narrow stripes on upper side may connect a lateral band to a dorsal saddle. Humeral area is darkened in many individuals. Ventral surfaces lack pigmentation.

A broad preorbital bar extends downward to lip but fails to meet counterpart. Suborbital bar is fairly distinct and a postorbital spot is present. An additional diagonal bar usually occurs on cheek.

Spiny dorsal fin supports a dark marginal band and 2 submarginal bands. Additional darkening may develop at base of each fin membrane. Such banding is incomplete in small individuals. Basal portion of soft dorsal fin is clear but outer three-quarters is darkened by pigment in and adjacent to rays, leaving a clear strip along center of each membrane. Darkening in caudal fin rays produces 3 or 4 wavy vertical bands. Caudal membranes may be lightly stippled. Anal, pelvic, and pectoral fins are clear or nearly so.

Nape, cheek, opercle, and prepectoral area are scaled; breast is naked. Lateral line is complete, with 46-53 scales. Fin counts usually are: dorsal X-XI, 10-12; anal II, 7-8; pectoral 13-14. Vertebrae number 37-39.

As with most snubnose darters, breeding males are very colorful, as seen in color plate. Breeding tubercles are absent; genital papilla is a small tube. Body pattern of breeding females is very bold, and dull red often appears in spiny dorsal fin. Genital papilla is a short tube, crenulate at tip.

Distribution. An endemic of the Coosa arm of the Alabama River basin in Alabama, Georgia, and Tennessee. Boschung (1961) cites collection records, mostly from the upper portion of the basin, where it is abundant.

Natural History. Like most members of *Ulocentra,* the Coosa darter generally occurs in clear streams of small to medium size where moderate current and gravel or rubble substrates are found. In large streams it is mainly limited to shallow gravelly portions of riffles.

We have found no reference to the ecology of this darter. Some ripe females were present in collections we made during early May in northwestern Georgia. The scarcity of such females indicates that most spawning activity occurs earlier. By chance we collected virtually at the type locality for the Coosa

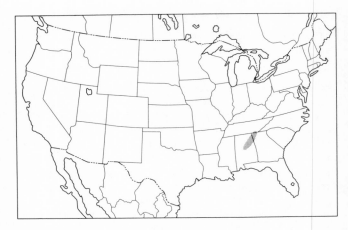

Distribution of *Etheostoma coosae*

darter and found it to be common there. It may be taken with most other darters of the Coosa basin including *P. nigrofasciata* and *P. palmaris.*

Abundance. Although geographically confined, the Coosa darter appears to be in no danger of extirpation and is locally abundant.

Name. The trivial name given this darter by Fowler (1945) is in obvious reference to the river basin of capture. Subsequent clarification of its full range proves the choice to have been appropriate.

Etheostoma duryi Henshall   Plate 11
Blackside Snubnose Darter   Subgenus *Ulocentra*

Description. A robust moderate sized darter reaching a maximum length of about 60 mm SL. It is placed in subgenus *Ulocentra* by the presence of a blunt snout, small mouth, broadly joined gill membranes, 5 branchiostegal rays, fully scaled belly, humped nape, and 8 or 9 squarish dorsal saddles. It differs from *E. simoterum,* which occurs in part of its range, in lacking a frenum; it has much brighter male coloration than a more golden snubnose darter with which it shares the downstream portion of its range. In mature individuals *E. duryi* has a much heavier midlateral band than most snubnose darters, named or unnamed.

Back is crossed by 8, rarely 9, squarish saddles, the fourth typically being the boldest and extending ventrally to join 1 of about 10 lateral blotches. These tend to be joined into a fairly continuous jagged band. Several additional dorsal saddles may fuse with lateral blotches. Lower side and belly are unpigmented.

Diffuse preorbital bar fails to join counterpart on snout. Suborbital bar is weakly to moderately well developed. Cheek bears a rather large postorbital spot.

A marginal to submarginal dark band occurs in spiny dorsal fin. Darkening in spines and adjacent parts of membranes

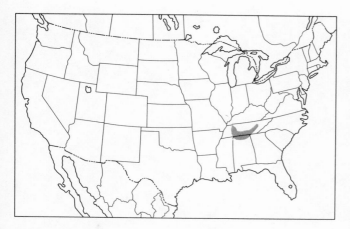

Distribution of *Etheostoma duryi*

large yolky eggs on April 21, 1968, in southern Tennessee. Presumably this is the height of the breeding season. More life history data are needed on the blackside snubnose darter.

Abundance. The species seems safe from extermination and yet is fragmented into isolated populations along the length of Kentucky and Pickwick lakes.

Name. Named in honor of its field collector, C. Dury.

Etheostoma etnieri Bouchard   Plate 11
Cherry Darter   Subgenus *Ulocentra*

Description. A robust moderate sized darter reaching a maximum size of 64 mm SL. It is placed in subgenus *Ulocentra* because of a blunt snout, small mouth, broadly joined gill membranes, fully scaled belly, humped nape, and 8 or 9 squarish dorsal saddles. It differs from *E. atripinne* in lacking a frenum or having one quite weakly developed. Gill membranes may be moderately joined.

The first and fourth of 8 dorsal saddles are the most prominent. Upper side is covered with small dark spots which may be aligned in stripes. A narrow midlateral band tends to fuse the 8 or 9 lateral blotches. Humeral area is somewhat darkened, and anterior half of unpigmented lateral line often appears as a thin light stripe dividing lateral band.

Diffuse preorbital bar does not meet counterpart on lip. A suborbital bar is prominent. A postorbital spot and several horizontal or diagonal streaks on upper cheek and opercle complete head markings.

Membranes of spiny dorsal fin contain dark spots which form 1 or more horizontal bands. Membranes of soft dorsal fin are lightly stippled in small individuals but larger specimens show much heavier membrane pigmentation. Wavy vertical bands are faintly developed on caudal fin. Anal, pelvic, and pectoral fins are little if at all pigmented.

Belly, nape, prepectoral area, and opercle are scaled. Cheek scales may be embedded or occasionally absent dorsally. Breast may support a few embedded scales near pelvic fin insertions. Complete lateral line contains 47-52 (45-57) scales. Fin counts are: dorsal XI (IX-XII), 11 (10-12); anal II, 7 (6-8); pectoral 14 or 15. Vertebrae number 38-39.

Breeding males are quite colorful, sometimes even more so than shown in color plate. Genital papilla is a small round tube. Breeding females often have a red spot in first membrane of spiny dorsal fin and isolated reddish scales beneath and parallel to midlateral band. Genital papilla is a round tube posteriorly recurved in the 1 gravid specimen we have seen.

Distribution. Restricted to Caney Fork of the middle Cumberland River basin. The species has not been captured in the cool, slightly acidic eastern headwaters which descend from the sandstones and shales of the Cumberland Plateau nor from near the mouth of Caney Fork, where *E. atripinne* occurs.

produces a number of interrupted bands in remainder of fin. Rays of soft dorsal fin are alternately light and dark, membranes are clear to stippled, and banding is not apparent. Darkening which is restricted to rays produces weak vertical bands in caudal fin. Anal and pelvic fins are clear; pectoral fin is very lightly stippled and not banded.

Nape, opercle, and prepectoral area are scaled. Cheek is well scaled along posterior margin but anteriorly scales are small and may be partly embedded. Breast is naked or rarely scaled posteriorly. Complete lateral line consists of 44-50 (38-54) scales. Fin counts usually are: dorsal XI-XII, 11-12; anal II, 7; pectoral 14. Vertebrae number 37-39.

Breeding males are brightly colored, as shown in color plate. Genital papilla is a short thin tube. Body pattern intensifies in breeding females and body may develop a yellow hue. First membrane in spiny dorsal fin may bear a red spot, less intense than in males, and reddish brown marks may be scattered throughout fin. Genital papilla is a round tube, longer and thicker than that of male.

Distribution. Occurs in the middle Tennessee basin downstream almost to the Kentucky border. In the lower basin it is confined mainly to eastern tributaries of the Tennessee, including the upper Duck River, and in the middle basin principally to tributaries entering from the north, such as the Sequatchie River, Elk River, and Shoal Creek. It continues up the Tennessee River to about the mouth of the Clinch River.

Natural History. The blackside snubnose darter is locally abundant where clear streams of small to medium size flow over gravel or rubble substrate. In the eastern part of its range it comes in contact and presumably into competition with *Etheostoma simoterum*. Further examination of the interaction of these species is certainly warranted. The "golden snubnose darter," an unnamed form, occurs throughout the downstream range of *E. duryi*. Absence of reported hybrids between the blackside snubnose and either *E. simoterum* or the "golden snubnose" indicates that behavioral and genetic isolation are well established.

We encountered brightly colored males and females with

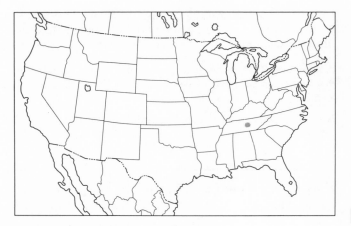

Distribution of *Etheostoma etnieri*

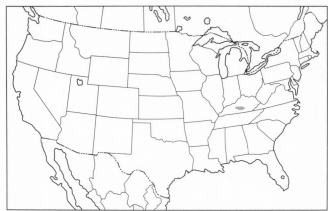

Distribution of *Etheostoma rafinesquei*

Natural History. The cherry darter typically inhabits gravel riffles in small to medium sized streams. It may also occur in the vicinity of springs and in shallow margins of riffles in Caney Fork and its principal tributaries. Common darter associates recorded in our collections are *Etheostoma blennioides* and *E. virgatum*. It should occur in places with another Caney Fork endemic, *E. olivaceum*. The cherry darter seems not to have been taken with *E. atripinne;* competitive exclusion may be the explanation.

Based on ripe females, we surmise that breeding is optimal during April and early May. Although the natural history of the cherry darter has not been investigated, some additional observations are included with the species description of Bouchard (1977).

While not at maximum breeding coloration, our photographed specimen nonetheless represents a lucky find. David Etnier and Raymond Bouchard informed us of the species' existence and of localities where it might be captured. Kuehne with James Small finally captured the specimen near dusk as Cherry Creek was rising rapidly from heavy downpours.

Abundance. Abundant locally but an endemic of quite restricted distribution. This species is vulnerable to decimation by any drastic changes in land use and should be monitored carefully.

Name. The name refers to both the type locality and the prominent red wedges in the soft dorsal and anal fins. The scientific name honors David Etnier, ichthyologist and aquatic ecologist who has trained a number of students at the University of Tennessee.

Etheostoma rafinesquei Burr & Page   Plate 11
Kentucky Snubnose Darter   Subgenus *Ulocentra*

Description. A moderate sized darter, 49.6 mm SL in our largest specimen, with characteristics typical of subgenus *Ulocen-*

tra. It is intermediate in robustness, has a narrow frenum, and has fairly broadly connected gill membranes.

The 8 or 9 squarish dorsal saddles are not very prominent, the one located between dorsal fins being best developed. Eight or 9 lateral blotches are weakly connected by midlateral stippling that does not produce a distinct band. Clusters of tiny spots occur on lower side; belly is clear.

Preorbital and suborbital bars and a postorbital spot are distinct.

Each membrane of spiny dorsal fin contains several spots or diagonal dashes. Soft dorsal fin is clear at base and usually at outer margin but is variably darkened between. Vertical banding is poorly developed in caudal fin. Anal and pelvic fins are clear; pectoral rays are slightly darkened but not banded.

Opercle and nape are scaled. Cheek has small scales, sometimes absent along posterior margin. Scales from prepectoral area and belly may encroach a bit on otherwise naked breast. Complete lateral line usually consists of 38-43 scales. Fin counts usually are: dorsal X-XII, 10-11; anal II, 7; pectoral 14. Vertebral number is not known.

Breeding males are brightly colored, as seen in color plate. Genital papilla is a short round tube. Mature females have bold body markings but develop little coloration except a red to reddish brown spot on first 2 membranes of spiny dorsal fin. Appearance of the genital papilla in breeding females is not known to us.

Distribution. Has been collected in the upper Green River and its tributaries at least as far downstream as the Nolin River. Additional records are needed to determine its exact limits.

Natural History. The Kentucky snubnose darter occurs most commonly in clear streams with substrates of fine to coarse gravel. In the Green River it may be taken from shallow portions of riffles when gravel habitat is available. In small streams this darter is common in unsilted pools. It may be associated with virtually all other *Etheostoma* found in the upper Green River. We have never found it to be the most common darter at any spot where encountered.

Winn (1958a) observed spawning in aquarium-held specimens and reported no significant difference from the behavior of *E. barrenense*. Males of both forms would attempt to breed with females regardless of species. Some cross-fertilized eggs were hatched but not reared. Specimens collected in early April were close to spawning condition. We have encountered gravid females of this species in both April and May.

Natural hybrids of the two snubnose darters of the Green and Barren rivers are not reported, but Winn's experiments would suggest that laboratory hybridization is not difficult to achieve.

Abundance. Parts of the upper Green River watershed are well vegetated and harbor stable populations of this darter. Dams, siltation, channelization, and oil brine contamination have taken a toll on some streams, but this species is not threatened with extirpation. Our most colorful specimens came from Bylew Creek, a Nolin River tributary just north of Mammoth Cave National Park. This picturesque brook harbors a remarkably diverse assemblage of fishes.

Name. Named in honor of Constantine S. Rafinesque, who named many species of Kentucky fishes while a professor at Transylvania University and who essentially initiated study of the Ohio River basin fish fauna. The common name used unofficially for many years was retained by Page and Burr (1982).

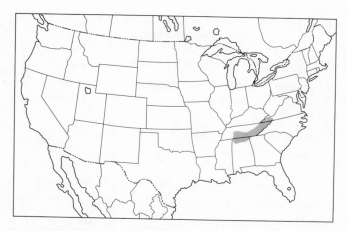

Distribution of *Etheostoma simoterum*

Etheostoma simoterum (Cope)   Plate 12
Tennessee Snubnose Darter   Subgenus *Ulocentra*

Description. A robust moderate sized darter reaching a maximum of about 60 mm SL. It is put in subgenus *Ulocentra* by virtue of a blunt snout, small mouth, broadly joined gill membranes, 5 branchiostegal rays, fully scaled belly, humped nape, and 8 or 9 squarish dorsal saddles. It differs from *E. duryi* and the unnamed "golden snubnose darter" in having a frenum, which is narrow but distinct and consistently present. It differs slightly from *E. atripinne,* which usually has 9 dorsal saddles, in usually having 8, rarely 7 or 9.

The fourth saddle, lying between dorsal fins, is the most prominent and sometimes extends downward to fuse with 1 of about 8 vertically elongated blotches that overlie a narrow midlateral band. Anterior lateral blotches may be divided into dorsal and ventral portions. Upper side is dusky to spotted. Lower side and belly are clear to lightly stippled. Last lateral blotch may extend onto caudal fin but does not appear to be a caudal spot.

Preorbital bar is distinct in small specimens, sometimes fusing with counterpart on upper lip; in larger individuals it tends to be more diffuse. Suborbital bar is prominent and a postorbital spot is present.

A narrow marginal dark band in spiny dorsal fin may be virtually absent. Pigment in rays and spots in membranes pro-

duce a blotchy appearance. There may be a dark basal band. Pigmentation in both rays and membranes of soft dorsal fin produces a series of bands parallel to fin margin. Vertical banding in caudal fin is weak to absent. Anal, pelvic, and pectoral fins are virtually devoid of pigmentation.

Nape, opercle, and cheek are scaled, the latter often with small or partly embedded scales. Breast usually is naked in specimens from upper Tennessee basin, but a few scales near pelvic fins may be present in individuals from lower basin. Complete lateral line usually consists of 45-53 scales. Fin counts are: dorsal X-XII, 10-12; anal II, 6-8; pectoral usually 14. Vertebrae number 38-40.

Breeding males are strikingly colored, as seen in color plate. Genital papilla is a small round tube. Body of breeding females often becomes slightly yellow and usually is darkly patterned. A little reddish brown pigment may appear in spiny dorsal fin. Genital papilla is a longer thicker tube than that of male.

Distribution. This is the only *Ulocentra* of the extreme upper Tennessee River basin, where it is widespread and abundant. It becomes rarer in the middle Tennessee basin and is absent from the montane areas of North Carolina. It reaches its downstream limit in Duck River. Bouchard (1977) treats specimens from the middle and lower Tennessee basin as *Etheostoma atripinne* and shows them to be intermediate between *atripinne* and *E. simoterum* of the upper Tennessee basin. His views set the stage for possible consideration of these 2 darters as a single species.

Natural History. The Tennessee snubnose darter may occur abundantly in small clear streams with gravel bottom or bedrock strewn with rubble. In larger streams it is confined to the shallow gravel-bedded portions of riffles. In the middle Tennessee basin it is sometimes caught with either *Etheostoma duryi* or the unnamed "golden snubnose darter." In this region of overlap the Tennessee snubnose darter seems to be considerably less abundant and widespread, and it usually moves into swifter water than that of its congeners. Almost any of the numerous stream darters of the upper Tennessee

River basin can be captured with it, but especially the rainbow darter, *E. caeruleum*, in our experience.

It is always a thrill to see this brilliant little fish. More information needs to be gathered on its life habits.

Abundance. In spite of local habitat losses and range fragmentation by dams, *E. simoterum* remains abundant at many spots.

Name. *Simoterum* can be translated broadly as snub-nosed.

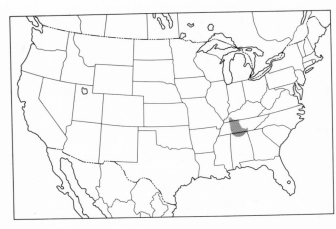

Distribution of "golden snubnose darter" *(Ulocentra)*

Etheostoma species   Plate 12
"Golden Snubnose Darter"   Subgenus *Ulocentra*

Description. A moderate sized robust darter, 50 mm SL in our largest specimen, with characteristics typical of subgenus *Ulocentra*. A frenum is absent. Gill membranes are rather broadly attached, the bridge forming a shallow V.

Back supports 8 rather distinct squarish saddles. The fourth saddle, between dorsal fins, is boldest and largest. Upper side is dusky, sometimes with dark scales which bridge the space between 1 or more dorsal saddles and 1 of the 8 lateral blotches, which are narrowly connected by a midlateral band. Unpigmented lateral line scales anteriorly divide lateral band and blotches. Small spots occur at dorsal and ventral base of caudal fin. Ventral surfaces are pale.

Diffuse preorbital bar does not meet counterpart on snout. Suborbital bar is not intense, but small postorbital spot is. A few dark spots occur on chin.

Spiny dorsal fin supports a narrow dark band near its base. Diagonal dark streaks occur in membranes and a marginal band is confined to posterior half of fin. Membranes of soft dorsal fin are stippled basally but tend to become clear toward margin. Caudal fin has weak vertical banding. Anal, pelvic, and pectoral fins are clear or virtually so.

Cheek, opercle, nape, and prepectoral area are well scaled; breast is naked. Complete lateral line usually consists of 45-52 scales. Fin counts usually are: dorsal X-XII, 10-12; anal II, 6-8; pectoral 14-15. Vertebral counts are not known.

As seen in color plate, this species lacks array of colors characteristic of subgenus *Ulocentra*, although orange on lips, yellow over body, and bold pattern make this a very handsome darter. Male genital papilla is a short thin tube. Breeding females develop a faint yellow cast. Genital papilla is a rather short tube, thicker than that of male.

Distribution. With the possible exception of *E. atripinne*, the "golden snubnose darter" is probably the only member of *Ulocentra* to occur within both the Cumberland and Tennessee river systems. In the Cumberland it is in the Harpeth, Red, and Little rivers of Tennessee and Kentucky. In the Tennessee River it is distributed about as far upstream as Chattanooga.

Natural History. The "golden snubnose darter" is a common inhabitant of clear streams where gravel- or rubble-strewn riffles exist. This preference brings it in contact with other spe-

cies of subgenus *Ulocentra* and with other darters, such as *Etheostoma caeruleum* and *E. rufilineatum*. This meager information is all we have at present for this very handsome darter.

The "golden snubnose" seems to be specialized in that it does not develop the bright breeding colors of other *Ulocentra*. There exists the possibility that its reproductive behavior also is specialized.

Abundance. Many flourishing populations of this darter persist and it seems in no danger of extirpation.

Etheostoma species   Plate 12
"Redbelly Snubnose Darter"   Subgenus *Ulocentra*

Description. A moderate sized darter, 46.6 mm SL in our largest specimen, with characteristics of the subgenus *Ulocentra*. The body is not as robust and the snout not as blunt as most snubnose darters. A frenum is absent. Gill membranes are moderately to fairly broadly connected.

Eight small dorsal saddles and 8 lateral blotches are best developed in small individuals. The first 2 saddles may fuse in large females; saddles of large males are ill defined. In females lateral blotches may be poorly separated; in males they fuse into a band that weakens posteriorly and appears split anteriorly by pallid lateral line. Upper side is speckled, particularly in females. Lower side and belly lack pigmentation.

Preorbital bar almost meets counterpart on upper lip. Suborbital bar is faint or reduced to a spot comparable to postorbital spot. Upper cheek and opercle may support 1 or 2 blotches.

Spiny dorsal fin in males is weakly darkened along margin and has 2 median bands. Spiny dorsal and soft dorsal fins in females lack a distinct pattern. Soft dorsal fin in males bears a submarginal and a darker basal band. Caudal fin has weak vertical banding. Anal, pelvic, and pectoral fins are clear or lightly stippled in most males. All fins are rather small for a snubnose darter.

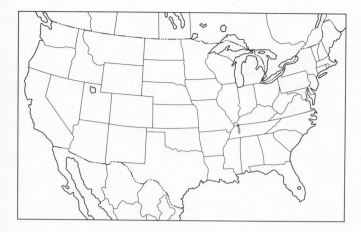

Distribution of "redbelly snubnose darter" *(Ulocentra)*

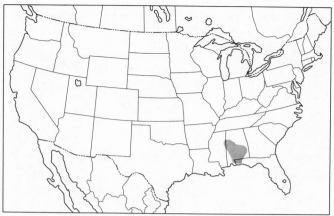

Distribution of "Gulfcoast snubnose darter" *(Ulocentra)*

Scalation is heavy; nape, opercle, cheek, and prepectoral area are prominently scaled. Posterior two-thirds of breast has small scales, sometimes partially embedded. Complete lateral line usually consists of 42-49 scales. Fin counts usually are: dorsal IX-XI, 10-13; anal II, 6-8; pectoral 14-15. Vertebral number is not known.

Breeding males are quite colorful, as shown in color plate. Genital papilla is a thin short tube. Females apparently do not develop breeding colors. Genital papilla is a small rounded tube directed posteriorly in a mature specimen examined by us.

Distribution. Has been taken from the western tributaries of the lower Tennessee River in Kentucky and Tennessee.

Natural History. We have taken the "redbelly snubnose darter" from slowly flowing gravel-bedded riffles. Its range includes no upland streams. Adaptation to slowly flowing streams and occupation of rivers adjacent to the Mississippi River may be setting the stage for extension of subgenus *Ulocentra* west of the great river, where they are yet to be found.

Life history and behavioral data are needed to determine any modifications which may have accompanied the invasion of lowland streams by this and similar forms of *Ulocentra*.

Abundance. This species has probably been hurt by numerous channelization projects within its range, but it is locally common and in no immediate danger of extinction.

Etheostoma species   Plate 12
"Gulfcoast Snubnose Darter"   Subgenus *Ulocentra*

Description. A moderate sized darter reaching 49.1 mm SL in our largest specimen, with characteristics of the subgenus *Ulocentra*. A frenum is absent. Gill membranes are less broadly connected than in many members of the subgenus.

Back is crossed by 8 squarish saddles, the last and those

beneath spiny dorsal fin sometimes poorly developed. First 3 lateral blotches are narrow and vertically elongated while remaining 5 are larger, extending far lower on side. Remaining ventral surfaces are pale.

Preorbital bar is short and indistinct; suborbital bar and postorbital spot are not prominent. Tiny blotches may be present on upper cheek and opercle.

Membranes of spiny dorsal fin in males are darkened basally, most prominently the first 2. Soft dorsal fin of males is darkened basally. Both dorsal fins of females are little pigmented or entirely clear. In both sexes caudal fin is little pigmented and displays no pattern. Anal, pelvic, and pectoral fins of females are clear but those of males are stippled with black.

Cheek, opercle, nape, and prepectoral area are scaled; breast is naked. Complete lateral line usually contains 41-47 scales. Fin counts usually are: dorsal X-XI, 11-12; anal II, 6-8; pectoral 14. Vertebral number is not known.

Breeding males become colorful, perhaps more so in some individuals than is seen in color plate. Genital papilla is a short round tube. Females apparently lack breeding colors. Genital papilla is a narrow tube, posteriorly bent in the 1 specimen we have seen.

Distribution. Certainly the characteristic if not the only *Ulocentra* occurring below the Fall Line along the eastern Gulf Coast. It occurs from the Mobile basin eastward to the Choctawhatchie system. Further collecting is needed to establish its presence in additional basins.

Natural History. The upland type of riffle in which many species of *Ulocentra* flourish is extremely scarce within the range of the "Gulfcoast snubnose darter." This species occupies areas of steady current over gravel or sand substrates, or favors the protection provided by debris and aquatic plants. Our most colorful specimens were taken in mid-March but we have no gravid females among the few individuals retained. The reproductive behavior of this species should be studied because it may differ from upland members of *Ulocentra*.

Bailey, Winn, and Smith (1954) recorded this darter from 5 of their Escambia River stations and listed it as the "orange-stripe darter." Still earlier reference to the species as *Etheostoma simoterum* was made by Gilbert (1891).

Abundance. This species is abundant locally but suitable habitat is absent in many areas. An intensive study is needed to determine its exact status, although it is in no apparent danger of extirpation.

Distribution of "Black Warrior snubnose darter" *(Ulocentra)*

Etheostoma species   Plate 12
"Black Warrior Snubnose Darter" Subgenus *Ulocentra*

Description. A robust moderate sized darter, 60.2 mm SL in our largest specimen, with the characteristics of subgenus *Ulocentra*. A frenum is absent. Gill membranes are broadly connected.

Back is crossed by 8 squarish saddles, although fusion or splitting occasionally produces 7 or 9. First saddle is large and very dark; fourth is bold also. Usually there are 8 blotches along and extending below lateral line. Various scales on upper side are blackened, sometimes producing 1 or more horizontal bands. Lower side and belly are lightly stippled in males, clear in females.

Preorbital bar does not fuse with counterpart on snout but may be joined by stippling on upper lip. A postorbital spot and 1 or 2 spots behind that complete head pattern.

Submarginal and basal bands in spiny dorsal fin are best developed in males. Membranes of soft dorsal fin are spotted in females; in males they are dusky basally and grade to clear marginally. Caudal fin rays are darkened to produce weak vertical bands. All remaining fins are clear except for some spotting in anal and pelvic fins of males.

Cheek, opercle, nape, and prepectoral area are scaled; breast is naked. Complete lateral line usually contains 48-52 scales. Fin counts usually are: dorsal XI-XII, 10-11; anal II, 7-8; pectoral 14. Vertebral counts are not known.

Breeding males are strikingly colored, as seen in color plate. Genital papilla is a short thin tube. Breeding females may develop a dull red spot at origin of spiny dorsal fin but lack bright colors. Genital papilla is a short tube directed posteriorly in some individuals.

Distribution. Occurs in the Black Warrior component of the Mobile basin. It may live elsewhere in the basin but is not likely to occur below the Fall Line.

Natural History. Our specimens of the "Black Warrior snubnose darter" came from a clear spring-fed creek near Pinson, Alabama. *Percina nigrofasciata* was the abundant darter found in steady current over gravel and rubble substrate. A few *Etheostoma jordani* were encountered, and the snubnose darters were caught near banks protected by shoreline brush and tree roots.

Abundance. This form of *Ulocentra* was sought at a number of places but proved to have a spotty distribution. A compre-

hensive study might reveal areas of abundance, but our initial impression is that this species is already very restricted and bears careful watching.

Etheostoma species   Plate 12
"Upland Snubnose Darter"   Subgenus *Ulocentra*

Description. A moderate sized darter, 48 mm SL in our largest specimen, with characteristics typical of subgenus *Ulocentra*. This species is not particularly robust or deep bodied. A frenum is absent. Gill membranes are broadly connected.

There are usually 8 squarish dorsal saddles, the first and the one between dorsal fins being most distinct. Side is characterized by 5 vertically elongated bands on posterior half of body. Upper side is blotchy. Lower side and belly are pale.

Spiny dorsal fin supports a dark basal band and a faint marginal band, with horizontal or diagonal streaks in intervening portions of each membrane. Soft dorsal fin is dusky basally, clear along margin. Caudal fin banding is weak. Anal and pelvic fins are clear and pectoral fins are very weakly banded.

Preorbital bar nearly converges with counterpart on upper lip. Suborbital bar and postorbital spot are distinct.

Cheek, opercle, nape, and prepectoral area are scaled; breast is naked. Complete lateral line usually has 47-49 scales. Fin counts usually are: dorsal X-XI, 10-12; anal II, 7; pectoral usually 14. Vertebral number is not known.

Breeding males are brightly colored, probably more so than specimen shown in color plate. Females apparently do not develop coloration. Well developed genital papillae have not been seen for either sex.

Distribution. Apparently confined to upland portions of the Coosa River system above the Fall Line in Alabama, Georgia, and Tennessee. Its occurrence at present seems to be quite spotty but more collecting is needed to establish the actual distribution. Boschung (1961) reports several collections of a

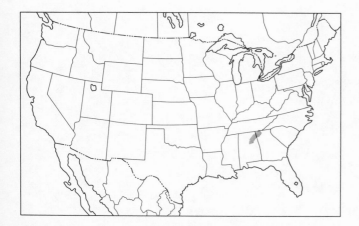

Distribution of "Upland snubnose darter" *(Ulocentra)*

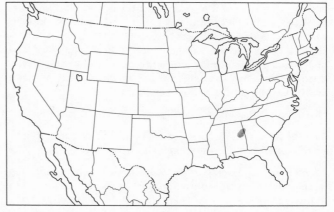

Distribution of "Tallapoosa R. snubnose darter" *(Ulocentra)*

"broadband snubnose darter" in the Coosa basin but the status of that form is unknown to us and seems not to be the upland form discussed here. The broadband form may be a variant of *Etheostoma coosae.* Smith-Vaniz (1968) refers briefly to this upland form without suggesting its range, while Ramsey (in Boschung, 1976) confirms the range we have indicated.

Natural History. This snubnose darter seems to require clear, cool upland streams of intermediate to fairly large size. David Etnier (personal communication) has taken specimens over clean gravel adjacent to swift riffles. Our specimens were captured in Alabama under similar conditions, with *Percina palmaris* as the sole darter associate. Additional ecological information is needed for this darter.

Abundance. Apparent restriction of this darter in Alabama to Shoal Creek of the Coosa basin prompted Ramsey (in Boschung, 1976) to list it as being of special concern in that state. It is not so listed nationally, probably because additional populations are found in headwater areas in Georgia and Tennessee.

Etheostoma species   Plate 13
"Tallapoosa Snubnose Darter"   Subgenus *Ulocentra*

Description. A moderate sized robust darter, 53.3 mm SL in our only adult male specimen, with characteristics typical of subgenus *Ulocentra*. A frenum is absent. Gill membranes are moderately to broadly connected.

Back is crossed by 8 saddles, the last 5 or 6 having narrow ventral extensions that serve as narrow bands separating the 8 lateral blotches.

Preorbital bar fails to join counterpart on snout. Suborbital bar and postorbital spot are well developed. Two additional spots are present on each cheek.

Membranes of spiny dorsal fin are darkened to produce a

submarginal and a basal band. Membranes of soft dorsal fin are darkly stippled basally and become steadily less so toward clear margin. An opaque wedge, expanding posteriorly, starts at about third membrane. Faint vertical bands exist in caudal fin. Anal, pelvic, and pectoral fins are clear except for some stippling in anal and pelvic fins in males.

Cheek, opercle, nape, and prepectoral area are scaled; breast is naked. Complete lateral line usually consists of 48-51 scales. Fin counts usually are: dorsal X-XI, 11-12; anal II, 7-8; pectoral 14-15. Vertebral counts are not known.

Males probably exceed brightness shown in color plate. Genital papilla is a short thin tube. Females apparently lack breeding colors. Genital papilla is a narrow tube directed posteriorly at tip.

Distribution. Seems to be restricted to the Tallapoosa River above the Fall Line in Alabama and Georgia.

Natural History. Our specimens were taken over riffles in a creek with clear gravel and rubble substrate. Several attempts to locate specimens in somewhat turbid streams had failed. Our material, including 1 gravid female with genital papilla extended, was collected on April 9, 1972. We are indebted to John Ramsey for notes on collecting sites for this darter.

This snubnose darter should be closely examined to determine if it is distinct from the "Gulfcoast snubnose darter," which lives just downstream and below the Fall Line from it.

Abundance. If the Tallapoosa form is specifically distinct, then its survival status is questionable because little suitable habitat exists.

Etheostoma species   Not illustrated
"Yazoo Darter"   Subgenus *Ulocentra*

Description. A moderate sized darter known to us only by an illustration in Deacon et al. (1979). It has the appearance of an *Ulocentra* type that is not very robust or deep bodied. Lateral blotches tend to form a confluent band anteriorly. Preorbital bar, suborbital bar, and postorbital spot are present. Males have a dark band near base of both spiny and soft dorsal fins. Other fins seem to be poorly if at all pigmented. Females lack fin markings, and body pattern is weakly developed. Reddish brown along side and orange on belly of males are the only bright coloration seen in either sex.

Distribution. Presumably confined to the Yazoo River basin.

Natural History. We have not collected this darter and have no natural history information on it.

Abundance. Apparently restricted and but rarely constituting large populations, this darter is listed by Deacon et al. (1979) as threatened.

Etheostoma species
"Lowland Snubnose Darter"
and other unnamed forms

Not illustrated

Subgenus *Ulocentra*

Description. A "lowland snubnose darter" has been mentioned to us by David Etnier, Raymond Bouchard, and Melvin Warren. It occurs in rivers of western Tennessee directly tributary to the Mississippi River and may just enter western Kentucky. Its southward limits are not established. This form differs from the "redbelly snubnose darter" in having a completely scaled rather than partly scaled breast and perhaps in important breeding color differences of which we are unaware.

Whether or not this darter is the same form as the "Yazoo darter" is also a matter of conjecture. The possibility exists that additional snubnose darters occupy streams entering the Mississippi south of the confluence of the Ohio River and also in rivers of the Gulf Coast between the Mississippi River and the Mobile River basin.

Etheostoma jessiae (Jordan & Brayton)
Blueside Darter

Plate 13

Subgenus *Doration*

Description. A rather small darter, 58 mm SL in our largest specimen. It resembles a member of subgenus *Boleosoma* but males are tuberculate and have a red and a blue stripe in the spiny dorsal fin. It is quite similar to *E. stigmaeum* but has a sharper snout, larger mouth, and more scales in the lateral series. A narrow frenum usually is present. Branchiostegal membranes are slightly joined. Supratemporal and infraorbital canals are complete.

Lightly speckled back has 6 saddles, and side bears 9-10 blotches sometimes resembling letters V or W but often appearing as more solid vertical bands. Belly is clear. Diffuse preorbital bar does not meet counterpart on snout. A weak suborbital bar may extend to lower cheek margin. Chin, throat, and breast lack pigmentation.

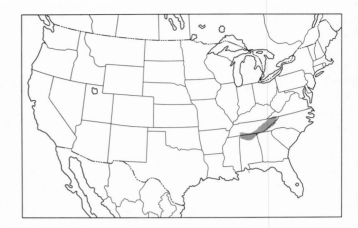

Distribution of *Etheostoma jessiae*

Narrow marginal and submarginal bands in spiny dorsal fin are faint; much darker basal portion of fin typifies males, while light stippling characterizes females. Soft dorsal fin rays are narrowly edged in black, giving fin a dusky appearance. Similar effects are found in caudal, anal, and pelvic fins, while pectoral fin is clear.

Cheek may be naked but usually has a few scales beneath and behind eye. Opercle and nape are scaled. Lateral line ends beneath soft dorsal fin. Lateral scale series numbers 53-62, 5-14 being unpored. Fin counts are: dorsal XI-XII, 11-12; anal II, 8-9; pectoral 13-15. Vertebrae number 40-42.

Breeding males are colorful, as shown in color plate, and closely resemble *E. stigmaeum*. Based on the male available to examine, breeding tubercles are not as well developed as in *E. stigmaeum*. Genital papilla is a wedge-shaped flap. Females are not colorful. We have not examined a breeding female for appearance of genital papilla.

Distribution. Confined to the middle and upper Tennessee basin and to the Stones River in the Cumberland basin where recorded once. It is absent from Virginia and higher elevations of eastern Tennessee and all of North Carolina. Confusion of this darter with *E. asprigene* is responsible for old erroneous records from Illinois.

Natural History. Reproduction in the blueside darter probably occurs mostly in March and April. It seems to favor deeper riffles for breeding than does *E. stigmaeum* and may persist in these during the warmer months. Detailed comparison of the 2 forms needs to be made.

Abundance. The blueside darter remains locally common within the Tennessee basin, although extensive habitat alterations have undoubtedly reduced its abundance.

Name. The trivial name honors Mrs. Jessie D. Brayton, wife of one of the describers of this species.

Etheostoma stigmaeum (Jordan)
Speckled Darter

Plate 13

Subgenus *Doration*

Description. A rather small slender darter probably not exceeding 50 mm SL. It resembles a member of subgenus *Boleosoma* but differs in that breeding males are tuberculate and have a red and a blue stripe in the spiny dorsal fin. This species is quite similar to *E. jessiae,* which has a sharper snout, larger mouth, and more scales in the lateral series. A vestige of a frenum is found in some individuals. Branchiostegal membranes are slightly to moderately joined; supratemporal and infraorbital canals are complete.

Stippled upper side separates 6, rarely 5, dorsal blotches from 9-11 lateral markings that consist of zigzag lines sometimes resembling letters V or W. Belly and ventral area are normally unpigmented. A dark basicaudal spot may be flanked by pale spots above and below. Preorbital bar nearly meets counterpart on snout. Suborbital bar is a large blotch in most populations but may be long and fairly distinct in some. A dark spot represents postorbital bar. Upper opercle is conspicuously darkened. Chin, throat, and breast are clear to lightly stippled.

Spiny dorsal fin has a narrow marginal dark band and variable stippling in membranes of lower half to three-quarters of fin. Soft dorsal fin is moderately stippled near base, becoming consistently less so toward margin. Margins of caudal rays are dark but fin lacks a pattern. Anal and pelvic fin membranes are lightly stippled basally. Pectoral fins are pale.

Cheek is naked or has a few partly embedded scales beneath and behind eye; opercle is scaled. Nape is scaled posteriorly but is naked or has fine embedded scales anteriorly. Breast is naked. There are 40-53 scales in lateral series, but 5-31 are unpored; lateral line ends beneath soft dorsal fin. Fin counts are: dorsal XI-XII (X-XIII), 10-12; anal II, 8-10; pectoral 13-14. Vertebrae number 38-40 (38-42).

Breeding males become colorful and show darkening of fins and body, as shown in color plate. Coloration varies considerably. Specimens from upper Cumberland River have orange lips, while some from upper Mobile basin have bluish green lips. Breeding tubercles develop on belly, pelvic fin, and anal fin, but belly tuberculation may be lacking in some southern populations. Male genital papilla is a wedge-shaped flap. In mature females soft dorsal, caudal, and pectoral fins show some banding. Body markings are more pronounced than in males but coloration does not develop. Female genital papilla is a long oval tube.

An analysis of variations found in the speckled darter would solve nomenclatural problems. Deacon et al. (1979) list an unnamed species of subgenus *Doration* as being of special concern in Tennessee, while Lee et al. (1980) have resurrected the name *E. meadiae* (Jordan & Evermann) for this or another member of the subgenus in the Clinch and Powell rivers of Tennessee and Virginia. Populations of the upper Cumberland are distinctive and may represent yet another valid species or subspecies.

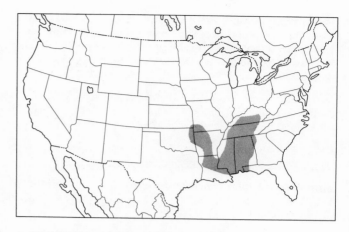

Distribution of *Etheostoma stigmaeum*

Distribution. East of the Mississippi extends from the Green and upper Cumberland rivers southward in most drainages to the Gulf, and eastward through the Mobile basin to but not including the Escambia River. It is virtually replaced by *E. jessiae* in the middle and upper Tennessee basin. West of the Mississippi it is found in the southward flowing lowland and Ozark streams of Missouri and Arkansas, southeastern Kansas, eastern Oklahoma, and Louisiana west to the Sabine River.

Natural History. The speckled darter most characteristically is found in clear, medium sized streams with moderate gradient but has been occasionally taken from sluggish murky streams. It can be found below riffles. In Kentucky we have found it over shallow gravel riffles throughout the warmer months. Cross (1967) and other writers have reported it over riffles mainly during its breeding season. This is usually March in the south and April in the northern range. At such seasons one is likely to encounter brilliant males and ripe females where shallow water is dancing over clean gravel.

Winn (1958a) observed aquarium spawning of speckled darters to resemble that of *E. spectabile* and *E. caeruleum*. A large male mounts a female with vents apposed, head to head when she stops over gravel. Several eggs are deposited and fertilized each time, but total egg counts, presumably in the hundreds, are not reported. Vibration of the pair causes them to embed in the gravel, where the eggs settle. Limited field observation indicates that males have shifting territories over breeding riffles, as do males of *E. caerulum*.

This species could be the subject of a fine life history study because it is poorly known, widespread, and locally abundant. We have noted that it sometimes replaces *E. nigrum* with stream size increase, and a possible interaction of the 2 species could result in this allocation of habitat. Food habits are not known and may be quite variable since the fish is sometimes found over riffles and sometimes in pools with variable water velocity and clarity.

Abundance. The speckled darter is locally common and in no danger of extirpation. Regionally it has suffered losses and the restricted variants perhaps worthy of species status are in a more precarious position. The northern limit of its range is interestingly abrupt on both sides of the Mississippi, giving the impression of a southern species extending to its limits of tolerance.

Name. *Stigmaeum* means speckled. Unfortunately some other darters equal or exceed *E. stigmaeum* in degree of stippling.

Etheostoma longimanum Jordan   Plate 13
Longfin Darter   Subgenus *Boleosoma*

Description. A rather large member of the subgenus reaching about 68 mm SL but seldom exceeding 62 mm SL. Thin flexible anal spines, rounded snout, absence of frenum, absence of breeding tubercles, a complete or nearly complete lateral line, and a flat bilobed genital papilla in females mark this species as a member of subgenus *Boleosoma*. It differs from all members but *E. podostemone* in having considerable coloration in breeding males, and from that species in having more lateral line scales but lacking a distinct suborbital bar. Branchiostegal membranes are moderately joined. Supratemporal and infraorbital canals are complete, but the latter may be deeply embedded and difficult to see.

Six dark dorsal saddles contrast well with intervening light areas. Anterior light areas often appear as pale oval spots. Eight to 11 lateral blotches and a basicaudal spot separate irregularly spotted upper side from virtually unmarked lower side and belly. A diffuse prepectoral spot is usually present.

Preorbital bar extends forward and downward, almost meeting counterpart on lip. A suborbital spot and usually additional spots occur on cheek. Opercle is darkest behind eye. Ventral surfaces of head and breast are immaculate.

Spines of first dorsal fin are clear; each membrane contains 4 or 5 oblong spots becoming smaller and fainter toward margin. Rays of soft dorsal fin are clear and membranes are marked like those in spiny dorsal fin. Soft dorsal fin is not exceptionally long in females or juveniles but in breeding males is rivaled for length only by that of *E. cinereum*. Anal and pelvic fins lack much pigmentation; somewhat expansive pectoral rays are stippled near base.

Opercle is scaled but cheek, nape, and breast are naked. Belly is naked anteriorly. Lateral line typically is complete with 42-46 (39-52) scales. Fin counts are: dorsal IX-X (VIII-XI), 11-12 (10-13); anal II, 7 (5-9); pectoral usually 11-12. Vertebrae number 37-39.

As seen in color plate, breeding males are among the most striking of all darters. Breeding tubercles are absent; genital papilla is short and conical. Basic body pattern of females is augmented by a slight darkening but no coloration appears. Genital papilla is short, bifurcate, and with terminal lobes.

Distribution. An endemic of the upper James River system in Virginia and a small piece of West Virginia, where it commonly occurs in clear streams of various sizes in both montane and Piedmont portions of the basin.

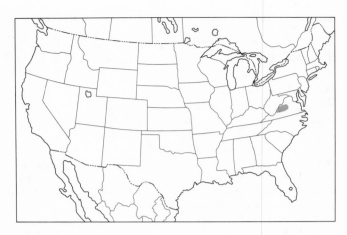

Distribution of *Etheostoma longimanum*

Natural History. The longfin darter is an inhabitant of swift water to a greater degree than other members of subgenus *Boleosoma*. We captured 2 exceptional breeding males in early June from a tributary of Craig Creek. The strongly flowing riffle was about 30 cm deep with a coarse gravel and rubble substrate. The breeding sites apparently were 2 large flat rocks; several ripe females were caught in calmer waters nearby. Spawning probably occurs earlier in most cases since the tributary was exceptionally cool. In Craig Creek *Etheostoma longimanum* was commonly taken near the foot of riffles along with *E. flabellare* and *Percina roanoka*. Cole (1971) reports *E. nigrum* also to be an associate of the longfin darter. Raney and Lachner (1943) found *E. longimanum* to live about 2 years, females producing from 50 to 300 eggs per season. This unusual species deserves additional study.

In habit and to some extent appearance we find this species to resemble members of the subgenera *Etheostoma* and *Ulocentra* more than its fellow members of *Boleosoma, E. nigrum, E. olmstedi,* and *E. perlongum*.

Abundance. Locally abundant and well distributed through the upper James River, *E. longimanum* is in no danger of extirpation. Gross alterations within the basin could change its prospects greatly, however.

Name. *Longimanum* means long hand and refers to the long pectoral fins, though the soft dorsal fin of large males is the species' most spectacular characteristic.

Etheostoma nigrum Rafinesque   Plate 13
Johnny Darter   Subgenus *Boleosoma*

Description. A small member of the subgenus reaching about 60 mm SL but seldom much exceeding 50 mm SL. A thin flexible anal spine, rounded snout, absence of frenum, almost complete lateral line, absence of breeding tubercles, and flat bilobed genital papilla in females place it in subgenus *Boleosoma*. The combination of blunt snout, interrupted supratemporal and infraorbital canals, 1 anal spine, and lack of body coloration distinguishes *E. nigrum* from its congeners. The gill membranes are moderately to slightly connected.

Six, sometimes 7, dorsal saddles and 7-10 lateral blotches are principal markings. Lateral blotches may resemble letters W, V, or X. Lower side bears only small spots and belly is devoid of pigmentation. Most specimens have a fairly distinct basicaudal spot. Preorbital bar is directed downward, failing to meet counterpart on lip. A suborbital spot and other small spots appear on cheek. Upper opercle varies from dark to stippled. Breast and throat are clear; chin and lower jaw often are blotchy.

Elongated black spots occur on spines of first dorsal fin and rays of second dorsal sufficiently to produce a weakly banded appearance in the latter. Dorsal fins are more widely separated than is usual in darters. Caudal rays are pigmented enough to produce vertical bands. Anal, pelvic, and pectoral fins are almost without pigmentation.

Nape, cheek, and breast are naked in most populations but are variably scaled toward north and northeast parts of range. Opercle is variably well to lightly scaled. Belly is naked anteriorly. Lateral line consists of 37-52 (35-59) scales and may lack pores on last 1-3 scales. Fin counts are: dorsal VIII-IX (VI-X), 11-13 (9-15); anal I (rarely II), 7-8 (6-9); pectoral usually 11-12. Vertebrae usually number 37-38.

Though colors do not appear, breeding males darken at least on head and sometimes are darkly stippled over entire body. Four to 8 vertical bands are seen in many breeding individuals. Body of post-reproductive males is bowed and such individuals swim feebly at surface of stream before dying. Genital papilla is a short conical tube. Breeding females retain typical body and fin markings, usually somewhat intensified, and body takes on a yellowish cast. Female genital papilla is a bilobed flap, sometimes distended into a short thick tube with grooves. Juveniles are not well marked and are easily confused with several other species of darters, particularly *Etheostoma chlorosomum, E. stigmaeum, P. copelandi,* and *E. vitreum.*

Regional variation has led to the proposal of subspecies. Underhill (1963) concluded that the separation of *E.n. nigrum* and *E.n. eulepis* is based on genetic differences too minor to warrant taxonomic recognition, but Cole (1971) continues to recognize *eulepis.* Kott and Humphreys (1978) note a cline of decreasing lateral line scales in *E.n. nigrum* from northwest to southeast. Starnes and Starnes (1979b) argue for retention of *E.n. susanae,* a form with reduced scalation isolated in the Cumberland River above the falls.

Distribution. The range of the johnny darter is quite large, perhaps rivaling that of *Percina caprodes.* In Canada it occurs in Hudson Bay drainages from eastern Saskatchewan as far north as the Churchill River drainage through much of Manitoba and western Ontario, as well as the St. Lawrence drainage at least as far east as Lake Champlain. Scott and Crossman (1973) indicate that a problem exists in eastern Canada in distinguishing *E. olmstedi* (itself once treated as a subspecies of *E. nigrum*) from the johnny darter. From central Canada *E. nigrum* extends southward through the eastern Dakotas to eastern Oklahoma and west central Arkansas. In the Platte

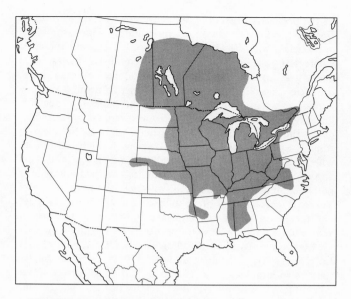

Distribution of *Etheostoma nigrum*

River basin it continues westward into Wyoming and Colorado to elevations of 1,500 meters. Cross (1967) reports early records in the Kansas River system fully 150 km west of the present limits of occurrence. The species is well distributed within the upper Mississippi basin, the Great Lakes region, and the Ohio River basin. Jenkins, Lachner, and Schwartz (1971) list it as being present in the upper reaches of several Atlantic drainages from the York southward to the Neuse. It also occupies much of the Mobile basin. Eastern stocks of the johnny darter received close attention from Cole (1971). In spite of lower lateral line counts and some other meristic differences, he considered them all to be *E.n. nigrum* which are rather recent invaders from the Ohio River basin.

That the johnny darter is a highly invasive species is shown by its postglacial dispersal in Canada, both through the eastern Great Lakes portal into the St. Lawrence drainage and through the Red River into Hudson Bay rivers. Entrance by stream capture into the Mobile basin is the apparent cause for the species' presence there.

Natural History. The johnny darter has been taken in streams of various size, gradient, substrate, and clarity. Trautman (1957) considered it to be the Ohio darter most tolerant of diverse conditions. The species has even been reported to inhabit shallow lakes in eastern South Dakota (Bailey and Allum, 1962). It is not a riffle species and is most frequently encountered in small to medium sized streams of moderate clarity, where it lives in pools over sand or solid bedrock. No single compendium of knowledge exists for the johnny darter but it has been the subject of numerous articles of more limited scope.

Winn (1958b) reported that considerable upstream and downstream movements precede spawning. Males establish territories around partially embedded rocks or occasionally other materials beneath which they can squeeze. A nest site is prepared by turning upside down and rubbing the area with the caudal, anal, and pelvic fins while balancing with the aid of the pectorals. Intruding males are approached with dorsal fins erect, and presumably are intimidated. Ripe females are approached with fins lowered and are led beneath the rock, where nest polishing is resumed. The female may then join the male, head to head, and deposit 30-200 eggs over an hour's time, occasionally interrupted by return to normal posture. Females lay 5 or 6 such egg clutches and males may accumulate a thousand or more eggs from several females. Males guard the eggs until hatched but may eat those attacked by fungus. Spear (1960) observed spawning in Michigan to start when water temperature exceeded 15°C, as early as mid-April and continuing well into June. Females spawned a year after hatching and the next spring, although survival was low. Year-old males are not often successful in attaining territories and most breeding is accomplished by males in their second year. Survival to a third year apparently is quite unlikely.

Many investigators, including Turner (1921), Karr (1963), Lotrich (1973), and Smart and Gee (1979), agree in general that chironomidae, tiny crustacea, and small insect larvae constitute the principal food of johnny darters. The last authors above found johnny darters to be daytime benthic feeders and to compete minimally with *Percina maculata* that occupied the same stream. Smith (1979) reports that johnny darters react to the smell, or perhaps taste, of skin extract from compatriots by remaining quiet. He concluded that this was an alarm reaction, as previously demonstrated in minnows. A large number of parasites variously reported in the johnny darter have been summarized by Hoffman (1967).

Aside from their broad environmental tolerances, the ability to sequester eggs beneath stones probably contributes to the success of johnny darters, particularly where murky water predominates. Local and regional disappearance of the species may be associated with siltation in many cases rather than with the presence of toxic substances.

Abundance. The johnny darter remains a common and widespread species in spite of local setbacks and the loss of distribution on the western margins of its range. Only the subspecies *E. nigrum susanae* is threatened by the pervasive stripmining and attendant siltation within the upper Cumberland River basin.

Name. This little fish was among the first American species described by Rafinesque (1819), who like many observers since was impressed by the black head and darkened body of the nuptial male and accordingly offered the trivial name *nigrum*. *Eulepis* means well-scaled; *susanae* honors Susan B. Jordan.

Etheostoma olmstedi Storer   Plate 14
Tesselated Darter   Subgenus *Boleosoma*

Description. The second largest member of the subgenus, reaching a maximum size well over 70 mm SL but usually less than 65 mm SL. Thin flexible anal spines, somewhat rounded snout, absence of frenum, almost complete lateral line, ab-

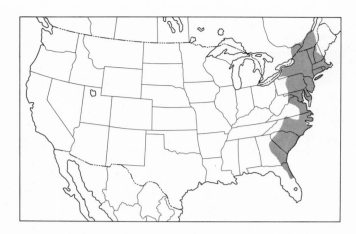

Distribution of *Etheostoma olmstedi*

sence of breeding tubercles, and flat bilobed genital papilla in females place it in the subgenus *Boleosoma*. It lacks body coloration and has fewer lateral line scales than *E. perlongum*. It is quite similar to *E. nigrum* but has a less rounded snout, complete supratemporal and infraorbital canals, usually 1 or 2 more lateral blotches, and 2 anal spines except for 1 subspecies. Gill membranes are narrowly joined.

Six dorsal saddles are not very dark and are separated by weakly stippled paler zones. Side bears 9-11 dark blotches, often in the shape of letters X, V, or W. Upper side is weakly and irregularly spotted, while lower side and belly bear little or no pigmentation. A faint basicaudal spot is often present.

Moderately developed preorbital bar extends downward and forward, failing to meet counterpart on lip. Suborbital bar is of variable length and intensity and usually directed slightly posteriorly. Chin, throat, and breast are virtually devoid of pigment.

Membranes of first dorsal fin are clear but spines are alternately dark (usually brown) and pale. Soft dorsal fin is similarly marked, its banding much more obvious than that of spiny dorsal. Caudal rays are darkened to produce several wavy vertical bands. Other fins are virtually clear.

Scalation is extremely variable. Nape usually is naked; cheek usually is naked or has a few scales. Opercle is scaled; breast usually is naked. Belly is quite variable, ranging from naked to fully scaled. Lateral line is complete and contains 34-64 scales, but most collections display less than half this variability. Fin counts are: dorsal VIII-X, 11-14 (10-16); anal I (regionally II), 7-9 (5-10); pectoral 12-13. Vertebrae number 37-39.

Although pattern darkens considerably in breeding males, and dorsal, anal, and pelvic fins develop much black, body does not blacken to the extent seen in *E. nigrum*. Male genital papilla is short, conical, and slightly bilobed terminally. A darkening of body pattern is the principal change in breeding females. Genital papilla is a bilobed flap. The poorly marked juveniles are easily confused with other *Boleosoma*.

Distribution. From scattered populations along the St. Lawrence River in Quebec, the tesselated darter extends southward into New York, including the Lake Ontario shore. It occurs rarely in Vermont and New Hampshire but becomes common in southern New England. From Chesapeake Bay to the Santee basin it is far more abundant below the Fall Line than above. It then continues coastally to the St. Johns basin in northern Florida. Though its range is narrow, the tesselated darter displays one of the greatest north-south distributions found among the darters.

Cole (1967) presents morphological evidence for the recognition of 4 subspecies, 2 existing in relative geographic isolation and 2 in relative ecological isolation from one another. From the Cape Fear basin in North Carolina southward the only form is *E.o. maculaticeps,* which is easily identified by having the belly devoid or nearly devoid of scales and by consistently having 2 anal spines. In the upper Rappahannock basin of Virginia a dwarf form, *E.o. vexillare,* exists to the apparent exclusion of others. It never reaches 50 mm SL, has only 34-42 lateral line scales, lacks scales on cheek, nape, and breast, and usually has reduced numbers of dorsal, pectoral, and anal rays. *E.o. atromaculatum* occurs in the lower Rappahannock and in some but not all sluggish coastal streams from Albemarle Sound to the Hudson River. It is most common in the lower Hudson and Delaware rivers and in the lower reaches of streams entering Delaware Bay, even in slightly brackish water. Cheek, nape, belly, and breast are usually fully scaled, and mean counts for lateral line scales, dorsal rays, pectoral rays, and anal rays are higher than those for the other forms. The nominate form, *E.o. olmstedi,* occurs from the New River in North Carolina to the upper Connecticut River valley. It is virtually absent from the Chesapeake Bay area, and southern populations are generally coastal. From upstate New York and into Canada tesselated darters seem to be intergrades between *E.o. olmstedi* and *E.o. atromaculatum.* The typical *E.o. olmstedi* has a naked or weakly scaled nape and breast.

Zorach (1971) tends to discount the idea that *E.o. olmstedi* and *E.o. atromaculatum* are genetically distinct subspecies, citing the peculiar and discontinuous range of the latter. Scott and Crossman (1973) note the polymorphism of all johnny darters and continue to consider all Canadian specimens *E. nigrum* until a firm genetic basis is demonstrated for recognizing *E. olmstedi* and its subspecies. Obviously, the systematics of the johnny and tesselated darters is not a completely settled matter.

Natural History. *Etheostoma olmstedi* probably exploits a greater variety of environments than any other darter. It thrives from cold Canadian streams to the tepid waters of northern Florida and from poorly mineralized streams to brackish parts of Chesapeake Bay. Bailey et al. (1954) took *E. fusiforme* in slightly brackish water but Cole's (1967) record of *E.o. atromaculatum* existing at 2.4 parts per thousand salinity is the most dramatic example of salt tolerance for a darter. This is not a species of swift currents; rather it occupies slow runs, pools, and backwaters, sometimes living among aquatic plants or debris over sand or silt bottom.

Raney and Lachner (1943) and Layzer and Reed (1978) studied aspects of the life history of tesselated darters and agreed closely in findings that show chironomidae to predominate as a food source. The latter authors report that trichop-

tera larvae become important locally in autumn. The 2 studies agree that tesselated darters of both sexes can spawn after 1 year, incur great losses in numbers during the second year, and can live into or through a third year. By the end of a second year of growth males are larger than females. Tsai (1972) reports that 93% of breeding females in his study population were hatched the year before. Older females produced more eggs, which partially offset their drastic decrease in numbers. Tsai reports adult males to be far less numerous than females.

Spawning behavior has been described by Hankinson (1932) and Atz (1940). Males defend small territories established and maintained during April and May around flat nesting stones. Females lay 1 to several eggs on the underside of the stone, which has been cleaned by the male. Spawning is accomplished upside down with the partners usually head to head beside one another. Fifty to several hundred eggs may be deposited by a female, and each male presumably spawns with several females.

Tsai (1968c) observed all species of fish present to be adversely affected by chlorinated sewage outfalls into the Patuxent River basin, but reports the tesselated darter to be among the more resistant species. Raney and Lachner (1942) report the tesselated darter to be an important food of young walleye in New York.

In lowland streams *E. olmstedi* may live adjacent to *E. vitreum* or several of the swamp darters. In upland streams it occurs with various upland darters; toward the limits of its northern range it may be the only darter present.

Abundance. Tesselated darters have been extirpated or much depleted in urbanized and industrialized areas of the East, yet remain among the most abundant of darters generally.

Name. This fish was named in honor of Charles Olmsted, a natural historian of the Connecticut valley. *Atromaculatum* means black spotted; *maculaticeps* means spotted head; *vexillare,* standard bearer, refers to the high fins.

Etheostoma perlongum (Hubbs & Raney) Plate 14
Waccamaw Darter Subgenus *Boleosoma*

Description. Consistently the largest *Boleosoma,* reaching 75 mm SL and often exceeding 60 mm SL. Thin flexible anal spines, somewhat rounded snout, absence of frenum, almost complete lateral line, absence of breeding tubercles, and flat bilobed genital papilla in females place it in the subgenus. It is unique in the combination of a high number of lateral line scales and a high number of dorsal saddles. The snout is more pointed than in other *Boleosoma;* though a frenum is absent, a flap overlying the upper lip is slightly attached at the midline. Gill membranes are slightly joined. Infraorbital and supratemporal canals are complete.

Six to 11 dorsal saddles fail to stand out boldly. Usually 9 oblong lateral blotches are present, seldom developing any resemblance to letters V, W, or X. Additional stippling is present from back to lower side, which along with belly is pale. A

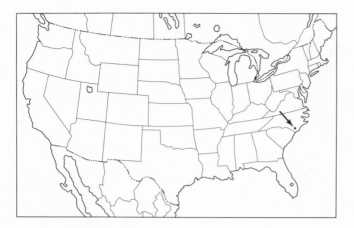

Distribution of *Etheostoma perlongum*

faint humeral spot is usually present; a basicaudal spot is fairly large and diffuse and might be counted as another lateral blotch.

Preorbital bar extends forward and slightly downward, not meeting counterpart on snout. Weak suborbital bar extends downward to angle of jaw. Breast and ventral surface of head are pale.

Spines of first dorsal fin are sparingly streaked with dark, while membranes are stippled along basal half and margin. Soft dorsal fin rays are alternately light and dark, and membranes are stippled to produce a banded effect. Darkened caudal fin rays produce several wavy vertical bands. Anal and pelvic fins are rather pale, stippled lightly in membranes. Pectoral fin shows some vertical banding from stippling in membranes.

Opercle and cheek are scaled. Nape may lack a few scales and belly may be partly naked on midline. Embedded or exposed scales appear on posterior half of breast. Lateral line is complete with 54-66 scales. Fin counts are: dorsal IX-XII, 13-15; anal II (rarely I), 8-9; pectoral 12-14. Vertebrae number 39-40.

Collette (1965) reports that dorsal, anal, and pelvic fins in males darken and that pelvic spine and rays develop fleshy terminal pads, though our specimens taken in March show no modifications. Lindquist, Shute, and Shute (1981) verify Collette's statements and present detailed information on the appearance of the genital papillae of both sexes (typical for the subgenus) and a comparison of the pelvic fin pads of males within members of *Boleosoma*.

Distribution. Restricted to Lake Waccamaw in the Coastal Plain of North Carolina.

Natural History. This is the only darter totally restricted to a lacustrine habitat. Lake Waccamaw is late Pleistocene in origin and contains at least 2 other endemic fishes, *Fundulus waccamensis* and *Menidia extensa,* both closely related to nearby species having extensive distributions. *Etheostoma perlongum* is similar to and probably derived from the stock of *E. olmstedi. E. fusiforme* occurs locally in Lake Waccamaw but is not an associate of *E. perlongum.*

We caught specimens over clean sand in less than 1m of water in late March. They usually were near old tree stumps and embedded pieces of wood. Lindquist, Shute, and Shute (1981) report that males precede females from deep water to shallow areas in spring; nesting occurs in April, May, and early June. Males excavate nests beneath sticks and similar debris, guard the nest, engage in complex courtship rituals with females, and spawn with them in upside-down positions, head to head, or more rarely head to tail. These authors suggest that males may use pelvic fins to prepare and clean nests. Females lay about a third of their initial egg complement (150 eggs) in each mating event but may produce a second batch of eggs. Predation on eggs by the tiny catfish *Noturus gyrinus* is possible.

Abundance. Deacon et al. (1979) list *E. perlongum* as threatened, probably because of gradually induced changes to its sole habitat. Its well-being undeniably is linked to continuing control of development of the Lake Waccamaw shoreline.

Name. *Perlongum* alludes to the considerable length of this darter compared with other species of *Boleosoma.*

Etheostoma podostemone Jordan & Jenkins Plate 14
Riverweed Darter   Subgenus *Boleosoma*

Description. A moderate sized robust *Boleosoma* reaching 65 mm SL but seldom exceeding 60 mm SL. A somewhat rounded snout, absence of frenum, thin flexible anal spines, nearly complete lateral line, lack of breeding tubercles, and bilobed genital papilla of females mark this as a *Boleosoma*. It differs from most of its congeners in having some breeding coloration, and from *E. longimanum* in the presence of a distinct suborbital bar rather than a spot. Gill membranes are moderately connected. Supratemporal and infraorbital canals are complete but the latter may be difficult to see.

Dorsum bears 6 dark broad saddles, the first being smallest but often the most intense. Areas between saddles may appear as wedge-shaped pale spots. First 3 or 4 of about 8 lateral blotches are poorly defined, while remainder may resemble letters V, W, or X. Wedge-shaped dark spots tend to form horizontal bands on upper side, in some cases continuing below midline on posterior third of body. Belly is without such markings. Basicaudal spot is of variable intensity, sometimes vertically elongated or divided in 2. Often a humeral spot is present. One or more dark markings may be present anterior and posterior to pectoral fin base.

Preorbital bar almost meets counterpart on snout. Suborbital bar is distinct and is curved anteriorly. Cheek is pale, sometimes creamy. Chin and throat may be stippled; breast is clear.

Membranes of spiny dorsal fin are darkened at margin, middle, and base to produce faint horizontal bands; spines lack appreciable pigmentation. Three to 5 faint bands are produced in soft dorsal fin by darkening of membranes and adjacent parts of rays. Caudal fin membranes are darkened to

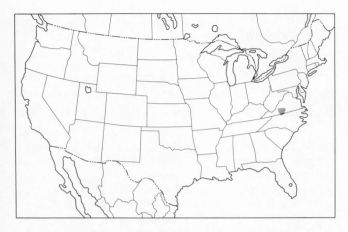

Distribution of *Etheostoma podostemone*

form several wavy vertical bands. Anal and pelvic fins lack much pigmentation; anal spines are particularly short and weak. Darkening in pectoral rays causes vertical banding, best developed basally.

Opercle is scaled but cheek, nape, and breast are naked. Belly is naked anteriorly. Lateral line is typically complete with 36-41 scales. Fin counts usually are: dorsal IX-X, 12-13; anal II, 6-7; pectoral 12-13. Vertebrae number 36-37 (35-38).

Breeding males develop some body and fin coloration as shown in color plate. Fins, particularly soft dorsal, are somewhat elongated. Genital papilla is a short conical tube. Breeding females become somewhat darker and pattern intensifies, but colors do not develop and fins are not much elongated. Genital papilla is short and terminally lobed.

Distribution. Endemic to the Roanoke River system and often abundant in clear headwater streams, especially where water plants grow adjacent to riffles. It is less common in Piedmont tributaries and is probably absent below the Fall Line.

Natural History. We collected riverweed darters in mid-May from the South Fork of the Roanoke River. They were fairly common in riffles 5-10 cm deep over clean gravel and rubble. Gravid females were quite evident but colorful males were rare; we assume that their breeding period was ending. *Etheostoma podostemone* were about equal in numbers to *E. flabellare* and more common than *Percina roanoka* or *P. rex*.

Riverweed darters were also caught in the upper Blackwater River over predominantly sandy and gravelly riffles with only moderate current. *E. vitreum, E. olmstedi,* and *Percina roanoka* occurred in the same area. During summer they may congregate among submerged aquatic plants. We were strongly reminded of *Ulocentra* darters on first capturing this robust, blunt snouted, and rather colorful species.

Breeding behavior probably resembles that of *E. nigrum*. Life history, behavior, and population dynamics of this interesting endemic are in need of study.

Abundance. The riverweed darter is found in enough different streams to be safe from immediate threat, but its abundance should be monitored closely for change.

Name. The name is taken from that of the riverweed, *Podostemum,* with which this darter may be associated in clear streams with steady current.

Etheostoma vitreum (Cope)
Glassy Darter

Plate 14
Subgenus *Ioa*

Description. A moderate sized slender darter reaching about 55 mm SL. It is uniquely different from species in subgenera *Boleosoma, Doration,* and *Vaillantia* in that the anus is surrounded by villi, breeding tubercles are present in both sexes, and spawning is communal. It is further characterized by its slender body, maximum depth being one-seventh of SL, and by an elongated snout. A frenum is lacking; gill membranes are separate or but slightly connected; supratemporal and infraorbital canals are not interrupted. Eyes are closely set high on the head.

Dorsum is stippled, tending to form 7-8 faint blotches. Upper side is stippled, spots sometimes aligning in 1 or more short horizontal stripes. Midlateral markings consist of 7-9 interrupted stripes or thin blotches. Ventral surface of body is unpigmented. Individuals are partially transparent in life but turn opaque in preservatives. Head bears a few blotches; a postorbital stripe is consistently developed.

Spines of first dorsal fin are somewhat darkened marginally but remainder of fin is virtually clear. Similarly, rays of soft dorsal are lightly edged and fin is otherwise clear. Caudal fin may appear faintly vertically banded or simply be somewhat darker at base and tip than in intervening space. Anal, pelvic, and pectoral fins are clear or faintly patterned like dorsal fins.

Cheek and opercle are heavily scaled. Breast is naked but prepectoral area sometimes has embedded scales. Anterior portion of nape is naked or has embedded scales. Midline of belly lacks several scale rows. Lateral line is complete or virtually so with 50-62 scales. Fin counts are: dorsal VII-IX, 11-14; anal II (sometimes I), 6-9; pectoral 12-14. Vertebrae number 37-39.

Breeding males and to a lesser extent breeding females become dusky, a condition not well shown in color plate. Pelvic spines and ventralmost 2 or 3 pectoral rays are expanded and fleshy, particularly in males. Breeding tubercles develop on outer surface of pectoral fin rays and inner surface of pelvic rays but not on body according to Jenkins (1971). Fleshy villi surrounding anus apparently are better developed in females than in males.

Distribution. Confined to Atlantic coastal drainages from the Patuxent in Maryland to the Neuse in North Carolina. It is common and widespread below the Fall Line and occurs in the Piedmont where sandy substrate prevails.

Natural History. The study of Winn and Picciolo (1960) presents a wealth of information on the ecology of glassy darters. The fish remain inactive and hidden in pools during the winter

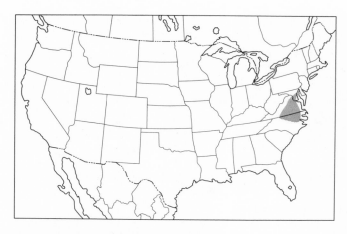

Distribution of *Etheostoma vitreum*

but begin to move upstream to breeding sites as water temperatures exceed 5°C. Spawning occurs in March and early April at water temperatures of 10-18°C and always at sites with a steady current. Egg deposition may occur upstream from rocks, beneath logs, or even on the face of concrete spillways. Aggressiveness among males is limited to nudging or butting, and suitable breeding grounds are often occupied by many males that refrain from combat as females enter 1 or 2 at a time. About 100 eggs are laid singly in a series of passes over the communal nest, and in each the female is accompanied by 1 or 2 males which align with her and keep in contact with her with their fins. An active breeding aggregation seems to attract more participants and a single nest may accumulate 30,000 to 50,000 eggs. Breeding aggregations have not been reported for other darters.

For the remainder of the growing season glassy darters live singly or in small groups. Feeding habits, life history, and other aspects of species ecology need elaboration. The glassy darter appears to be specialized for sandy streams which are periodically turbid and afford few of the conditions favored by most darters. In this regard the glassy darter has evolved parallel attributes to those of the sand darters, *Ammocrypta,* including the habit of burrowing in clear sand with only part of the head exposed as noted by Lee and Ashton (1979). These authors followed radioactively tagged glassy darters for 10 months. Individuals were nomadic and always sought out areas with clean sandy substrate, where they nested beneath the surface unless engaged in morning or evening foraging. Extreme cold or flooding caused glassy darters to burrow as deeply as 30 mm. *Etheostoma olmstedi* often is found in areas which support glassy darters but does not exploit the same microhabitat.

Abundance. The glassy darter seems to be in no danger of extirpation, but it should be noted that females produce few eggs, breeding sites are not numerous, and the range is small. Thus local populations might be subject to rapid extermination.

Name. The epithet *vitreum* obviously refers to the clear or vitreous appearance of living specimens. Preservation of the species in formaldehyde causes the flesh to whiten much as egg albumen does on heating.

Etheostoma chlorosomum (Hay) Plate 14
Bluntnose Darter Subgenus *Vaillantia*

Description. A moderate sized darter of delicate appearance, probably never larger than 50 mm SL. It closely resembles members of subgenus *Boleosoma* but differs from them primarily in having an incomplete lateral line ending beneath the spiny or soft dorsal fin. It differs from *Etheostoma davisoni* in having breeding tubercles and perhaps in other minor regards. The snout is quite short, gill membranes are separate, infraorbital canal is widely interrupted, and the supratemporal canal is narrowly interrupted or further reduced to disjunct segments.

There are 6 or 7 faint dorsal markings but only 5 usually appear to be true saddles. Side bears 8-10 diffuse blotches, the last few occasionally resembling letters V, W, or X. Small blotches on upper side may be randomly scattered or may tend to be arranged in short wavy horizontal lines. Belly and lower flank lack markings. A weak humeral spot and a dark basicaudal spot are usually present. Preorbital bar fuses with counterpart to form a semicircular band around snout. Pale cheek is usually stippled to produce a weak suborbital bar and postorbital blotch. There is a diffuse dark spot on opercle. Ventral portions of head and breast lack markings.

Membranes of spiny dorsal fin may be clear or lightly stippled along margin; median and basal bands may be weakly developed. Dorsal spines are alternately light and dark, usually producing 3 weak horizontal bands. Soft dorsal fin has a short base and is separated by a distinct gap from spiny dorsal; membranes are lightly stippled, and rays are darkened to produce 3 or 4 weak diagonal bands. Three or 4 rather faint vertical bands are produced by local darkening of caudal rays. Small anal, pelvic, and pectoral fins are pale and without markings.

Cheek, opercle, and prepectoral area are well scaled. Nape is naked anteriorly and bears normal or embedded scales posteriorly. Breast is well scaled posteriorly and may bear embedded scales anteriorly. Belly is completely scaled. Usually only half of the 50-60 scales of lateral series are pored, but as many as 36 scales may have pores. Fin counts are: dorsal VIII-IX, 9-11; anal I (rarely II), 7-8; pectoral 13. Vertebrae number 38-40.

Males may darken more than is shown in color plate. Spiny dorsal fin membranes in particular become darker. In some males breeding tubercles occur on ventral surfaces of pelvic rays and first few anal rays. Tips of pelvic spine and first few rays are fleshy. Genital papilla is short and conical. Breeding females are not much darkened. Genital papilla is a swollen pad with a rugose margin. Young of *E. chlorosomum* are not well marked and are easily confused with those of *E. nigrum, E. stigmaeum,* and perhaps other darters.

Distribution. Occurs in streams adjacent to the Mississippi River from extreme southern Minnesota to the Gulf Coast.

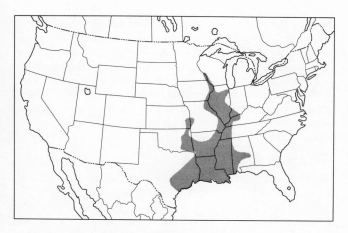

Distribution of *Etheostoma chlorosomum*

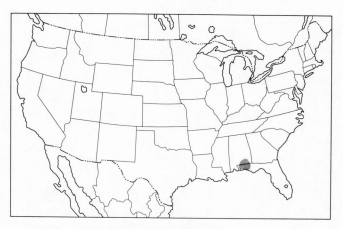

Distribution of *Etheostoma davisoni*

Below the Fall Line it extends eastward, except in the Escatawpa (Beckham, 1977), to streams in the Mobile basin of Alabama and westward to the Guadalupe River in Texas. Arkansas River basin populations in Kansas, Missouri, and Oklahoma are rather isolated from the rest.

Natural History. The bluntnose darter typically inhabits sluggish streams of low gradient and shows little aversion to clay or organic substrates. Forbes and Richardson (1920) noted that this species occurred in oxbows and differed in habitat preference from *Etheostoma nigrum*.

Cross (1967) collected gravid females from Kansas streams in April, when they presumably start spawning. Smith (1979) suggests that May is the spawning month in Illinois. Clark Hubbs (personal communication) indicates that this species lays eggs on plants or debris.

Abundance. Although the bluntnose darter lives in many streams with mud substrate, its abundance has been locally diminished by man's activities. Forbes and Richardson (1920) knew it from many Illinois streams where it is now rare or absent. Pflieger (1971) found the species to be rare in northeastern Missouri apparently due to siltation or other effects of intensive agriculture. The future of isolated Arkansas basin populations is not secure. Nevertheless, the bluntnose darter is common in many parts of its range and is not a species of particular concern.

Name. *Chlorosomum* refers to a greenish yellow color which appears in subdued tones on many individuals.

Etheostoma davisoni Hay   Not illustrated
Choctawhatchee Darter   Subgenus *Vaillantia*

Description. A rather small and delicate darter probably not exceeding 50 mm SL. It differs from species in subgenus *Boleosoma* mainly in having an incomplete lateral line, ending beneath the soft dorsal fin. It is tenuously distinct from *E.*

chlorosomum in that males apparently lack breeding tubercles. Though this form has been raised from the synonymy of *E. stigmaeum,* it lacks breeding colors and many other traits of that species and certainly does not belong in subgenus *Doration.* Smith-Vaniz (1968) treats *E. davisoni* as a species, while Howell (in Lee et al., 1980) notes it placement in *Vaillantia.*

E. davisoni may differ from *E. chlorosomum* in additional ways but has not been carefully described.

Distribution. Restricted to Gulf Coast drainages from the Escambia to the Choctawhatchee rivers in Alabama and Florida.

Natural History. The species presumably is similar to *E. chlorosomum* but needs study to verify its ecology and life history.

Abundance. The Choctawhatchee darter seems to be common and widely distributed within its range.

Name. The species was named for one of its collectors, D.M. Davison.

Etheostoma acuticeps Bailey   Plate 14
Sharphead Darter   Subgenus *Nothonotus*

Description. A moderate sized, fairly robust darter reaching 68 mm SL. It has the compressed body, deep caudal peduncle, horizontal banding, closely set pelvic fins, complete lateral line, frenum, and absence of breeding tubercles which characterize subgenus *Nothonotus,* but differs from other members in havng an elongated and exceptionally pointed snout. Gill membranes are separate to slightly connected.

Side usually bears 11 or 12 narrow vertical bands, several of which may fuse dorsally with saddles. An additional broad terminal band encircles caudal peduncle. At caudal fin base is a large dark spot with very pale areas above and below. Horizontal dark stripes are most distinct on caudal peduncle but extend forward almost to origin of spiny dorsal fin. Lower

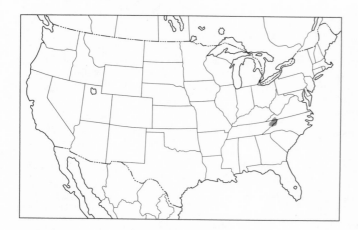

Distribution of *Etheostoma acuticeps*

side and belly are pale to dusky. There is usually a diffuse humeral spot.

Preorbital bar and suborbital bar are poorly developed. A narrow postorbital bar is better defined. Lower portion of head is clear to stippled.

Membranes of spiny dorsal fin are dark basally, becoming clear toward margin, which may be narrowly edged with black in males. The first 2 membranes are darkened enough to produce an obvious spot at fin base. Darkening in soft dorsal fin is confined to basal half of membranes. Basal half of caudal fin is darkest, pigment being deposited in narrow horizontal stripes. Anal, pelvic, and pectoral fins are virtually clear.

Cheek, opercle, nape, and breast are unscaled. Lateral line consists of 55-65 scales. Fin counts are: dorsal XI-XIII, 11-13; anal II (I-II), 7-9; pectoral 12-14. Vertebrae number 38-39.

Breeding males are not gaudily pigmented, though they may become brighter blue than specimen shown in color plate. It seems unlikely that females develop appreciable coloration. We presume that genital papilla of both sexes resembles that of other *Nothonotus*.

Distribution. Before the rediscovery of the sharphead darter, the species was known only from 37 preserved specimens taken originally from the South Fork of the Holston River in Virginia and Tennessee and from the North Toe River in North Carolina. Subsequently the Toe River received great amounts of silt from mining and the Holston River type locality cited by Bailey (1959) was inundated by a large reservoir. Many attempts to capture the species failed and a general belief emerged among ichthyologists that the species was extinct. Jenkins and Burkhead (1975) obtained specimens upstream from the type locality, however, and Bryant, Beets, and Ryon (1979) again report it from North Carolina in a tributary of the Nolichucky River.

Natural History. The sharphead darter inhabits strongly flowing water in riffles and chutes of medium sized to large upland rivers where substrate consists of coarse gravel, rubble, or boulders. Most specimens have been captured when low-water conditions prevail. By reexamining much of the preserved material, Jenkins and Burkhead determined some aspects of the

biology of the species to complement their field observations. Spawning probably does not occur until mid-June. Prespawning females contain many very small eggs plus some of intermediate size and about 100 larger yolky eggs. They probably lay the large eggs in a first spawning and perhaps a second batch later if favorable conditions persist. The smallest eggs are probably a year removed from maturity. Examination of scale annuli indicates that some individuals reach 3 years of age but none 4. The largest 3-year-old specimens are always males.

Stocking of sharphead darters in additional sites seems to be out of the question due to the small numbers available. As matters stand now, a single pollution event could wipe out 1 of the 2 known populations, a most precarious situation. Robert Jenkins provided us with information about this species and furnished the color slide illustrated.

Abundance. This species fully deserves its rare and endangered status (Deacon et al., 1979), and chances for its survival remain quite uncertain. Former distribution of the sharphead darter must have been fairly extensive within the upper Tennessee River basin before impoundments destroyed so much big-river habitat.

Name. *Acuticeps* means sharp or pointed head.

Etheostoma aquali Williams & Etnier   Plate 15
Coppercheek Darter   Subgenus *Nothonotus*

Description. A moderate sized robust darter reaching 67 mm SL. It has the compressed body, deep caudal peduncle, horizontal banding, closely set pelvic fins, complete lateral line, and absence of breeding tubercles which typify subgenus *Nothonotus*. Gill membranes are separate. Most similar to those of *E. maculatum sanguifluum,* males have reddish marks on the cheek but lack a distinct suborbital bar. Females are easily confused with other *Nothonotus* that lack a suborbital bar.

Body lacks well defined vertical bands or lateral blotches, appearing instead to support numerous large spots, often nearly square, which overlie horizontal dark stripes. A large basicaudal spot may be broken into several discrete spots. Lower side and belly are dusky or bear tiny dark spots. Humeral bar is small but quite apparent.

Preorbital bar is poorly defined, suborbital bar is absent, and a postorbital spot or diagonal dash is present. One or 2 wavy reddish lines run diagonally across cheek in males, whereas cheek and opercle are speckled in females. Ventral head surface is dusky.

Males have a black spot at anterior base of spiny dorsal fin and considerable darkening near base of all subsequent membranes; fin becomes clear toward margin. Lacking an anterior spot, soft dorsal fin is otherwise similar to spiny dorsal. Caudal, anal, and pelvic fins are also dark basally. Pectoral fin is virtually clear. In females all fins appear speckled.

A small patch of scales, sometimes partly embedded, oc-

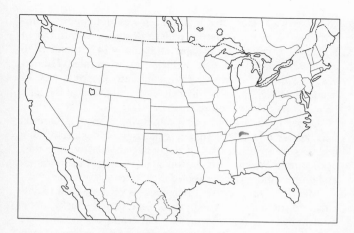

Distribution of *Etheostoma aquali*

curs on cheek. Opercle is well scaled. Nape, breast, and pre-pectoral area are naked. Belly is scaled or is naked just behind pelvic fins. Complete lateral line contains 57-62 scales. Fin counts are: dorsal XII-XIV, 11-14; anal II, 8-10; pectoral 13-14 (12-16). Vertebrae number 38-40.

Mature males are brightly colored, often more so than shown in color plate. Females do not develop bright colors. We do not know the appearance of genital papilla in either sex.

Distribution. Confined to the Duck and Buffalo rivers of the lower Tennessee basin in west central Tennessee.

Natural History. The coppercheek darter usually occurs in the riffles of large streams where flow is moderate to swift and depths range from 0.3 to 1 m. The bottom preference is for gravel and coarse stones. The species being newly described and poorly known, Williams and Etnier (1978) limit their discussion to its threatened status resulting from proposed construction of reservoirs on the Duck River. They note that *Nothonotus* darters generally have been much reduced in range by reservoirs and are not tolerant of tailwaters.

Abundance. The extremely restricted range of this darter has led to its inclusion on the list of threatened species by Deacon et al. (1979).

Name. *Aquali* is a shortening of the Cherokee word for cheek, "agaquali." We feel the full word would be more appropriate, though admittedly difficult to pronounce.

Etheostoma bellum Zorach   Plate 15
Orangefin Darter   Subgenus *Nothonotus*

Description. A moderate sized robust darter reaching 65 mm SL. It has the compressed body, deep caudal peduncle, horizontal banding, closely set pelvic fins, complete lateral line, and absence of breeding tubercles which typify subgenus *Nothonotus*. The snout is more rounded than in most of its

congeners. Gill membranes are separate to slightly joined. A dark uninterrupted suborbital bar distinguishes it from *E. camurum* and *E. rufilineatum*. It can be captured with and easily distinguished from the sharp-snouted *E. maculatum* and the miniature *E. tippecanoe*, which lacks pronounced horizontal body stripes.

There are usually 8 dorsal saddles, the last 4 appearing boldest. The first 4 of 8-9 midlateral blotches are sometimes indistinct but next 3-4 are prominent, often vertically elongated. Last blotch usually fuses with terminal dorsal saddle and almost meets its counterpart ventrally to nearly encircle caudal peduncle. Ventral body surface is virtually unpigmented. Up to 11-13 distinct horizontal lateral bands occur from beneath spiny dorsal fin to caudal fin base, decreasing to 8-9 on caudal peduncle. Large opaque zones lie above and below a large but rather diffuse basicaudal spot. Vertically elongated humeral spot is distinct.

Head markings include a spot above each eye and 1 or 2 spots on snout. Diffuse preorbital bar fails to join counterpart on lip. Suborbital bar is bold and long enough almost to meet counterpart ventrally. A sharp postorbital bar, horizontal opercular dash, and dusky ventral surface complete head pigmentation.

In males spiny dorsal fin is lightly stippled except for a dark basal band and narrow dark marginal band. In females this fin is less darkened except that marginal band is represented by a series of dark spots. Soft dorsal fin pigmentation is similar, but marginal band is wider in males and more intensely spotted in females. A vertical dark band marks end of caudal fin; a large dark area occupies center of fin. Anal fin may be pale but can be darkened basally or along margin. Pelvic fin is almost unpigmented and pectoral fin shows weak vertical banding, most evident in females.

Cheek is naked; opercle is scaled. Nape is naked anteriorly. Breast and prepectoral area are naked and belly is fully scaled. Lateral line is complete or nearly so with 51-60 (48-63) scales. Fin counts are: dorsal XII (X-XIII), 11-12 (10-13); anal II, 7-8 (6-9); pectoral 14 (13-15). Vertebrae number 37-38 (36-39).

Breeding males are brightly colored as shown in color plate. Both body and fins retain at least a little coloration throughout the year. Genital papilla is small and subtriangular, sometimes divided into 3 lobes. Breeding females usually develop dull orange in dorsal fins, which also bear numerous dark spots, in contrast to males. Female genital papilla is a large round fleshy pad.

Variations between upper Green River and Barren River populations are too slight to warrant racial recognition.

Distribution. Endemic to the Green and Barren rivers in Kentucky and Tennessee upstream from their confluence. One cannot yet preclude its presence in a few tributaries immediately downstream from its presently established range. It is identified as *E. camurum* or perhaps *E. rufilineatum* in older keys. Neither of these species occurs in the Green River system.

Natural History. The orangefin darter is locally quite abundant in small to medium sized clear streams over gravel sub-

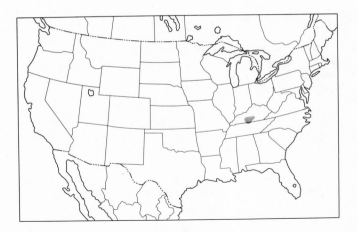

Distribution of *Etheostoma bellum*

strate. It is confined to riffle margins in the Green and Barren rivers proper. Among the *Nothonotus* darters only *E. rufilineatum* so readily enters and thrives in creeks. We have captured the orangefin with virtually all other darters of the upper Green and Barren rivers.

Having caught this species before becoming familiar with *E. camurum*, we made the characteristic misidentification. Zorach (1968) described this distinctive form to end such confusion. Though it is readily collected in numbers, its ecology remains unstudied.

Abundance. Widely distributed within streams of the Green River basin and locally abundant, *E. bellum* is in no way threatened. But construction of 2 major reservoirs and extensive channel modification of headwater streams have undoubtedly eliminated or reduced populations locally.

Name. *Bellum* was chosen to call attention to the beautiful fins of this darter.

Etheostoma camurum (Cope)   Plate 15
Bluebreast Darter   Subgenus *Nothonotus*

Description. A robust, rather large member of the subgenus occasionally reaching 60 mm SL and rarely almost 80 mm SL. It has the compressed body, deep caudal peduncle, horizontal banding, closely set pelvic fins, complete lateral line, frenum, and absence of breeding tubercles which characterize subgenus *Nothonotus*. The snout is wide and rounded, lips are heavy, and frenum is wide. Gill membranes are separate to slightly connected. It is most similar to *Etheostoma bellum* and *E. chlorobranchium*. Males of the former lack the crimson body spots of *E. camurum*, and *E. chlorobranchium* males have small, rather obscure red spots. When captured together, *E. camurum* is quickly distinguished from *E. maculatum* by its much broader snout.

Eight or 9 small dorsal saddles lack intensity. Nine (8-11) lateral blotches appear as squarish spots in juveniles but be-

come vertically elongated in adult females and appear as distinct bands in most mature males. Posterior two-thirds of body has horizontal dark stripes, maximally 14 but reduced to about 9 on caudal peduncle. Belly is clear to stippled. Humeral spot is distinct. A rather diffuse midlateral spot at base of caudal peduncle may be divided and is flanked above and below by pale cream-colored areas.

Upper head is dark, partly obscuring a short preorbital bar. Suborbital bar is diffuse in females and little developed in males. A postorbital and an opercular spot are visible even against dark background. Lower lip, throat, gill membranes, and prepectoral area are stippled most intensely in males.

Margin of spiny dorsal fin in males is variably clear to narrowly edged in black; remainder of fin is usually dusky, darkest near base. A spot is formed by blackening at base of first 2 or 3 membranes. In females spiny dorsal fin is darkened marginally and basally; remainder of fin usually has a number of small dark blotches. Soft dorsal fin in males is dusky except for a narrow submarginal strip. In females this fin is darkened primarily toward base. Caudal fin is dusky, more so in males, except for a narrow clear margin. Anal fin in males is dusky with a submarginal clear area; this pattern is obscure in less dusky anal fin in females. Pelvic fin in males is dusky except near tip but is virtually clear in females. In both sexes rays of pectoral fin are darkened and membranes are clear.

Cheek, breast, prepectoral area, and nape are naked. Opercular scales are confined to a central patch and are often embedded. Lateral line consists of 47-70 scales. In the Tennessee and Cumberland basins the number is 55-62 (52-70), elsewhere 50-60 (47-64). Typically as much as one third of caudal fin may be covered with tiny scales. Fin counts are: dorsal XI-XII (IX-XV), 11-13 (10-14); anal II, 7-8 (6-9); pectoral 14 (13-15). Vertebrae number 37-39 (36-40).

Breeding males are colorful and have well developed red spots on body as shown in color plate. These colors are at least partially developed during much of the year. Breast coloration is variably dark blue to bluish green. Male genital papilla is short, subtriangular, and grooved. Females may develop a few brownish body spots, never red ones. Female genital papilla is an elevated oval pad, sometimes grooved.

Distribution. Has been widely captured in the Ohio River basin. Records, often from the last century, exist for most of the major northern tributaries from the Allegheny drainages of northwestern Pennsylvania to tributaries of the Wabash River in Illinois. The species persists locally in Pennsylvania, Ohio, and Illinois but has not been reported from Indiana for many years. Bluebreast darters occur in some southern tributaries of the Ohio from the Monongahela basin in West Virginia to the Tennessee basin in Virginia, Tennessee, and North Carolina. The Big Sandy, Licking, and Salt rivers apparently do not harbor the species. Old reports of the bluebreast darter in the Green River are misidentifications of *Etheostoma bellum*, which replaces and perhaps excludes *E. camurum*.

Natural History. The bluebreast darter almost always lives in medium sized to large rivers in moderately swift riffles with substrate of coarse gravel, rubble, or even boulders. Turbid streams with riffles partially impacted with silt and sand are

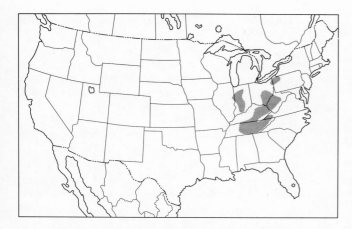

Distribution of *Etheostoma camurum*

Abundance. The bluebreast darter is regionally abundant only in the Allegheny system of northwest Pennsylvania, the middle Cumberland basin below the falls in Kentucky and part of Tennessee and the upper Tennessee basin including the Virginia headwaters. Other populations seem to be remnants of a once extensive range in the Ohio River basin. If the species is migratory, then the mainstream Ohio once served as an avenue of dispersal. We think it unlikely that all the remaining populations will be extirpated but see good reason for the bluebreast darter to be treated as rare and endangered regionally as in Illinois (P.W. Smith, 1979) and Ohio. In Ohio the bluebreast darter can be taken with relative assurance only in Big Darby Creek, which recently has been considered as an impoundment site for water supply to Columbus. The Vermilion River in Illinois retains what may be the last population in the Wabash basin.

Name. *Camurum* means blunt-headed, unfortunately a condition that exists in several darters of subgenus *Nothonotus*.

not likely to harbor this species. As reported by Trautman (1957), the bluebreast darter may be quite mobile, moving many kilometers upstream for spawning and downstream to larger rivers during lower water in summer or autumn. We have found the bluebreast darter to vary from rare to abundant when the same spot is visited over several years. Tagging will be required to determine the actual migratory capability of this darter.

Trautman has also documented the gradual disappearance of *E. camurum* from several rivers of Ohio starting in the latter part of the 19th century. Industrial wastes and domestic effluents have apparently done their share of damage, as has the increased siltation accompanying agricultural growth. Furthermore, navigation locks and low dams on major streams have rendered them unsuitable to the bluebreast darter and have impeded its movements, as well.

Mount (1959) described the reproductive behavior of bluebreast darters held in a circulating tank and observed their breeding activity in Big Darby Creek. Males tend to defend small, poorly defined territories in swift water around a stone and engage in fights which may include fin nipping. During April and May at temperatures of 10-23°C the female initiates breeding activity by swimming in short darts over the bottom of the tank, attracting a male from beneath his stone. After much swimming and chasing, the female burrows into gravel beneath or beside the nest stone. The male mounts and partially wraps around her while up to 100 eggs are laid and fertilized in a few seconds. The pattern is repeated once or twice at intervals of 3-5 minutes. Females may breed with more than 1 male. Eggs hatched in 7-10 days in the tank but young were not successfully reared. Under stream conditions reproductive activity reaches its peak in late May and early June and is completed by the end of June. Males are located around large rocks near the heads of riffles and are approached by females entering from the quieter water downstream.

Within *Nothonotus* the bluebreast darter often occurs with *E. maculatum* and less frequently with *E. tippecanoe, E. microlepidum,* and *E. rufilineatum.* It may also be captured with *E. blennioides, E. variatum, E. zonale,* and several species of *Percina*, depending on location.

Etheostoma chlorobranchium Zorach   Plate 15
Greenfin Darter   Subgenus *Nothonotus*

Description. A robust, rather large member of its subgenus occasionally exceeding 60 mm SL and maximally reaching 80 mm SL. It has the compressed body, deep caudal peduncle, horizontal banding, closely set pelvic fins, complete lateral line, frenum, and absence of breeding tubercles which characterize subgenus *Nothonotus*. The snout is short and rounded, lips are heavy, and the frenum is wide. Gill membranes are separate to slightly connected. It closely resembles *E. camurum,* especially in preservation, but breeding males have green in the dorsal fins instead of orange as in *E. camurum*.

Nine to 11 small dorsal saddles are often rather obscure; some tend to fuse with 10-12 vertically elongated lateral blotches. Posterior two-thirds of body bears maximally 12-15 dark horizontal stripes (reduced to about 9 on caudal peduncle). Belly is dusky, more so in males than in females. A diffuse basicaudal spot may be flanked by small spots above and below. Humeral spot is distinct.

A preorbital bar is absent to weakly developed. A suborbital bar and postorbital spot are moderately well developed in females, usually obscure in males. Ventral surface of head is dusky in males, lightly stippled in females.

In males spiny dorsal fin is darkly edged and rather dusky elsewhere except for a black spot in basal half of first 2 or 3 membranes. Spiny dorsal fin in females also is darkly edged but otherwise appears to have weak horizontal dark bands. Males have a marginal dark band and a submarginal clear zone in soft dorsal fin, the remainder being rather dusky. Soft dorsal fin in females is banded much like spiny dorsal. In both sexes caudal fin is darkly edged and has a submarginal clear zone; remainder of fin is dusky; median fin rays may be enough darkened to produce horizontal bands. Dark margin and clear submarginal zone are repeated in anal fin. Pelvic fin is dusky except near tip in males but is clear in females. Pec-

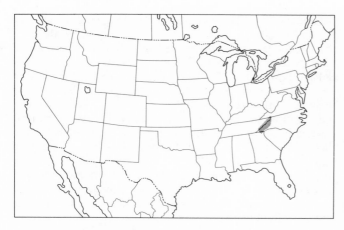

Distribution of *Etheostoma chlorobranchium*

toral fin rays may be darkened but not enough to produce a distinct pattern.

Cheek, nape, breast, and prepectoral area are scaleless. A small patch of partly embedded scales occurs on opercle. Lateral line consists of 52-72 scales; 56-64 is typical of specimens from the French Broad and Little Tennessee rivers, and 63-70 is typical of individuals from the Watauga and Nolichucky rivers. Small scales may extend over as much as basal third of caudal fin. Fin counts are: dorsal XI-XII (X-XIV), 12-13 (11-14); anal II, 7-10; pectoral 14 (13-15). Vertebrae number 38-40.

Breeding males are somewhat less colorful than in most species in *Nothonotus*. Genital papilla is small and triangular. Females lack bright coloration except for rusty brown in dorsal fin and a few reddish brown spots on side. Genital papilla is a rounded pad.

Distribution. Has been taken only from the Watauga-Nolichucky drainages of North Carolina and Tennessee and the French Broad and Little Tennessee drainages of North Carolina, Tennessee, and Georgia. It is associated with rivers which drain the higher mountains of that region.

Natural History. The greenfin darter inhabits clear fast riffles of moderate sized to large streams. It is usually captured over substrates of gravel and rubble at depths of 10-30 cm. Little is known of its behavior other than observations accompanying the species description. Zorach (1972) saw a bright green mature male follow 2 females beneath a rock, undisturbed by his presence. Discovery of another male beneath a stone led him to believe that the basic spawning behavior might be like that of *E. camurum*. Sympatric species of *Nothonotus* listed by Zorach are *E. acuticeps, E. maculatum,* and *E. rufilineatum. Percina aurantiaca* and *P. evides* inhabit strong riffles which may also be favored by the greenfin darter.

The only mature male we have caught came from the Pigeon River, where the swift water and rounded slippery rocks made collecting difficult. James W. Small, Kuehne, and John Kuehne had visited the spot a week earlier during a flood so powerful that stones could be heard grinding against one another. The survival of fish and other aquatic life in such streams is remarkable.

Abundance. Although its numbers probably are small, *E. chlorobranchium* lives in a region in which many watersheds are protected by federal and state governments. At present there is no reason to consider it endangered.

Name. *Chlorobranchium* calls attention to the green fins of mature males.

Etheostoma jordani (Gilbert)   Plate 15
Greenbreast Darter   Subgenus *Nothonotus*

Description. A moderate sized member of the subgenus reaching 66 mm SL but appearing more slender than most. Compressed body, deep caudal peduncle, closely set pelvic fins, complete lateral line, and absence of breeding tubercles characterize it as a member of *Nothonotus,* but it lacks the horizontal bands typical of all other members except *E. tippecanoe,* which has an incomplete lateral line. The frenum is broad. Gill membranes are slightly joined.

The first 2 of about 8 dorsal saddles are distinct; remainder are distinct in juveniles, becoming obscure in adults. The first 2 or 3 of 9-12 vertically elongated lateral blotches are small but distinct; remainder are usually fragmented into 2 or more spots, and side may appear checkered in adult females. Belly varies from pale to stippled. Median caudal area has 2 vertically arranged dark spots, and an additional spot may occur above or beneath these. Vertically elongated humeral bar lies entirely below lateral line.

Preorbital bar is distinct to diffuse, not meeting counterpart on snout. Suborbital bar is short, broad, often diffuse. There is a small, horizontally elongated postorbital bar. Ventral head surface is lightly stippled in females, more heavily stippled in males.

There is a narrow marginal to slightly submarginal dark band in spiny dorsal fin in males; dark pigment lies in a vertical band in each membrane, leaving a corresponding clear band. The first 2 or 3 membranes are blackened to produce a noticeable spot. Spiny dorsal fin in females lacks a distinct marginal band and is less richly pigmented. Soft dorsal fin in males has a dark marginal and a clear submarginal band; rays are stippled and membranes become darker toward base. Marginal and submarginal band are much less distinct in females; rays are stippled and membranes are spotted. In both sexes caudal fin has a narrow dark margin and a submarginal clear zone; basally fin rays only are darkened, continuously in males and intermittently to produce weak vertical banding in females. Anal spines and rays are clear; membranes are dusky toward base in females and almost to fin margin in males. Pelvic fin is pigmented much like anal fin, although there may be almost no pigmentation in females. Pectoral fin membranes are clear in both sexes; rays are darkened, most notably in males.

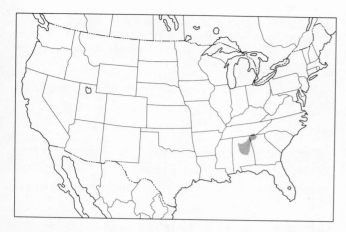

Distribution of *Etheostoma jordani*

Additional life history information on this species would be a welcome addition to the darter literature, particularly since this is an abundant species.

Abundance. Neither rare nor endangered, the greenside darter should nonetheless be watched closely because its only center of abundance is the upper Coosa basin.

Name. Named for David Starr Jordan, first president of Stanford University and probably the greatest ichthyologist of his day.

Etheostoma juliae Meek   Plate 15
Yoke Darter   Subgenus *Nothonotus*

Description. A rather large and very robust member of the subgenus reaching 74 mm SL. Compressed body, deep caudal peduncle, closely set pelvic fins, complete lateral line, and absence of breeding tubercles characterize it as a member of *Nothonotus*. It is unusual in that many individuals lack horizontal banding on the body, and is distinct in that gill membranes are moderately connected. A frenum is well developed.

A dark dorsal saddle crosses nape and extends to lateral line. Three small additional saddles are confined to back. In males there are 7-9 vertically elongated lateral blotches, the 3 most prominent usually being those which touch last 3 dorsal saddles. Body scales may be darkened to produce weak horizontal bands. In females lateral markings are small and more oval than those in males. Distinct horizontal bands are lacking. In both sexes humeral bar is continuous with first dorsal saddle. A green spot appears on humeral region, brightest in males, and humeral scales tend to overlie a fleshy distension of body. There are usually 2 small basicaudal spots. Belly is pale or lightly stippled.

Preorbital bar is short and contrasts poorly with darkened head. Suborbital bar is broad and usually distinct, sometimes dusky. Postorbital bar is variably developed, often extending diagonally upward. Lower cheek and opercle may have 1 or more dark spots in females. Ventral surface of head and breast is stippled.

In some individuals margin of spiny dorsal fin is clear and darkening is greatest through middle of fin, particularly at anterior end. Alternatively, stippling may become gradually more intense toward fin base. Soft dorsal fin rays are somewhat darkened and contrast with lightly stippled membranes. Caudal fin pigmentation is similar to that of soft dorsal. Anal fin membranes are lightly stippled; spines and rays are rather distended and opaque. Pelvic fin membranes are stippled in females and much darker in males; spine and rays are distended and opaque. Pectoral fin membranes are almost clear; rays are of normal thickness on dorsal half of fin but become progressively thicker and more opaque ventrally. This thickening of spines and rays is more pronounced in males than in females and is not apparent in juveniles.

Cheek, breast, and prepectoral area are unscaled. Nape is

Cheek, prepectoral area, and breast are naked. Opercle has a few exposed scales, a few embedded scales, or rarely is naked. Nape is naked anteriorly but supports some scales posteriorly. Belly often lacks scales immediately adjacent to pelvic fin insertions. Lateral line consists of 46-52 (43-56) scales. Fin counts are: dorsal X-XI (VII-XII), 11-12 (10-13); anal II, 7-8 (6-9); pectoral 12-14. Vertebrae number 36-37 (34-39).

As seen in color plate, breeding males become quite colorful. Male genital papilla is small and triangular. Breeding females may become yellowish but lack distinct colors. Genital papilla is a small wedge-shaped flap but is seen to become longer, tapered, and grooved in a spawning female. Zorach (1969) noted that lateral line scale counts are higher in the Black Warrior basin (46-56) than in the Tallapoosa basin (43-50). Black Warrior populations are characterized by no scales or few embedded scales on opercle, while greenbreast darters elsewhere have a distinct patch of opercular scales. These differences Zorach deemed not sufficient for taxonomic recognition.

Distribution. Inhabits the Black Warrior, Cahaba, Coosa, and Tallapoosa rivers of the Mobile basin in Alabama, Georgia, and Tennessee, normally above the Fall Line. The species' absence from the Tombigbee River, spotty occurrence in the Black Warrior, and relative abundance in the Coosa basin lend weight to the idea that ancestors of *E. jordani* gained access to the Mobile system via the Tennessee drainage.

Natural History. Almost nothing has been written on the ecology of the greenbreast darter. Like most other members of *Nothonotus* it inhabits riffles of clear streams, seeking moderately strong current and a gravel or rubble substrate. In the West Branch of the Sipsey River, a tributary of the Black Warrior, we caught greenbreast darters with *Percina nigrofasciata* and *Etheostoma stigmaeum*. In the Coosa basin we took it most frequently with *P. nigrofasciata* and *P. palmaris* but also with *E. rupestre* and *E. coosae*. One female taken on May 5, 1968, had the elongated genital papilla normally associated with spawning activity. Thus this species may reproduce a full month earlier than the *Nothonotus* of more northern rivers.

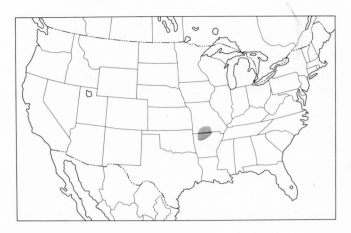

Distribution of *Etheostoma juliae*

scaled; opercle usually has a patch of partially embedded scales but occasionally is naked. Belly lacks a few scales immediately behind pelvic fins. Lateral line consists of 56-65 scales, the last often unpored. Several rows of small scales cover basal portion of caudal fin. Fin counts usually are: dorsal X-XI, 10-11; anal II, 6-8; pectoral 13-14. Bailey and Gosline (1955) report 35-36 vertebrae but Hill (1968) found a few specimens with as few as 29.

Breeding males are handsomely colored as seen in color plate. Genital papilla is small and triangular. Pelvic spine and rays and ventral pectoral rays are greatly thickened. Breeding females are less colorful than males but still showy. Head is darker, side is brown, and creamy white dots are common on caudal peduncle. Genital papilla is a round pad with deep radiating grooves.

Distribution. Restricted to the upper White River basin in Arkansas and Missouri, including principal tributaries downstream to the North and Buffalo rivers.

Natural History. The yoke darter is typically found in strong currents of medium sized to large clear streams over substrates of gravel and rubble, particularly where boulders break the river's surge. We have taken the fish under such conditions at depths of .5 m or more. *Etheostoma blennioides, E. caeruleum,* and *E. zonale* were present locally but never ventured into the turbulent world of the yoke darter. Hill (1968) took yoke darters from shallow riffles in some cases and resorted to electrofishing to obtain them from more turbulent rapids. He found ripe males already present in autumn but reported breeding in Arkansas to occur between April and early July. Pflieger (1975) reported breeding in Missouri during May over swift riffles. Both the above authors found yoke darters to be locally abundant and the only darter in turbulent waters. Additional life history data are needed.

Abundance. The yoke darter is locally abundant and not to be considered threatened within its rather limited range. But several dams on the White and North rivers have eliminated a great deal of former habitat. Our first encounter with large-scale pollution from animal wastes occurred while seeking the

yoke darter on Kings River and War Eagle Creek in northern Arkansas, both badly degraded by chicken wastes and possibly by chemicals used to control diseases in the enormous poultry rearing operations of the area.

Name. Named in honor of Julia Gilbert, wife of a prominent American ichthyologist.

Etheostoma maculatum Kirtland   Plate 16
Spotted Darter   Subgenus *Nothonotus*

Description. A rather long slender member of the subgenus, often exceeding 60 mm SL and reaching 70 mm SL. It has the compressed body, deep caudal peduncle, horizontal banding, closely set pelvic fins, complete lateral line, and absence of breeding tubercles which typify subgenus *Nothonotus*. Except for *Etheostoma acuticeps* it has the sharpest snout seen in the subgenus; when viewed from above the snout is extremely narrow, as well. The frenum is narrow. Gill membranes are separate to slightly joined. Subspecific differences are noted below as necessary.

Back is quite dusky; saddles are indistinct. In subspecies *maculatum* there may be a light stripe from snout to spiny dorsal fin. In males lateral blotches are indistinct and vary in number. At least posterior half of body has dark horizontal bands. Red spots with dark encircling rings are scattered over body; in preservation spots are pale. In some females there are up to 11 vertically elongated lateral blotches, but more typically small black spots form a checkered pattern on side. Horizontal bands may develop on posterior third of body, and in subspecies *sanguifluum* and *vulneratum* there are also a few poorly developed reddish brown spots. In both sexes lower side and belly are dusky. Narrow humeral bar is partly hidden behind pectoral fin.

Preorbital bar and postorbital spot are best developed in subspecies *maculatum*. Suborbital bar is weak to absent in this subspecies, weak in *sanguifluum,* and fairly distinct in *vulneratum*. Ventral head surface is dusky, more so in males than in females.

In males spiny dorsal fin has a clear margin and becomes consistently darker toward base; a dark spot at base of first 2 membranes is much less distinct in *maculatum* than in other 2 subspecies. In females fin is mottled below clear margin. In both sexes margin of soft dorsal fin is clear; remainder is dusky in males, spotted in females. Caudal fin also has a clear margin; in males it is characterized by a large dusky spot near base but in females it tends to appear vertically banded. In females remaining fins are clear to slightly dusky and are spotted. In males anal fin is dark basally and clear marginally, except for a dark marginal band in subspecies *vulneratum*. In all males pelvic fin spine and rays are clear and membranes dusky, particularly toward base. Pectoral fin rays are somewhat darkened and membranes are clear.

Cheek, breast, and prepectoral area are naked. Opercle is scaled, belly is scaled, and nape has scales at spiny dorsal fin origin. Lateral line is complete or lacks 1 or 2 pores at end.

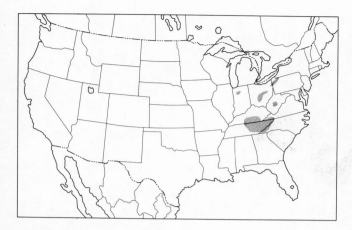

Distribution of *Etheostoma maculatum*

Small scales extend out as much as one-third the length of caudal fin. Lateral line counts usually are 56-65 in *maculatum,* 54-61 in *sanguifluum,* and 55-61 in *vulneratum.* Fin counts are: dorsal XII-XIII (X-XV), 11-13 (10-14); anal II, 8-9 in *maculatum* and *sanguifluum,* 7-8 (7-10) in *vulneratum;* pectoral 13-14 (12-15). Vertebrae number 37-39 in *maculatum,* 38-40 in *sanguifluum,* 39-41 in *vulneratum.*

As seen in color plate, males are handsomely colored but less brilliant than some members of *Nothonotus;* these colors tend to persist through much of the year. Genital papilla is subtriangular. Females may develop weak coloration on body and fins but are never bright. Genital papilla is an oval fleshy pad.

Distribution. Has been recorded widely in the Ohio River basin and has a range similar to that of *Etheostoma camurum* and *E. tippecanoe.* It is common at a few sites in tributaries of the Allegheny River in northwest Pennsylvania and was formerly recorded in the Mahoning River across the Ohio border. Other Ohio records are from the Muskingum and Scioto rivers but recent captures are limited to Big Darby and Deer creeks in the Scioto basin. The type locality record from the Tippecanoe River in northern Indiana has not been followed by new ones, and the spotted darter probably is now extinct in the entire Wabash system. Records from the Licking River in Kentucky and the lower Kanawha River in West Virginia have not been matched with recent collections. Spotted darters may still be taken in the Green River. All the above records are of subspecies *maculatum.* Subspecies *sanguifluum* is widely distributed through the middle Cumberland River basin below the falls. Subspecies *vulneratum* has been taken in the upper Tennessee River system in Virginia, Tennessee, and North Carolina. David Etnier (personal communication) has taken spotted darters from the Duck River, a lower Tennessee tributary; he assigns them to *vulneratum.*

Natural History. The spotted darter characteristically inhabits the strong riffles of large streams, where it is found over coarse gravel and rubble. *Etheostoma camurum* and *E. tippecanoe* are well known associates at some localities. Spotted darters have been captured with *E. rufilineatum, E. bellum,*

and the endangered *E. acuticeps.* They probably occur with *E. chlorobranchium* and *E. microlepidum,* as well. Associates among darters other than *Nothonotus* would probably encompass a majority of the Ohio basin species including several *Percina,* with which *E. maculatum* often shares habitat.

Raney and Lachner (1939) observed breeding activity of spotted darters in Pennsylvania and contributed additional life history information. Nests were beneath rocks near the heads of riffles, where current was steady but not excessively turbulent. Nests were located about 1 m apart, suggesting that territoriality is operative, and were exposed to current from upstream. The authors did not report fighting or aggressive displays between males, however. Spawning occurred during the entire month of June at water temperatures exceeding 17°C. In from 2 to 4 spawnings females normally laid the full complement of ovarian eggs, 288-352, although about a third became fungus covered and died. Eggs are large, about 2 mm in diameter, and were laid on the underside of stones in wedge-shaped masses several layers deep, reaching maximum dimensions of 2 cm by 3.5 cm. The spawning act was not observed. Spotted darters are 5-6 mm long at hatching and reach about 25 mm SL by the first autumn. Some cannibalism of young was observed. Normal diet for adults consisted almost entirely of insects. The authors projected a maximum lifespan of 4 years for both males and females. Adults were observed to winter in somewhat deeper and slower waters near the spawning riffle.

Winn (1958a) states that certain darters which nest beneath stones, such as *Etheostoma nigrum, E. flabellare,* and the spotted darter, produce few eggs each year but lay all of these. He found that these 3 species establish very small territories in aquariums and stated that more dispersed territories in nature might simply reflect scarcity of suitable nest rocks. Trautman (1957) stated that his observations on the spotted darter agreed generally with those of Raney and Lachner.

Abundance. The spotted darter is now absent from much of its former range and remains common at very few sites, fortunately at widely scattered ones that give hope for survival of all 3 subspecies. Continued existence of the species, however, presupposes the protection of the majority of streams in which it now flourishes. Otherwise the species may soon be worthy of rare and endangered status.

Name. *Maculatum* means spotted and refers to the conspicuous red spots on the body of males. *Sanguifluum* means "red one of the river," again in reference to the spots. An analogy between the red spots and droplets of blood is construed from *vulneratum,* meaning wounded.

Etheostoma microlepidum Raney & Zorach   Plate 16
Smallscale Darter   Subgenus *Nothonotus*

Description. A moderate sized and moderately robust member of the subgenus reaching about 60 mm SL. It is placed in *Nothonotus* because of the compressed body, deep caudal peduncle, horizontal banding, closely set pelvic fins, complete lateral line, and absence of breeding tubercles. Females are easily confused with those of several other *Nothonotus* species. Males differ from *Etheostoma aquali* in not having wavy copper colored lines on the cheek, from *E. maculatum* in having a less pointed snout, and from other *Nothonotus* in lacking a dark margin on the soft dorsal, caudal, and anal fins. The snout is pointed; frenum is broad. Gill membranes are slightly joined.

Eight or 9 small dorsal saddles vary from faint to distinct. Most of about 9 midlateral blotches are small and poorly defined; last 2 or 3 appear as vertical bands; only the terminal one is ever sharp. Dark horizontal bands lie along posterior third of body. On dorsal half they may continue somewhat anteriorly. In preservation scattered red spots on side in males appear as unpigmented spots. Side in females appears blotchy or checkered. In both sexes belly varies from pale to dusky. A humeral bar is strongest in females. In males a large dusky spot with creamy zones above and below lies partly on body midline and partly on caudal fin. In females this area usually supports 2 smaller, more distinct spots, and adjacent creamy areas may each have a small spot.

Diffuse preorbital bar fails to meet counterpart on lip. Suborbital bar is narrow and directed somewhat posteriorly. Postorbital spot is dull. Orbital bars are sharpest in females. Ventral head surface is virtually clear in females, stippled in males, particularly the breast.

In males a black basal spot occurs in first 2 or 3 membranes of spiny dorsal fin. Spines are weakly pigmented and membranes elsewhere are stippled basally and clear marginally. A thin marginal dark band may appear along last 2 membranes. Spiny dorsal fin is less darkly pigmented in females and may be spotted. In males soft dorsal fin has a narrow marginal dark band, a clear submarginal zone, and a dusky appearance to remainder. This fin is almost clear in females except for about 4 series of horizontally aligned black spots. In males a large central portion of caudal fin is dark; remainder is pale or creamy in appearance except for a narrow dark band on posterior margin. Caudal fin in females is clear and supports 4-5 vertical rows of black spots. In both sexes anal fin is similar to soft dorsal fin. Pelvic and pectoral fins in females are virtually clear but are spotted like soft dorsal fin. In males pelvic spine and rays are clear and membranes are dusky except toward tip. By contrast pectoral rays are finely stippled and membranes are clear.

Cheek is scaled; opercle, prepectoral area, breast, and nape are naked. Belly is scaled except for a few scales missing behind pelvic fin insertions. Lateral line consists of 58-68 (55-71) scales. Small scales continue onto caudal fin. Fin counts are: dorsal XII-XIV (XI-XV), 11-13; anal II, 8-9 (7-9); pectoral 13-14 (12-15). Vertebrae number 38-39 (38-40).

Breeding males are handsomely colored as shown in color plate. Breeding females may develop subdued colors such as reddish brown spots on side and a green humeral bar. We have not observed genital papilla of females but that of males is typically short and subtriangular.

Distribution. Has been taken only in the Cumberland River drainage from the Stones River in Tennessee downstream to

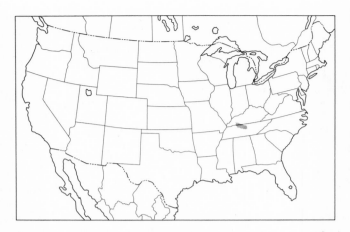

Distribution of *Etheostoma microlepidum*

the Little River in Kentucky. Raney and Zorach (1967) mention specimens from the Duck River (Tennessee drainage), but these are now referable to *Etheostoma aquali*.

Natural History. The smallscale darter occurs in medium sized to fairly large streams over strongly flowing riffles with gravel and rubble substrates. Typical depth of capture during normal discharge is about .5 m. Smallscale darters have been taken with 3 other *Nothonotus, Etheostoma camurum, E. rufilineatum,* and *E. tippecanoe,* and likely might be captured with *E. maculatum.*

The male we illustrate was taken in late April and already shows good coloration. Though most *Nothonotus* are presumed to be late spawners, a mature female taken in early April from East Fork, Stones River, had rather large yolky eggs and was beginning to show roundness of belly. Certainly this handsome fish of which we know so little deserves a life history study.

Abundance. We have only caught the smallscale darter on 2 occasions and feel that it is not an abundant species. The main channel of the Cumberland River is now unsuitable habitat due to impoundments. Given its restricted fragmented range it deserves close monitoring, although not at present listed as rare and endangered.

Name. *Microlepidum* means small scaled and aptly refers to the high mean value for lateral line scales, matched in *Nothonotus* only by *E. chlorobranchium.*

Etheostoma moorei Raney & Suttkus   Plate 16
Yellowcheek Darter   Subgenus *Nothonotus*

Description. A rather small but fairly robust member of the subgenus reaching 57 mm SL. It has the compressed body, deep caudal peduncle, horizontal banding, closely set pelvic fins, complete lateral line, and absence of breeding tubercles typical of subgenus *Nothonotus*. A combination of characteristics such as bold suborbital bar, virtual absence of red spots on side, and horizontal bands on posterior half of body serve to distinguish it from its congeners. The frenum is rather narrow. Gill membranes are slightly joined.

Eight or 9 dorsal saddles are variably developed, seldom any of them prominently. About 13 small lateral blotches have dark extensions forming vertical bands, the last producing a prominent caudal band. About 12 dark horizontal bands are confined to posterior half of body. Horizontal bands are weakly developed in females, and side has a somewhat checkered appearance. Belly is clear in females, somewhat dusky in males. Dark humeral bar is elongated. Caudal fin base is cream colored with a dark spot at both dorsal and ventral midlines. A large midcaudal spot, often partially subdivided, extends onto caudal fin and fades gradually.

Distinct preorbital bar does not meet counterpart on lip. Prominent suborbital bar slants backward across cheek, sometimes meeting counterpart at union of gill membranes, and has a short anterior extension. Narrow postorbital bar is best seen in females. Ventral surface of head and breast are pale in females, darker particularly on breast in males.

In males spiny dorsal fin is narrowly edged in black and has a broad submarginal pale zone; remainder of fin darkens steadily toward base and has a black spot in basal half of first 2 membranes. Spiny dorsal fin in females is clear and supports marginal, median, and basal dark bands. In males soft dorsal fin is similar to spiny dorsal except that blackening is virtually confined to middle portion of each membrane and there is no anterior basal spot. Soft dorsal in females is dusky at base and supports 2 or 3 rows of black spots in clear portion. Caudal fin in males is black at tip and clear or cream colored elsewhere except for darkening posterior to basicaudal spot. In females blackened and creamy portions are confined to base; posteriorly fin is clear with 2 or 3 vertical rows of black spots. Anal fin in males is dark basally and clear marginally except for a narrow black edge along posterior portion. Females have a few black spots in otherwise clear anal fin. Pelvic fin is dark basally and clear marginally in males; in females it may have a few dark spots. In males pectoral fin is clear on ventral half but darkly edged along dorsal rays. In females pectoral fin is spotted basally.

Cheek is naked or has 1 to several tiny scales behind eye. Opercle is scaled. Nape, breast, and prepectoral area are naked. Lateral line consists of 53-57 (51-60) scales. Scales of decreasing size extend outward about one-third the length of caudal fin. Fin counts are: dorsal XI (X-XII), 11-12 (9-12); anal II, 7-8 (6-8); pectoral 12-14. Vertebrae number 35-37.

Breeding males are brightly colored as shown in color plate. Colors tend to persist during all but the warmest months. Genital papilla is small and subtriangular. In females orange may develop slightly on dorsal fins and behind pectoral fin during breeding season. Genital papilla is more tubular than is typical for *Nothonotus*.

Distribution. Restricted to the principal upstream tributaries of the Little Red River in north-central Arkansas. Even this small range is fragmented by Greers Ferry Reservoir.

Natural History. The yellowcheek darter occurs in moderate numbers where riffles are deep and substrate is composed of

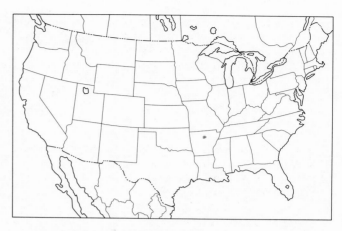

Distribution of *Etheostoma moorei*

clean gravel, rubble, or boulders. The aquatic plant *Podostemum* often grows in such clear riffles. Other darters captured in areas adjacent to *Etheostoma moorei* habitat are *E. blennioides, E. caeruleum, E. euzonum, E. zonale,* and *Percina nasuta.*

Little is known about the habits of yellowcheek darters, and their numbers are too small to invite investigation at this time. Buchanan (1974) notes that Greers Ferry Reservoir covers the early collecting sites of *E. moorei*. He believes that aquarium-reared young or perhaps adults might be introduced into unoccupied streams in the Little Red River basin to better assure survival of this darter.

Abundance. Deacon et al. (1979) list the yellowcheek darter as threatened. The immediate problem is an encroachment of resort developments on some good habitat.

Name. Named in honor of George A. Moore, teacher, past president of the American Society of Ichthyologists and Herpetologists, and a noted specialist on fishes of the mid-South.

Etheostoma rubrum Raney & Suttkus   Plate 16
Bayou Darter   Subgenus *Nothonotus*

Description. A small member of the subgenus reaching 46 mm SL but seldom exceeding 40 mm SL. The compressed body, deep caudal peduncle, horizontal banding, closely set pelvic fins, complete lateral line, and absence of breeding tubercles place it in subgenus *Nothonotus*. It is unique within the subgenus in having the anterior half to one-third of the belly naked, although less extensive scaleless patches exist in some other *Nothonotus*. The frenum is broad. Gill membranes are slightly to moderately joined.

Eight dorsal saddles are distinguished in some individuals but only the last is always prominent. Dark nape, split by a light transverse band, is counted as first 2 saddles. All but last 2 of 9-12 vertically elongated lateral blotches are poorly de-

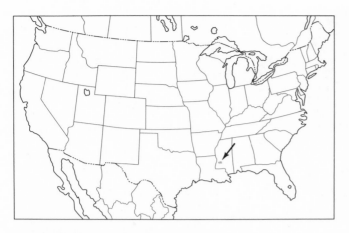

Distribution of *Etheostoma rubrum*

fined. Last dorsal saddle and last pair of lateral blotches encircle caudal peduncle. Well developed horizontal bands are found on posterior third of body in males; such bands are weak to absent in females, side having instead a checkered appearance. Vertically elongated humeral bar is not strongly developed. Cream colored base of caudal fin is virtually divided by a large median spot which extends onto caudal fin base. Median spot may in turn be subdivided, especially in females.

Preorbital bar fails to meet counterpart on lip, which itself is darkened to angle of jaw. Moderately distinct suborbital bar extends diagonally backward, almost meeting counterpart at junction of gill membranes; a short extension runs anteriorly beneath eye. A postorbital and an opercular dash vary from faint to distinct. Ventral head surface is lightly to moderately stippled, usually with darkest effects on midline posterior to lower lip. Breast is variably stippled.

In males spiny dorsal fin bears a quite narrow marginal dark band and a fairly wide submarginal clear zone. Basally membranes are dusky except for a rather narrow clear zone; basal half of first 2 membranes is black. In females marginal band usually is lacking on anterior half of spiny dorsal fin, and dusky areas are patchy; dark anterior spot is weak to absent. A narrow marginal band and clear submarginal zone also characterize soft dorsal fin in males, but dusky pigmentation in remainder of fin is heaviest in 2 horizontal bands. Dark fin margin is weak to absent in soft dorsal in females; remainder of fin appears clear with 3 or 4 rows of horizontally arranged black spots. In males caudal fin has a narrow marginal band and a clear submarginal zone followed by a broad dusky vertical band and darkening from basicaudal spot. Caudal fin is clear in females, with 3 or 4 vertical rows of black spots. A marginal dark band, submarginal clear zone, and dusky median band characterize anal fin in males; that in females is clear with 2 or 3 imperfectly arranged rows of black spots. In males pelvic spine and rays are clear and membranes are dusky except along margin; conversely, pectoral rays are dusky and membranes are clear. Pelvic and pectoral fins in females are spotted, with spots of pectoral fin vertically arranged.

Cheek has several exposed scales. Opercle is well scaled and opercular spine is often prominent. Breast, nape, and pre-pectoral area are naked. About anterior third of belly is naked. Lateral line consists of 50-53 (45-55) scales. Small scales cover basal portion of caudal fin. Fin counts are: dorsal X-XII, 11-12 (10-13); anal II, 7-8 (5-9); pectoral 13-14 (12-15). Vertebrae number 36-37 (35-38).

Breeding males are handsomely colored as shown in color plate. Genital papilla is short, subtriangular, and slightly grooved. Females may develop tinges of color on body and fins but no bright colors. Genital papilla is a short grooved tube, terminally rounded.

Distribution. Known only from Bayou Pierre in southwest Mississippi and from its principal tributaries. This is the southernmost distribution for a species of *Nothonotus*. The bayou darter is the only member of the subgenus to occur to any extent below the Fall Line.

Natural History. We captured the bayou darter at the type locality in a long riffle that crossed over poorly consolidated sandstone overlain locally by gravel, sand and scattered stones. The water was murky and free of aquatic plants. We caught this species sparingly over gravel at 10-20 cm depth, along with *Etheostoma zonale*. We also captured *E. histrio*, *Percina sciera*, and *P. ouachitae* in other parts of this riffle. The locality is rich in darters, Raney and Suttkus (1966) and Neil Douglas (personal communication) having listed there also *Ammocrypta asprella, A. beani, A. vivax, E. stigmaeum,* and *E. whipplei*. The status of the bayou darter virtually precludes extensive ecological study at this time. The size distribution of specimens led Raney and Suttkus to state that bayou darters probably spawn in their second year and live to be 3 years old.

The bayou darter is a *Nothonotus* living well outside the range and somewhat outside the environmental conditions associated with the subgenus. Displacement of some ancestral form down the Mississippi River, perhaps during a cool glacial epoch, is a plausible explanation for its occurrence in southern Mississippi. The upper and middle reaches of Bayou Pierre are not totally unlike most streams above the Fall Line because of the gently rolling uplands of that region. The bayou darter has speciated and persisted under these very localized conditions, adjusting to murky water and warm temperatures. That the species represents a tightly inbred stock is suggested by the small variation in meristic data presented in its description.

Abundance. There is no doubt that the bayou darter deserves its status as a threatened species (Deacon et al. 1979), particularly after considering the status report by Suttkus and Clemmer (1977) detailing recent and proposed changes in the Bayou Pierre drainage system. They confirm the steady disappearance of riverweed, *Podostemum,* and of rock or stable gravel riffles since the mid-1960s, as a consequence of gravel mining along the main channel, road grading, cutting of riparian timber, and institution of clean farming to the river bank in some places. Headwater flood and recreation dams, proposed by the Soil Conservation Service, could further modify flow and water quality as well as encourage more timber clearing for farming.

Name. *Rubrum* probably refers to the red on all median fins and touches of red on the paired fins instead of the rather unimpressive red spots on the body, but the original description does not specify.

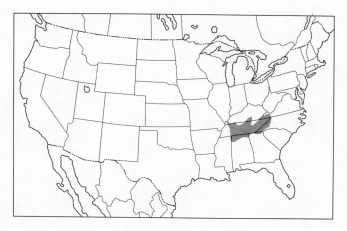

Distribution of *Etheostoma rufilineatum*

Etheostoma rufilineatum (Cope)
Redline Darter

Plate 17

Subgenus *Nothonotus*

Description. A rather large robust member of the subgenus reaching 75 mm SL. It is placed in *Nothonotus* because of the compressed body, deep caudal peduncle, horizontal banding, closely set pelvic fins, complete lateral line, and absence of breeding tubercles. Several dark spots or dashes on the cheek and opercle distinguish it from its congeners.

Back bears 8-10 squarish saddles, only the first 2 always distinct. Eight to 11 vertically elongated lateral blotches are usually broken into 2 or 3 segments; the last joins ventrally with its counterpart and dorsally with last saddle to form a circumcaudal band. This is followed by a pale creamy band that also encircles tail. Anterior three-fourths of body supports up to 14 dark horizontal bands, weak to virtually absent in females. Alternating patches of light and dark on side may be staggered to produce a checkered pattern. Belly is pale. A large humeral mark is partly hidden by pectoral fin.

Preorbital bar reaches lip but does not meet counterpart. Suborbital bar is represented by a spot beneath eye and another beneath and somewhat posterior to it. Postorbital spot is followed by 1 or 2 on opercle. An additional horizontal dash on cheek and 1 or 2 more on opercle contrast strongly with their cream colored background. Ventral head surface is lightly stippled in females and duskier in males.

In males margin of spiny dorsal fin is clear, or is narrowly edged in black along posterior third; remainder of fin appears dusky except for a black or merely dusky area at base of first 2 membranes. Fin margin is dark in females and has alternating clear zones and spotty or dusky bands; an anterior basal spot may be present in breeding females. Soft dorsal fin is narrowly edged with black in males and has a submarginal clear band underlain by a broad dusky zone; a few dark spots may be present. Beneath dark margin in females, fin is clear with numerous dark spots tending to lie in 2-3 bands. In males base of caudal fin supports a large dusky spot which dissipates into dusky pigment on membranes; a clear zone and dark vertical margin complete pattern. In females basal spot is smaller and remainder of caudal fin is clear with 3 or 4 vertical rows of dark spots. In both sexes pigmentation in anal fin resembles that of soft dorsal fin. Pelvic fin is usually clear in females and dusky near base in males. Dull spots in vertical rows characterize pectoral fin in females. In males pectoral fin is slightly dusky, sometimes faintly spotted, and may have a narrow dark margin.

Cheek, breast, and prepectoral area are naked. Nape is naked except just anterior to spiny dorsal fin. Opercle is scaled. Lateral line consists of 43-64 scales, usually 47-57 in the Tennessee River basin and 50-57 in the Cumberland River basin. Small scales continue outward a short distance onto caudal fin. Fin counts are: dorsal XI-XII (IX-XIII), 11-13 (9-14); anal II, 7-8 (6-9); pectoral 13-14 (12-15). Vertebrae number 36-40, usually 38-39 in the Tennessee River basin, 37-38 in the Cumberland River basin. In a detailed analysis of variation, Zorach (1970) concluded that differences were too slight to warrant recognition of subspecies.

Males reach brilliant coloration during breeding season as shown in color plate. Some coloration tends to persist throughout the year. Genital papilla is small and wedge shaped. Breeding females are not colorful but are distinctly patterned on body and fins. A little yellow or orange may appear in caudal, anal, pelvic, and pectoral fins. Genital papilla is a short, somewhat flattened, and slightly grooved tube.

Distribution. Is abundant through much of the Tennessee and Cumberland basins. In the latter it occurs from the junction of the Big South Fork in Kentucky downstream almost to the mouth. The redline darter is abundant throughout most of the Tennessee basin but absent in western tributaries of the lower Tennessee in that state. Clay (1975) reports it from Clarks River in Kentucky, the final tributary of the Tennessee River.

Natural History. The redline darter is easily the most abundant *Nothonotus* of the Cumberland and Tennessee basins, favoring large creeks and small to medium sized rivers. In its exploitation of rather small stream habitats it is matched only by *Etheostoma bellum* among *Nothonotus*. We have taken it over a variety of substrates including clean gravel, rubble, and exposed slabs with scattered rubble. In bigger streams with powerful currents redline darters typically are found in shallow gravelled margins of riffles. It has been collected with *Etheostoma acuticeps, E. aquali, E. chlorobranchium, E. maculatum vulneratum* and *E.m. sanguifluum, E. microlepidum,* and *E. tippecanoe,* and is anticipated to occur with *E. camurum.* Among darters other than *Nothonotus* it has been captured with the majority of species in the Cumberland and Tennessee basins.

A prime target for study, the redline darter has nonetheless not been the subject of a detailed life history. In terms of diet, behavior, and perhaps other aspects of its ecology, it may differ from the rest of its subgenus.

Abundance. Locally the most abundant darter, this species is in no danger of extirpation.

Name. *Rufilineatum* means red-lined.

Etheostoma tippecanoe Jordan & Evermann Plate 17
Tippecanoe Darter   Subgenus *Nothonotus*

Description. A moderately robust darter but the smallest member of its subgenus, reaching only 35 mm SL. It belongs in *Nothonotus* because of the compressed body, deep caudal peduncle, closely set pelvic fins, and absence of breeding tubercles. It lacks horizontal banding found in other *Nothonotus* except for *E. jordani,* and is subgenerically unique in having an incomplete lateral line. The frenum is broad. Gill membranes are separate to slightly joined.

Eight or 9 dorsal saddles are quite poorly developed except for first 2 and the last. Side is dusky with scattered dark spots. Lateral blotches are absent on anterior half of body and in females may be lacking entirely. In males posterior half of body supports 3-6 dark vertical bands plus a terminal band which is continuous with its counterpart, forming a circumcaudal ring. Just posterior to this ring there are dorsal and ventral pale oval spots. A distinct midcaudal spot may be present. A short humeral bar originates beneath lateral line.

Head is particularly dark between eyes. Distinct preorbital bar fails to meet counterpart on lip, which itself is often dark toward angle of jaw. Suborbital bar and postorbital spot are diffuse in males, more distinct in females. An additional spot on opercle or running diagonally upward at back of eye may be present. Ventral head surface and breast are clear to lightly stippled in females, dusky in males.

In males margin of spiny dorsal fin is clear or only lightly flecked with black; remainder of fin appears dusky except for a black spot at base of first 2-3 membranes. In females a narrow clear margin is underlain by stippled membranes, sometimes forming several faint horizontal bands. In males soft dorsal fin lacks a basal spot but otherwise is similar to spiny dorsal fin. In females soft dorsal fin also is similar to spiny dorsal fin except that clear marginal zone varies from narrow to absent. In males caudal fin may be clear along margin or narrowly edged in black and with a broader clear submarginal zone; most of remainder is dusky but a dark vertical band may develop just posterior to pale basal area. Caudal fin in females has dark spots in membranes arranged in a series of about 5 wavy vertical bands. Margins of anal and pelvic fins in males are clear and fins become steadily more dusky toward base; pectoral fin is virtually unpigmented. In females anal fin has dusky spots arranged in 2-3 poorly defined rows; pelvic and pectoral fins have a few dusky spots.

Cheek is naked or has several scales behind eye; opercle is scaled. Nape, prepectoral area, and breast are naked. Belly lacks scales just behind pelvic fin insertions and occasionally along midline. Lateral line is incomplete, pored scales ending about beneath soft dorsal fin origin. There are 45-52 (40-56) scales in lateral series, the last 13-27 lacking pores. Fin counts

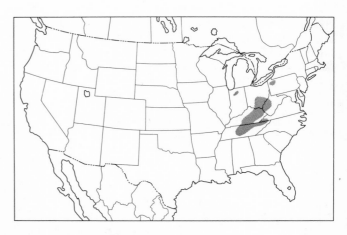

Distribution of *Etheostoma tippecanoe*

are: dorsal XI-XIII (X-XIV), 11-13 (10-13); anal II, 7-8 (7-10); pectoral 12-13 (11-14). Vertebrae number 35-37.

Breeding males are richly garbed in orange as shown in color plate. Having seen breeding specimens from a number of major river systems, we can state that the degree of body and fin coverage by orange pigments is quite variable. Male genital papilla is a thin short grooved tube. Breeding males have ventralmost pectoral rays bent downward and terminally expanded, and have distended pouches at base of spiny dorsal fin. Breeding females develop little yellow, remaining mostly brown to olivaceous. Genital papilla is short, flattened, and subtriangular.

Zorach (1969) noted that Tennessee River specimens may have cheek scales, lacking in other populations. This and other small differences he deemed unworthy of taxonomic recognition.

Distribution. Has been recorded quite sporadically over the Ohio River basin from the Allegheny River in Pennsylvania to the Wabash River in Indiana and then southward to the middle Cumberland basin, Duck River, and upper Tennessee rivers in Tennessee and Virginia. Old records exist for several river systems in which Tippecanoe darters no longer occur. Several populations remain in Pennsylvania. Distribution in Ohio may now be reduced to Big Darby and Deer creeks of the Scioto basin. Specimens from the Wabash River basin predate 1940. Strangely enough, discovery of the Tippecanoe darter in the Kentucky, Green, Cumberland, and Tennessee basins did not occur until after World War II. Coarse meshed seines normally used in strong rapids allow this tiny fish to escape.

Natural History. Typical habitat of the Tippecanoe darter is the riffle areas of rivers or large creeks adjacent to such rivers. Moderate current, clean gravel substrate, and depths of 10-50 cm are preferred. Trautman (1957) recorded vast fluctuations in numbers in Big Darby and Deer creeks. These Ohio populations are big in a year immediately following high survival of young from the previous autumn. Conversely, rarity immediately follows a summer with poor survival of offspring. These observations lead one to believe that the species is short-lived. Trautman also observed males to abandon their territories at turbidity levels that had not begun to deter other darter species. Thus Tippecanoe darters probably are abundant every few years and are easily missed during collecting in other years. The sudden appearance of populations some distance from previously known sites, as further reported by Trautman, suggests the possibility of extensive migrations.

In collections we made in the South Fork of the Kentucky River in mid-August 1972, males remained brightly colored but females were emaciated and reproductively spent. As with several other *Nothonotus* the Tippecanoe darter may spawn in late spring and early summer. Other species of the subgenus with which it does or might be expected to occur are *Etheostoma bellum, E. camurun, E. maculatum, E. microlepidum,* and *E. rufilineatum.* In the South Fork, Kentucky River, we observed it with *Percina caprodes, P. maculata, P. sciera, E. baileyi, E. blennioides, E. caeruleum, E. flabellare, E. variatum,* and *E. zonale.*

The Tippecanoe darter displays a number of neotenic traits, particularly dwarf size, reduction of belly scalation, incomplete infraorbital canal, and marked reduction of pored lateral line scales. Such modifications typically are associated with darters which exploit special habitats such as swamps, springs, and weedy lakes, but are unusual for a species which challenges the open river. Obviously much work could profitably be done to understand the behavior and ecology of this strange little fish.

Abundance. We feel that the Tippecanoe darter is probably threatened, though it is not so listed by Deacon et al. (1979). Persistence in so few places over such a large area is evidence that this darter has suffered enormous losses. Siltation and more dramatic forms of pollution have been most severe in major rivers where this species dwells. Trautman's findings were that the Tippecanoe darter in Ohio breeds at the head of riffles where unimpacted gravel and rubble exist.

Name. *Tippecanoe* is taken directly from the river of first capture of this species.

Etheostoma edwini (Hubbs & Cannon)   Plate 17
Brown Darter   Subgenus *Villora*

Description. A fairly slender darter, the smaller member of its subgenus, probably never exceeding 45 mm SL. It is weakly associated with *E. okaloosae* in subgenus *Villora* by possession of embedded scales on cheek and opercle, arched anterior end of the lateral line, broad frenum, uninterrupted sensory canals on the head, separate to narrowly connected gill membranes, some stippling on the body, and 3 basicaudal spots. The gill membranes are separate and often overlap anteriorly. The lateral line is well arched anteriorly. Page (1981) suggests that *Villora* should contain only *E. edwini.*

Some individuals, particularly females, only partially develop the 8-10 tiny dorsal saddles found in others. Eight to 12 small lateral blotches may be partly joined by numerous rows of small spots lying on upper two-thirds of body. Belly is pale

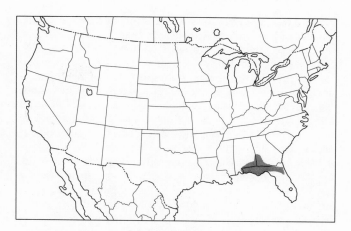

Distribution of *Etheostoma edwini*

and overlain with a few irregularly shaped spots. There may be a single basicaudal spot but usually there is also a smaller spot above and another below. Humeral bar is reduced to a dark spot.

Broad preorbital bar is partly fused with dark pigment on head and almost meets counterpart on snout. Postorbital bar is broad but rather diffuse. Suborbital bar is narrow, usually starting well below eye level. Lower half of head is pale and overlain by several small blotches. Usually there is a large spot on opercle and another in front of pectoral fin. Breast and ventral surface of head are lightly stippled but may have a few spots.

In males spiny dorsal fin is very lightly stippled and each membrane bears 2-5 oval dark spots. In females spiny dorsal fin is more nearly clear and oval spots are fewer and far less distinct. Soft dorsal fin membranes in males have smaller oval spots which are most intense near base but fade out toward margin. In females basal spots are slightly developed in soft dorsal fin membranes but remainder of fin appears weakly banded by darkening in rays. Caudal fin appears vertically banded in both sexes. Anal fin may be spotted basally in males and is clear in females. Unlike that in *E. okaloosae,* first anal spine is shorter than second. Pelvic fin is dark basally in males, clear in females. Pectoral fin is weakly barred in both sexes.

Cheek, opercle, prepectoral area, and nape have scales, sometimes embedded in nape. Breast bears few to many scales. Belly may lack a few scales immediately behind pelvic fin insertions. Lateral line is incomplete, consisting of 36-40 (34-42) scales, the last 7-15 (4-18) unpored. Fin counts are: dorsal VIII-X (VIII-XI), 10-12 (9-13); anal II, 6-8 (5-9); pectoral 12-14. Vertebrae number 36-38 (35-38).

Breeding males are not highly colorful but distinctive red spots on body may be brighter than shown in color plate. Male genital papilla is an elongated wedge. Females lack breeding colors. Genital papilla is a short tube, somewhat expanded and deeply grooved near tip.

Distribution. Found in Alabama, Florida, and Georgia from the Perdido River to the St. Johns River. In the Apalachicola River basin this darter is found northward to the Fall Line.

Natural History. The brown darter is generally found in small streams of low gradient with clear to slightly turbid water and depths of less than 1 m. Most often it is secluded among or beneath aquatic plants outside the main channel. Another habitat occupied by this species is the spring-fed alkaline rivers of northern Florida. It may dwell at somewhat greater depths here but still is associated with aquatic vegetation. Silt, sand, and gravel are the principal substrates. Eggs are laid on aquatic plants; this seems to be an excellent adaptation to an area where shifting substrates are so common.

Percina nigrofasciata is consistently found in streams that contain the brown darter, and *Etheostoma fusiforme* frequently is. *E. davisoni, E. parvipinne,* and the "Gulfcoast snubnose darter" are found within its range. Brown darters seem to have been accidentally introduced into the restricted range of *E. okaloosae* and have replaced that species locally.

Abundance. This is a successful species in much of its range and is free of any immediate threats to its survival.

Name. Hubbs and Cannon (1935) named this darter in honor of Edwin P. Creaser of Wayne State University, who provided them with initial specimens.

Etheostoma okaloosae (Fowler)
Okaloosa Darter

Plate 17

Subgenus *Villora*

Description. A rather small, moderately robust darter reaching 50 mm SL. It is weakly associated with *E. edwini* in subgenus *Villora* by possession of embedded scales on cheek and opercle, arched anterior end of the lateral line, broad frenum, uninterrupted sensory canals on the head, narrowly connected gill membranes, some stippling on the body, and 3 basicaudal spots. The lateral line is but slightly arched and *E. okaloosae* differs in several other basic respects from *E. edwini.* Page (1981) recommends placing *E. okaloosae* in his proposed subgenus *Belophlox.*

Dorsum is rather pale with 7-10 small dark blotches along midline in most individuals. Side supports 9-10 vertically elongated blotches which sometimes appear to be fused by numerous small spots that often lie in horizontal bands. Lower side and belly are pale and lightly stippled. There is a dark humeral spot. Preorbital and postorbital bars are not distinct. Suborbital bar is narrow but distinct. Cheek and opercle are speckled. Breast and ventral surface of head are lightly stippled. A distinct prepectoral spot is usually present.

Spiny dorsal fin in females supports 2-3 weak irregular horizontal bands. In males pigmentation is heavier, there being 2 large dark spots at posterior end of spiny dorsal fin. In females soft dorsal fin is spotted to produce about 4 horizontal bands; in males this fin is darkly spotted in more random fashion. Short horizontal dark stripes along margins of caudal rays tend to appear as wavy vertical bands. Anal fin is somewhat darkened basally and in mature males is very dark anteriorly; second spine is quite thin and is shorter than the first. Pelvic fin rays are edged with a little dark pigment in fe-

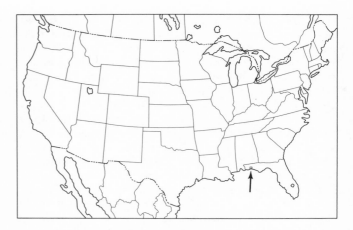

Distribution of *Etheostoma okaloosae*

males; additional darkening occurs in membranes of males. Pectoral fin is weakly pigmented toward base.

Cheek and opercle are scaled. Breast and prepectoral area may have a few scales. Nape is scaled posteriorly and may have some embedded scales anteriorly. Belly often lacks a few scales just posterior to pelvic fin insertions. Lateral line is complete or nearly so, consisting of 32-37 scales, up to 4 being unpored. Fin counts are: dorsal IX (VIII-X), 11-12 (10-13); anal II, 7 (6-8); pectoral 12-14. Vertebral counts are not known.

Bright breeding colors fail to develop, though more red may appear as a submarginal band in spiny dorsal fin than appears in color plate. Breeding tubercles apparently do not develop. Male genital papilla is an elongated wedge; that of females is a rounded tube deeply grooved at tip.

Distribution. Confined to Okaloosa and Walton counties, Florida, where it lives in Turkey Creek, Rocky Creek, and a few more small streams all of which enter an arm of Choctawhatchee Bay. Such a small range, entirely confined to streams of recent origin, is initially puzzling. Collette and Yerger (1962) surmise that the Okaloosa darter has been extirpated from an originally larger range, probably by competition from *E. edwini.*

Natural History. Okaloosa darters are locally common in clear sandy streams of small to medium size and slow to moderate current. It is usually found near banks among aquatic plants to depths of .5 m. Collette and Yerger (1962) observed males apparently breeding with females on a sandy substrate but eggs of this species were found to have been laid on aquatic plants. The exact breeding season may vary in response to mildness or severity of winters.

Percina nigrofasciata is the principal darter associate but prefers deeper or swift water. Mettee, Yerger and Crittenden (1976) initiated studies on the exact distribution and abundance of the Okaloosa darter. They discovered that *Etheostoma edwini* has apparently been introduced into part of its range and appears to be replacing it. Yerger (in Gilbert, 1978) gives a further update on the species, and the Florida Game and Freshwater Fish Commission continues studies.

Abundance. Deacon et al. (1979) accord threatened status to the Okaloosa darter. In spite of further reductions in range it is common in those streams where it persists. Some of the remaining populations are on Eglin Air Force Base, and cooperation by state and federal agencies may save this species for the foreseeable future.

Name. Fowler (1941) simply named the species from the county of capture, probably unaware that the entire species range is so nearly confined to that boundary.

Etheostoma boschungi Wall & Williams   Plate 17
Slackwater Darter   Subgenus *Ozarka*

Description. A moderate sized member of the subgenus reaching 62 mm SL but seldom exceeding 51 mm SL. It is placed in *Ozarka* by its combination of dusky, irregularly placed blotches on the ventral half of head and body, separate or nearly separate gill membranes, cheek and opercle without exposed scales, terminal mouth with broad frenum, incomplete lateral line, and in males a strong suborbital bar, red or orange belly, and breeding tubercles on ventral scales and anal and pelvic fins. Gill membranes are separate, sometimes overlapping. It has over 30 pored lateral scales in contrast to either *Etheostoma cragini* or *E. pallididorsum*.

Back is crossed by 3 distinct saddles, some individuals having 1 or 2 additional weak ones. Middorsal area is pale but not to the extent seen in *E. pallididorsum*. Dark upper half of body may obscure 9-12 lateral blotches. In some specimens blotches tend to fuse into a band on posterior half of body and end in a poorly defined caudal spot. Ventral half of body is pale but overlain by irregular dusky spots and finer stippling. An extremely prominent humeral bar extends downward behind pectoral fin.

Preorbital and postorbital bars are present but not strongly developed. Broad suborbital bar curves posteriorly. Cheek and opercle are mottled; ventral surface of head and breast are finely spotted.

Spiny dorsal fin has a narrow dark border, additional dark spots forming a median band, and isolated dark spots lie along base. Dark spots in soft dorsal fin form 2 or 3 poorly defined bands. More conspicuous spots form several poorly defined vertical bands in caudal fin. Remaining fins, particularly pectoral, bear a few blotches.

Cheek and breast are naked. Opercle has 1 or more embedded scales. Nape has embedded scales posteriorly. Lateral line contains 44-53 (43-58) scales, the first 30-44 pored. Fin counts are: dorsal X-XI (IX-XII), 11-12 (10-13); anal II, 8-9 (6-10); pectoral 13 (12-14). Vertebrae number 35-37.

As seen in color plate, breeding males develop more blue in spiny dorsal fin than is typical of other *Ozarka*. Breeding tubercles may develop on anal fin spine and rays, 2 of pelvic rays, and body scales surrounding anus. Females may develop dull coloration on spiny dorsal fin and belly. Genital papillae are presumed to be typical for *Ozarka*: short and subtriangular in males; longer, rounder, and perhaps pointed in females.

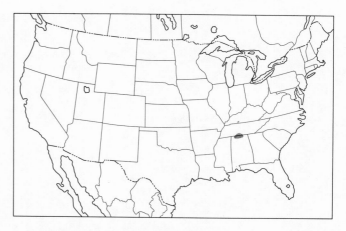

Distribution of *Etheostoma boschungi*

Distribution. Narrowly confined to the middle portion of the Tennessee River basin, where it occurs in several streams rising in Tennessee and entering the river in Alabama. A disjunct population exists in the head of the Buffalo River, just north of the principal range.

Natural History. Wall and Williams (1974) found a few specimens of this species in much the same habitat as first reported for *Etheostoma pallididorsum*, shallow creeks with accumulations of organic material. Subsequently Boschung (1979) reports that breeding individuals leave such creeks to breed in seepages in open pastures, areas which literally become dry land during summer. Adults and newly hatched young return to adjacent creeks for the remainder of the year. One is led to surmise that *E. boschungi*, *E. pallididorsum*, and perhaps *E. trisella* and *E. cragini* have carried the exploitation of small streams to a new extreme.

Darter associates of the slackwater darter are *E. caeruleum*, *E. duryi*, *E. flabellare*, *E. simoterum*, and *E. squamiceps*, with *E. neopterum* a possibility.

Scarcity of specimens precludes experimental studies on the fascinating reproductive habits of this species.

Abundance. Deacon et al. (1979) list the slackwater darter as being threatened. All evidence points to its being highly vulnerable.

Name. Named in honor of Herbert T. Boschung of the University of Alabama, who has contributed to several aspects of ichthyology in the southeastern United States and trained a number of active ichthyologists.

Etheostoma cragini Gilbert   Plate 17
Arkansas Darter   Subgenus *Ozarka*

Description. A moderate sized member of its subgenus reaching 60 mm SL. It is placed in *Ozarka* by the combination of dusky, irregularly placed blotches on the lower half of head

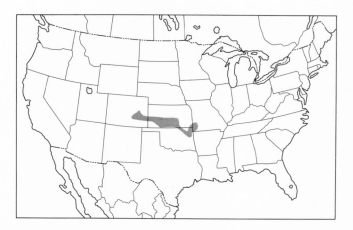

Distribution of *Etheostoma cragini*

and body, separate or slightly connected gill membranes, cheeks and opercles without exposed scales, terminal mouth with broad frenum, incomplete lateral line, and in breeding males a strong suborbital bar, red or orange belly, and breeding tubercles on ventral scales and on anal and pelvic fins. Gill membranes are separate or narrowly connected. In *Ozarka* only *E. pallididorsum* with a pale dorsal stripe has a lateral line with so few pored scales.

Six to 9 small dorsal saddles vary in intensity. Nine to 12 lateral blotches may be distinct or partly obscured by mottling that continues downward to belly. Pored lateral line scales tend to be unpigmented. Humeral bar is small and dark.

Preorbital bar almost meets counterpart on snout. Broad suborbital bar is directed somewhat posteriorly and is strong in males. Postorbital bar varies from distinct to a dusky spot. Cheek, opercle, and lip are mottled. Breast and ventral surface of head are finely stippled.

Spiny dorsal fin is darkly edged and bears a dusky band just above base. Dusky spots in soft dorsal fin tend to lie in about 3 horizontal bands, and caudal fin bears 5-7 similar vertical bands. Diffuse spots tend to lie in 2 bands in anal fin. Pelvic fin is clear to weakly spotted; pectoral fin is somewhat more heavily spotted.

Cheek and opercle are naked or have a few embedded scales. Nape scales are exposed to partly embedded. Breast is naked. Lateral line consists of 42-57 scales, the first 7-25 pored. Fin counts are: dorsal VIII-X (VI-XI), 10-12 (10-15); anal II, 6-7 (5-8); pectoral 11 (9-13). Vertebrae number 33-36.

Breeding males are brightly colored and darkly pigmented as shown in color plate. Breeding tubercles may be found on ventral belly scales, anal fin rays, and occasionally pelvic fin rays. Genital papilla is short, flattened, and subtriangular. Mature females lack bright colors. Genital papilla is a short tube.

Distribution. Confined to the Arkansas River basin of southwestern Missouri, northeastern Oklahoma, northwestern Arkansas, Kansas, and Colorado, where reported as far west as Canon City.

Natural History. Arkansas darters live in spring-fed creeks and seeps where watercress or native aquatic plants often are present. In the western part of its range it is the only darter, but eastward it may be taken with *Etheostoma spectabile* and less commonly with other darters of the region (Blair and Windle, 1961). Breeding observations have been recorded by Ellis and Jaffa (1918), Blair (1964) and Distler (1971). A female leaves protective vegetation, burrows into gravel, and is mounted by 1 of several males, which show no territoriality. The spawning act is brief and may be repeated with different males. When frightened, Arkansas darters have been seen to burrow into silt, clouding the water above them. Breeding colors are brightest in April and May, presumably peak spawning months.

Abundance. Arkansas darters are apparently rare through the western part of their range. Cross (1967) has found the species common in Kansas only in Crooked Creek of the Cimarron River basin. He did not find it at the type locality, which has been grossly altered. Heavy demands for water have probably dried up many springs that once supported the species. It is somewhat more common in Oklahoma, the principal sites noted by Blair (1959). It is locally common in extreme southwest Missouri according to Pflieger (1975). This species bears close observation because of its shrinking range.

Name. Named for F.W. Cragin, who collected the species when director of the Washburn College Laboratory.

Etheostoma pallididorsum Distler & Metcalf

Plate 18

Paleback Darter   Subgenus *Ozarka*

Description. A small member of its subgenus reaching 47 mm SL. It is placed in *Ozarka* by the combination of dusky, irregularly placed blotches on the ventral half of head and body, separate or nearly separate gill membranes, cheek and opercle without exposed scales, terminal mouth with broad frenum, incomplete lateral line, and in males a strong suborbital bar, red or orange belly, and breeding tubercles on ventral scales and anal and pelvic fins. Gill membranes are slightly connected. Like *Etheostoma cragini* it has a quite incomplete lateral line but in addition has a pale dorsal stripe.

Distinctly pale dorsum is crossed by up to 6 small dusky saddles. Upper side is dark, often appearing faintly banded; lower side and belly are pale but stippled. Midlateral markings consist of a faint band, sometimes expanded into blotches posteriorly. Basicaudal area is darkened. A dark humeral bar extends ventrally from lateral line behind pectoral fin.

Preorbital bar fails to meet counterpart on snout. Strong suborbital bar may be curved posteriorly. There is a short postorbital bar. Lower half of head is mottled. Breast and ventral surface of head are stippled.

Spiny dorsal fin is darkly edged and additional darkening may occur near base. Soft dorsal fin is spotted. Spots in caudal fin form several vertical bands. Diffuse spots tend to lie in 2 bands in anal fin. Pelvic and pectoral fins are clear to very lightly pigmented.

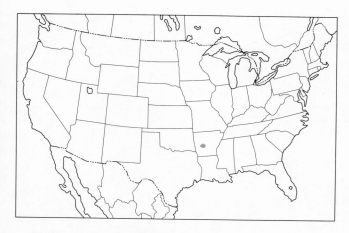

Distribution of *Etheostoma pallididorsum*

Cheek, opercle, breast, and anterior part of belly are naked. Nape has embedded scales. Lateral line consists of 43-55 scales, only the first 8-19 pored. Fin counts are: dorsal IX-X (VII-XI), 11-12 (10-14); anal II, 7-9; pectoral 11-12 (10-13). Vertebrae number 34-36.

Breeding males usually display stronger shades of reddish orange than shown in color plate. Breeding tubercles may develop on belly scales and anal and pelvic fin rays. Genital papilla is somewhat flattened and triangular. Mature females may develop a little color. Genital papilla is a large tube, constricted and pointed at tip.

Distribution. Initially reported only from the upper Caddo River basin in southwestern Arkansas. Robison (1974c) found another population in the upper Ouachita River, master stream of the Caddo.

Natural History. Distler and Metcalf (1962) described the paleback darter from few individuals, all captured in very shallow water with organic debris. The few subsequent reports of this species mention the same conditions. Neil Douglas (personal communication) indicates that these darters enter streamside seeps in the spring, perhaps to breed. *Etheostoma radiosum* is the darter most likely to be captured with or near the paleback darter.

Hambrick and Robison (1979) discuss the habitat in greater detail. They report a sex ratio of 1:1.5 in favor of females, which tend to be larger than males. March is the peak spawning month; survival is for 2 or perhaps 3 years. Adults and larvae of aquatic diptera, mayfly larvae, and cladocera are the principal food items.

Blair (1964) saw distinct differences between aquarium-held individuals of *E. pallididorsum* and *E. cragini,* the former tending to drape themselves over strands of vegetation and the latter resting on the substrate. Though similar and geographically close, early doubts about the validity of the paleback darter seem to have been dispelled. Its method of arrival in the upper Ouachita River system remains a mystery.

Abundance. Listed by Deacon et al. (1979) as threatened, the paleback darter has questionable chances for survival. The presence of suitable habitat is in its favor but the small range, further broken by 2 reservoirs, leaves the individual populations vulnerable to extinctions without chance of reinvasion. Few specimens have been captured, which suggests that individual populations are quite small. Channel modification is a particular threat.

Name. *Pallididorsum* means pale back.

Etheostoma punctulatum (Agassiz)   Plate 18
Stippled Darter   Subgenus *Ozarka*

Description. A robust darter, the largest in its subgenus, reaching 88 mm SL though seldom exceeding 60 mm SL. It is typical of *Ozarka* in possessing dusky, irregularly placed blotches on the lower half of head and body, separate or slightly connected gill membranes, cheek and opercle without exposed scales, terminal mouth with broad frenum, incomplete lateral line, and in breeding males a strong suborbital bar, red or orange belly, and breeding tubercles on ventral scales and anal and pelvic fins. Gill membranes are separate. The lateral line is incomplete but includes 58 or more scales in contrast to other species in *Ozarka*.

One or more of 4 small dorsal saddles may be poorly developed or divided. Upper side is dusky to fairly dark. Mottling on lower half of body contrasts with pale background. Midlateral blotches are small and partly obscured by mottling anteriorly but may be enlarged, more visible, and sometimes vertically elongated on caudal peduncle. Humeral bar is reduced to a dark spot.

Dorsal half of head is dark and ventral half is light but overlain with small blotches and fine stipples. Preorbital bar is difficult to distinguish. Suborbital bar is broad and in males very dark. Postorbital bar is usually short and dark. Ventral surface of head and breast are stippled.

In males spiny dorsal fin bears a dark marginal band or slightly submarginal dark band and a median dark band. Additional darkening occurs near fin base and sometimes in a weak band between the other 2. In females marginal and median bands are interrupted and are not intense. Dark spots in soft dorsal fin usually are arranged in poorly defined horizontal bands. Three to 5 vertical bands in caudal fin are similarly produced. Anal and pelvic fins have dark spots usually not forming distinct bands. Pectoral fins are vertically banded in females but stippled in males.

Cheek, opercle, and breast are naked or have few embedded scales. Nape is scaled. Lateral line consists of 58-80 scales, more than 30 of which are pored. Fin counts are: dorsal X-XI, 13-15; anal II, 7-9; pectoral 12-14. Vertebrae number 36-38.

Breeding males are handsomely colored as shown in color plate. Breeding tubercles on belly are most numerous just anterior to genital papilla, which is short, flattened, and subtriangular. Tubercles may also occur at base of anal fin, on pelvic fin, and sometimes on the ventralmost caudal fin ray. Females develop a little orange in spiny dorsal fin, and more

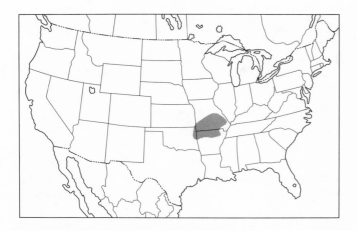

Distribution of *Etheostoma punctulatum*

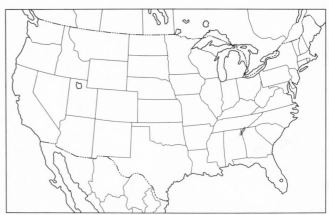

Distribution of *Etheostoma trisella*

heavily spotted fins than males. Genital papilla is a rounded tube.

Distribution. Essentially restricted to streams rising in and adjacent to the Ozark region in Missouri, Arkansas, Oklahoma, and Kansas.

Natural History. Found most often in clear, permanently flowing small streams and spring-fed brooks where it frequents unsilted areas. It often hides beneath rocks, undercut banks, or vegetation and debris in quiet backwaters. Cross (1967) took stippled darters in riffles during May in Kansas and surmised that breeding occurred then.

In a stroke of luck we caught *Etheostoma punctulatum, E. cragini, E. spectabile,* and in adjacent quiet water *E. microperca* in late May from a spring-fed run near the Spring River, Missouri. Some individuals of all species were in breeding condition. Throughout its range, *E. spectabile* is the most common darter associate of the stippled darter.

Abundance. Locally abundant in the western part of its range, the stippled darter is rare in the eastern Ozarks, perhaps indicating a decrease in abundance since 1900 (Pflieger, 1971, 1975). Despite the probability of local extinctions this species remains common.

Name. *Punctulatum* means with little spots, in reference to the fine stippling and perhaps the coarser mottling on the body.

Etheostoma trisella Bailey & Richards   Plate 18
Trispot Darter   Subgenus *Ozarka*

Description. The smallest member of its subgenus, reaching 40 mm SL. It is placed in *Ozarka* by the combination of dusky, irregularly placed blotches on the ventral half of head and body, separate or nearly separate gill membranes, the presence of a frenum, and a well developed suborbital bar.

Williams and Robison (1980) were guided by choice of habitat and geographic considerations in transferring this species from subgenus *Psychromaster* to *Ozarka*. It has some cheek and opercle scales, a complete lateral line, and 1 anal spine, and has not been shown to have breeding tubercles. Nonetheless the trispot darter fits *Ozarka* better than any other subgenus in *Etheostoma*.

Rather pale dorsum is crossed by 3 small dusky saddles. Side is mottled and posteriorly may support several blotches; when well developed, last blotch may join its counterpart across back as a fourth saddle. Ventral half of body is pale overlain by some mottling. Humeral spot is small and diffuse.

Preorbital bar does not meet counterpart on snout. Postorbital bar is dark initially but fades posteriorly. Suborbital bar varies from faint to distinct. Cheek and opercle are pale, with a dark wedge on the latter. Lips and ventral surface of head have a few dark spots.

Spiny dorsal fin is edged in dark, but line may be intermittent. Interrupted dark streaks are again found near fin base. Soft dorsal fin is darkened along margins of rays to produce several weak irregular bands. Similar and better defined vertical bands occur in caudal fin. Anal and pelvic fins are little pigmented; pectoral fin is very weakly banded.

Cheek and opercle are scaled but the former is naked ventrally. Breast is naked. Small scales may occur on dorsolateral portion of head. Nape is well scaled. Lateral line is complete or nearly so with 44-52 scales in series. Fin counts are: dorsal VIII-X, 10-11; anal I, 8-9; pectoral 13-14. Vertebral counts are not known.

Color plate illustrates a female trispot darter. Breeding males develop 4 lateral green blotches, yellow lips, and yellow or orange ventrally on caudal peduncle. Breeding tubercles have not been described. Female genital papilla is a short tube, terminally bilobed; that of males is presumed to be small and subtriangular.

Distribution. Has been taken at a few sites in the upper Coosa River basin in Tennessee, Georgia, and Alabama.

Natural History. This species was named by Bailey and Richards (1963) on the basis of a single specimen taken in

1947. Howell and Caldwell (1967) and Etnier (1970) have added new collecting sites and made habitat notes. In the Conasauga River the species lives at the edge of the stream or in quiet backwaters of it. Sluggish tributaries of this river may support populations, as well, primarily in vegetated pools. A gravid female and colorful males have been taken in April. It is possible that the species spawns in shallow water or enters adjoining seeps, but additional life history data are not available.

Abundance. Deacon et al. (1979) list the trispot darter as threatened. The type locality is inundated by a large reservoir and additional streamside alteration presents a threat to the species' persistence. Its only center of relative abundance is the Conasauga River and sluggish tributaries in the vicinity of the Tennessee-Georgia border, where the stream leaves the hills of its origin.

Name. *Trisella* means three spotted and draws attention to the 3 dorsal saddles.

Etheostoma australe Jordan   Plate 18

Conchos Darter   Subgenus *Austroperca*

Description. A moderate sized robust darter reaching 50 mm SL. Its characteristics and appearance fit subgenus *Oligocephalus* except for the presence of a single thick anal spine, which to us appears as though it might be a fusion of the second spine with the first. Page (1981) recommends the submergence of the monotypic subgenus *Austroperca* in *Oligocephalus*. The frenum is fairly broad; gill membranes are slightly to moderately joined. The supratemporal canal is interrupted; infraorbital canals are complete or interrupted.

Dorsum bears 6-9 small saddles which are darker than but usually continuous with 9-11 broad vertical bands on side. Central portion of nape usually appears as a light oval. Lateral bands extend almost to ventral midline in males but in females only those on caudal peduncle do so. Upper side is considerably darkened, lower side dusky, and belly pale or stippled. Humeral bar is fairly prominent. Small basicaudal spot may be flanked by a smaller spot above and below.

Preorbital bar is diffuse, not meeting counterpart on snout. Suborbital bar is fairly broad but diffuse. Short postorbital bar is prominent. Ventral surface of head and breast are pale or lightly stippled.

Spiny dorsal fin is narrowly edged in black, the band becoming somewhat broader posteriorly; membranes are slightly darkened, often forming narrow median and basal bands. Membranes of soft dorsal fin support dark spots, and margins of rays are sometimes darkened, but there is no distinctive pattern.

Cheek, opercle, breast, and prepectoral area are naked. Nape is naked or has a few embedded scales near spiny dorsal fin. Belly is naked immediately behind pelvic fin insertion but fully scaled otherwise. Counts based on a series of 20 fish are as follows: Lateral line contains 54-68 scales, 32-47 of them

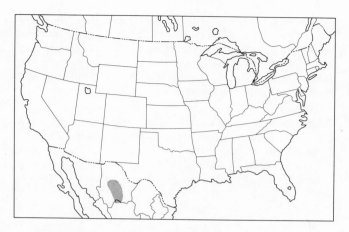

Distribution of *Etheostoma australe*

pored. Fin counts are: dorsal XI-XII (X-XIII), 10-11 (9-12); anal I, 7 (6-8); pectoral 11 (10-12). Vertebrae number 37.

Breeding males become more colorful than specimen shown in color plate. Breeding tubercles occur on ventral belly scales. Genital papilla is short, flattened, and terminally rounded or slightly bilobed with grooves or pits radiating from base. Females apparently lack bright coloration and breeding tubercles. Genital papilla is a short, somewhat flattened tube.

Page (1981) has collected and described colorful males of *E. australe*. Spiny dorsal fin has a narrow blue margin, a blue basal band, and a red median band. Other fins are yellow except that anal and pelvic fins have green near base. Green lateral bands are separated by areas of yellow or reddish brown. Breast and belly are green. Breeding tubercles occur on pelvic and anal fins and ventral scales of caudal peduncle as well as belly. Females are green dorsally and yellow ventrally.

Distribution. Found only in the upper Rio Conchos basin in the states of Chihuahua and Durango, Mexico. Local occurrence in the lower Rio Conchos basin is an unverified possibility.

Natural History. The Conchos darter apparently is a typical riffle inhabitant over sand and gravel substrate. Clear cool streams occur locally in the upper Rio Conchos, which exceeds 1,000 m in elevation. Meek (1902) said that the species was abundant and could be captured with *E. pottsi*. Meek (1904) stated that May and June were breeding months but Page (1981) has found prespawning males in late February in a rubble-strewn riffle. Additional life history information is badly needed for the Conchos darter. In terms of reproductive physiology it remains a cool temperate region species which is narrowly confined to suitable water and is forced to breed early in the year.

Wet periods of the Pleistocene undoubtedly afforded darters the chance to spread into the present-day Chihuahuan Desert where suitable habitat persists locally. Geological changes also have occurred at a rapid pace so that our knowledge of the origins, spread, and diversification of desert fishes awaits the accumulation of much additional knowledge.

Abundance. Contreras-Balderas (in Deacon et al., 1979) recommends treating the Conchos darter as a truly endangered species, though it remains common in perhaps a few spots. Intensified modern agriculture in arid portions of Mexico places top priority on irrigation water and there is a question as to whether any natural stream segments will persist.

Name. *Australe* means southern. *Austroperca* means southern perch. Because *Ethestoma australe* is not part of the fish fauna of the United States or Canada, it has no common name sanctioned by the American Fisheries Society. The appropriate name Conchos darter has been taken from Deacon et al. (1979).

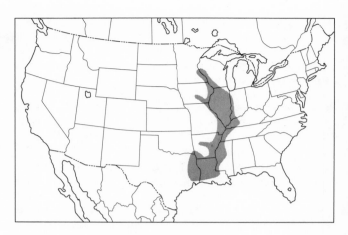

Distribution of *Etheostoma asprigene*

Etheostoma asprigene (Forbes)   Plate 18
Mud Darter   Subgenus *Oligocephalus*

Description. A moderately large robust member of the subgenus reaching 70 mm SL but seldom exceeding 55 mm SL. It is typical of its subgenus in having a conical head, frenum, 2 anal spines, separate or slightly connected gill membranes, and in breeding males a blue marginal and a red submarginal band in the spiny dorsal fin. Gill membranes are completely separate, even overlapping. It is sometimes difficult to distinguish from *E. collettei,* which is more slender and tuberculate in breeding males. It also can be confused with *E. swaini,* which is more slender and has less prominent cheek scales.

Eight or 9 dorsal blotches are uniformly subdued in appearance. The first 2 or 3 lateral markings are mere midlateral blotches; remaining 6-8 markings become more vertically elongated; those on caudal peduncle are distinct bands. Dark areas on upper side may produce a weak interconnecting pattern between dorsal and lateral markings. A small basicaudal spot sometimes is partly fused with last lateral band. Humeral bar is usually small but may continue ventrally behind pectoral fin.

Preorbital bar meets counterpart on snout. Suborbital bar is moderately to rather prominently developed and sometimes anteriorly directed. Postorbital bar may be short, or longer and directed upward. Lower surface of head is pale, and usually stippled, as is breast.

Spiny dorsal fin has a narrow dark border, sometimes a median dark band, and a broad dusky area at base. Stippling in membranes of soft dorsal fin may be random but often produces 3-4 faint bands. Several dark vertical bands in caudal fin lack intensity. Remaining fins are clear except in mature males, which have darkened anal and pelvic fins.

Cheek and opercle are conspicuously scaled. Prepectoral area and nape are scaled, and breast has a few scales. Lateral line consists of 44-57 scales, the last 3-19 unpored. Fin counts are: dorsal IX-XI, 11-13 (10-14); anal II, 7-8; pectoral 14 (11-15). Vertebrae number 37-38 (36-39).

Breeding males become fairly colorful, sometimes brighter on body than individual shown in color plate. Breeding tubercles are absent in this species. Male genital papilla is a broad flap which supports a smaller terminal section. Females do not develop appreciable coloring. Genital papilla is a circular pad which may elongate into a short tube.

Distribution. Found in lowland streams adjacent to the Mississippi River from Louisiana to southern Minnesota. It also occurs in the Sabine and Neches rivers in eastern Texas. In the lower Ohio basin a few populations are known to occur as far east as the lower Green River.

Natural History. The mud darter is found most commonly in sluggish murky streams, oxbow lakes, and even the arms of some reservoirs, often in association with organic debris. But it is not precluded from clear streams where it inhabits pools. It may be associated with *Percina maculata, P. ouachitae, Ammocrypta clara, A. vivax, Etheostoma fusiforme, E. gracile,* and occasionally other species. Forbes and Richardson (1920) report that mud darters eat mayfly and midgefly larvae.

The mud darter seems to be most closely related to *E. swaini* of the eastern Gulf Coast. Superficially it resembles *E. collettei,* with which it is occasionally captured. We hope more life history information will soon appear on this interesting species.

Abundance. The mud darter seems safe from major threats at this time. Smith (1979) notes serious loss in abundance within Illinois and attributes this to the greatly reduced summer flow of streams during drought. Various drainage schemes elsewhere may be causing similar reductions in abundance.

Name. *Asprigene* means a variety of *Asper,* a European genus of the perch family. The species author probably was not implying close relationship by the choice of name.

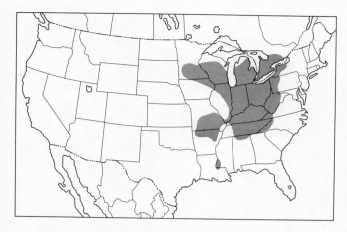

Distribution of *Etheostoma caeruleum*

Etheostoma caeruleum Storer   Plate 18
Rainbow Darter   Subgenus *Oligocephalus*

Description. A fairly large and robust member of the subgenus reaching 65 mm SL. It is typical of *Oligocephalus* in having a conical head, frenum, 2 anal spines, separate to slightly connected gill membranes, and in breeding males a blue marginal and a red submarginial band in the spiny dorsal fin. The infraorbital canal is complete in contrast to the incomplete canal of *Etheostoma spectabile,* the species most often confused with *E. caeruleum.*

Dorsum bears 6-10 squarish saddles, the boldest 2 just anterior and posterior to spiny dorsal fin. There are 9-14 lateral blotches which are more vertically elongated toward tail, especially in males, in which blotches meet their counterparts on belly and sometimes also across back. A humeral bar is present, never large or prominent. Body is free of much additional pattern in some specimens but in many individuals bears numerous small spots.

Preorbital bar is diffuse, sometimes meeting counterpart on snout. Postorbital bar is usually short and diffuse. Suborbital bar also is variably developed but never very bold. Breast and lower half of head may be lightly stippled.

In males spiny dorsal fin has a narrow dark marginal band; usually there is a dark median band and additional darkening along fin base. In females these bands are poorly developed, the median one often deleted. In males soft dorsal fin has a faint dark margin and is darkened near base; additional stippling occurs in membranes and often along margins of rays. In females marginal band of soft dorsal is weak to absent; elsewhere fin appears weakly banded due to clustered stippling in membranes. Males have 2-3 dusky vertical bands in caudal fin; females have several narrow vertical bands. In mature males bases of anal and pelvic fins are darkened but otherwise these fins are virtually clear, as is pectoral fin in all cases.

Cheek and breast are naked or rarely have embedded scales. Opercle is scaled. Nape is naked or supplied with embedded scales posteriorly. Lateral line consists of 37-50 scales,

the first 18-34 pored. Fin counts are: dorsal X-XI (IX-XII), 13 (12-15); anal II, 7-9; pectoral usually 13. Vertebrae number 36-37 (34-38).

The above description best fits populations in the Ohio River basin. Leslie Knapp (personal communication) indicates that specimens from the isolated southern part of the range and those from the White River basin in Arkansas and Missouri probaby represent separate unnamed subspecies. The remainder of the range seems to contain a single subspecies divisible into 3 races based on slight variation.

Breeding males are among the most striking of darters, as show in color plate. Details of color pattern vary somewhat but males are not easily confused with other species. Breeding tubercles may develop on belly scales, around anal fin base, and for a short distance between anal fin and caudal peduncle. Genital papilla is a broad flap, rounded and often with a small nipple at tip. Breeding females may develop patches of dull orange and blue on body. Female genital papilla is a short, posteriorly bent, rather flattened tube.

Distribution. Occurs widely in the Ohio River basin and the Great Lakes region north through the lower peninsula of Michigan and eastward to Lake Ontario. It is common in the upper Mississippi River basin but virtually absent in prairie regions or in lowlands bordering the lower Mississippi and Ohio rivers. It is again common in the Ozarks of Missouri and Arkansas. A few eastern tributaries of the Mississippi River in Louisiana and southern Mississippi contain the species. Stauffer and Hocutt (in Lee et al., 1980) verify the presence of rainbow darters in the upper Potomac River basin.

This distribution pattern clearly reflects the influence of Pleistocene glaciation. Relict populations in the South, successful reinvasion of the southern and eastern Great Lakes region, and failure to cross into the Arctic drainage in northern Minnesota are clearly seen in the distribution pattern.

Natural History. Rainbow darters typically inhabit creeks and small rivers of moderate gradient and riffles composed of coarse gravel and rubble. They are sometimes the most abundant darter under such conditions, and are captured with a greater variety of other darters than any species with the possible exception of *E. flabellare.* Their abundance is a good omen for the presence of a variety of small fishes.

Rainbow darters feed on a variety of aquatic insect larvae. Turner (1921) reports that they capture small snails and tiny crayfish; Winn (1958b) observed them to eat minnow and lamprey eggs. In turn they may be utilized to a limited extent as food by game fish. Adamson and Wissing (1977) show a strong selectivity for caddisfly larvae and demonstrate feeding peaks in morning and evening, as well as seasonal variations in food consumed.

Winn (1958a,b) reports further on breeding and ecology of the rainbow darter. Breeding reaches its peak as water temperature reaches 17-18°C. Males have shifting, ill defined territories and practice intimidation on intruding males. Females enter from pools downstream and lay eggs in gravel at the foot of riffles. The spawning act with the male mounted on the female's back is repeated several times as she moves upstream. Several days are required for a female to deposit a maximal 800 eggs. Cooper (1979) describes the appearance of eggs and the early larval stages of the rainbow darter.

This species is relatively well known, having appeared on wildlife stamps and in popular magazines. When placed in the home aquarium males are found to lose bright colors gradually. In experimental tanks with controlled temperature and light cycle the rainbow darter is more responsive and undergoes considerable seasonal change. If darters become popular with fish hobbyists, the rainbow darter will be one of the important species.

Abundance. The rainbow darter is one of our most abundant species. Although local reductions and extirpations have occurred, there is no present reason for concern for its well-being. The isolated southern populations are probably the ones most in need of careful protection.

Name. *Caeruleum* means blue or a shade thereof.

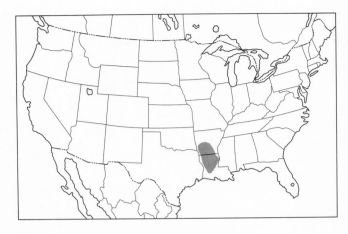

Distribution of *Etheostoma collettei*

Etheostoma collettei Birdsong & Knapp   Plate 19
Creole Darter   Subgenus *Oligocephalus*

Description. An average sized but not very robust appearing member of its subgenus reaching 62 mm SL. It is typical of *Oligocephalus* in having a conical head, frenum, 2 anal spines, separate to slightly connected gill membranes, and in breeding males a blue marginal and a red submarginal band in the spiny dorsal fin. Some individuals have slightly connected gill membranes, others have separate and overlapping gill membranes. It is superficially similar to but more slender than *E. asprigene.*

There are up to 9 small dorsal saddles but as few as 4 may be distinct. Five to 8 vertically elongated lateral blotches are usually developed but only the last 2 are bold. Small, horizontally aligned dark spots are usually found on upper two-thirds of body. There is a small dusky prepectoral spot, and a distinct humeral bar that usually continues downward behind pectoral fin.

Preorbital bar joins counterpart on snout. Postorbital bar is short but distinct, and suborbital bar is usually intense but sometimes is reduced to a dusky spot. Lower surface of head and breast are pale.

Spiny dorsal fin is darkly edged; membranes at base are darkened. Soft dorsal fin has a dark margin, a submarginal clear zone, and some darkening toward base. Darkening in caudal fin produces weak vertical bands. Remaining fins are clear or lightly stippled except for darkening near base of anal and pelvic fins in mature males.

Cheek scales may be partly embedded; opercle is scaled; nape is scaled posteriorly. Breast and prepectoral area are naked. Belly scales may be embedded just behind pelvic fin insertions. Lateral line consists of 47-52 (44-60) scales, 32-42 (28-46) of them pored. Fin counts are: dorsal X-XI (VIII-XII), 12-14 (11-14); anal II, 6-8; pectoral 12-13 (11-14). Vertebrae number 36-38.

Breeding males are very colorful as shown in color plate.

Breeding tubercles may develop on midventral line of belly and for a short distance along base of anal fin. Genital papilla is a broad flap, rather prominently developed. Females do not become colorful but body may develop touches of dull blue and orange. Genital papilla is a short, somewhat flattened tube.

Distribution. Occurs in the Ouachita and Red rivers of Arkansas and Louisiana and westward in the latter state to the Sabine River. Its occurrence in adjacent portions of Oklahoma and Texas is to be expected.

Natural History. The Creole darter occurs typically in headwater streams of second to fourth order over a variety of substrates. In Louisiana Neil Douglas (in Birdsong and Knapp, 1969) found it in heavily vegetated streams of moderate current and soft substrate. We have taken it in southwestern Arkansas from a small creek with clay substrate flowing through open pasture. In the headwaters of the Ouachita it may live in upland riffles with gravel and rubble substrate, preferably where aquatic plants are common. Common darter associates are *Etheostoma blennioides, E. radiosum,* and *E. whipplei* in upland streams, and more often *E. chlorosomum, E. gracile, E. proeliare, Percina maculata,* and *P. sciera* in various lowland streams. Additional information is needed on this regionally important darter.

Name. Named in honor of Bruce B. Collette, U.S. Bureau of Commercial Fisheries, for his contributions to the systematics and phylogeny of percid fishes.

Etheostoma ditrema Ramsey & Suttkus   Plate 19
Coldwater Darter   Subgenus *Oligocephalus*

Description. A rather small but fairly robust species of *Oligocephalus* reaching almost 49 mm SL in our largest specimen. It is typical of the subgenus in having a small conical head, frenum, 2 anal spines, separate or slightly connected gill mem-

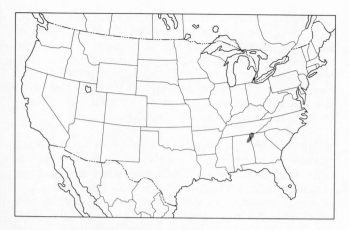

Distribution of *Etheostoma ditrema*

branes, and in breeding males a blue marginal and a red submarginal band in the spiny dorsal fin. The lateral line is somewhat arched anteriorly. The frenum is often narrow; gill membranes are separate and overlapping anteriorly. This species was initially thought to be unusual in having 2 coronal pores on the head (Ramsey and Suttkus, 1965), but some populations discovered subsequently have the single pore typical of most darters. It differs from *E. nuchale* in having more scales encroaching on the head and generally higher counts for fin rays, fin spines, and lateral line scales.

Dorsum is uniform in appearance in contrast to blotchy and darker side, along which lateral line is seen as a pale stripe. Belly is pale but overlain by a few irregularly shaped spots. All 3 vertically aligned basicaudal spots are usually well developed. Usually there is a pale area along center of nape. There is no humeral bar.

Preorbital bar meets counterpart on snout. Suborbital bar is narrow but long and well defined. Postorbital bar is long and often well defined. Cheek and opercle often bear a few small blotches. Breast and ventral surface of head are pale or lightly stippled.

Spiny dorsal fin has a narrow dull marginal band, darkening at base, and often a median dark band. Membranes of soft dorsal fin are variably stippled but darkening in rays produces several horizontal bands. Vertical bands are similarly formed in caudal fin. There are fainter markings on basal half of anal fin. Pelvic and pectoral fins are virtually unpigmented.

Cheek, opercle, and prepectoral area are scaled; some cheek scales may be embedded. Nape is naked or has a few embedded scales posteriorly. Breast is scaled posteriorly. Body scales encroach on dorsolateral surface of head. Lateral line consists of 44-50 (41-54) scales, 22-32 (19-35) of them pored. Fin counts are: dorsal X-XI (VIII-XII), 10-11 (9-12); anal II, 6-7 (6-8); pectoral 12-13 (11-13). Vertebrae number 35-37.

Breeding males are quite colorful as shown in color plate. Genital papilla is a small subquadrate flap. Males apparently lack breeding tubercles. Females may develop a touch of fin and body coloration. Genital papilla is a short crenulated tube.

Distribution. Restricted to a few springs and associated pools above the Fall Line in the Coosa basin of Alabama, Georgia, and Tennessee.

Natural History. The coldwater darter lives among aquatic plants or coarse organic debris at depths of 1 m or less. It may perch on clumps of vegetation well off the bottom, much as *E. nuchale* does. Ramsey and Suttkus (1965) found gravid females from April to July. They state that males may be colorful during a much greater part of the year. They suggest that this species may be a paedomorphic offshoot of *E. swaini*, retaining certain juvenile traits of the latter, including a reduced number of pored lateral line scales, incomplete development of cephalic canals, and weakly developed dorsal spines.

This species seems to be slightly different at each spot where it occurs. The actual place of its origin and the history of its spread to the widely isolated sites it inhabits remain matters of speculation.

We found this species hard to collect. The type locality experienced a severe flood on our arrival there, and 2 springs visited on other trips yielded no specimens. It was finally taken near the Georgia-Tennessee border from a spring-fed pond we had passed but overlooked several times before.

Abundance. Listed by Deacon et al. (1979) as threatened, the coldwater darter can only be maintained by protection of the springs in which it dwells. The large spring near Anniston, Alabama, has long been used as the water supply for that city, but this darter apparently persists there. Careful management gives hope for the immediate future, at least.

Name. *Ditrema* denotes 2 pores. The first collection sites yielded specimens preponderantly with 2 coronal pores, but some populations have principally 1 pore, as do most darter species.

Etheostoma exile (Girard)   Plate 19
Iowa Darter   Subgenus *Oligocephalus*

Description. A moderate sized, very slender species of *Oligocephalus* reaching 68 mm SL but seldom exceeding 55 mm SL. It is typical of the subgenus in having a small conical head, broad frenum, 2 anal spines, separate or slightly connected gill membranes, and in breeding males a blue marginal and a red submarginal band in the spiny dorsal fin. The lateral line is somewhat arched anteriorly. The Iowa darter is not likely to be confused with other members of the subgenus within its range, nor does that range overlap that of *E. fusiforme*, which has an arched lateral line and slender shape. This species undoubtedly shares characteristics with subgenus *Hololepis*, and Page (1981) recommends inclusion of the 2 groups in a subgenus *Boleichthys*.

Rather light dorsum is crossed by 7-10 small dusky saddles, which may be indistinct. Nine to 14 vertically elongated lateral blotches are usually distinct in males, and indistinct in females, especially posteriorly. Belly is clear. A small basicau-

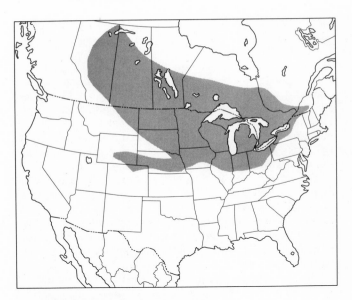

Distribution of *Etheostoma exile*

dal spot is usually flanked by 1 spot below and occasionally 1 above. Humeral bar is absent.

Preorbital bar almost meets counterpart on snout. Suborbital bar is of variable width and length but is always distinct. A short postorbital bar may in males have another lying above it. An opercular blotch and a few tiny blotches on lower cheek and opercle complete head markings. Breast is pale.

In males margin of spiny dorsal fin is dark; there is a broad basal band which is dusky and usually a median dark band. In females 2 or 3 horizontal dark streaks are faintly developed. In both sexes there are several weak diagonal bands in soft dorsal fin, and vertical counterparts in caudal fin. Anal and pelvic fins are clear and pectoral fins are stippled, often producing vertical bands.

Cheek, opercle, and nape are scaled; cheek scales are often embedded. Breast is naked or has a few scales. Lateral line consists of 45-63 scales, the first 18-29 of them pored. Fin counts are: dorsal VIII-X (VII-XI), 10-12 (9-13); anal II (I-II), 7-8 (6-8); pectoral 12-14. Vertebrae number 36-39 (34-40).

Breeding males become much brighter than individual shown in color plate. Reddish brown on side appears to be overlain by prominent lateral blotches. Lower side is heavily flecked with reddish orange pigment. There may be a red prepectoral spot. Spiny dorsal fin is edged with dark blue and has a broader dark blue base; between these is a fairly broad red band. Reddish brown spots occur in soft dorsal and caudal fins. The color illustration of an exceptional Iowa darter presented in Forbes and Richardson (1920) and used by Hubbs and Lagler (1947 and subsequent editions) is familiar to many biologists. Breeding tubercles do not develop. Male genital papilla is a small squarish flap. Females do not develop bright colors. Female genital papilla is a short tube, grooved near tip.

Scott and Crossman (1973) discuss geographic variability in the Iowa darter but do not recommend subspecific recognition.

Distribution. Extends from Lake Champlain and Lac St. Pierre in Quebec west and north to the headwaters of Hudson Bay drainages and on to the Mackenzie basin. A record near the northern boundary of Alberta is the northernmost known occurrence for any darter. In the United States it extends from New York to Illinois and westward to Wyoming and Montana. No other darter penetrates so close to the Continental Divide in the United States and Canada.

Natural History. The Iowa darter is an inhabitant of clear but sluggish vegetated streams and weedy portions of glacial lakes, marshes, and ponds. Forest clearing and drainage practices have reduced habitat and warmed the remaining waters enough to eliminate this species at many of its southernmost strongholds. Trautman (1957) describes its gradual disappearance from Buckeye Lake and other Ohio localities. Bailey and Allum (1962) comment on its decline in South Dakota, and P.W. Smith (1979) on depletions in Illinois. In the United States it is now common only in nonagricultural regions.

Darters associated with *Etheostoma exile* include *E. microperca* and *Percina caprodes* in lakes, and *E. nigrum* and *E. flabellare* in streams. Turner (1921) reports young to consume microcrustacea principally, whereas midge larvae, mayfly larvae, and amphipods are very important to adults. Hoffman (1967) discusses parasites of the Iowa darter.

Winn (1958a,b) observed on-shore movement from deeper lake water in March and April, and spawning among fibrous root material in May and June. Larger males chase other males; dominant males are most successful at courting females. The male's pelvic fins are placed over the female's dorsal fin and his caudal peduncle wraps around to meet hers. Only a few eggs are laid in each spawning act. In a crowded stream environment Winn did not observe territoriality or much combativeness. Breeding occurs in sandy areas or beneath stream banks.

Abundance. There is no reason to consider the Iowa darter threatened. However, as noted earlier, it has become rare in many parts of the United States and survives best in Canada.

Name. *Exile* means slender.

Etheostoma fricksium Hildebrand   Plate 19
Savannah Darter   Subgenus *Oligocephalus*

Description. A darter of moderate size and average robustness for *Oligocephalus,* reaching 60 mm SL. It is typical of the subgenus in having a small conical head, frenum, 2 anal spines, separate or slightly connected gill membranes, and in breeding males a blue marginal and a red submarginal band in the spiny dorsal fin. Gill membranes are slightly connected; lateral line is gently arched upward and nearly complete. Combined with the speckled soft dorsal fin and distinctly barred caudal fin, these traits serve to separate it from other members of *Oligocephalus*. Bailey and Richards (1963) verified the validity of this species.

Dorsum usually has 6 faint saddles and is lighter than

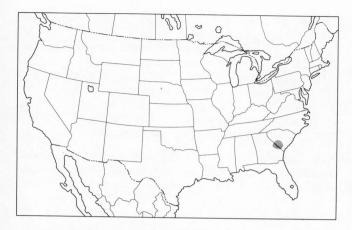

Distribution of *Etheostoma fricksium*

aquatic vegetation. Fallen logs and associated debris sometimes produce both steady flow and suitable protection for this darter. Its only associate in *Oligocephalus* is *E. hopkinsi*. We found it to be less abundant than *Percina nigrofasciata*, *E. olmstedi,* or *E. fusiforme* when all were captured together.

We caught 2 ripe females in late March, which suggests that *E. fricksium* breeds fairly early in Georgia. Additional information is needed for this species.

Abundance. There is no reason to believe that the Savannah darter is threatened. However, it has a small range and is apparently not abundant by comparison with other local darters.

Name. Named by Hildebrand (1923) in honor of L.D. Fricks, surgeon of the U.S. Public Health Service in charge of a malaria control program. The darter's discovery was an accidental by-product of a study to control malaria by use of mosquitofish.

Etheostoma grahami (Girard)   Plate 19
Rio Grande Darter   Subgenus *Oligocephalus*

Description. A rather small but moderately robust member of its subgenus reaching 49 mm SL in our largest specimen. It conforms to *Oligocephalus* traits in having a small conical head, broad frenum, 2 anal spines, and separate to slightly connected gill membranes. The reddish orange spiny dorsal fin of breeding males, however, lacks the marginal blue band and submarginal red band of most members of *Oligocephalus*.

Dorsum may support a number of small saddles but only 1-2 on nape and 2-4 posterior to soft dorsal fin are distinct. Ten or 11 midlateral blotches may be present; anterior blotches are small and very ill defined, but the last 3 on caudal peduncle appear as distinct bands. Numerous dark spots are densest on upper half of body but even belly is spotted. Basicaudal spot is poorly developed or absent. Humeral bar is always apparent.

Preorbital bar is short and postorbital bar is usually only a dark spot. Suborbital bar is dusky but contrasts well with cheek. Lower surface of head is lightly stippled, breast somewhat more so.

Spines of spiny dorsal fin are alternately clear and dark; membranes are darkest toward base, often with individual spots in males. Soft dorsal fin is similar to spiny dorsal fin but lacks dark margin. Caudal fin has a few dusky markings on outer third but is nearly clear basally in males; females have a series of weak vertical bands. Remaining fins are not heavily pigmented but are usually somewhat darkened near base.

Cheek is naked or has embedded scales behind eye. Opercular scales are exposed. Nape bears exposed or embedded scales posteriorly. Breast is naked. Lateral line consists of 44-58 scales, the last 2-13 unpored. Fin counts are: dorsal IX-XII, 11-12 (10-13); anal II, 7-8 (7-10); pectoral 11 (11-13). Vertebrae number 36-37.

sides. There are 8-9 vertically elongated lateral blotches, the posterior few appearing as well defined bands. Spots on upper side sometimes form a scalloped margin with paler dorsum. Additional densely set spots usually form a horizontal lateral band. Lower side has dark spots but belly is clear. Three basicaudal spots are poorly to well defined. There is a small dusky humeral bar.

Head is distinctly dark above, pale below. Preorbital bar and postorbital bar are distinct; suborbital bar is thin, dusky, and posteriorly recurved. Ventral portion of head is clear; breast is clear or stippled.

Spiny dorsal fin has a dark marginal band; basally each membrane has both a vertical dark and a vertical light zone. In females marginal band is faint and rest of fin is very lightly stippled. In males soft dorsal fin rays and adjacent membranes are darkened to form numerous dark spots, sometimes aligned in 2 or 3 bands. In females spots are less prominent, the darkening limited mostly to rays. Caudal fin has 4-5 vertical bands in both sexes. Remaining fins are virtually clear except for some spots in anal fin in males.

Cheek is naked. Nape is scaled posteriorly. Opercle and prepectoral area have some scales. Breast is naked; belly lacks a few scales immediately behind pelvic fin insertions. Lateral line consists of 37-42 (35-45) scales, the last 0-4 (0-9) unpored. Fin counts are: dorsal IX-XII, 9-12; anal II, 7-8; pectoral 13-15. Vertebrae number 37-39.

Males become colorful as shown in color plate. Collette (1965) found breeding tubercles only on anal fin rays but had too small a sample to preclude their presence on belly or pelvic fin. Genital papilla is a triangular flap. Females may develop a little red in spiny dorsal fin, particularly at posterior end. Rusty spots may be present on body. Genital papilla is a round tube, sometimes almost as long as first anal spine.

Distribution. Occurs in the Savannah, Broad, Combahee, and Edisto drainages below the Fall Line in Georgia and South Carolina.

Natural History. The Savannah darter lives in small to medium sized streams, usually in fairly strong current over sand and gravel substrate. It is usually caught in or near areas of

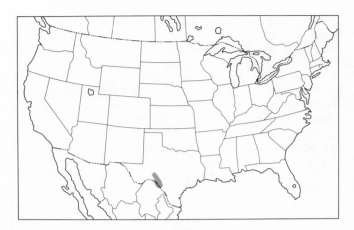

Distribution of *Etheostoma grahami*

Breeding males are handsomely colored, often with lighter green vertical bands on side than those shown in color plate. Breeding tubercles have not been reported. Male genital papilla is a triangular flap. Breeding females may develop dull green vertical bands on body and dull orange spots in soft dorsal fin. Genital papilla is a short round tube.

Distribution. Limited in the United States to the lower Pecos River, a short stretch of the Rio Grande, the lower Devils River, San Felipe Creek, Dolan Creek, and Howard Springs in western Texas. It almost certainy occurs in a few streams and springs in nearby Coahuila, Mexico, and according to Harrell (in Lee et al., 1980) is found in Rio Salado and Rio San Juan in Nuevo Leon.

Natural History. The Rio Grande darter still occurs in riffles of large streams but now is found most frequently in and near springs in the Edwards Plateau. It may be taken from gravel and rubble areas and from vegetated pools. We found specimens hidden among leaves and twigs.

Strawn (1955-56) observed aquarium-held individuals. Breeding activity started as water temperature approached 21°C and success was greatest when very hard water was used. Males displayed some fighting over spots in the tank. Females laid about 10 eggs at a time, apparently on plants, and these apparently were sight detected and fertilized by a male. Males chewed the fins of breeding females. Both sexes ate young but those that were protected and given live food grew rapidly to breeding size in 6 months. Strawn's color description is in close agreement with our specimens except that he noted a red throat and breast in aquarium-reared individuals. He also reared hybrids between *E. grahami* and *E. lepidum*. Subsequently Clark Hubbs and his graduate students conducted numerous experimental studies with this and other Texas darters.

Abundance. The Rio Grande darter is not listed by Deacon et al. (1979). It remains common at a few sites in the United States and Mexico but its future prospects are not bright.

In the late 1960s riffles in Devils River ceased flowing in summer due to upstream pumping for irrigation of alfalfa

and perhaps other crops. This change will quickly relegate *E. grahami* to isolated springs in the river valley. We were directed to such a small spring for specimens by a rancher, Mr. Baker, who explained the rapid change of the region from cattle ranching at the beginning of the century to goat and sheep raising and commercial deer hunting today on what has become brushlands in that short time. Such accelerated change in semiarid regions must be the cause of the rapid endangerment of many species, particularly aquatic ones.

Name. Named in honor of J.D. Graham of the U.S. Boundary Survey, which was responsible for obtaining specimens of this fish.

Etheostoma hopkinsi (Fowler) Plate 19
Christmas Darter Subgenus *Oligocephalus*

Description. An average sized, fairly robust *Oligocephalus* reaching about 60 mm SL. It is typical of the subgenus in having a small conical head, broad frenum, 2 anal spines, and in breeding males a blue marginal and a red submarginal band on the spiny dorsal fin. It differs from its congeners in that the gill membranes are slightly to moderately connected.

Dorsum supports 7-8 small saddles, often quite distinct but sometimes almost obscure. Up to 10 midlateral blotches may be present, those toward tail tending to form distinct vertical bands. In females this lateral pattern is less distinct. A small dark humeral bar may be present. There may be 3-4 basicaudal spots but only the one nearest midline is strong. Numerous spots on body become less frequent ventrally. Belly is clear. A small prepectoral spot is usually present.

Preorbital bar usually meets counterpart on snout. Suborbital bar is diffuse but rather distinct on pale cheek. Postorbital bar is long and distinct, often accompanied by a short line extending diagonally upward. Breast and ventral surface of head are clear to lightly stippled.

Males have a narrow dark marginal band on spiny dorsal fin and a broader dark basal band. In females this fin is stippled on both spines and membranes but is not distinctly patterned. Soft dorsal fin appears lightly banded in both sexes. Caudal fin has wavy vertical bands in both sexes. Basal half of anal fin is somewhat darkened in males, and rays have some dark spots in females. Pelvic fins are clear or darkened slightly on last few membranes. Pectoral fins are lightly darkened, usually producing weak vertical bands.

Squamation is variable and forms the basis for separation into subspecies *E.h. hopkinsi* and *E.h. binotatum* by Bailey and Richards (1963). In the nominate form cheek, opercle, prepectoral area, and nape are usually fully scaled, belly is naked anteriorly, and breast is naked or has a few scales. Lateral line consists of 40-47 (39-50) scales, the last 2-11 (0-14) unpored. In *E.h. binotatum* opercle and breast are naked, prepectoral area and nape are usually naked, cheek is naked to partly scaled (fully scaled rarely), and belly is naked anteriorly. Lateral line consists of 41-49 (39-52) scales, the last 8-13 (3-15) unpored. First 2 dorsal saddles are rather large and

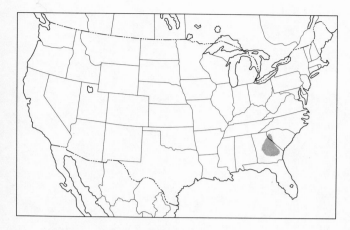

Distribution of *Etheostoma hopkinsi*

prominent in contrast to small markings on a pale background that typify *E.h. hopkinsi.*

Breeding males are colorful, usually showing more red or bright yellow between green or blue vertical bands than is shown in color plate. Breeding tubercles develop to varying degrees but may occur on pelvic fin, on posterior scales of belly back to anal fin, and on anal spines and rays. Genital papilla is a short tube. Females develop some green on body and dull red at end of spiny dorsal fin. Genital papilla is a slender tube of moderate length, slightly crenulate.

Distribution. *Etheostoma h. hopkinsi* occurs in the Altamaha and Ogeechee drainages of Georgia both above and below the Fall Line. *E.h. binotatum* occurs in the Savannah River basin of Georgia and South Carolina, most commonly above the Fall Line.

Natural History. The Christmas darter has been captured from a variety of habitats. It may live, as at the type locality, in spring-fed streams with cool water, sandy substrate, and abundant aquatic vegetation. It also frequents creeks and small rivers, especially where stronger currents produce coarser substrate. We have taken the nominate form below a small spillway around tree roots by an overhanging bank. The subspecies *binotatum* is common in the vicinity of the Fall Line, where one is likely to find riffles with some gravel and rubble, and again in headwater creeks of the Savannah River system. We have taken ripe females in mid-March from the Ocmulgee River in Georgia. Little additional ecological information seems to be available for this species. We are impressed with the strong difference between males of the 2 subspecies, and wonder if they are not specifically distinct.

Abundance. This species is in no present danger, but its areas of abundance are often widely separated from one another, and various types of watershed alterations could cause serious range shrinkages in the future.

Name. Named for the original collector, N.M. Hopkins, Jr., by H.W. Fowler (1945). *Binotatum* refers to the 2 large saddles on the nape.

Etheostoma lepidum (Baird & Girard)   Plate 20
Greenthroat Darter   Subgenus *Oligocephalus*

Description. A rather small and slender member of the subgenus reaching 64 mm SL but seldom exceeding 50 mm SL. It is typical of the subgenus in having a small conical head, frenum, separate to slightly connected gill membranes, 2 anal spines, and in males a blue marginal and a red submarginal band in the spiny dorsal fin. Within its range it is easily confused only with the orangethroat darter, which has less well developed banding on the caudal peduncle. Also, the lateral line is almost complete in *E. lepidum*.

Six to 9 small dorsal saddles vary from very distinct to diffuse. In males 9-12 lateral blotches are rather small and indistinct anteriorly but on posterior half of body are thin vertical bands. In females lateral blotches are less distinct. Small spots are abundant on upper side but become still smaller ventrally and are virtually absent on belly. There is a humeral bar, sometimes appearing as a ventral extension of first dorsal saddle. A basicaudal spot is present, often accompanied by another spot above.

Preorbital bar almost meets counterpart on snout. Suborbital bar is diffuse. Postorbital bar is a dark spot, usually matched by another on opercle. Breast and ventral portion of head are clear.

Spiny dorsal fin has a narrow dark band on margin and a broader dusky median band in males; this pattern is less distinct in females. In both sexes soft dorsal fin has scattered spots but little tendency to be banded. Caudal fin has quite weak vertical bands. Remaining fins are virtually clear except in mature males, which have base of anal and pelvic fins darkly stippled.

Cheek usually is naked; opercle usually is naked but is scaled in specimens from the San Saba River. Nape is scaled posteriorly. Breast is naked. Lateral line consists of 46-61 (43-67) scales, usually the last 2-4 unpored. Fin counts are: dorsal VIII-X (VII-XI), 10-13 (8-14); anal II, 6-8 (4-9); pectoral 11-13. Vertebral counts are not known.

Breeding males are colorful, often brighter than specimen shown in color plate. Breeding tubercles do not develop. Genital papilla is a triangular flap. Breeding females lack bright breeding colors. Genital papilla is a short, rather flat tube.

Distribution. Found in 2 distinct areas, the Pecos River of southeastern New Mexico, and streams of the Edwards Plateau of Texas from the Nueces basin north to the Colorado system.

Natural History. The greenthroat darter is a typical riffle species occurring over gravel and rubble, especially when aquatic vegetation is present. It also lives in spring areas, sometimes in cool vegetated pools.

Hubbs (1967) hybridized *Etheostoma lepidum* and *E. spectabile* readily but these forms do not cross frequently in nature. Strawn (1955-56) found that 18-22°C was optimal spawning temperature. Hubbs et al. (1969) studied developmental temperature requirements.

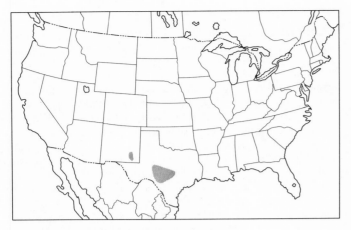

Distribution of *Etheostoma lepidum*

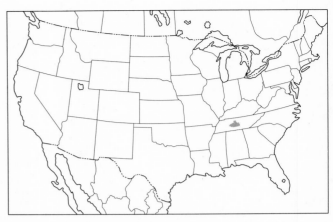

Distribution of *Etheostoma luteovinctum*

In the Colorado and Guadalupe *E. lepidum* is virtually confined to springs and the areas immediately downstream , whereas *E. spectabile* occurs widely throughout the remaining systems. In the Nueces River *E. spectabile* is absent, whereas *E. lepidum* occurs widely and is not confined to spring regions.

Abundance. The greenthroat darter is in no immediate danger of extirpation. Some populations are in a precarious position, however. Hubbs and Echelle (1972) report water supply and habitat problems leading to declines.

Name. *Lepidum* denotes pretty. This darter is a colorful addition to the local fauna.

Etheostoma luteovinctum Gilbert & Swain   Plate 20
Redband Darter   Subgenus *Oligocephalus*

Description. A moderate sized robust member of *Oligocephalus,* 51 mm SL in our largest specimen but probably approaching 60 mm SL maximally. It is typical of its subgenus in having a small conical head, broad frenum, 2 anal spines, and in breeding males a blue marginal and a red submarginal band in the spiny dorsal fin. In some individuals the gill membranes are slightly connected, a condition which helps distinguish nonbreeding populations from those of *E. caeruleum* and *E. spectabile,* both of similar appearance.

Dorsum is rather pale and crossed by 6-7 small distinct saddles. Side bears 8-10 blotches. Those on anterior half of body do not extend far ventrally and often appear to be divided by unpigmented lateral line. Posteriorly blotches are more elongated, almost reaching ventral midline on caudal peduncle. A few dorsal saddles may connect with lateral blotches via narrow, diagonally descending lines. A dark humeral bar continues ventrally behind pectoral fin as a thin line. There is a small dark basicaudal spot, sometimes divided. Belly is clear or sparingly spotted.

Preorbital bar is poorly developed; suborbital bar is very distinct. Postorbital bar may be a spot or may extend posteriorly and dorsally onto head. Upper portions of cheek and opercle are dusky and contrast with pale lower portions. Ventral surface of head and breast are lightly stippled, more heavily so in males.

A narrow dark band in spiny dorsal fin is submarginal anteriorly but is marginal toward end of fin; it is separated by a clear zone from broad dusky basal band. In females dark bands may be represented by interrupted clusters of dark pigment. Soft dorsal fin supports about 3 poorly defined horizontal bands in both sexes. Likewise caudal fin has several wavy vertical bands. Remaining fins are virtually clear except for darkening in basal portion of anal and pelvic fins in mature males.

Cheek is naked ventrally and covered by embedded scales dorsally; opercle is well scaled. Nape is scaled; breast is occasionally naked but usually has a few embedded scales posteriorly. Lateral line consists of 50-56 scales with a mean of 35 pored scales. Fin counts usually are: dorsal X, 13-14; anal II, 6-7; pectoral 11-12. The above counts are mostly those made by David Etnier. Vertebrae number 37 (36-38).

Breeding males are brightly colored as shown in color plate. Breeding tubercles may develop on pelvic fin rays, ventral midline of belly, anal fin spines and rays, base of anal fin, and sometimes on caudal peduncle plus ventral caudal rays. Male genital papilla is a triangular flap. Females may develop tinges of red on spiny dorsal fin and body but are not colorful. Genital papilla is a short round tube.

Distribution. Restricted in central Tennessee to the Caney Fork and Stones River in the Cumberland basin and the Duck River in the Tennessee basin.

Natural History. The redband darter is an inhabitant of springs, spring-fed brooks, and somewhat larger creeks. Near springs it occurs in both pools and riffles, often associated with algae and aquatic plants. In small streams it is common in gravel and rubble riffles during spring but seeks the deeper portions of pools during summer, often finding shelter around rocks or steeply sloping banks. Our casual observation is that individuals in springs are smaller on the average than those in pools and tend to develop richer colors. We have observed it to tolerate heavy stream use by cattle, which often foul the water. Additional information is needed for this interesting endemic species. Its occurrence in adjacent portions of the Tennessee and Cumberland basins suggests recent faunal exchange, quite possibly by way of subterranean change of flow in this region, which is so rich in springs and caves. It frequently is associated with *E. squamiceps,* less frequently with *E. striatulum* or other darters.

Abundance. This species is not in immediate danger. Locally it still occurs in large numbers. But the isolated Stones River stock is very restricted and the species may be undergoing range fragmentation. Deacon et al. (1979) list the redband darter as a species of special concern.

Name. *Luteovinctum* means yellow band, perhaps in reference to the dorsal band in males just reaching or just past optimal breeding coloration.

Etheostoma mariae (Fowler)　　　　　　Plate 20
Pinewoods Darter　　　　　　Subgenus *Oligocephalus*

Description. A moderate sized robust member of its subgenus reaching a maximum size of about 60 mm SL. It is typical of *Oligocephalus* in having a small conical head, broad frenum, 2 anal spines, and in breeding males a blue marginal and a red submarginal band in the spiny dorsal fin. In this species, however, the marginal band fuses into the red band and gill membranes are usually moderately rather than than narrowly connected. Black spots on the cheek, opercle, and prepectoral area are unique traits of this darter.

Dorsum is rather pale and may be subdivided by a narrow dark stripe. There are about 8 pairs of dark spots along base of dorsal fins. Ten to 12 lateral blotches are confined mostly to upper half of body and often appear to be split by pale lateral line. Humeral bar may be poorly developed but often continues ventrally behind pectoral fin. Lower side is abruptly lighter, marked only with a few scattered dark spots. There are 1 or 2 small basicaudal spots.

Dark preorbital bar is narrowly separated from counterpart on snout. Suborbital bar is dark, directed somewhat posteriorly. Postorbital bar is dark and extends across cheek and opercle. Two or 3 black spots on cheek, sometimes fused into a band, plus similar spots on lower opercle and prepectoral area, complete the distinctive head pattern.

Spiny dorsal fin has both a broad marginal and a basal dark band, each darkest at beginning of fin. In females spiny dorsal fin is more spotted than banded. In both sexes soft dorsal and caudal fins are spotted to produce a banded effect, most intense in females. Remaining fins are virtually clear except for dusky bases of anal and pelvic fins in males.

Cheek is finely scaled along posterior margin or bears additional tiny embedded scales anteriorly. Opercle is scaled. Nape has a few scales, often embedded, posteriorly. Prepectoral scales are few and often embedded. Lateral line consists

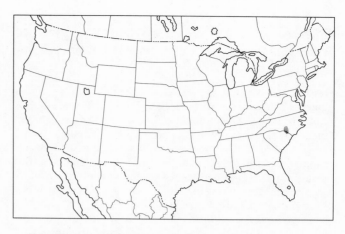

Distribution of *Etheostoma mariae*

of 34-42 scales, the last 1-4 unpored. Fin counts are: dorsal IX-XI, 11-12; anal II, 8-9; pectoral 11-13. Vertebrae number 36-38.

Breeding males are handsomely but not brightly colored, as shown in color plate. Breeding tubercles are not described and are apparently absent. Male genital papilla is a small triangular flap. Breeding females are heavily patterned but not colored. Genital papilla is an abruptly tapered cone, quite broad at base.

Distribution. Narrowly confined to the Little Pee Dee River system in North Carolina and South Carolina. It is found both above and below the Fall Line. Moore (1968) and Menhinick, Burton, and Bailey (1974) corrected the error of Fowler (1947), who had indicated the Cape Fear drainage as the range of this species.

Natural History. The pinewoods darter typically inhabits creeks where riffles contain gravel or rubble. It may be found in quiet sandy or silty pools, especially when aquatic vegetation is present. *Etheostoma fusiforme* and *E. olmstedi* are common darter associates, the latter usually in considerably greater numbers than the pinewoods darter in our experience. Our capture of females with large yolky eggs in late March suggests that breeding occurs fairly early in spring. Menhinick, Burton, and Bailey (1974) indicate that *E. mariae* is abundant in riffles. More information is needed for this darter.

Abundance. The pinewoods darter is locally common within its tiny range and is not considered threatened. Its status should be monitored closely, however.

Name. Named in honor of Mrs. Emlen P. Darlington, who sponsored H.W. Fowler's southern trip.

Etheostoma nuchale Howell & Caldwell   Plate 20
Watercress Darter   Subgenus *Oligocephalus*

Description. A small and rather slender member of its sub-genus reaching 45 mm SL but usually less than 40 mm SL. It is typical of *Oligocephalus* in having a small conical head, broad frenum, separate to slightly connected gill membranes, 2 anal spines, and in breeding males a blue marginal and a red submarginal band in the spiny dorsal fin. It is difficult to distinguish from *E. swaini* but has fewer pored scales in the lateral line and usually fewer dorsal spines and pectoral rays. It obviously is derived from *E. swaini*.

There are up to 9 dorsal saddles but as few as 3 may be clearly defined. Midline of nape is pale. Anteriorly upper part of body bears clusters of spots which are hardly grouped enough to constitute lateral blotches. Posteriorly, particularly in males, spots coalesce into vertically expanded lateral bands. Belly is clear to stippled. There is a narrow vertical humeral bar. Usually there is a single basicaudal spot, sometimes flanked by a smaller spot above and 1 below.

Top of head is rather pale with a dark area posterior to eyes. Preorbital bar usually meets counterpart on snout. Suborbital bar is diffuse, sometimes short. Postorbital bar is distinct, often matched by 1 or 2 horizontal bars on opercle. Breast and ventral surface of head are pale in females, finely stippled in males.

Spiny dorsal fin in males bears a narrow marginal dark band and a wider band above base; often there is an intervening dark band. In females membranes of this fin are stippled, most heavily posteriorly. Males have 2 poorly defined bands in soft dorsal fin with additional darkening at base. In females rays of this fin are darkened to produce a banded appearance. Caudal fin rays in females are darkened, producing vertical bands. In males caudal fin has 2-3 broad dusky vertical bands. Remaining fins are virtually clear except for a broad dusky band in anal fin and a dusky base in pelvic fin of mature males.

Cheek has a few exposed or embedded scales behind or beneath eye. Opercle usually has exposed scales. Breast and midline of nape are naked. Lateral line consists of 35-42 scales, the last 15-27 unpored. Fin counts are: dorsal IX (VIII-XI), 11 (10-12); anal II, 7 (6-8); pectoral 11-12. Vertebrae number 34-35.

Breeding males are handsomely colored as shown in color plate. Breeding tubercles are not present. Genital papilla is a small triangular flap. Breeding females may develop some dull red in spiny dorsal fin and on body. We have not seen genital papilla of a mature female.

Distribution. Howell and Caldwell (1965) found watercress darters only in Glenn Springs within the city of Bessemer, Alabama. Howell and Black (1976) found additional small populations in 3 more springs in the same small stream basin. Attempts to establish this darter in springs a few miles distant did not succeed. Platania (in Lee et al., 1980) reports a sizable population discovered in Roebuck Springs a number of kms south of the type locality.

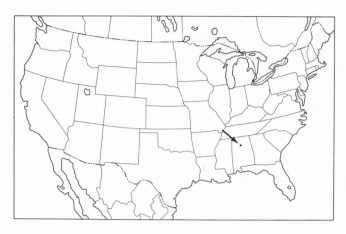

Distribution of *Etheostoma nuchale*

Natural History. *Etheostoma nuchale* inhabits springs and the small streams immediately below them. It has usually been taken from mats of watercress where it rests on stems and leaves well above the soft substrate. It may also occur in flowing water where vegetation offers protection. Since watercress is an introduced plant it is not surprising that this darter occurs in beds of native aquatic plants, as well. Platania (in Lee et al., 1980) reports that snails, crustacea, and insect larvae are food items of the watercress darter and that females are gravid from March to July. Additional studies are being conducted on this darter.

Abundance. The watercress darter is listed by Deacon et al. (1979) as endangered. Its abundance at the type locality has been decreasing as urbanization has surrounded the spring. Increased surface runoff is robbing the spring of flow during summer. The species is common only at Roebuck Springs. The present distribution pattern suggests that many additional sites once existed.

Name. *Nuchale* refers to nape, calling attention to a hump on the nape, a condition found in adult males of a number of darters.

Etheostoma parvipinne Gilbert & Swain   Plate 20
Goldstripe Darter   Subgenus *Oligocephalus*

Description. A rather small and slender species regarded as a member of *Oligocephalus*. It reaches a maximum size of 56 mm SL but usually is less than 50 mm SL. It fits the subgenus in having a small conical head, broad frenum, and 2 anal spines. There is virtually no sign of blue or red in the spiny dorsal fin in breeding males, however, and gill membranes are moderately connected. These and other differences prompted Page (1981) to place *E. parvipinne* alone in a new subgenus *Fuscatelum*, a decision that may gain wide acceptance.

Dorsum is pale with small spots but no saddles. There may be a dark middorsal stripe. Side is densely spotted on upper

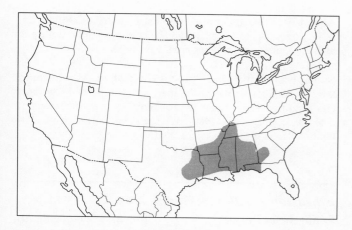

Distribution of *Etheostoma parvipinne*

two-thirds of body. Lateral line appears as a thin golden stripe against dark background. Belly is clear. In mature individuals there may be 10-12 lateral blotches divided into dorsal and ventral components at the level of lateral line. One or 2 (sometimes 3 or 4) small dark spots occur at base of tail. There is no distinct humeral bar. Belly is pale.

Short preorbital bar often meets counterpart on snout. Suborbital bar is prominent, often tapering to a point on ventral surface of head. Postorbital bar is of variable width, often extending across cheek and opercle. Top of head is rather pale but also stippled. Lower cheek, opercle, and often prepectoral area are flecked with dark pigment. Ventral surface of head and breast are clear to lightly flecked with black.

Spiny dorsal fin usually has a dusky margin and dark pigment adjacent to each spine; males have a dark basal spot in the first 1 or 2 membranes. Soft dorsal fin has dark spots scattered on membranes and rays but is not distinctly banded. Caudal fin has poorly defined vertical bands created by numerous dark spots. Anal fin is darkened toward base in males and bears several spots in females. Pelvic and pectoral fins are clear in females; pelvic fin base is dusky in mature males.

Cheek has some scales, often embedded; opercle is scaled. Nape has scales, sometimes embedded anteriorly. Breast is variably scaled, sometimes fully so. Lateral line consists of 48-58 scales, usually fewer than the last 7 unpored. Fin counts are: dorsal VIII-IX, 9-10 (9-12); anal II (I-II), 7-9; pectoral 12-14. Vertebrae number 35-38.

Breeding males do not develop bright colors but may become more golden than the mature female shown in color plate. In males breeding tubercles are restricted to anal fin. Genital papilla is a triangular flap. Female genital papilla is a thick tube, pointed at tip.

Etheostoma parvipinne is variable and worthy of taxonomic investigation. Early confusion existed; Jordan and Evermann (1896) treated it as a mere race of *E. squamiceps,* with which it has scant affinity. Hubbs and Black (1941) and Moore and Cross (1950) reestablished the validity of the goldstripe darter.

Distribution. Is essentially a lowland species occurring almost always below the Fall Line from the lower Brazos River in Texas northeastward to the head of the Mississippi Embayment in Missouri and Kentucky, then southeastward to the Apalachicola and Altamaha drainages in Georgia.

Natural History. The goldstripe darter occurs in or near springs, in small sluggish streams, and occasionally in seepages adjacent to small streams. It may be associated with detritus and aquatic vegetation in some places, sluggish gravel riffles in others. In the case of seepages it must migrate back to streams in summer or be able to survive in crayfish burrows. In Louisiana, Douglas (1974) found it in association with the creek chub in tiny streams tributary to upland creeks, but not in swampy lowlands.

Some darter associates are *Etheostoma collettei, E. proeliare,* and *E. whipplei* in Arkansas, and *E. swaini* and *Percina nigrofasciata* elsewhere. Robison (1977) has studied the goldstripe darter in Arkansas but work is needed from other parts of its range.

Abundance. Seldom collected in numbers, this species is nonetheless widely distributed and in no overall danger of extirpation. But local extinctions are a real threat, as noted for Oklahoma by Robison et al. (1974) and for Missouri by Pflieger (1975).

Name. *Parvipinne* means small fin. The pectoral fin is responsible for the name, being short and rounded. the spiny dorsal fin also has a short base and little height, and may have been in the authors' minds, too.

Etheostoma pottsi (Girard)   Plate 20
Chihuahua Darter   Subgenus *Oligocephalus*

Description. A small, moderately robust member of its subgenus probably not much exceeding 45 mm SL. It is typical of the subgenus in having a small conical head, broad frenum, separate or slightly joined gill membranes, 2 anal spines, and in breeding males a blue marginal and a red submarginal band in the spiny dorsal fin. Its only known congener in Mexico is *E. australe,* which has 1 anal spine. *Etheostoma pottsi* is a poorly known species.

In long-preserved specimens examined by us, dorsum is pale with 6-8 small saddles of variable intensity. Side bears about 10 small blotches, sometimes indistinct. Above and below these are very lightly pigmented zones. Upper side is dark and lower side bears scattered dark scales. Belly is clear. There is a small humeral spot and sometimes 2 faint basicaudal spots.

Prominent preorbital bar fails to meet counterpart on snout. Suborbital bar is weak. Chin is stippled but remainder of ventral part of head and breast are clear.

Spiny dorsal fin has a narrow dark marginal band and a dark basal band. A series of dark spots in each membrane of soft dorsal fin may produce a weakly banded effect. Vertical bands are similarly formed in caudal fin. Anal and pelvic fins

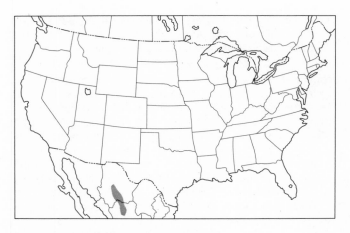

Distribution of *Etheostoma pottsi*

Abundance. Deacon et al. (1979) list *E. pottsi* as threatened. Irrigation agriculture, pesticides, expanding population, and alteration of stream courses are the probable reasons.

Name. Named for John Potts of Chihuahua, who obtained the specimens from which the species was described. The species does not occur in the United States and is therefore not listed in Robins et al. (1980). We use the common name Chihuahua darter given in Deacon et al.

Etheostoma radiosum (Hubbs & Black)   Plate 21
Orangebelly Darter   Subgenus *Oligocephalus*

Description. A rather large member of its subgenus reaching 71 mm SL but usually less than 60 mm SL. It is typical of *Oligocephalus* in having a small conical head, broad frenum, 2 anal spines, and in breeding males a blue marginal and a red submarginal band in the spiny dorsal fin. Some individuals have gill membranes slightly connected. Quite similar in scale and fin counts to *E. whipplei*, it has a weaker suborbital bar than the latter.

Dorsum usually bears 8-9 small indistinct saddles. A like number of lateral blotches are variable, anterior ones sometimes being indistinguishable from dusky background. Some may appear divided into dorsal-ventral pairs but those on caudal peduncle usually form distinct vertical bands. Lower side is less darkened and belly is clear. A small dark humeral spot is evident on almost all individuals.

Dusky preorbital bar does not meet counterpart on snout. Suborbital bar is moderately developed at best. Postorbital bar is usually a diffuse spot matched by another spot on opercle. Ventral surface of head and breast are clear to lightly stippled.

Spiny dorsal fin has a narrow dark border, additional dark pigment at base, and often a dusky median band. Soft dorsal fin has a narrow dark marginal band, a submarginal clear zone, and stippled membranes toward somewhat darker base. A dark vertical band on caudal fin is followed by a clear zone; remainder becomes more heavily stippled toward base. Basal portion of anal fin is dusky and there may be a narrow dark marginal band in mature males. Pelvic fin may be darkened some at base in mature males but otherwise this and pectoral fin are clear.

Cheek has exposed scales posteriorly but embedded ones or no scales anteriorly; opercle has larger exposed scales. Nape may be naked anteriorly but has embedded or exposed scales near dorsal fin. Scales on breast are embedded. Lateral line consists of 47-66 scales, 26-60 of them pored; variability is much less in any local population. Fin counts are: dorsal IX-XII, 11-17; anal II, 6-9; pectoral 10-13. Vertebrae number 35-38.

Hubbs and Black (1941) named this species as a subspecies of *Etheostoma whipplei*. Moore and Rigney (1952) recognized *E. radiosum* as a species with 3 subspecies. *E.r. radiosum* has sharpest shout; *E.r. cyanorum* is on average largest, has fewest unpored lateral line scales, and has bluntest snout; *E.r.*

are clear or lightly stippled at base only. Pectoral fin has a little pigment lying on or adjacent to rays but no distinct banding.

Cheek, opercle, and breast are naked. Nape is naked or has a few embedded scales just anterior to spiny dorsal fin. Belly is fully scaled. Lateral line consists of about 34-45 scales, the last 11-27 unpored (Moore, 1968). Five specimens examined from the Rio Nazas basin had 44-50 scales, the last 12-17 unpored. Fin counts are: dorsal X-XIII, 9-12; anal II, 6-9; pectoral 10 or 11. Vertebrae number 35-36 (34-37).

Breeding males are rather colorful as shown in color plate. We are not familiar with tuberculation, stated by Collette (1965) as absent, and have not seen genital papilla of breeding individuals of either sex.

Distribution. The only early information on the distribution of this species and of *E. australe* was that of Meek (1902, 1904). This range information agrees with that given by Page (1981). Chihuahua darters occur in the Rio Conchos, Rio Nazas, upper Rio Aguanaval, and Rio Mezquital, all in the states of Chihuahua and Durango, Mexico. The headwaters of the Rio Mezquital have been changed by recent volcanic activity with the result that the Chihuahua darter is the only darter to have gained natural access to a Pacific drainage of North America.

Natural History. *Etheostoma pottsi* seems to be a typical riffle darter confined to streams with suitably swift and cool characteristics. Meek (1902) indicated it to be common and to occur with *E. australe*. Page (1981) indicates that the 2 species are seldom found together.

During wetter Pleistocene stages many rivers of northern Mexico were interconnected via lakes which now are dry. The spread of *E. pottsi* must have occurred during such a wet period.

Deacon et al. (1979) imply that the populations of each river basin constitute separate species and that another species exists in Cuatro Cienegas east of the range of *E. pottsi*. We have no evidence for or against these ideas.

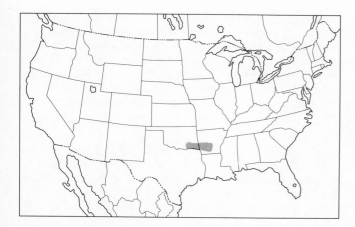

Distribution of *Etheostoma radiosum*

paludosus is palest subspecies and has blue spots on margin of spiny dorsal fin.

Breeding males are colorful as shown in color plate. Breeding tubercles develop on ventral belly scales, on several scale rows on either side of anal fin, and on several scale rows on ventral caudal peduncle. Genital papilla is an elongated triangular flattened tube. Breeding females develop little coloration. Genital papilla is a short pointed tube.

Distribution. Found in Oklahoma and Arkansas in tributaries of the Red River and in the headwaters of the Ouachita River in Arkansas. Strays, if not established populations, are to be expected in northeastern Texas. Subspecies *cyanorum* is found in the Blue River basin in Oklahoma; subspecies *paludosus* occurs in the Clear Boggy and Kiamichi basins of Oklahoma; subspecies *radiosum* occupies the remainder of the range.

Natural History. The orangebelly darter is most often found in riffles of streams ranging from small creeks to moderate sized rivers. Specimens have been captured occasionally in sluggish streams or from quiet backwaters. Gravel and rubble riffles are preferred in most cases. The most common darter associates are *Etheostoma blennioides* and *E. spectabile*.

Scalat (1972) reports on food habits during the first summer of life and the progression in size and variety taken. Adult population density as high as 2.66 per sq m has been measured over riffles (Scalat, 1973b). According to Scalat (1973a) orangethroat darters first breed at 1 year of age and live as long as 4 years. Males hold breeding territories in riffles or raceways. Breeding occurs from March through May. A female enters a territory, is followed by the male, and initiates spawning by plunging into gravel. Eggs are laid in a few seconds while she is mounted by the male. The act is repeated, probably with various males, until as many as 270 eggs are laid. A second batch of eggs may reach maturity and be laid the same season. Scalat (1971) notes some parasites of *E. radiosum*.

Linder's (1953) paper on care of laboratory-maintained darters includes preliminary observations on breeding behavior. Linder (1955) reports natural hybrids between *E. radio-*

sum and *E. spectabile,* a cross observed many times since. Low fertility in parental backcrosses was measured by Linder (1958). Branson and Campbell (1969), Echelle, Schenck, and Hill (1974), and Echelle et al. (1975) continued these studies to evaluate the importance of introgression on the species involved, particularly on *E. radiosum* as the more restricted species. The last named of these authors used isozyme analyses from various parts of the range of *E. radiosum* to conclude that gene flow between populations was slight and that hybridization was not of great importance in determining the difference in various stocks.

This was the first darter we caught and photographed outside Kentucky, and in a sense it initiated the photographic series primarily used in this book.

Abundance. Within its rather limited range *E. radiosum* is well distributed and often the most abundant darter at a particular site. The western localities are those most likely to suffer habitat changes detrimental to this darter.

Name. *Radiosum* refers to the high number of soft dorsal rays found in some individual orangebelly darters. *Cyanorum* and *paludosus* refer to the Blue River and Boggy River, respectively.

Etheostoma spectabile (Agassiz)　　　　　Plate 21
Orangethroat Darter　　　　　Subgenus *Oligocephalus*

Description. A robust average sized member of its subgenus reaching a maximum of 64 mm SL. It is typical of *Oligocephalus* in having a small conical head, broad frenum, separate to slightly joined gill membranes, 2 anal spines, and in breeding males a blue marginal and a red submarginal band in the spiny dorsal fin. It is very easily confused with *Etheostoma caeruleum* but differs in having the infraorbital sensory canal narrowly interrupted. Breeding males are quickly separated on the basis of red pigmentation in the anal fin of *E. caeruleum*.

Dorsum bears up to 10 squarish saddles which are sometimes indistinct. Up to 11 lateral blotches may be present but anteriorly these may be small and difficult to distinguish from general background. Posteriorly blotches are vertically elongated and more distinct but do not form bands as in *E. caeruleum*. Many body scales bear a dark spot; in some individuals these align to form horizontal rows on upper half of body. There is a small humeral spot and a basicaudal spot, the latter sometimes horizontally elongated and often diffuse. Females often appear somewhat mottled, never as distinctly patterned as males.

Preorbital bar, sometimes diffuse, does not meet counterpart on snout. Suborbital bar is moderately well developed. Postorbital bar may be a mere spot or may extend across both cheek and opercle. Breast and ventral surface of head vary from clear to lightly stippled.

In males a broad dark outer band in spiny dorsal fin is separated by a narrow clear zone from a broad dark basal band. In females there usually are narrow marginal, median, and

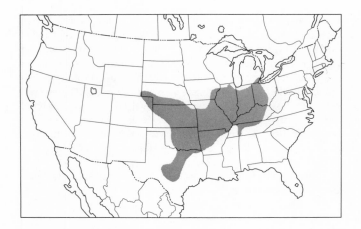

Distribution of *Etheostoma spectabile*

basal bands. In males soft dorsal fin has a broad dusky marginal band, stippling beneath, and a dusky base. In females soft dorsal fin has a series of 3-4 weak bands; caudal fin is similarly banded vertically. Caudal fin is stippled to dusky in males. In females remaining fins are clear, except for dark spots on pectoral rays. In males anal and pelvic fins are dusky basally and pectoral fin is virtually clear.

Cheek is usually naked but may have embedded or even a few exposed scales in some populations. Opercle and nape vary from well scaled to naked in a few cases. Breast usually is naked. Lateral line consists of 35-61 scales, 10-42 of them pored. Variation in scalation is not so great in local populations. Higher counts tend to occur in western and southwestern areas and lower counts in eastern populations. Fin counts are: dorsal IX-XI (VIII-XII), 12-13 (10-15); anal II, 6-7 (4-8); pectoral 11-13. Vertebrae number 35-37.

Distler (1968) recognized 2 widely distributed and 3 narrowly restricted subspecies. He presents good color illustrations of males. *E.s. spectabile* occurs in the White, Black, and Osage systems and some other Ozark streams. All populations to the north and east of the Ozarks are also this form. The subspecies has some racial variation, especially in eastern populations. Prairie and Great Plains streams from Nebraska south to Texas contain subspecies *pulchellum*. The above 2 subspecies intergrade in the Missouri River. Arkansas River tributaries draining the Springfield Plateau contain subspecies *squamosum,* probably derived from *pulchellum*. Subspecies *uniporum* is restricted to the Spring, Eleven Point, and Current rivers in Missouri and Arkansas. It is probably a neotenic form derived from subspecies *spectabile*. Subspecies *fragi* is restricted to the Strawberry River in Arkansas. Possible hybridization with *E. asprigene* and *E. caeruleum* was discussed as a cause for the distinctiveness of subspecies *fragi* and *squamosum*. Distler presents an excellent exposition of the changes in drainage patterns in the western part of the orangethroat darter's range and Pleistocene changes elsewhere in its range as they have contributed to the variations we now see. Electrophoretic patterns produced by the various subspecies have been compared by Wiseman, Echelle, and Echelle (1978); these are in close agreement with Distler's interpretation.

Breeding males are colorful as shown in color plate. Breeding tubercles may develop on anal spines and rays, pelvic spine and rays, lower caudal fin rays, lower pectoral fin rays, and ventral scales of belly and caudal peduncle. Genital papilla is flattened and triangular. Breeding females may develop yellow in spiny dorsal fin and dull red on body but are not bright. Genital papilla is short, tubular, and rounded at tip.

Distribution. Barely enters the Great Lakes basin in southeastern Michigan and northwestern Ohio. From middle Ohio it extends westward through Nebraska to Wyoming, then southward to the Guadalupe River basin in Texas and northeastward through Arkansas, Tennessee, and Kentucky.

Natural History. The orangethroat darter inhabits slow to swift riffles of headwater streams with sand, gravel, rubble, or bedrock substrates. It occasionally enters spring runs or is found in pools or quiet backwaters. It is most abundant in alkaline waters and seems to avoid rivers with powerful currents. In the eastern parts of its range it may be found in a limestone stream only to be absent in an adjacent stream flowing over shale or sandstone.

Daiber (1956) studied seasonal feeding in orangethroat darters. Small (1975) analyzed seasonal differences in feeding, growth rates, production by dry weight and kilocalories per sq m, and differences associated with stream order in probably the most complex such study involving darters.

Winn (1958b) studied some aspects of reproductive behavior. Spawning occurs in April and May over much of the range, but Hubbs and Armstrong (1962) noted breeding in Texas from November through April. Spawning usually occurs in slowly flowing riffles. Males display aggressive behavior toward each other, smaller individuals usually failing to establish breeding sites. A female burrows into gravel, is mounted by a male, and lays several eggs in each spawning act. Hubbs, Stevenson, and Peden (1968) found that females may produce over 1,200 eggs in a spawning season.

In central Kentucky we have observed *E. spectabile* to occur in spring-fed first-order streams and limestone-bedded second-order streams to the exclusion of *E. caeruleum*. The latter is more abundant in third-order streams and is the only one of these 2 species in larger streams. Pflieger (1975) has noted the separation of these 2 species in Missouri.

Hubbs (1967) demonstrated interspecific darter crosses involving *E. spectabile*. While natural hybrids seem rather common, separation of this species from others primarily by behavioral means rather than genetic incompatibility appears to be effective in maintaining its integrity.

Abundance. The orangethroat darter is locally common east of the Mississippi River but achieves greater abundance west of it. Extirpations have occurred locally, as noted for southeastern Iowa by Distler (1968). Conversely Trautman (1957) states that orangethroat darters may have become more abundant relative to rainbow darters in parts of Ohio due to increases in turbidity.

Name. *Spectabile* means conspicuous and is appropriate for breeding males. By coincidence this may be the most conspicuous darter in terms of scientific studies as well as appearance. *Fragi* refers to the Strawberry River. *Uniporum* means one pore, in reference to a modification of pores in the infraorbital canal. *Squamosum* means scaly, indicating the increased anterior scalation of this form. *Pulchellum* means beautiful.

Etheostoma swaini (Jordan)
Gulf Darter

Plate 21
Subgenus *Oligocephalus*

Description. A moderate sized and moderately robust member of its subgenus reaching a maximum of 60 mm SL. It is typical of *Oligocephalus* in having a small conical head, broad frenum, separate to slightly joined gill membranes, 2 anal spines, and in breeding males a blue marginal and a red submarginal band in the spiny dorsal fin. It resembles *E. nuchale* and *E. ditrema,* which have more unpored scales in the lateral series, and *E. asprigene,* which has a much stronger suborbital bar.

Dorsum may be crossed by 7-9 squarish saddles but these are not always distinct. Many scales on side bear a large black spot; spots tend to form about 3 horizontal bands above and the same number below lateral line. Spots on lower side are less perfectly aligned than those above. Belly is clear to stippled. Lateral blotches are poorly defined except for 3-6 weak vertical bands on caudal peduncle. Usually 3 vertically arranged basicaudal spots are distinct. Humeral bar is distinct, running diagonally downward behind pectoral fin.

Preorbital bar fails to meet counterpart on snout. Suborbital bar is dusky and sometimes forms a wedge-shaped spot. Postorbital bar may be a spot or may extend across cheek and opercle. An additional spot on lower cheek and 1 on prepectoral area are often present. Also a dark bar may extend diagonally upward and backward from eye. Two dark spots usually occur beneath lower jaw. Other ventral surfaces of head and breast are clear to stippled.

Spiny dorsal fin has a dark margin and a median dark band, best defined in males. Soft dorsal fin has a narrow dusky margin, a clear submarginal zone, and usually increasing stippling toward base. Caudal fin rays bear numerous dark spots; membranes are stippled but only weakly banded. Remaining fins are virtually clear except for darkening at tips of anal and pelvic fins in mature males.

Opercle is scaled; cheek scales may be embedded. Nape is naked anteriorly but may have a few embedded scales posteriorly. Breast is naked. Lateral line consists of 35-57 scales, only the last 1-12 unpored. Fin counts are: dorsal X-XI (IX-XII), 11-12 (10-14); anal II, 6-8; pectoral 12-14. Vertebrae number 35-37.

Breeding males are brightly colored as shown in color plate. Breeding tubercles are not present. Genital papilla is small and triangular. Females do not develop bright colors. Female genital papilla is a short tube.

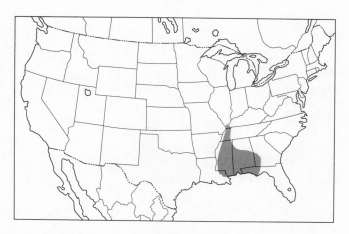

Distribution of *Etheostoma swaini*

Gulf darters have been compared with *Etheostoma nuchale* by Howell and Caldwell (1965) and with *E. ditrema* by Ramsey and Suttkus (1965).

Distribution. Occurs almost entirely below the Fall Line in Gulf Coast streams from Lake Ponchartrain in Louisiana to the Ochlockonee River in Florida. It also occurs in eastern tributaries of the Mississippi River north to Kentucky. Starnes (in Lee et al., 1980) reports its entry in the Tennessee system via Bear Creek about on the Mississippi-Alabama border.

Natural History. The Gulf darter is principally an inhabitant of riffles in clear creeks and small rivers. It is often associated with vegetation, brush, or rocks that give protection. It may also be found over clean sand and gravel in slower currents. We have caught it with *Etheostoma zonale* and *E. stigmaeum* in larger streams and with *Percina nigrofasciata* in small streams.

We have captured brightly colored males and gravid females in March and April in Louisiana and southern Mississippi. A detailed life history of this species is needed.

Abundance. The Gulf darter is locally abundant and in no danger of extirpation. Channelization to drain valleys for farms and pastures has eliminated or depleted this species in many localities, however.

Name. Named in honor of the important 19th-century American ichthyologist Joseph Swain.

Etheostoma whipplei (Girard)
Redfin Darter

Plate 21
Subgenus *Oligocephalus*

Description. A rather robust darter, the largest in its subgenus, reaching 80 mm SL in our largest specimen. It is typical of *Oligocephalus* in having a small conical head, broad frenum, 2 anal spines, and in breeding males a blue marginal and a red submarginal band in the spiny dorsal fin. It is not

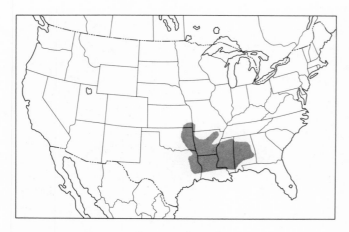

Distribution of *Etheostoma whipplei*

typical in that gill membranes may be moderately connected. It is similar to *Etheostoma radiosum* but has a stronger suborbital bar.

Some individuals have 8-10 small dorsal saddles but a majority have a mottled or reticulated appearance to dorsum and side. In mature males caudal peduncle usually has 4-5 vertically elongated blotches. There is a small humeral spot, and a basicaudal spot which often appears to be expanded into a vertical band. Belly varies from clear to stippled.

Preorbital bar is distinct but fails to join counterpart on snout. Suborbital bar is dark and posteriorly recurved. Postorbital bar sometimes is short but may extend across cheek and upper opercle. Ventral surface of head and breast are clear to lightly stippled.

Spiny and soft dorsal fins have fairly wide marginal and basal dark bands separated by a median clear zone. In females pattern is rather obscure. There is a dusky band at or near tip of caudal fin, the remainder being clear except for a dusky area near base. Remaining fins are rather clear except for a dark base and dusky margin in anal fin of mature males.

Cheek is typically naked, rarely having embedded scales. Opercle has some scales, often embedded. Nape scales are occasionally embedded anteriorly. Breast typically is naked. Lateral line consists of 45-75 scales, the last 7-17 (0-21) unpored. Fin counts are: dorsal IX-XII, 12-14 (11-16); anal II, 7-9; pectoral usually 12-13. Vertebrae number 36-39.

The redfin darter is variable and is discussed here as consisting of 3 subspecies, *E.w. whipplei, E.w. artesiae,* and *E.w. montanus.* Subspecies *artesiae* has about 10 fewer lateral line scales on the average than the nominate form, and subspecies *montanus* averages about 5 more lateral line scales. We have seen only 1 breeding male of subspecies *artesiae*; it differed in several respects from the nominate form, though admittedly it was not at the height of coloration. Robison (1974b) suggests that the Red River basin in southern Arkansas should be a good spot to study the 2 stocks. If intergradation occurs, the subspecies arrangement is probably valid. Douglas (1974) notes the presence of both stocks in Louisiana and treats them as subspecies. The possibility of returning subspecies *artesiae* to species status deserves attention.

Breeding males are extremely colorful as shown in color

plate. Breeding tubercles develop on belly scales and sometimes along anal fin base to caudal peduncle. Genital papilla is a small squarish flap. Breeding females may display a little red or yellow on fins and body but are not colorful. Genital papilla is a short, rather flattened tube.

Distribution. *Etheostoma w. whipplei* occurs in the Arkansas River basin in Kansas, Missouri, Oklahoma, and Arkansas. It continues northeastward into the lower White River system and southward in the lower Red River and the Ouachita River basin. *E.w. montanus* is confined to 1 Arkansas River tributary in western Arkansas. The western range of *E.w. artesiae* is not accurately established, particularly in the Red River basin, where it contacts the range of the nominate form. In general it extends from the Neches-Angelina basin in eastern Texas across southern Louisiana, most of Mississippi (probably excluding the Pascagoula basin), and through most of the the Mobile basin, excluding the upper Tallapoosa and Coosa rivers.

Natural History. The redfin darter typically inhabits riffles in small to medium sized streams over a wide range of gradients and degrees of clarity. Blair (1959) found it to enter the smallest brooks and to prefer gravel riffles. It breeds during April in Kansas, where it is sporadic in occurrence (Cross, 1967). In such regions of unpredictable drought the effects of dams, stream alterations, and organic pollution by runoff from cattle feedlots are sadly documented for the Neosho River by Cross and Braasch (1968). There remain many interesting questions on the ecology of the redfin darter.

Abundance. Robison (1974a) indicates that *E.w. montanus* in Arkansas is rare. Local reductions and extirpations are known for *E.w. whipplei* and are likely to have occurred with *E.w. artesiae.* The latter two are abundant enough in places to be considered safe, however.

Name. *Whipplei* honors A.W. Whipple, officer in charge of the survey that produced the first specimens of this species. Specimens said to have come from an artesian well gave rise to the name *artesiae.* Hilly terrain and the swift water associated therewith are suggested by *montanus.*

Etheostoma barbouri Kuehne & Small   Plate 22
Teardrop Darter   Subgenus *Catonotus*

Description. A rather small member of the subgenus reaching 60 mm SL but usually less than 50 mm SL. It is typical of *Catonotus* in having a deep caudal peduncle, rather low spiny dorsal fin, frenum, interrupted supratemporal and infraorbital canals, and closely set pelvic fins. Its cheek bar, suborbital bar, and virtually unpored lateral line are distinctive. The frenum is broad. Gill membranes are separate to slightly connected.

Dorsum may be stippled but more often bears 8-9 small

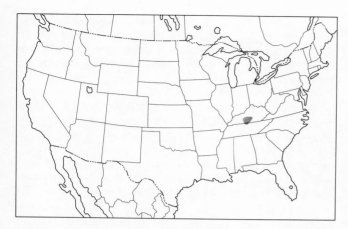

Distribution of *Etheostoma barbouri*

m. In Bylew Creek near Mammoth Cave National Park we have encountered it thriving with 2 other *Catonotus* darters, *Etheostoma flabellare* and *E. squamiceps*. *E. nigrum* and *E. caeruleum* are the most common additional associates throughout its range.

Flynn and Hoyt (1979) report spawning in pools between March and late May at temperatures of 12-15.5°C. Females spawning at 1 year's age produce an average of only 19 ova; those few females surviving to 2 years produce an average of 35 mature ova. A higher percentage of males survive to their second year and these are reproductively more successful than younger smaller males. Chironomids, cladocerans, copepods, and blackfly larvae make up the bulk of the diet. Some cannibalism of young was observed. Winter and spring are the season of heaviest feeding. Heavy infestations of the parasite blackspot are reported.

The strong tendency toward neotony found in the subgenera *Hololepis* and *Microperca* is also seen in *E. barbouri* and to a lesser degree in other barcheeked members of *Catonotus*. About 10% of specimens from the Green River and about one-third of those from the Barren River have no pores in the lateral line series, a reduction matched only in *E. microperca* and *E. fonticola*.

Abundance. The teardrop darter is abundant in many headwater streams within its rather small range. Channel clearing and straightening to facilitate farming are the main disturbances to the species. Ironically such practices lead to the appearance of lateral gullies and slumping banks, both detrimental to permanent agriculture as well as to aquatic resources.

Name. Named in honor of R.W. Barbour for his teaching and research contributions to the natural history of Kentucky. The common name stems from the presence of a distinct suborbital bar in contrast to other species of barcheeked darters.

saddles. About 10 lateral blotches tend to be vertically elongated, and 1 or more may connect with a dorsal saddle via a diagonal dark streak. Belly is pale. A dark humeral bar continues beneath pectoral fin, sometimes to fin base.

Preorbital bar fails to meet counterpart on snout. A prominent suborbital bar is directed somewhat posteriorly. Postorbital bar is directed upward around prominent cheek patch before crossing upper cheek and opercle. Remainder of cheek and opercle is clear to stippled, and ventral surface of head and breast are clear or stippled in mature males.

Spiny dorsal fin is stippled in membranes and bears some dark spots in spines; fin is dusky toward base in mature males. Soft dorsal fin is lightly pigmented to produce weak horizontal barring. Similar wavy vertical bands occur in caudal fin. Anal and pelvic fins are clear except for a few spots and stippling toward base of anal fin in males. Pectoral fin displays weak vertical banding.

Cheek, opercle, nape, and breast are naked. Belly is naked anteriorly, often scaled posteriorly. Lateral line consists of 40-49 scales, only the first 0-12 (mean about 3) pored. Fin counts are: dorsal VIII-X, 12-13 (11-15); anal II, 8-9 (7-10); pectoral usually 12. Vertebrae number 35-37.

Breeding males are brightly colored on fins as shown in color plate. Genital papilla is a short triangular tube. Breeding females are not colorful. Genital papilla is a fleshy pad with radiating grooves.

Specimens from the Barren River have fewer pored scales and less variability in number of pored scales in lateral series than have specimens from the Green and Nolin rivers.

Distribution. Restricted to the upper Green River and Barren River in Kentucky and Tennessee. The most plausible method of entrance from the Cumberland River basin that houses the other barcheeked darters is via subterranean stream capture in the karst area of Logan and Simpson counties, Kentucky.

Natural History. The teardrop darter inhabits pools in small upland streams, most commonly those free of silt. It frequently stays close to the stream margin where rocks, overhanging banks, or brush offer protection. It is common only in second-, third-, and fourth-order streams at depths of less than 1

Etheostoma flabellare Rafinesque   Plate 22
Fantail Darter   Subgenus *Catonotus*

Description. A fairly slender and sometimes large member of its subgenus reaching 70 mm SL but usually not exceeding 60 mm SL. It is typical of *Catonotus* in having a deep caudal peduncle, a low spiny dorsal fin, frenum, interrupted infraorbital canal, and closely set pelvic fins. Supratemporal canal is occasionally uninterrupted. Gill membranes are rather broadly joined; this trait, along with the absence of a distinct submarginal band in the spiny dorsal fin and the presence of greatly enlarged tips of that fin's spines, serves to distinguish it from *Etheostoma kennicotti*.

The fantail darter is the most variable of all darters. Some of this variability exists within individual populations but much is regional and represents a serious taxonomic problem. Additional subspecies probably can be named and perhaps some variants are worthy of specific recognition. A small un-

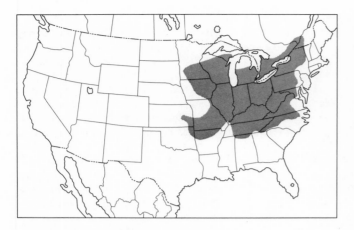

Distribution of *Etheostoma flabellare*

named *Catonotus* darter in the upper Tennessee basin, superficially similar to *E. flabellare,* awaits formal recognition.

Dorsum bears an average of 8 saddles in younger individuals which tend to become continuous with a like number of lateral blotches in adults, especially males. Anteriorly 1 or 2 blotches are never in contact with a saddle. Some individuals, especially females, are not so consistently banded, or have pattern partly obscured by a generally mottled appearance. Lower side is spotted and belly is clear to stippled. Many scales on upper half of body have dark central spots and in some populations these may create horizontal lines. Humeral area usually is slightly elevated and covered by a dark mark which may continue ventrally behind pectoral fin. A basicaudal spot may not develop, may be distinct, or may be divided into separate dorsal and ventral spots.

Preorbital bar is dark to diffuse and does not meet counterpart on snout. Suborbital bar is a small, usually diffuse spot, sometimes absent. Postorbital bar is dark to dusky, crossing cheek and opercle. Ventral surface of head and breast are stippled to varying degrees.

Spiny dorsal fin stands but half as high as soft dorsal fin; in adult males each spine is expanded at tip. In breeding males epidermis at base of fin becomes thickened and turgid, perhaps producing a substance protective of eggs in the nest. In some cases there is a dusky submarginal band, in others a dusky basal band. Females usually have a dusky basal band. In both sexes rays and membranes of soft dorsal fin bear scattered dark markings often producing weak horizontal bands. Fan-shaped caudal fin has 5-7 bold dark wavy vertical bands. Anal fin varies from clear to basally darkened. Pelvic and pectoral fins are clear or slightly darkened basally.

Cheek, opercle, breast, nape, and anterior half of belly are naked. Lateral line consists of 45-55 (44-59) scales, the first 14-40 pored. Fin counts are: dorsal VIII (VI-IX), 13-14 (12-15); anal II, 7-9; pectoral usually 13. Vertebrae usually number 33-34 in subspecies *lineolatum* and 34-36 in subspecies *flabellare,* though Scott and Crossman (1973) report 32-34 for Canadian specimens of the latter.

Subspecies *flabellare* has well developed vertical bands on body and shows little tendency toward development of horizontal bands except to an increasing extent westward along

the lower Ohio River basin. Subspecies *lineolatum* displays horizontal bands prominently. Subspecies *brevispina* has a light body coloration against which saddles and vertical bands stand out; also snout is more rounded and mouth more nearly horizontal.

Breeding males are not colorful, as shown in color plate, but are extremely modified in shape of head, nape, and spiny dorsal fin. Some individuals develop a dark head and yellowish body, others become fairly dark all over. Male genital papilla is a flattened triangular tube, much smaller than in most darters. Breeding females are not colorful nor altered in head shape, though often distended in belly to a degree unusual among darters. Genital papilla is a circular pad.

Distribution. The only member of subgenus *Catonotus* with an extensive range, the fantail darter occurs from southern Quebec across the southern Great Lakes to the head of the Mississippi basin in Wisconsin and Minnesota, southward to northern Arkansas, and eastward throughout the Ohio River basin. It occurs in rivers of the Atlantic slope from the Pee Dee north to the upper Hudson. However, its absence in the Rappahannock, York, and Delaware rivers and its probably recent appearance in the Susquehanna suggests that the more northerly of these basins may have gained this species by recent introduction. Populations in western North Carolina seem long established and need taxonomic study.

Populations in the Pee Dee, Roanoke, and New rivers and parts of the upper Tennessee have been referred to subspecies *brevispina*. Other Atlantic coast populations and those of the St. Lawrence basin and virtually all of the Ohio basin are considered to be subspecies *flabellare*. Populations west of the Mississippi are generally considered to be subspecies *lineolatum*. Pflieger (1975) indicates that isolated populations in the southeastern Ozarks are subspecies *flabellare*. Jenkins, Lachner, and Schwartz (1971) and Clay (1975) mention a *lineolatum* type in the Guyandot and Big Sandy rivers.

Questions concerning the fantail darter and possible relatives remain the largest species problem among darters of the genus *Etheostoma*.

Natural History. The fantail darter occupies riffles with gravel or rubble substrate in streams of first through eight order; it lived in the Ohio River before canalization. In large streams it is found in shallow areas away from main currents. In tiny streams it may sometimes be scooped from beneath riffles that have virtually ceased to flow. Ultsch, Boschung, and Ross (1978) have demonstrated that it tolerates low oxygen levels for short periods, greatly aiding its survival during low flow. Trautman (1957) reports its former abundance in prairie streams of northwestern Ohio and in the shoals around western Lake Erie islands. Scott and Crossman (1973) state that Canadian populations breed in small streams but overwinter in deeper pools downstream. Fantail darters occur at higher elevations in the eastern mountains than do most darters. We are able to take specimens in winter in Kentucky when sculpins are the only other active fish.

Breeding behavior is described in part by Lake (1936) and more completely by Winn (1958a,b). Males establish and defend territories around rocks with some clearance above a silt-free substrate. The spiny dorsal fin is used to clean the underside of the rock. A female moves under the rock and lays an average of 38 eggs in a single layer. Spawning position is head to tail, the female inverted and the male upright except at the moment of fertilization. About 450 eggs per female are laid, several spawnings with the same or different males being required. Lake (1936) and Cross (1967) add more observations, and Cooper (1979) has studied eggs and larval development.

Karr (1964) found larger but fewer males than females in Iowa. By contrast Baker (1978) found males to be more numerous and to outlive females by 6 months, reaching 2.5 years.

Turner (1921) reported midge larvae and other aquatic insects to be the principal dietary components. Small (1975) found isopods and amphipods to be seasonally important; he determined growth rates and production by dry weight and kilocalories per sq m, as well as changing relationships of the above factors associated with stream order. Adamson and Wissing (1977) used their electivity index to determine real food preferences, and found morning and evening to be feeding peaks.

The external and internal parasites of fantail darters are summarized by Hoffman (1967). This darter may occasionally serve as food for sculpins and for game fishes but is not important in this regard.

Abundance. The fantail darter is the most abundant darter locally and is common throughout much of its range.

Name. *Flabellare* means fanlike, in reference to the caudal fin. *Lineolatum* means "with fine lines" and refers to the horizontal bands on the body. *Brevispina* means short spine, calling attention to the spiny dorsal fin of fantail darters generally.

Etheostoma kennicotti (Putnam) Plate 22
Stripetail Darter Subgenus *Catonotus*

Description. An average sized, rather slender member of its subgenus reaching 69 mm SL but not often exceeding 50 mm SL. It is typical of subgenus *Catonotus* in having a deep caudal peduncle, a low spiny dorsal fin, frenum, interrupted supraorbital and infraorbital canals, and closely set pelvic fins. Gill membranes are moderately connected. A prominent submarginal dark band in the spiny dorsal fin is the principal feature distinguishing this species from *Etheostoma flabellare.*

Back has about 7 small saddles, often poorly defined. Small individuals usually have 11-12 evenly spaced lateral blotches which tend to become vertically elongated in adults. Irregularly placed dark areas on upper side obscure pattern in many cases. Some individuals tend to have spots arranged in horizontal lines along upper half of body. Belly is clear. A basicaudal spot varies in size and intensity and may be flanked above and beneath by less prominent spots. There is a prominent humeral spot.

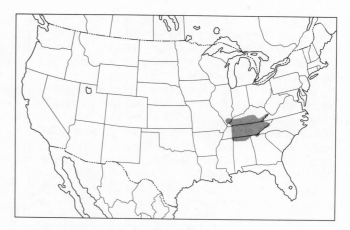

Distribution of *Etheostoma kennicotti*

Distinct preorbital bar fails to meet counterpart on snout. Suborbital bar is often absent in western populations, weakly developed in eastern populations. Postorbital bar is short and distinct. Lower cheek, opercle, ventral surface of head, and breast are stippled with dark pigment.

Spiny dorsal fin has a narrow submarginal dark band which is quite prominent in males; basally fin is clear to stippled. In males tips of spines are expanded into knobs; females are unusual in that tips of spines are also expanded, though not to the degree found in males. Soft dorsal fin is diagonally banded due to dark pigment in rays and associated portions of membranes. Fan-shaped caudal fin has 5-7 prominent vertical bands formed similarly to those in soft dorsal fin. Anal and pelvic fins are clear; pectoral is clear to weakly banded.

Cheek, opercle, nape, and breast lack scales. Anterior half of belly is naked or incompletely scaled. Lateral line consists of 40-49 scales, the first 20-25 pored. Small specimens are incompletely developed and have fewer pored scales. Fin counts are: dorsal VII-VIII, 10-12; anal II, 7-8; pectoral usually 13. Vertebrae number 34 (32-35).

Variability in size and to some extent pattern is great, particularly when comparing populations from western Kentucky or southern Illinois with those of the upper Cumberland River basin. Page and Smith (1976) found the variation to be clinal and recommended that no subspecies be recognized.

Breeding males are not brightly colored but touches of yellow and orange develop on body and fins as shown in color plate. As in *Etheostoma flabellare,* head and nape may become swollen. Male genital papilla is flat and pointed, very much smaller than that in most darters. Females do not develop breeding colors. Genital papilla is a circular pad with deep radiating grooves.

Distribution. Occurs from the southern tip of Illinois southward and eastward to the head of the Green and Cumberland rivers and almost to the head of the Tennessee River. Gaps in this range occur in the lower Green and middle Cumberland basins.

Natural History. The stripetail darter usually is found in small shallow streams with rocky substrate and moderate gradient. In riffles it is found where rubble offers good protection. In pools protection is sought beneath stones or undercut banks. In the lower Tennessee River basin this species occurs in gravel- or sand-bedded streams, often where overhanging vegetation occurs at poolside.

Page (1975a) conducted stream and aquarium studies on the stripetail darter. The sex ratio among young specimens favored females 1.4:1.0. Mortality rates were high for both sexes. Males grew faster and lived longer, almost to their third year. Large males usually attracted breeding females before smaller males did and were able to obtain good breeding sites through combative behavior. Courtship preceded spawning, which occurred head to tail or head to head beneath flat stones. Females laid 1-2 eggs at a time until 20-80 were placed in a single layer on the underside of the stone. Nests contained 50-400 eggs. Aquarium-held specimens were daylight spawners. Competition for nest sites with *Etheostoma squamiceps* is possible. Adults fed on immature insects and crustaceans.

In the upper Cumberland basin the stripetail darter is associated with *E. baileyi, E. caeruleum, E. nigrum,* and *E. sagitta.* In the rest of its range it usually comes into contact with 1 or more other members of subgenus *Catonotus.* Its uniform abundance in the upper Cumberland basin contrasts with its sporadic abundance elsewhere and suggests the possibility of severe competition with its close relatives.

Abundance. This species is in no danger of extirpation. Channel modification poses the main threat to western populations, and stripmining to certain eastern populations.

Name. Named in honor of Robert Kennicott, who first caught the species in southern Illinois.

Etheostoma neopterum Howell & Dingerkus Plate 22
Lollypop Darter   Subgenus *Catonotus*

Description. A robust, average sized member of its subgenus reaching 65 mm SL in males and about 50 mm SL in females. It is typical of subgenus *Catonotus* in having a deep caudal peduncle, a low spiny dorsal fin, frenum, interrupted supratemporal canal, and closely set pelvic fins. The infraorbital canal is sometimes uninterrupted. Gill membranes are separate, usually overlapping anteriorly. The soft dorsal fin apparently is unique among darters.

Dorsum is crossed by 6-11 poorly defined saddles. Several oval blotches contrast poorly with dusky side. Breeding males become very dark, sometimes developing 10-12 dark vertical bars on side. Humeral spot is small, usually quite dark. Basicaudal spot is small and poorly defined.

Distinct preorbital bar does not meet counterpart on snout. Dusky suborbital bar is fairly long and directed somewhat posteriorly. Postorbital bar extends almost across cheek and is narrowly separated from a weaker continuation across opercle. Cheek and opercle become steadily lighter ventrally. Ventral surface of head and breast vary from almost clear to dusky in mature males.

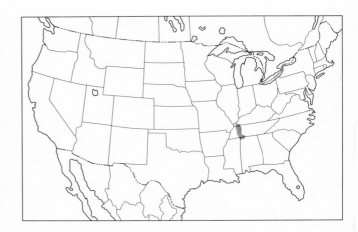

Distribution of *Etheostoma neopterum*

In specimens other than breeding males, spiny dorsal fin has clear spines and mottled membranes; soft dorsal fin is weakly banded and has a scalloped margin caused by rays extending a little beyond membranes; rounded caudal fin has broad wavy vertical dark bands; anal and pelvic fins are clear to basally dusky; and pectoral fin supports weak vertical bands. In breeding males spiny dorsal fin is dark except for white or yellow knobs at tips of spines; elongated tips of soft dorsal fin are yellow and expanded into terminal knobs. Membranes are dark except for occasional clear oval windows, and membranes are restricted to basal half of rays; anal and pelvic fins are dark but caudal and pectoral fins differ little from nonbreeding individuals.

Cheek varies from naked to scaled. Opercle has few to many exposed scales. Nape is scaled but anterior scales may be embedded. Breast is naked; belly is fully scaled. Lateral line consists of 46-51 (41-58) scales, the last 11-18 (7-27) unpored. Fin counts are: dorsal VIII-X, 11 (9-12); anal II, 7 (6-9); pectoral usually 12. Vertebral number is not reported.

Breeding males develop black and yellow pigmentation but are not colorful, as shown in color plate. Genital papilla is small, flattened, and triangular. Breeding females are not colorful. Female genital papilla is a rounded grooved pad.

Distribution. Restricted to tributaries of the lower Tennessee River from Shoal Creek in Alabama and Tennessee northward to the mouth of the river in Kentucky.

Natural History. The lollypop darter usually inhabits spring- or seepage-fed creeks with depths of less than 1 m. It is rather secretive, living beneath undercut banks, especially where leaf litter, detritus, or tree roots offer additional protection. Sandy substrates characterize most sites of capture. *Etheostoma duryi, E. simoterum,* and *E. squamiceps* were reported as darter associates at the type locality by Howell and Dingerkus (1978), who offer some ecological information. Kuehne and James Small captured the male illustrated here with several females, *E. nigrum,* and the "redbelly snubnose darter" on a 1970 trip but never pursued the problem of this strange darter. Page and Mayden (1979) found eggs to be laid on undersides of flat rocks.

Abundance. The lollypop darter appears to be in no danger of extirpation. It is sporadically distributed and should be carefully monitored.

Name. *Neopterum* means new fin in reference to the unique soft dorsal fin of breeding males. The unusual common name refers to the same knobbed structures.

Etheostoma obeyense Kirsch   Plate 22
Barcheek Darter   Subgenus *Catonotus*

Description. A rather large slender member of its subgenus reaching 68 mm SL in our largest specimen. It is typical of *Catonotus* in having a deep caudal peduncle, a low spiny dorsal fin, frenum, interrupted supratemporal and infraorbital canals, and closely set pelvic fins. Gill membranes are separate. Lack of both suborbital bar and horizontal lines on body distinguishes it from other barcheeked darters except for *E. smithi*, which differs in usually having fewer pored lateral line scales.

Most individuals have 6-7 dorsal saddles, 1 or more of which may be indistinct. Saddle on nape may be broken into blotches. Nine to 11 vertically elongated lateral blotches may in many cases be joined to saddles by zigzag lines of dark pigment on upper side. A distinct humeral bar continues ventrally behind pectoral fin.

Preorbital bar fades near snout and does not meet counterpart. Suborbital bar is absent or represented only by slight stippling. Postorbital bar passes above cheek bar before crossing cheek and opercle. Lower cheek and opercle are stippled, or in mature males reticulated. Lower surface of head and breast are clear to stippled.

Only membranes in spiny dorsal fin are pigmented, and these most strongly near base. Males have a dark spot at anterior base of this fin. Pigment in membranes of soft dorsal fin produces several weak diagonal bands. Vertical bands in caudal fin are virtually absent in some males. Anal fin has a dusky border in mature males but otherwise lacks pigmentation; anal spines are unusually short. Pelvic fin is clear and with its partner may form a cuplike structure. Weak vertical banding in pectoral fin is entirely absent in 3 ventralmost rays and membranes.

Cheek, opercle, nape, breast, and at least anteriormost portion of belly are naked. Lateral line consists of 41-52 scales, only the first 6-21 pored. Fin counts are: dorsal VII-IX, 12-15; anal II, 7-10; pectoral 12-13. Vertebrae number 35-36.

Breeding males become rather colorful as shown in color plate. Genital papilla is a small triangular flap. Breeding females may develop traces of yellow on body, cheek bar, and appropriate fins but are not colorful. Genital papilla is a circular pad with radiating grooves.

Distribution. Occurs in tributaries of the Cumberland River from the Big South Fork in Kentucky to the Obey River in Tennessee. A downstream population discussed and briefly

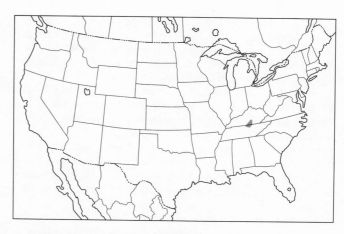

Distribution of *Etheostoma obeyense*

characterized by Kuehne and Small (1971) is now considered to be *Etheostoma smithi*.

Natural History. The barcheek darter is common in pools in creeks up to third order but is quite rare in larger streams. It usually occurs in association with rubble, organic debris, or steep banks which afford some protection. In spring this species may be common in steadily moving currents, where we have observed males establishing territories and guarding nests beneath flat rocks. In Kentucky it breeds in April and May, sometimes in close proximity with *Etheostoma flabellare*.

E. obeyense seems to occur to the exclusion of other barcheeked darters, though it is in close proximity to *E. virgatum* and *E. smithi*. The situation suggests that intense competition and competitive exclusion are involved. Page and Schemske (1978) note this exclusion among pool-dwelling members of *Catonotus* where competition for breeding sites may be intense.

Etheostoma blennioides, *E. caeruleum*, *E. flabellare*, *E. nigrum*, and *E. rufilineatum* are the common darter associates of the barcheek darter in its small-stream habitat.

Abundance. The barcheek darter occurs in most small streams within its restricted range and often is the most abundant darter present. It seems to be safe from threats.

Name. *Obeyense* calls attention to the fact that the type specimens were captured in small streams within the Obey River basin.

Etheostoma olivaceum Braasch & Page   Plate 22
Sooty Darter   Subgenus *Catonotus*

Description. A robust and rather large member of its subgenus reaching 67 mm SL in our largest specimen. It is typical of subgenus *Catonotus* in having a deep caudal peduncle, a low spiny dorsal fin, frenum, interrupted supratemporal canal, and closely set pelvic fins. Infraorbital canal is uninterrupted. Gill membranes are slightly connected. It differs from *Etheostoma squamiceps* in lacking scales on cheek and opercle, and from *E. neopterum* in the absence in males of expanded tips on the soft dorsal fin.

In many individuals 5-7 ill-defined dorsal saddles lie between middle of spiny dorsal fin and caudal peduncle. In other specimens dorsum has irregular small blotches. Side is mottled and may also bear 8-9 broad vertical bands. Anterior part of lateral line may be unpigmented and appear as a clear line. Humeral spot is well developed but does not contrast well with side. There usually is a prominent vertical bar at base of caudal fin. Belly and ventral surface of caudal peduncle are pale.

Distinct preorbital bar does not quite meet counterpart on snout. Bold postorbital bar crosses cheek and often continues across part of opercle. There is no suborbital bar. Lower cheek, opercle, ventral surface of head, and breast are pale but stippled.

Dark submarginal and basal bands are poorly developed in spiny dorsal fin, which otherwise is lightly stippled. In males tips of spines are bent posteriorly but are not expanded. Rays of soft dorsal fin protrude slightly above margin of membranes; rays and sometimes adjacent membranes are alternately light and dark, producing a series of diagonal bands. Six to 9 vertical bands lie in caudal fin, pigmentation concentrated in and adjacent to rays. Anal fin varies from clear to moderately stippled at base; first anal spine is much longer than second spine, following which there is a distinct notch in fin margin. Pelvic fin is clear to basally dusky and with its partner forms a slightly cup-shaped structure. Pectoral fin bears 6-9 faint vertical bands.

Cheek and opercle are naked. Nape often is naked anteriorly but has exposed or embedded scales posteriorly. Prepectoral area varies from poorly to well scaled; breast has scattered scales or is naked. Belly is fully scaled. Lateral line consists of 44-58 scales, the first 13-46 pored. Fin counts are: dorsal VIII-X, 12-13 (11-14); anal II, 7-8 (6-9); pectoral 11-13. Vertebral number is not reported.

Breeding males do not develop bright colors, instead darkening considerably as shown in color plate. Specimen illustrated is the extreme example in our experience, relief offered only in cream or yellow fin margins and in caudal fin. Genital papilla of males is a short wide flap with a posteriorly directed median nipple. Breeding females, usually much smaller than adult males, do not develop bright colors. Genital papilla is a raised oval pad with alternating ridges and grooves.

Distribution. Restricted in the middle Cumberland River basin of Tennessee to tributaries of the Caney Fork and to a few short Cumberland River tributaries near the mouth of Caney Fork.

Natural History. The sooty darter inhabits small streams, usually being found in rocky pools less than 1 m deep. Less often it occurs in shallow runs or riffles with protective rubble. Its usual darter associates are *Etheostoma atripinne* and *E. flabellare,* both of which are far less common.

Page (1980) found that males establish and defend territo-

Distribution of *Etheostoma olivaceum*

ries around flat rocks. Most successful males are in their second year but do not survive to a third year. Most egg production is accomplished by 1-year-old females, few of which survive to their second year. Egg production is low, probably no more than 112 eggs. Males protect the nest, which may contain as many as 1,500 eggs, but not the young. Aquatic insects and small crustaceans are the main food items. Occasional parasites include a spiny-headed worm and the metacercariae of flukes.

Abundance. Locally abundant within its narrow range, the sooty darter is not in present danger of extirpation. Valley farms and hillside pastures in the area are eroded in many cases but the impact is not apparent on this darter. Its very short lifespan and low reproductive potential could quickly change its status if conditions favoring reproduction were altered.

Name. *Olivaceum* calls attention to the tan mottled appearance of this species. David Etnier, when he called our attention to its existence, spoke of the then-unnamed species as a "dirty darter" because of its unkempt appearance. That name was used in the species description but altered to sooty darter in Robins et al. (1980).

Etheostoma smithi Page & Braasch   Plate 23
Slabrock Darter   Subgenus *Catonotus*

Description. A rather small slender member of its subgenus reaching 52 mm SL. It is typical of subgenus *Catonotus* in having a deep caudal peduncle, a low spiny dorsal fin, frenum, interrupted supratemporal and infraorbital canals, and closely set pelvic fins. Gill membranes are separate to slightly joined. Lack of horizontal banding and a suborbital bar distinguish it from barcheeked darters other than *Etheostoma obeyense,* which has a higher average number of pored lateral line scales.

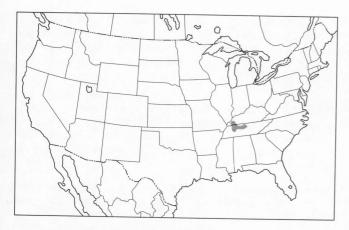

Distribution of *Etheostoma smithi*

the habitat of other barcheeked darters. *Etheostoma squamiceps* and *E. kennicotti* are occasional associates of the slabrock darter.

Page and Burr (1976) found this to be a short-lived species, 2 years maximally. Males grow faster but only constitute about 40% of hatchlings and do not survive as well into the second year. Females lay only 19-69 eggs in a season spanning April to mid-June. Much of this species' behavior resembles that reported for *E. kennicotti*.

Abundance. The slabrock darter is common at widely separated places but rarity or absence in intervening areas cannot be attributed to human interference. Possibly competitive exclusion by other members of subgenus *Catonotus* accounts for sporadic occurrence of this species, which is in no present danger of extirpation, however.

Name. Named in honor of Philip W. Smith of the Illinois Natural History Survey, contributor to several fields of vertebrate natural history.

Dorsum usually bears 6-8 small rectangular saddles; the first may be missing and others occasionally contrast poorly with cross-hatching which extends onto back from side. There are 8-12 lateral blotches, the anterior ones small and oval and those toward tail vertically elongated. Lower side is lightly stippled and belly is clear. A prominent humeral bar continues ventrally behind pectoral fin.

Preorbital bar is prominent, not quite meeting counterpart on snout. Postorbital bar is narrow and recurved upward along margin of cheek bar, not quite reaching opercle. Suborbital bar is virtually absent, fused into anterior margin of cheek bar. Ventral surface of head and breast are clear to lightly spotted.

Spiny dorsal fin membranes are lightly stippled except for a distinct dark spot at anterior base, best seen in males. Several weak diagonal bands cross soft dorsal fin, and rather weak vertical bands cross caudal fin. Anal fin is clear except for basal darkening in males. Pelvic fins are clear or weakly stippled near base in males. Weak vertical bars are confined to dorsal half of pectoral fin.

Cheek, opercle, nape, breast, and anterior part of belly are naked. Lateral line consists of 41-54 scales of which only the first 5-11 (2-13) are pored. Fin counts are: dorsal VIII-X, 13-15; anal II, 8-10; pectoral 11-13. Vertebral number is not reported.

In breeding males coloration is most intense on head and fins, as shown in color plate. Genital papilla is a small triangular flap much widened at base. Breeding females may develop a little yellow or orange in fins and on cheek bar but are not colorful. Genital papilla is a circular pad with radiating grooves.

Distribution. Occurs sporadically in the lower Cumberland River basin from below Caney Fork in Tennessee to the mouth of the river in Kentucky. It extends up the Tennessee River basin to tributaries of the lower Duck River.

Natural History. The slabrock darter typically lives in shallow pools of small streams. It may be captured beneath rocks, brush, and overhanging banks. We have seen it in streams lacking a rocky substrate and with murkier water than typifies

Etheostoma squamiceps Jordan   Plate 23
Spottail Darter   Subgenus *Catonotus*

Description. A robust darter and the largest of its subgenus, reaching 85 mm SL. It is typical of subgenus *Catonotus* in having a deep caudal peduncle, a low spiny dorsal fin, frenum, interrupted supratemporal and infraorbital canals (infraorbital rarely uninterrupted), and closely set pelvic fins. Gill membranes are separate, sometimes overlapping anteriorly. Prominent basicaudal spots and heavy scalation on the head are unique characteristics for the subgenus.

Dorsum supports 6-8 small saddles which may be rather obscure. Upper side is variously stippled, mottled, or covered with zigzag open V-shaped lines. Likewise the rest of body, save clear belly, may be mottled or covered with wavy bands or may support poorly defined vertical bands. A distinct midcaudal black spot usually is flanked above and below by lesser spots. Small humeral spot is not prominent.

Preorbital bar does not meet counterpart on snout. Suborbital bar varies from diffuse to prominent, sometimes posteriorly directed at tip. Postorbital bar is distinct, sometimes flanked above by a parallel band. Particularly in males, cheek has several horizontal or diagonal marks. Ventral surface of head and breast are clear to stippled.

Spiny dorsal fin has clear to lightly stippled membranes and alternately light and dark spines; in breeding males fin darkens and develops somewhat expanded tips. Soft dorsal fin membranes also are clear and rays are alternately light and dark; in breeding males fin darkens, leaving unpigmented oval windows. Caudal fin membranes are clear; alternate light and dark marks on rays produce prominent vertical bands. Anal and pelvic fins are clear, or are stippled in mature males.

Cheek is partly naked but is scaled behind eye. At least upper part of opercle is scaled. Nape may have embedded

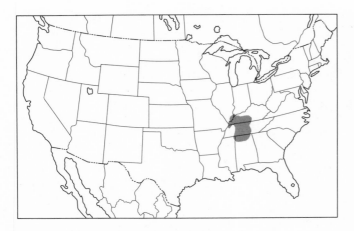

Distribution of *Etheostoma squamiceps*

Catonotus darters, including young crayfish in early spring.

The spottail darter may be found with several of its congeners in various parts of its range and is competitively successful in such situations. Darter associates include most small stream species within its range.

Abundance. Locally abundant, the spottail darter is in no danger of extinction or even serious depletion. It is one of the few fishes that are common in the coalfields of western Kentucky, and does better than most small-stream fish in agricultural regions.

Name. *Squamiceps* means scaled head, referring to the scales on the cheek, opercle, and breast, an exceptional condition among *Catonotus*.

scales toward head but has exposed scales posteriorly. Breast and prepectoral area have small scales, sometimes partly embedded. Lateral line consists of 40-57 scales, the first 19-42 pored. Fin counts are: dorsal VIII-IX (VII-X), 11-14; anal II, 6-8; pectoral usually 12. Vertebrae number 36 (35-38).

Spottail darters differ somewhat in different parts of their range but subspecies have not been proposed.

Breeding males do not develop bright breeding colors, as shown in color plate. They become quite dark; head blackens and becomes swollen. Most breeding males are old individuals much larger than gravid females. Modified tips of dorsal spines and rays are unusual but not unique for the subgenus. Genital papilla is a small triangular flap. Breeding females are not at all colorful. Genital papilla is an oval pad, radially grooved.

Distribution. Widely but sometimes sporadically distributed through the Green River in Kentucky and southward through the lower and middle portions of the Cumberland and Tennessee basins as far south as northern Alabama. The spottail darter enters southern Illinois and Indiana. Short eastern tributaries of the Mississippi River from the confluence of the Ohio River to Reelfoot Lake contain this or a closely related unnamed form.

Natural History. An inhabitant of small to medium sized streams of low to moderate gradient, the spottail darter may be found in quiet pools beneath stones, brush, aquatic vegetation, or undercut banks. It is quite tolerant of murky conditions but not of excessive amounts of silt. This species is also found in large river backwaters.

Page (1974b) found this to be a long-lived *Catonotus* darter, reaching 4 years in males and perhaps 3 years in females. An initial sex ratio of 2:1 in favor of females results in a few old breeding males reproducing with numerous smaller and younger females. Spawning occurs beneath flat rocks in pools or riffles with slow current. Females may produce as many as 357 ova, and nests may contain up to 1,500 eggs. Spawning occurs upside down, head to head. March and April are peak spawning months but small males may nest successfully in May. Diet is more varied than in certain other

Etheostoma striatulum Page & Braasch   Plate 23
Striated Darter   Subgenus *Catonotus*

Description. A small slender member of its subgenus reaching 47 mm SL. It is typical of *Catonotus* in having a deep caudal peduncle, a low spiny dorsal fin (sometimes rather arched), frenum, interrupted supratemporal and infraorbital canals, and closely set pelvic fins. Gill membranes are separate. It appears most similar to *Etheostoma barbouri* but has only a weak suborbital bar at best.

Dorsum is crossed by 6 small rectangular saddles; a seventh saddle may develop on nape. Pigment running through scales produces horizontal banding along side; a secondary diagonal pattern may develop. Nine to 11 oval midlateral blotches and a dark humeral bar with a ventral extension behind pectoral fin complete body pattern.

Prominent preorbital bar fails to meet counterpart on snout. Suborbital bar is weak or reduced to a spot. Postorbital bar follows margin of cheek bar upward and ends before reaching opercle. Ventral surface of head is often stippled and breast is lightly stippled.

Spines of spiny dorsal fin are clear and membranes are lightly stippled except for a dark spot well behind anterior margin of fin base; there may be a narrow marginal dark band, as well. Soft dorsal fin supports 3-4 diagonal dark bands and some additional darkening along base. There are 4-5 weak vertical bands in caudal fin. Anal fin varies from clear to stippled, darkening confined mostly to base. Pelvic fin is clear or has some pigmentation along anterior margin. Weak banding in pectoral fin excludes lower 3 rays and membranes.

Cheek, opercle, nape, and breast are naked. Belly is fully scaled. Lateral line consists of 40-46 (38-50) scales, only the first 6-12 (2-18) pored. Fin counts are: dorsal VIII-IX, 12-14; anal II, 8-9 (7-10); pectoral 10-12. Vertebral number is not reported.

Breeding males develop bright colors on fins and some on body as shown in color plate. Genital papilla is a small triangular flap. Breeding females develop touches of dull orange or yellow on appropriate fins and cheek bar but are not colorful. Genital papilla is an oval pad with radiating grooves.

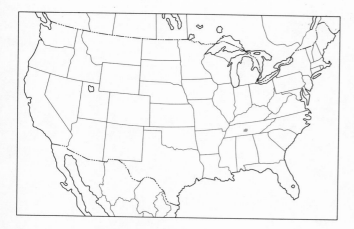

Distribution of *Etheostoma striatulum*

Distribution. The most restricted darter in subgenus *Catonotus,* the striated darter is found in tributaries of the Duck River in Bedford and Marshall counties, Tennessee.

Natural History. The striated darter occurs in shallow pools of limestone-bedded creeks and seeks shelter beneath stones, brush, and ledges. Habitat information presented by Page and Braasch (1976) is expanded by Page (1980). Striated darters usually live a single year, only a few living to reproduce a second time. Spawning beneath stones was not directly observed but probably resembles that of other barcheeked species. Females carry up to 108 eggs, and a nest contains an average of only 155 eggs. Females slightly outnumber males. Food is principally aquatic insect larvae and small crustacea. Ectoparasites are also reported.

Abundance. Page (1980) states that the striated darter is rare except at a few sites and that agricultural practices have led to altered stream conditions that do not favor this darter. On a recent trip Kuehne was unable to get a specimen at the type locality or elsewhere and observed heavy use of local streams by cattle. More than the physical disturbance of trampling, manure dropped directly into the stream creates severe oxygen problems that may be quite detrimental to the striated darter. Only *Etheostoma squamiceps* now is abundant in most of the headwater localities that formerly yielded striated darters.

Deacon et al. (1979) do not list the striated darter as rare or endangered. It should be so treated, in our opinion. Page (personal communication) also failed to capture specimens recently and is seriously concerned over this situation.

Name. *Striatulum* means striated.

Etheostoma virgatum (Jordan)   Plate 23
Striped Darter   Subgenus *Catonotus*

Description. A moderately large slender member of its subgenus reaching 65 mm SL in our largest specimen. It is typical of *Catonotus* in having a deep caudal peduncle, a low spiny dorsal fin, frenum, interrupted supratemporal and infraorbital canals, and closely set pelvic fins. Gill membranes are separate. It is most similar to *Etheostoma striatulum* only in that each has horizontal lines on the body; those of *E. virgatum* are less delicate in appearance.

Dorsum is crossed by 6-7 small faint saddles. In some individuals longitudinal bands occur on back, partly obscuring saddles. Eight to 11 small lateral blotches tend to be obscured by numerous horizontal dark bands. Banding weakens on lower side, and belly is clear.

A distinct humeral bar continues ventrally behind pectoral fin in most specimens. A distinct caudal spot is absent but there may be a concentration of spots at base of tail.

Preorbital bar initially is distinct but fades on snout, failing to meet counterpart. Suborbital bar is absent. Postorbital bar follows margin of cheek patch upward before crossing cheek and usually opercle. Lower cheek, opercle, ventral surface of head, and breast are usually clear but are stippled in mature males.

Spines of spiny dorsal fin are clear; membranes are stippled lightly at margin and a little more heavily toward base. There usually is a dark basal spot in the second, third, and fourth membranes. Soft dorsal fin has weak diagonal dark bands produced by stippling on membranes. Similar stippling produces weak vertical bands in caudal fin; caudal rays may be somewhat darkened basally. Anal fin usually is clear but in males is darkened basally and usually along margin. Pelvic fin is clear. Pectoral fin rays are slightly darkened basally but spots on rays produce vertical bands only in dorsal half of fin.

Cheek, opercle, nape, breast, and anterior half of belly are naked. Lateral line consists of 41-52 scales, the first 7-19 (4-21) pored, Fin counts are: dorsal VIII-IX (VII-X), 12-13 (10-14); anal II, 8-9 (7-10); pectoral 12-13. Vertebrae number 35-37.

Breeding males become colorful on fins, parts of body, and cheek bar, as shown in color plate. Genital papilla is a small triangular flap. Breeding females may develop touches of yellow or orange on fins, head, and body but are not colorful. Genital papilla is an oval pad with radiating grooves.

Western populations of *E. virgatum* have on the average fewer scales in lateral series than eastern populations, as noted by Kuehne and Small (1971), with an average decrease of about 5 pored scales. These 2 populations are separated by the range of *E. obeyense,* creating the possibility that *E. virgatum* may represent 2 subspecies or possibly 2 species.

Distribution. Abundantly distributed in the Rockcastle River, Buck Creek, and Beaver Creek of the Cumberland River basin in Kentucky. A downstream population occurs in the middle and lower Cumberland River basin from the Caney Fork to the Red River in western Tennessee and Kentucky.

Natural History. *Etheostoma virgatum* is common in second-, third-, and fourth-order creeks, where it usually is caught along protected banks or on sloping bottoms at depths of less than .5 m. In many areas it occurs in flat-bedded streams that flow over limestone but it is also common in streams flowing through sandstone or shale regions where pools are scoured to

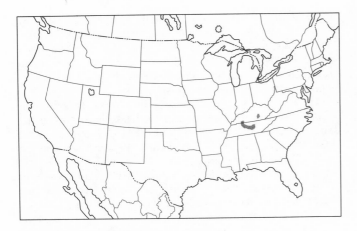

Distribution of *Etheostoma virgatum*

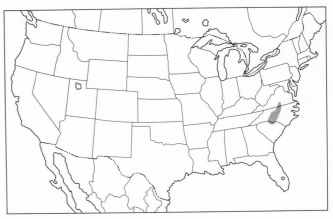

Distribution of *Etheostoma collis*

somewhat greater depths. We have noted this species to rein-vade silted stripmine streams of the Rockcastle basin more rapidly than other local darters. In April it is common in areas of steady current, sometimes entering the lower reaches of tiny woodland tributaries to spawn. Spawning tends to be delayed in murky silted streams until June, when reduced flow allows the water to lose turbidity.

Common darter associates include *Etheostoma baileyi, E. blennioides, E. caeruleum, E. nigrum,* and *Percina maculata* in the east, and additionally *E. etnieri, E. atripinne,* and *E. squamiceps* in western areas.

Abundance. Thriving in innumerable creeks and displaying adaptability to changing environmental conditions, the striped darter is in no present danger.

Name. *Virgatum* means streaked.

Etheostoma collis (Hubbs & Cannon)   Plate 23
Carolina Darter   Subgenus *Hololepis*

Description. An average sized member of its subgenus reaching 43 mm SL. It is typical of subgenus *Hololepis* in having a small head and mouth and a highly arched incomplete lateral line. The frenum is rather broad. Gill membranes are separate to slightly joined. The Carolina darter differs from most swamp darters in typically having 1 anal spine, but consistently differs from *E. saludae* only in lacking interorbital sensory pores. The 2 forms may not actually be specifically distinct.

Dorsum has only traces of saddles and is basically covered with small cross-hatched marks. Seven to 10 small lateral blotches are variously developed, sometimes not clearly separate from additional cross-hatching and stippling on body. Belly is clear or lightly stippled. A basicaudal spot is usually distinct and is flanked above and below by a spot of lesser intensity.

Preorbital bar is rather faint and does not quite meet

counterpart on snout. Suborbital bar varies from faint to distinct. Postorbital bar is faint, usually only a diffuse spot. Lower cheek, opercle, ventral surface of head, and breast usually are clear but are stippled in mature males.

In females there is only a little darkening on spines of spiny dorsal fin, but in males membranes are somewhat darkened above base, especially at anterior end. There is a black spot at anterior fin base in breeding males. Several weak diagonal bands in soft dorsal fin are best developed in males. Caudal fin rays are darkened to produce poorly defined vertical bands. In females remaining fins are clear; in males anal and pelvic fin membranes are stippled while pectoral fin bears a few dark spots. Pelvic fins in breeding males are unusually long and somewhat cupped, as they are in subgenus *Microperca*.

Cheek usually has small embedded scales. Opercle has exposed scales, sometimes few in number. Nape varies from scaleless to having a few embedded scales posteriorly. Breast and preopercular area vary from naked to weakly scaled. Lateral line consists of 35-49 scales, the first 9-21 (5-30) pored. Fin counts are: dorsal IX (VII-X), 11-13 (10-14); anal I (I-II), 7-8 (6-9); pectoral 11-12 (10-13). Vertebrae number 36-37 (35-37).

The Carolina darter exists as 2 subspecies according to Collette (1962). *Etheostoma c. collis* seldom develops scales on nape and lacks breast scales; *E.c. lepidinion* is characterized by a scaly nape in most individuals and breast scales in many.

Breeding males do not develop bright colors, as shown in color plate. They may develop breeding tubercles on pelvic fin spine and rays and on all anal fin rays. Genital papilla is a short pointed tube. Females do not develop breeding colors. Female genital papilla is a moderately elongated tube, somewhat rounded at tip.

Distribution. A species of the Atlantic coast Piedmont region. Subspecies *lepidinion* occurs in the Roanoke and Neuse basins, and according to Collette (1962) the Cape Fear River system. Subspecies *collis* lives in the Pee Dee and Catawba basins. The latter are part of the Santee River basin, which also contains *E. saludae,* but the species ranges do not overlap.

Natural History. This is typically a darter of small upland streams. It is found in areas of low current velocity, often against banks or in backwater areas. Murky water or fine sediments on the substrate do not preclude the Carolina darter's well-being. We have encountered specimens among brush and tree limbs fallen into a stream, which seemed to act as protection.

We have taken 2 gravid females in late March but know nothing else about reproduction in this species. We have not taken other darters with this species, though it seems plausible that *E. olmstedi* should be an occasional associate.

Abundance. This species perhaps is too little known to surmise its true abundance. We collected at several places before encountering *E.c. collis,* but it was fairly common in at least 1 spot. We have no first-hand information on *E.c. lepidinion.* The Carolina darter deserves a detailed study for range and abundance, since it may be a species which is disappearing.

Name. *Collis* pertains to upland, in reference to the species' occurrence above the Fall Line. *Lepidinion* means scaled nape.

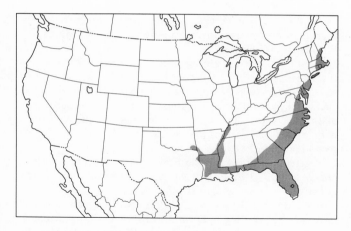

Distribution of *Etheostoma fusiforme*

Etheostoma fusiforme (Girard)   Plate 23
Swamp Darter   Subgenus *Hololepis*

Description. A rather large member of its subgenus reaching 50 mm SL. It is typical of subgenus *Hololepis* in havng a small head and mouth and a highly arched incomplete lateral line. The frenum is fairly broad. Gill membranes are slightly, sometimes moderately, connected. Its head scalation is sufficient to distinguish it from other species of *Hololepis* except for *Etheostoma serriferum,* which has a more nearly complete lateral line.

Dorsum may be poorly marked or may support about 9 small squarish saddles. Eight to 13 lateral blotches occur in varying sizes and intensities, sometimes merging into a continuous band. Lower side is spotted or stippled and belly is clear. A median caudal spot may be subdivided and in addition may occasionally have weak accompanying spots near dorsal and ventral bases of tail.

Preorbital bar is diffuse to distinct, not joining counterpart on snout. Suborbital bar may be continuous from eye or may start well below eye. Postorbital bar is usually a mere spot. Lower cheek and opercle are stippled or mottled, as are ventral surface of head and breast.

Spiny dorsal fin usually has alternately dark and clear spines; membranes are darkened at their contact with spines but a distinct pattern is not produced. Stippling against margins of rays in soft dorsal fin produces a weak banding. Caudal fin also is banded, weakly to moderately. Anal fin is clear or dusky near base. Pelvic fin is clear or a little darkened near base. Pectoral fin may be virtually clear but usually is weakly banded.

Cheek and opercle are scaled. Nape is partly to fully scaled. Breast and prepectoral area are scaled, though scales

may be partly embedded. Lateral line consists of 40-63 scales, of which 0-37 are pored. Lowest counts on pored scales occur in bay lakes of North Carolina. Maximum variation in all scale counts is never reached at any single locality. Subspecies *E.f. barratti* has a mean of 6 more pored scales and correspondingly fewer unpored scales than has *E.f. fusiforme.* Fin counts are: dorsal IX-XI (VIII-XIII), 10-11 (8-13); anal II, 7-8 (5-10); pectoral 12-14 (12-15). Vertebrae number 38-39 (37-40).

Hubbs and Cannon (1935) clarified many of the knotty problems dealing with *E. fusiforme* and other swamp darters, including undescribed forms on the Atlantic slopes. Collette (1962) further reviewed subgenus *Hololepis* and reduced *E. barratti* to its present status as a subspecies of *E. fusiforme,* while synonomizing certain other subspecies in *E.f. fusiforme.*

Neither breeding males nor breeding females develop bright colors, as shown in our color plate of a female *E.f. fusiforme.* Female genital papilla is a conical tube, rather enlarged at base. Males may develop breeding tubercles on pelvic and anal fin rays. Male genital papilla is a small, flattened triangular tube.

Distribution. *Etheostoma f. fusiforme* occurs primarily on the Atlantic coastal plain from southern Maine to the Cape Fear and Waccamaw rivers in North Carolina. Records exist for Long Island. In Virginia it may extend a bit above the Fall Line. It has been introduced into ponds in western North Carolina. *E.f. barratti* lives from the Pee Dee River in North Carolina virtually to the southern tip of Florida, the only darter with such an extensive range in the latter state. Westward it is narrowly confined to the Gulf coast until reaching the Mississippi embayment, where it occurs sporadically as far north as Kentucky. It also extends up the Red River drainage as far as northeastern Texas and southeastern Oklahoma, where it is rare (Robison, Moore, and Miller, 1974).

Natural History. The swamp darter is found in sluggish streams, swamps, bogs, and manmade ponds, especially where detritus or aquatic vegetation occurs. It lives in water with lower pH values than are tolerated by all but a few fishes, yet thrives in alkaline waters of north Florida, as well. The span of water temperature encountered between Maine and Florida also is impressive.

Small crustaceans are an important dietary element but complete food habits need clarification. Smith (1950) reports swamp darters to be an important element in the diet of young chain pickerel and young largemouth bass. Though some populations appear to have only a single adult size class, it is likely that most populations have some adults which survive to a second breeding season.

Darter associates include *Etheostoma serriferum* and *E. gracile* as well as *E. chlorosomum, E. olmstedi,* and less frequently other lowland species.

Collette (1962) presents field observations and describes breeding behavior for aquarium-held specimens. Initial courtship and physical contact did not result in spawning but females would later spawn with a male on aquatic plants. Specimens adjusted to artificial food and aquarium conditions with ease.

Abundance. There is no reason to suggest problems for this widespread and locally abundant darter. It thrives under a variety of conditions which include warm water, extreme murkiness or brown coloration, low pH, and low oxygen content. Such adaptability is an attribute beneficial to survival in our modern world.

Name. *Fusiforme* means long and cylindrical. *Barratti* is named in honor of John Barratt, a naturalist of South Carolina.

Etheostoma gracile (Girard)   Plate 24
Slough Darter   Subgenus *Hololepis*

Description. A moderate sized member of its subgenus reaching 50 mm SL. It is typical of *Hololepis* in having a small head and mouth and a highly arched incomplete lateral line. The frenum is fairly broad. Gill membranes are slightly connected, sometimes tending to be moderately connected. It may best be distinguished from most other members of *Hololepis* by the bright coloration seen in breeding males. From *E. zoniferum* specimens differ mainly in having a complete infraorbital sensory canal.

Eight to 11 small dorsal saddles vary from weak to prominent. Lateral blotches may be poorly developed, especially in females, but optimally consist of 8-10 roughly diamond-shaped marks lying beneath interspaces of dorsal saddles. Belly is clear. A small basicaudal spot is distinct.

Distinct preorbital bar almost meets counterpart on snout. Suborbital bar is diffuse, virtually absent in a few individuals. Postorbital bar varies from a mere spot to a line extending across cheek. Lower cheek, opercle, ventral surface of head, and breast usually are clear in females and stippled in males.

Membranes of spiny dorsal fin are weakly stippled and rays are clear in females. In males there usually is a weak dusky marginal band and somewhat heavier stippling at base

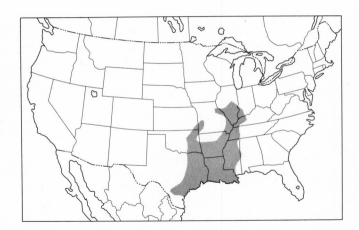

Distribution of *Etheostoma gracile*

of each membrane. In both sexes there are about 3 horizontal bands in soft dorsal fin produced by darkening of rays. Males may have lightly stippled membranes in addition. Caudal fin has about 4 similar bands which run vertically. In both sexes remaining fins are clear or virtually so.

Cheek and opercle are scaled. Scales often extend onto dorsolateral portion of head. Nape is naked anteriorly but may have scales posteriorly. Breast and prepectoral area are naked to weakly scaled. Lateral line consists of 42-52 (40-55) scales, the first 14-24 (13-27) pored. Fin counts are: dorsal IX-X (VII-XIII), 10-12 (9-14); anal II (I-II), 6-7 (5-9); pectoral 11-13. Vertebrae number 36-38.

Breeding males are unusual for subgenus *Hololepis* in having bright coloration. Breeding tubercles may develop on terminal portions of pelvic spine and rays as well as on outer portions of anal rays. The unusual development of 2-4 tubercles on each side of lower jaw is clearly seen in color plate, as are a few anal fin tubercles. Male genital papilla is a small flattened triangular tube. Breeding females are not colorful. Female genital papilla is a conical tube, terminally pointed and somewhat enlarged at base.

Distribution. Along the Gulf coast, occurs from the Pearl River in Mississippi westward to the Nueces River in Texas. The species extends northward well beyond the Mississippi Embayment into western Kentucky, southern Indiana and Illinois, and northeastern Missouri. It occurs also in the Red, Arkansas, and Osage rivers from eastern Texas to southwestern Missouri. Its presence in the Tombigbee arm of the Mobile River system suggests recent entry via stream capture or perhaps human introduction.

Natural History. The slough darter is found in pools of slowly flowing small streams, backwaters of major rivers, and occasionally oxbow lakes or swamps. It tolerates murky water and silt-bedded pools but favors areas of aquatic vegetation when available. It is easily maintained in aquariums.

The species may breed in early March in Texas and in May and early June in Illinois. Males develop coloration and breeding tubercles during winter. Braasch and Smith (1967) conducted extensive life history studies in Illinois. Males seem to be territorial, with 3-year-old individuals developing sexual characteristics earlier than younger males. At high population levels this would probably limit breeding to some extent. In years following severe drought conditions or winter kill from lack of oxygen, younger males presumably would find territories and be reproductive participants. The male mounts a female, rubbing her with his pectoral fins and chin tubercles. The female swims to twigs or aquatic plants to lay an egg, which is quickly fertilized. The site is passed by time and again until 30-50 eggs are aligned in a row.

Diet is determined in part by the ability to handle prey and in part by the availability or sheer abundance of species seasonally. Feeding is heavy during spring but becomes very light from July through September.

Braasch and Smith found slough darters to be in food competition with *Etheostoma chlorosomum*. Other darter associates were *E. nigrum, E. spectabile,* and *Percina maculata.* Elsewhere *E. asprigene, E. parvipinne, Ammocrypta vivax,* and occasionally *E. fusiforme* are found with the slough darter.

Braasch and Smith report a fluke, *Crepidostomum isostomum,* to be a common parasite of slough darters.

Abundance. This species remains common in many localities and is in no danger of extirpation, but many local extirpations or depletions have occurred. Pflieger (1971) describes a distribution pattern for Missouri that might be interpreted as a relict pattern. We were unable to find the species or even find suitable water at the type locality in the Nueces River basin. The slough darter should be monitored for further losses in the future.

Name. *Gracile* means slender.

Etheostoma saludae (Hubbs & Cannon)
Saluda Darter

Plate 24

Subgenus *Hololepis*

Description. A rather small member of its subgenus reaching 46 mm SL in our largest specimen. It is typical of subgenus *Hololepis* in having a small head and mouth and a highly arched incomplete lateral line. The frenum is narrow. Gill membranes are slightly connected. It is most similar to *E. collis,* differing principally in having interorbital sensory pores.

Dorsum is crossed by 7-9 narrow, poorly defined saddles, some of which may not be apparent. Eight to 10 diffuse lateral blotches usually are better defined in males than in females; blotches may be obscured by zigzag marks on upper side and cross-hatching on lower side. Belly is clear. A small distinct midcaudal spot usually is flanked by a smaller spot above and below.

Diffuse preorbital bar fails to meet counterpart on snout. Diffuse suborbital bar is directed slightly posteriorly. Postorbital bar may be a small spot or may continue across cheek. Cheek, opercle, ventral surface of head, and breast have widely scattered small spots.

Spiny dorsal fin membranes and spines are weakly stippled

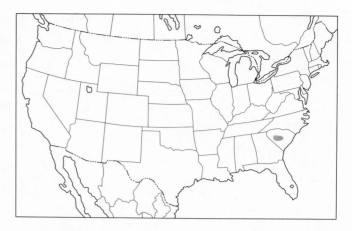

Distribution of *Etheostoma saludae*

or darkened, failing to produce a pattern; in males membranes are more heavily stippled, usually forming a distinct dark basal spot in the first 2 or 3 membranes. In both sexes rays and membranes of soft dorsal fin are darkened to produce 4-6 weak horizontal bands. Caudal fin membranes are clear and rays are darkened to produce several weak vertical bands. Anal fin membranes are clear in females, dusky in males; pelvic fin membranes are similar to anal membranes. Vertical banding in pectoral fin is weak.

Cheek usually has small embedded scales. Opercle is scaled. Breast is naked. Nape is naked or has a few embedded scales before dorsal fin. Lateral line consists of 38-45 (36-50) scales, the first 11-23 (5-29) pored. Fin counts are: dorsal IX (VIII-X), 11-12 (11-14); anal II (I-II), 7-8 (6-9); pectoral 11-12. Vertebrae number 36 (3 specimens only).

Breeding males do not develop bright colors, as shown in color plate. Breeding tubercles may develop on ventral surface of pelvic fin rays and along outer portion of anal fin rays. Genital papilla is a small flattened triangular tube. Females are not colorful. Genital papilla is a thick short cone with a blunt tip.

Distribution. Narrowly confined to tributaries of the Saluda and Broad rivers of the Santee River basin above the Fall Line.

Natural History. This is an inhabitant of small sluggish, often murky streams. Sand, gravel, and bedrock are cited as preferred substrates by Collette (1962), and we have taken the species over clay and silt substrate. There seems to be no information available beyond this meager amount.

Abundance. Deacon et al. (1979) list the Saluda darter as a species of special concern. Urban developments, reservoirs, and agricultural practices detrimental to water clarity have all played a part in eliminating the species from various spots where it once occurred. We searched long and hard for this species, taking it in what seemed an unlikely spot due to murkiness and siltation.

Name. Named for the river basin where the species was first captured.

Etheostoma serriferum (Hubbs & Cannon)   Plate 24
Sawcheek Darter   Subgenus *Hololepis*

Description. A large member of its subgenus reaching 60 mm SL. It is typical of subgenus *Hololepis* in having a small head and mouth and a highly arched incomplete lateral line. The frenum is rather broad. Gill membranes are slightly connected. It differs from other members of *Hololepis* in having a serrated rather than a smooth preopercle.

Dorsum is rather pale and has numerous dark mottlings but no true saddles. Midlateral blotches are poorly defined, tending to be connected into a distinct continuous band. Lower side and belly are clear or spotted. A colon-like pair of spots occurs at base of caudal fin.

Diffuse preorbital bar may meet counterpart on snout. Suborbital bar is diffuse, occasionally absent. Postorbital bar is continuous with an expanded band on opercle and then with lateral band of body. Cheek and opercle have scattered spots. Ventral surface of head and breast are clear or have an occasional dark spot.

In both sexes spines of spiny dorsal fin are somewhat darkened; in females basal stippling is the only pigmentation in membranes, but in males the same area is dark, especially in the first 3 membranes. Alternate light and dark rays of soft dorsal fin produce irregular banding, augmented in males by lightly stippled membranes. Caudal fin rays are similarly darkened to produce distinct vertical bands. Remaining fins are clear except for some basal darkening of rays and membranes in large males.

Cheek and opercle are scaled. Scales often occur laterally on breast and on prepectoral area. Nape usually is partially scaled. Scales occur on head behind and above eyes. Lateral line consists of 49-60 (44-66) scales, the first 28-40 (20-45) pored. Fin counts are: dorsal X-XII (IX-XIII), 12-15 (11-17); anal II, 6-8 (5-9); pectoral 12 (11-13). Vertebrae number 38-40.

Specimens from the Cape Fear drainage southward have a few more pored lateral line scales than northern populations, and some clinal north-south variation is seen in other measurements, but not enough to warrant subspecific recognition according to Collette (1962).

Breeding males are not colorful, as shown in color plate. Breeding tubercles may develop on pelvic and anal fin rays. Male genital papilla is small, flattened, conical, and tends to be bilobed at tip; base is encircled with tiny spots. Females are not brightly colored. Female genital papilla is unusual for the subgenus in being rather short, flattened, and bilobed at tip.

Distribution. Occurs from the Dismal Swamp and lower Roanoke River basin in Virginia to the Altamaha River in Georgia. It is essentially confined to the coastal plain but has been captured just above the Fall Line in North Carolina.

Natural History. The sawcheek darter is locally common in sluggish streams of small to medium size, especially where debris or aquatic plants offer protection. The species also occurs in quiet backwaters of rivers and swamps and occasionally in

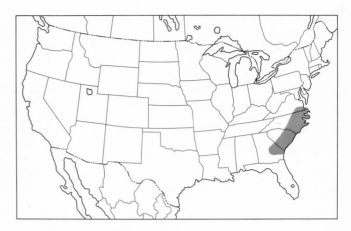

Distribution of *Etheostoma serriferum*

small natural lakes and artificial impoundments.

Sawcheek darters often are captured with *Etheostoma fusiforme* and not uncommonly with redfin pickerel, pirate perch, and several species of sunfish. *E. olmstedi, E. hopkinsi, E. fricksium,* and *Percina nigrofasciata* are other darter associates.

Gravid females are found in March which suggests that this species breeds during March and April. Collette (1962) did not find aquarium-held specimens to establish territories nor did they complete breeding activities. Some individuals were observed to rest on the bottom of the aquarium, others to perch on parts of aquatic plants. In the field Collette observed sawcheek darters to occur more frequently in current, especially among aquatic plants, than *E. fusiforme.* Additional life history information is needed for this species.

Abundance. The sawcheek darter is common at a number of spots and is in no immediate danger of extirpation. But we have captured it infrequently and feel that it may be sporadic in occurrence.

Name. *Serriferum* refers to the unusual sawtooth margin of the preoperculum.

Etheostoma zoniferum (Hubbs & Cannon)
Not illustrated

Backwater Darter   Subgenus *Hololepis*

Description. A small member of its subgenus reaching a maximum of 37 mm SL. It is typical of subgenus *Hololepis* in having a small head and mouth and a highly arched incomplete lateral line. The frenum is moderately broad. Gill membranes are slightly connected. It is most similar to *Etheostoma gracile* but differs in having an incomplete infraorbital sensory canal.

There are 8-11 weak to moderately well developed small dorsal saddles. Eight to 10 lateral blotches are developed to various degrees; in males the last 3-5 tend to be vertical bands.

Collette (1962) found only minor differences between *E.*

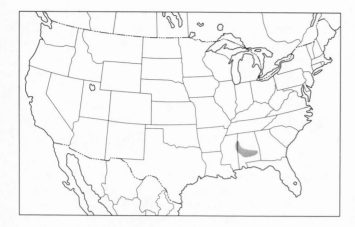

Distribution of *Etheostoma zoniferum*

zoniferum and *E. gracile* in body pattern, head markings, and fin pattern. He reviewed available information on breeding coloration of the 2 species, which is quite similar. Breeding tuberculation of *E. zoniferum,* including tubercles on lower jaw, is similar to that of *E. gracile,* and genital papillae are assumed to be similar.

Cheek and opercle are scaled. Nape usually is naked but sometimes is scaled posteriorly. Breast and prepectoral area are naked or weakly scaled. Lateral line consists of 45-50 (41-53) scales, the first 13-19 (7-20) pored. Fin counts are: dorsal IX-X (VIII-XI), 10-11 (9-13); anal II (I-II), 5-6 (4-7); pectoral 13 (12-15). Vertebrae number 37-38 (36-39).

Distribution. Found below the Fall Line in the Tombigbee and Alabama rivers of the Mobile drainage.

Natural History. *Etheostoma zoniferum* is an inhabitant of pools in small streams of slow to moderate current. It usually has been captured over sand or silt substrates and may be taken in aquatic vegetation.

Collette (1962) reported that aquarium-held specimens behaved much like *E. gracile.* The 2 forms have been reported from the Tombigbee River but there is no evidence that they occur together. Considerably more investigation is needed to determine the exact relationship between the species and to reveal more about the life history of the backwater darter.

We were given several localities for this species, but Kuehne and James Small did not obtain specimens, perhaps due to rather high water conditions.

Abundance. Smith-Vaniz (1968) does not state that the backwater darter is rare and it is not so indicated by Ramsey (1976). It has a restricted distribution, however, and should be carefully observed.

Name. *Zoniferum* means banded, calling attention to the lateral bands on the caudal peduncle of many individuals.

Etheostoma fonticola (Jordan & Gilbert)   Plate 24
Fountain Darter   Subgenus *Microperca*

Description. A minute but robust darter reaching 35 mm SL. Along with *Etheostoma microperca* it constitutes the smallest of all darters and one of the smallest species of freshwater fish. Adult males, which are smaller than the females, seldom exceed 27 mm SL. It is typical of subgenus *Microperca* in having a small head and mouth, few dorsal fin spines, fewer than 39 lateral line scales, of which no more than 9 are pored, and in males extreme modification of the pelvic fin. It is unique in the subgenus in almost always having 1 anal fin spine.

Dorsal pigmentation consists of tiny spots which may be densely arranged at base of each dorsal fin. Eleven to 16 small lateral blotches are developed in most individuals, resembling an interrupted dark band in many cases. Upper and lower side bear numerous tiny spots, often wedge-shaped. Belly is clear. There is a distinct basicaudal spot, sometimes isolated and sometimes partly fused with last lateral blotch.

Preorbital bar is dusky and may be connected with counterpart on snout via stippling on jaw. Suborbital bar is indistinct. Postorbital bar appears as a diffuse to distinct spot. A bar may extend diagonally upward and backward from eye. Tiny spots may be scattered on otherwise clear cheek, opercle, ventral surface of head, and breast.

In males margin of spiny dorsal fin is lightly stippled and basal portion of each membrane is dark; spines are clear. In females spines are alternately clear and slightly darkened; membranes are stippled, most strongly toward base. Soft dorsal fin appears distinctly banded in females and weakly banded in males. In both sexes caudal fin appears to be weakly banded. Remaining fins are clear except for stippling or a dusky appearance in anal and pelvic fins in males, and weak banding in pectoral fin in females. In males pelvic fins are long and pointed and appear cupped; effect is heightened by presence of a flap beside pelvic spine.

Cheek is naked. Opercle has a distinct patch of scales. Nape, breast, and prepectoral area are naked. Lateral line consists of 34-36 (31-37) scales, the first 1-3 (0-6) pored. Fin counts are: dorsal VII (VI-VIII), 10-11 (10-13); anal I (I-II), 6-7 (5-8); pectoral 9-10 (8-11). Vertebrae number 32-33 (31-34).

Breeding males have a red submarginal band in spiny dorsal fin but do not otherwise become brightly colored, as shown in color plate. Pointed breeding tubercles appear on ventral surface of pelvic spine and rays; smaller tubercles occur on anal spine and rays. Genital papilla is a tiny conical tube rounded at tip. Females display no bright colors. Genital papilla is a broad, somewhat flattened, terminally bilobed tube.

Distribution. Occurs in Texas in the spring at the head of the San Marcos River and downstream for 3-4 km. An introduced population exists at Dexter Fish Hatchery in New Mexico. The species originally occurred in the spring forming the Comal River about 30 km soutwest of the San Marcos site. Its disappearance there is attributed to rotenone treatment of the spring and river followed by drying of the various springs dur-

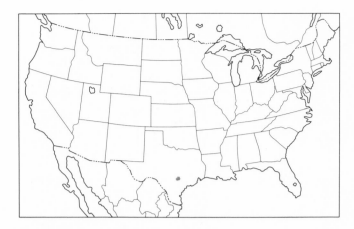

Distribution of *Etheostoma fonticola*

ing drought in the mid-1950s. Burr (1978) describes the slight differences between collections made at the 2 spring sites. Schenck and Whiteside (1976) reintroduced San Marcos River stock at Comal River springs.

Natural History. The fountain darter usually occurs amid dense beds of *Vallisneria, Elodea, Ludwigia* and other aquatic plants that flourish in the San Marcos and Comal springs. The substrate at such sites is normally mucky and the darters spend an arboreal-like existence among the plants. Early collections revealed the darter much farther downstream in the San Marcos River than now is the case, presumably because dense vegetation persisted farther downstream. Strawn (1955-56) gives preliminary information on breeding behavior of aquarium-held specimens, indicating spawning to occur on plants. Many aspects of life history are presented by Schenck and Whiteside (1976, 1977). Of special interest is their estimate that the San Marcos population consisted of 103,000 individuals and that the life span is only about 1 year.

Basing his conclusions on morphology, Burr (1978) concludes that *E. fonticola* and *E. proeliare* are more closely related to one another than either is to *E. microperca*. In addition, one can look at the present range of *E. proeliare* and imagine it or an ancestral stock extending a little westward to the Guadalupe River basin during a wetter portion of the Pleistocene and giving rise to *E. fonticola*. Electrophoretic evidence presented by Buth, Burr, and Schenck (1980) is in close correspondence with the above information.

Abundance. Deacon et al. (1979) list the fountain darter as endangered because the entire population is vulnerable to a single catastrophe. Restrictions on channel modification, streamside development, pollution, and excessive water usage have been recommended for the well-being of the species. Considering the steadily increasing use of the artesian system that feeds all the springs of the Balcones Escarpment, it is quite likely that the San Marcos spring may periodically suffer the same fate as befell the Comal spring in years of prolonged drought.

Name. *Fonticola* means fountain dweller. Before being inundated by a small dam and lake, the main spring at San Marcos was described as emerging like a fountain from a limestone basin.

Etheostoma microperca Jordan & Gilbert   Plate 24
Least Darter   Subgenus *Microperca*

Description. A minute but robust darter reaching 37 mm SL. Along with *Etheostoma fonticola* it is the smallest of all darters and one of the smallest of freshwater fish. Adult males, which are smaller than females, seldom exceed 30 mm SL. It is typical of subgenus *Microperca* in having a small head and mouth, few dorsal fin spines, fewer than 39 lateral line scales of which no more than 9 are pored, and in males extreme modification of the pelvic fin. It differs from *Etheostoma fonticola* in having the normal 2 anal fin spines and from *E. proeliare* in having fewer pored lateral scales and fewer and larger lateral blotches.

Background of dorsum is dusky, often with a narrow dark middorsal line on nape. Locally heavy stippling elsewhere fails to produce a discernible pattern. Nine to 11 small lateral blotches are obvious in most specimens but scales of mature males may be so covered with large spots as to obliterate pattern. One to 3 basicaudal spots are present in many individuals. Belly is clear.

Preorbital bar is distinct but fails to meet counterpart on snout. Suborbital bar is fairly distinct and posteriorly directed. Postorbital bar is reduced to a spot. In females cheek, opercle, ventral surface of head, and breast are lightly stippled; in males these areas are spotted or more darkly pigmented.

Dorsal fin spines are alternately clear and dark in females, clear in males. Spiny dorsal fin membranes are slightly dusky at base in females, much darker basally and often dusky along margin in males. In both sexes pigment in rays and membranes of soft dorsal fin produces several diagonal bands. Wavy vertical bands are fairly well developed in caudal fin. Remaining fins are virtually clear in females but anal and pelvic fins in males are darkened to varying degrees. Pelvic fins are highly modified in mature males; third ray is greatly elongated, spine has an auxiliary fold, and the 2 fins form a cup-shaped structure.

Cheek, nape, and breast are naked. Opercle has a few scales, sometimes partly embedded. Lateral line consists of 30-37 scales, the first 0-3 pored. Fin counts are: dorsal VI-VII (V-VIII), 9-10; anal II, 5-6 (4-7); pectoral 10 (9-11). Vertebrae number 33 (31-34).

Breeding males develop reddish spots in spiny dorsal fin and red or orange in anal and pelvic fins. Specimen in our color plate has brown in dorsal fin and reddish brown in anal and pelvic fins. Breeding tubercles develop on pelvic spine and rays and on lateral surfaces of anal spine. Males from the Ozarks may have tubercles on dorsal fins according to Burr (1978), a condition apparently unique among darters. Genital

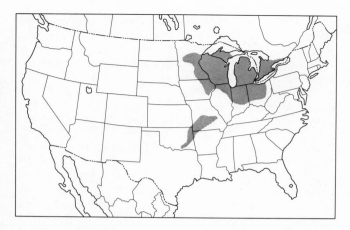

Distribution of *Etheostoma microperca*

Abundance. This darter remains common in many parts of its range and is in no danger of total extirpation. Trautman (1957, 1981) indicates that ditching and draining of northern Ohio streams have led to some population losses. This must be matched against discovery of undetected populations since 1930. P.W. Smith (1979) reports the same confusing picture in Illinois, where recent intensive collecting has turned up the species in new sites. It is a distinct possibility that the isolated Ozark populations until recently had at least some intervening populations between themselves and the northern stocks of this species.

Name. *Microperca* means little perch, a most appropriate epithet.

papilla is a tiny conical tube, rounded at tip. Females lack coloration. Genital papilla is a thick conical tube rounded at tip and deeply grooved on anterior half.

Distribution. Occurs from southern Ontario across the Great Lakes region to northwestern Minnesota, then southeastward to southern Ohio. Ozark populations from central Missouri to southeastern Oklahoma are isolated from the northern stocks. Buchanan (1973) reports the least darter from the head of the Saline River in Arkansas, but Burr (in Lee et al., 1980) excludes these records.

Natural History. Northern populations of the least darter occur in weedy portions of lakes and of clear streams with sluggish flow. Southern stocks live in vegetated portions of sluggish creeks, pools below springs, and quiet pools in stream floodplains.

Petravicz (1936) and Winn (1958a,b) observed aspects of breeding behavior. Males approach weedy shallows and establish loose territories. Females enter such a territory and lead its male to aquatic vegetation, where eggs are laid singly and in rows. The male uses his pelvic fins, placed over the female's dorsal fin, to hold position as the pair spawn vertically against the plant stem or blade. Females breed a number of times, producing as many as 800-900 eggs. Smaller males chase females along the bottom but the success of such ventures is not known.

Small crustacea living among aquatic plants are used as food but other items must also be taken by the least darter. It is fed on to some extent by small game fish.

Etheostoma exile is the typical darter associate of *E. microperca* in northern lakes and quiet streams. It may have other associates in the Ozark region. In a single short seine haul we once caught several least darters from brushy debris, and *E. cragini, E. punctulatum,* and *E. spectabile* from the adjacent riffle, the perfect example of beginner's luck. Blair and Windle (1961) have collected extensively in the region and found a high degree of mutual exclusion among the first 3 of the species mentioned. *Etheostoma gracile* is a potential associate of the least darter in the Neosho River basin.

Etheostoma proeliare (Hay)   Plate 24
Cypress Darter   Subgenus *Microperca*

Description. A minute but robust darter reaching 39 mm SL. It is typical of subgenus *Microperca* in having a small head and mouth, few dorsal fin spines, fewer than 39 lateral line scales of which not more than 9 are pored, and in males extreme modification of the pelvic fin. It differs from *Etheostoma fonticola* in having the normal 2 anal spines and from *E. microperca* in possessing a scaly cheek and smaller, more numerous lateral blotches.

Dorsum is marked by 8-9 dusky areas posterior to nape, but these hardly appear to be saddles. Nape is paler and often bears a narrow median dark stripe. Seven to 9 lateral blotches dominate body pattern; they tend to be horizontally elongated, and posteriorly several may almost join to form a band. Additional wedge-shaped spots above and below lateral blotches may be dense enough partly to obscure their discreteness. A small basicaudal spot usually is evident. Belly is clear to lightly stippled. Humeral area is often darkened in males.

Preorbital bar is short in some individuals but longer in others, sometimes meeting counterpart on snout. Suborbital bar is fairly distinct. Postorbital bar is reduced to a spot, sometimes obscure. Cheek, opercle, lower surface of head, and breast are clear in females, lightly stippled or spotted in males.

In females spiny dorsal fin is clear except for alternately light and dark spines. In males there is a dusky marginal dark band and considerable darkening of membranes toward fin base; base of first 3 membranes may be black. Soft dorsal fin is weakly banded in females, rather dusky in males, sometimes with dark spots in membranes. Dark wavy vertical bands are present in caudal fin and very weak vertical bands appear on pectoral fin in both sexes. In females anal and pelvic fins are clear or weakly stippled basally. In males these fins are dusky, pelvic fins are cupped, third pelvic ray is greatly elongated, and a flap lies against side of pelvic spine.

Cheek and opercle are scaled. Breast, prepectoral area, and nape are naked. Belly may lack some scales immediately posterior to pelvic fin insertions. Lateral line consists of 35-36

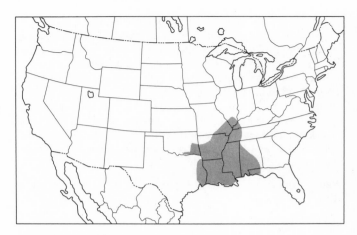

Distribution of *Etheostoma proeliare*

(33-38) scales, the first 2-4 (0-9) pored. Fin counts are: dorsal VII-IX, 10-11 (10-13); anal II, 5-6 (4-7); pectoral 9-11. Vertebrae number 35-36 (34-37).

Breeding males develop a little coloration, often more than is shown in color plate. Spiny dorsal fin has some red anteriorly and dull orange or red posteriorly. Amber or dull red bands appear in soft dorsal and caudal fins. Breeding tubercles develop on ventral surfaces of pelvic rays, anal spine, and anal rays except at base. Genital papilla is a tiny conical tube, rounded at tip. Females lack coloration. Genital papilla is a thick short tube, bilobed at tip and slightly grooved anteriorly.

Distribution. Occurs along the Gulf Coast from the Choctawhatchee River in Florida to the San Jacinto River in Texas. It occupies the Mississippi Embayment and the Mobile River system below the Fall Line. At the northern extreme it extends beyond the Fall Line into southern Illinois and adjacent portions of Kentucky and Missouri. In Arkansas and Oklahoma, particularly in the Arkansas River basin, the cypress darter extends northwest of the Fall Line.

Natural History. The cypress darter inhabits sluggishly flowing streams, sloughs, oxbows, and ponds, especially where aquatic vegetation or woody debris offers protection. *Etheostoma gracile, E. fusiforme, E chlorosomum, E. swaini,* and *Percina maculata* are common associates, although other species of darters may also be captured with it.

Burr and Page (1978) present life history information on the cypress darter at the northern end of its range. Both sexes reproduce at 1 year of age. Aquarium-held specimens bred during daytime, the female leading the male in quick dashes around the tank before approaching a leaf, twig, rock, or algae to lay 1-3 eggs. The male mounted the female with his pelvic fins placed over her dorsal fin and body wrapped around to fertilize the eggs. The authors note that the female always opened her mouth during the act and the male kept his closed. Spawning upside down on the underside of leaves was the most frequent method, but vertical posture was often assumed, as well. Females contain only 26-116 mature ova. The sex ratio of young is 1:1. Parental care is not apparent. Maximum lifespan is about 18 months. In vegetated areas of the study stream, darter density may be as high as 5.5 per sq m. Breeding occurs in April and May in Illinois, as early as January in Louisiana.

Burr and Ellinger (1980) describe some of the early development of eggs in *E. proeliare,* which like other species of subgenus *Microperca* and some species of subgenus *Hololepis* has deeply indented eggs. No present explanation of the developmental significance is available.

Abundance. There is no problem with survival for the cypress darter. Douglas (1974) and Pflieger (1975) state that this is locally an extremely abundant darter.

Name. *Proeliare* means pertaining to battle. The species was first taken from the Tuscumbia River close to the battlefield at Corinth, Mississippi.

References

Adamson, S.W., and T.E. Wissing. 1977. Food habits and feeding periodicity of the rainbow, fantail and banded darters in Four Mile Creek. Ohio J. of Science 77 (4):164-69.

Armstrong, J.G., and J.D. Williams. 1971. Cave and spring fishes of the southern bend of the Tennessee River. J. of the Tennessee Acad. of Science 46(3):107-15.

Atz, J.W. 1940. Reproductive behavior in the eastern johnny darter, *Boleosoma nigrum olmstedi* (Storer). Copeia 1940(2):100-106.

Bailey, J.R. 1950. A new subspecies of the darter *Hololepis barratti* from western North Carolina. Copeia 1950(4):311-16.

———, and D.G. Frey. 1951. Darters of the genus *Hololepis* from some natural lakes of North Carolina. J. of the Elisha Mitchell Scientific Soc. 67(2):191-204.

Bailey, R.M. 1940. *Hadropterus palmaris,* a new darter from the Alabama River system. J. of the Washington Acad. of Science 30(12):524-30.

———. 1941. *Hadropterus nasutus,* a new darter from Arkansas. Occasional Papers of the Museum of Zoology, Univ. of Michigan, no. 440. 8 pp.

———. 1948. Status, relationships, and characters of the percid fish, *Poecilichthys sagitta* Jordan and Swain. Copeia 1948(2):77-85.

———. 1959. *Etheostoma acuticeps,* a new darter from the Tennessee River system, with remarks on the subgenus *Nothonotus.* Occasional Papers of the Museum of Zoology, Univ. of Michigan, no. 603. 10 pp.

———, and M.O. Allum. 1962. Fishes of South Dakota. Misc. Publications, Museum of Zoology, Univ. of Michigan, no. 119. 131 pp.

———, J.E. Fitch, E.S. Herald, E.A. Lachner, C.C. Lindsey, C.R. Robins, and W.B. Scott. 1970. A list of common and scientific names of fishes from the United States and Canada. Amer. Fisheries Soc., Special Publication, no. 6, 3rd ed. 150 pp.

———, and W.A. Gosline. 1955. Variation and systematic significance of vertebral counts in the American fishes of the family Percidae. Misc. Publications, Museum of Zoology, Univ. of Michigan, no. 93. 44 pp.

———, and W.J. Richards. 1963. Status of *Poecilichthys hopkinsi* (Fowler) and *Etheostoma trisella,* new species, percid fishes from Alabama, Georgia, and South Carolina. Occasional Papers, Museum of Zoology, Univ. of Michigan, no. 630. 21 pp.

———, H.E. Winn, and C.L. Smith. 1954. Fishes from the Escambia River, Alabama and Florida, with ecologic and taxonomic notes. Proceedings of the Acad. of Natural Science of Philadelphia 106:109-64.

Baker, J.R. 1978. The fantail darter *Etheostoma flabellare* in the Salt River drainage, Kentucky. Transactions of the Kentucky Acad. of Science 39(3-4):150-59.

Bangham, R.V., and G.W. Hunter. 1939. Studies on the fish parasites of Lake Erie. Distribution studies. Zoologica 24(4):385-448.

Becker, G.C. 1965. The western sand darter, *Ammocrypta clara,* in the Great Lakes basin. Copeia 1965(2):241.

Beckham, E.C., III. 1977. A report on the Escatawpa River system of Alabama and Mississippi. Southeastern Fishes Council Proceedings 2(1):1-5.

———. 1980. *Percina gymnocephala,* a new percid fish of the subgenus *Alvordius,* from the New River in North Carolina, Virginia, and West Virginia. Occasional Papers of the Museum of Zoology, Louisiana State Univ., no. 57:1-11.

Birdsong, R.S., and L.W. Knapp. 1969. *Etheostoma collettei,* a new darter of the subgenus *Oligocephalus* from Louisiana and Arkansas. Tulane Studies in Zoology and Botany 15(3):106-12.

Blair, A.P. 1959. Distribution of the darters (Percidae, Etheostomatinae) of northeastern Oklahoma. Southwestern Naturalist 4(1):1-13.

———. 1964. Habitat and other notes on *Etheostoma pallididorsum* (Etheostomatini:Percidae). Southwestern Naturalist 9(2):105-7.

———. 1976. *Percina nasuta* and *P. phoxocephala* sympatric in Lee Creek. Proceedings of the Oklahoma Acad. of Science 56:9.

———, and J. Windle. 1961. Darter associates of *Etheostoma cragini* (Percidae). Southwestern Naturalist 6(3-4):201-2.

Boschung, H.T. 1961. An annotated list of fishes from the Coosa River System of Alabama. Amer. Midland Naturalist 66(2):257-85.

———. 1976. Endangered and threatened plants and animals of Alabama. Bull. Alabama Museum of Natural History, no. 2. 92 pp.

———. 1979. Notes on the distribution and life history of the slackwater darter, *Etheostoma boschungi* (Percidae). Assoc. of Southeastern Biologists Bull. 26(2):67.

Bouchard, R.W. 1974. The subgenus *Ulocentra* (Percidae, Etheostomatini) in western Kentucky, western Tennessee, and northern Mississippi. Assoc. of Southeastern Biologists Bull. 21(2):41.

———. 1977. *Etheostoma etnieri,* a new percid fish from the Caney Fork (Cumberland) River system, Tennessee, with a redescription of the subgenus *Ulocentra.* Tulane Studies in Zoology and Botany 19(3-4):105-30.

Braasch, M.E., and L.M. Page. 1979. Systematic studies of darters of the subgenus *Catonotus* (Percidae), with the description of a new species from Caney Fork, Tennessee. Occasional Papers of the Museum of Natural History, Univ. of Kansas, no. 78. 10 pp.

———, and P.W. Smith. 1967. The life history of the slough darter *Etheostoma gracile* (Pisces, Percidae). Illinois Natural History Survey Biological Notes, no. 58. 12 pp.

Branson, B.A. 1967. Fishes of the Neosho River system in Oklahoma. Amer. Midland Naturalist 78(1):126-54.

———. 1977. Threatened fishes of Daniel Boone National Forest, Kentucky. Transactions of the Kentucky Acad. of Science 38(1-2):69-73.

———, and J.B. Campbell. 1969. Hybridization in the darters *Etheostoma spectabile* and *Etheostoma radiosum cyanorum.* Copeia 1969(1):70-75.

———, J. Triplett, and R. Hartman. 1969. A partial biological survey of the Spring River drainage in Kansas, Oklahoma and Missouri. Part II: The fishes. Transactions of the Kansas Acad. of Science 72(4):429-72.

Brown, W.H. 1955. Egg production of the fish *Hadropterus scierus apristis* in San Marcos River, Texas. Copeia 1955(2):149-50.

Bryant, R.T., J.P. Beets, and M.G. Ryon. 1979. Rediscovery of the sharphead darter, *Etheostoma acuticeps* in North Carolina (Pisces, Percidae). Brimleyana, no. 2:137-40.

Buchanan, T.M. 1973. Key to the fishes of Arkansas. Little Rock: Arkansas Game and Fish Commission. 68 pp.

———. 1974. Threatened native fishes of Arkansas. In: Arkansas Natural Area Plan, 67-92. Little Rock: Arkansas Dept. of Planning. 248 pp.

Burr, B.M. 1978. Systematics of the percid fishes of the subgenus *Microperca,* genus *Etheostoma.* Bull. Alabama Museum of Natural History, no. 4. 53 pp.

———. 1979. Systematics and life history aspects of the percid fish *Etheostoma blennius* with description of a new subspecies from Sequatchie River, Tennessee. Copeia 1979(2):191-202.

———. 1980. A distributional checklist of the fishes of Kentucky. Brimleyana, no. 3:53-84.

———, and M.S. Ellinger. 1980. Distinctive egg morphology and its relationship to development in the percid fish *Etheostoma proeliare.* Copeia 1980(3):556-59.

———, and L.M. Page. 1978. The life history of the cypress darter, *Etheostoma proeliare,* in Max Creek, Illinois. Illinois Natural History Survey Biological Notes, no. 106. 15 pp.

Buth, D.G., B.M. Burr, and J.R. Schenck. 1980. Electrophoretic evidence for relationships and differentiation among members of the percid subgenus *Microperca.* Biochemical Systematics and Ecology 8:297-304.

Clay, W.M. 1975. The Fishes of Kentucky. Frankfort: Kentucky Dept. of Fish and Wildlife Resources. 416 pp.

Cloutman, D.G. 1970. Notes on the distribution of the Arkansas darter, *Etheostoma cragini* with a new record from Bluff Creek, Clark Co., Kansas. Transactions of the Kansas Acad. of Science 73(4):431-33.

Cole, C.F. 1965. Additional evidence for separation of *Etheostoma olmstedi* Storer from *Etheostoma nigrum* Rafinesque. Copeia 1965(1):8-13.

———. 1967. A study of the eastern johnny darter, *Etheostoma olmstedi* Storer (Teleostei, Percidae). Chesapeake Science 8(1): 28-51.

———. 1971. Status of the darters, *Etheostoma nigrum, E. longimanum* and *E. podostemone* in Atlantic drainages (Teleostei, Percidae, subgenus *Boleosoma*). In: The Distributional History of the Biota of the Southern Appalachians. Part III: Vertebrates, 119-38. Research Division Monograph 4, Virginia Polytechnic Institute, Blacksburg, Virginia.

Collette, B.B. 1962. The swamp darters of the subgenus *Hololepis* (Pisces, Percidae). Tulane Studies in Zoology 9(4):115-211.

———. 1963. The subfamilies, tribes, and genera of the family Percidae (Teleostei). Copeia 1963(4):615-23.

———. 1965. Systematic significance of breeding tubercles in fishes of the family Percidae. Proceedings of the U.S. National Museum 117(3518):567-614.

———. 1967. The taxonomic history of the darters (Percidae, Etheostomatini). Copeia 1967(4):814-18.

———, and P. Banarescu. 1977. Systematics and zoogeography of the fishes of the family Percidae. J. of the Fisheries Research Board of Canada 34(10):1450-63.

———, and L.W. Knapp. 1966. Catalogue of type specimens of the darters (Pisces, Percidae, Etheostomatini). Proceedings of the U.S. National Museum 119(3550). 88 pp.

———, and R.W. Yerger. 1962. The American percid fishes of the subgenus *Villora.* Tulane Studies in Zoology and Botany 9(4):213-30.

Cooper, J.E. 1978. Eggs and larvae of the logperch, *Percina caprodes* (Rafinesque). Amer. Midland Naturalist 99(2):257-69.

———. 1979. Description of eggs and larvae of fantail (*Etheostoma flabellare*) and rainbow (*E. caeruleum*) darters from Lake Erie tributaries. Transactions of the Amer. Fisheries Soc. 108(1):46-56.

Crawford, R.W. 1954. Status of the bronze darter, *Hadropterus palmaris.* Copeia 1954(3):235-36.

———. 1956. A study of the distribution and taxonomy of the percid fish *Percina nigrofasciata* (Agassiz). Tulane Studies in Zoology 4(11):1-55.

Cross, F.B. 1967. Handbook of fishes of Kansas. Univ. of Kansas Museum of Natural History, Misc. Publication no. 45. 357 pp.

———, and M.E. Braasch. 1968. Qualitative changes in the fish-fauna of the upper Neosho River system, 1952-1967. Transactions of the Kansas Acad. of Science 71(3):350-60.

Dahlberg, M.D., and D.C. Scott. 1971. The freshwater fishes of Georgia. Bull. of the Georgia Acad. of Science 29:1-64.

Daiber, F.C. 1956. A comparative analysis of winter feeding habits of two benthic stream fishes. Copeia 1956(3):141-51.

Danzman, R.G. 1979. The karyology of eight species of fish belonging to the family Percidae. Canadian J. of Zoology 57:2055-60.

Deacon, J.E., G. Kobetich, J.D. Williams, S. Contreras, et al. 1979. Fishes of North America endangered, threatened, or of special concern: 1979. Fisheries 4(2):29-44.

Denoncourt, R.F. 1976. Sexual dimorphism and geographic variation in the bronze darter, *Percina palmaris* (Pisces: Percidae). Copeia 1976(1):54-59.

———, W.A. Potter, and J.R. Stauffer, Jr. 1977. Records of the greenside darter *Etheostoma blennioides* from the Susquehanna River drainage in Pennsylvania. Ohio J. of Science 77(1):38-42.

———, and J.R. Stauffer, Jr. 1976. A taxonomic study of recently introduced populations of the banded darter *Etheostoma zonale* (Cope), in the Susquehanna River. Chesapeake Science 17(4):303-4.

Distler, D.A. 1968. Distribution and variation of *Etheostoma spectabile* (Agassiz) (Percidae, Teleostei). Univ. of Kansas Science Bull. 48(5):143-208.

———. 1971. Observations on the reproductive habits of captive *Etheostoma cragini* Gilbert. Southwestern Naturalist 16(3-4):439-41.

———, and A.L. Metcalf. 1962. *Etheostoma pallididorsum,*

a new percid fish from the Caddo River system of Arkansas. Copeia 1962(3):556-61.

Dobie, J. 1959. Note on food of northern log perch. Transactions of the Amer. Fisheries Soc. 88(3):213.

Douglas, N.H. 1968. A new record size for darters. Proceedings of the Louisiana Acad. of Sciences 31:41-42.

———. 1974. Freshwater fishes of Louisiana. Baton Rouge: Claitor's Publishing Division. 443 pp.

Echelle, A.A., A.F. Echelle, M.H. Smith, and L.G. Hill. 1975. Analysis of genic continuity in a headwater fish, *Etheostoma radiosum* (Percidae). Copeia 1975(2):197-204.

———, J.R. Schenck, and L.G. Hill. 1974. *Etheostoma spectabile-E. radiosum* hybridization in Blue River, Oklahoma. Amer. Midland Naturalist 91(1):182-94.

Eley, R.L., J.C. Randolf, and R.J. Miller. 1975. Current status of the leopard darter, *Percina pantherina*. Southwestern Naturalist 20(3):343-54.

Ellis, M.M., and B.B. Jaffa. 1918. Notes on Cragin's darter, *Catonotus cragini* (Gilbert). Copeia 1918:73-75.

Etnier, D.A. 1970. Additional specimens of *Etheostoma trisella* (Percidae) from Tennessee. Copeia 1970(2):356-58.

———. 1976. *Percina (Imostoma) tanasi*, a new percid fish from the Little Tennessee River, Tennessee. Proceedings of the Biological Soc. of Washington 88(44):469-88.

Ewers, L.A., and M.W. Boesel. 1935. The food of some Buckeye Lake fishes. Transactions of the Amer. Fisheries Soc. 65:57-70.

Flynn, R.B., and R.D. Hoyt. 1979. The life history of the teardrop darter, *Etheostoma barbouri* Kuehne and Small. Amer. Midland Naturalist 101(1):127-41.

Forbes, S.A., and R.E. Richardson. 1920. The fishes of Illinois. 2nd ed. Illinois Natural History Survey. 357 pp.

Fowler, H.W. 1941. A collection of fresh-water fishes obtained in Florida, 1930-1940, by Francis Harper. Proceedings of the Acad. of Natural Science of Philadelphia 92:227-44.

———. 1945. A study of the fishes of the Southern Piedmont and Coastal Plain. Monograph of the Acad. of Natural Science of Philadelphia, no. 7. 408 pp.

———. 1947. Description of a new species and genus of darter from the Cape Fear River basin of North Carolina. Notulae Naturae, Acad. of Natural Science of Philadelphia, no. 191. 3 pp.

Funk, J.L. 1955. Movement of stream fishes in Missouri. Transactions of the Amer. Fisheries Soc. 85:39-57.

Gerking, S.D. 1945. The distribution of the fishes of Indiana. Investigations of Indiana Lakes and Streams 3(1):1-137.

Gilbert, C.H. 1891. Report of explorations made in Alabama during 1889, with notes on the fishes of the Tennessee, Alabama, and Escambia rivers. Bull. of the U.S. Fish Commission, 1889, 9:143-59.

Goodrich, C., and H. van der Schalie. 1939. Aquatic mollusks of the upper peninsula of Michigan. Part II: The Naiades (freshwater mussels). Misc. Publications of the Museum of Zoology, Univ. of Michigan 43:35-45.

Graham, I.D. 1885. Preliminary list of Kansas fishes. Transactions of the Kansas Acad. of Science 9:69-78.

Guillory, V., Sr. 1976. Apparent absence of *Percina nigrofasciata* from the Mississippi Valley. Copeia 1976(4):804-5.

Hambrick, P.S., and H.W. Robison. 1979. Life history aspects of the paleback darter, *Etheostoma pallididorsum* (Pisces: Percidae), in the Caddo River system, Arkansas. Southwestern Naturalist 24(3):475-84.

Hankinson, T.L. 1932. Observations on the breeding behavior and habitats of fishes in southern Michigan. Papers of the Michigan Acad. of Science, Arts and Letters, 1931, 15:411-25.

Harlan, J.R., and E.B. Speaker. 1956. Iowa fish and fishing. 3rd ed. Ames: Iowa State Conservation Commission. 377 pp.

Hildebrand, S.F. 1923. Annotated list of fishes collected in vicinity of Augusta, Georgia, with description of a new darter. Bull. of the U.S. Bureau of Fisheries, 39:1-8.

———. 1932. On a collection of fishes from the Tuckaseegee and upper Catawba river basins, N.C., with a description of a new darter. J. of the Elisha Mitchell Scientific Soc. 48(1):50-82.

Hill, L.G. 1968. Inter- and intrapopulational variation of vertebral numbers of the yoke darter, *Etheostoma juliae*. Southwestern Naturalist 13(2):175-91.

Hobson, J.F. 1979. Life history of a percid fish, *Percina crassa roanoka*, the Piedmont darter. Bios 50(3):148-57.

Hocutt, C.H., and P.S. Hambrick, 1973. Hybridization between the darters *Percina crassa roanoka* and *Percina oxyrhyncha* (Percidae, Etheostomatini), with comments on the distribution of *Percina crassa roanoka* in the New River. Amer. Midland Naturalist 90(2):397-405.

Hoffman, G.L. 1967. Parasites of North American freshwater fishes. Los Angeles: Univ. of California Press. 486 pp.

Hogarth, W.T., and W.S. Woolcott. 1966. The mountain stripeback darter, *Percina notogramma montuosa*, n. ssp. from upper James River, Virginia. Chesapeake Science 7(2):101-9.

Horseman, N.D., and B.A. Branson. 1973. Fishes of Eagle Creek, northern Kentucky. Transactions of the Kentucky Acad. of Science 34(1-2):5-12.

Hough, J.L. 1963. The prehistoric Great Lakes of North America. Amer. Scientist 51(1):84-109.

Howell, J.F., Jr. 1971. The life history, behavior, and ecology of *Percina aurantiaca*. Unpublished doctoral diss. Univ. of Tennessee. 110 pp.

Howell, W.M., and A. Black. 1976. Status of the watercress darter. Southeastern Fishes Council Proceedings 1(3):1-3.

———, and R.D. Caldwell. 1965. *Etheostoma (Oligocephalus) nuchale*, a new darter from a limestone spring in Alabama. Tulane Studies in Zoology 12(4):101-8.

———, and ———. 1967. Discovery of a second specimen of the darter, *Etheostoma trisella*. Copeia 1967(1):235-37.

———, and G. Dingerkus. 1978. *Etheostoma neopterum*, a new percid fish from the Tennessee River system in Alabama and Tennessee. Bull. of the Alabama Museum of Natural History, no. 3:13-26.

Hubbs, C.L. 1922. Variations in the number of vertebrae and other meristic characters of fishes correlated with temperature of water during development. Amer. Naturalist 50:360-72.

———. 1936. *Austroperca*, a new name to replace *Torrenta-*

ria, for a genus of Mexican fishes. Occasional Papers of the Museum of Zoology, Univ. of Michigan, no. 341. 3 pp.

————, and J.D. Black. 1940. Percid fishes related to *Poecilichthys variatus,* with descriptions of three new forms. Occasional Papers of the Museum of Zoology, Univ. of Michigan, no. 416. 30 pp.

————, and ————. 1941. The subspecies of the American percid fish, *Poecilichthys whipplii.* Occasional Papers of the Museum of Zoology, Univ. of Michigan, no. 429. 27 pp.

————, and M.D. Cannon. 1935. The darters of the genera *Hololepis* and *Villora.* Misc. Publications of the Museum of Zoology, Univ. of Michigan, no. 30. 93 pp.

————, and K.F. Lagler. 1947. Fishes of the Great Lakes region. Bloomfield Hills, Mich.: Cranbrook Institute of Science, Bull. 26. 186 pp.

————, and E.C. Raney. 1939. *Hadropterus oxyrhynchus,* a new percid fish from Virginia and West Virginia. Occasional Papers of the Museum of Zoology, Univ. of Michigan, no. 396. 10 pp.

————, and M.B. Trautman. 1932. *Poecilichthys osburni,* a new darter from the upper Kanawha River system in Virginia and West Virginia. Ohio J. of Science 32(1):31-38.

Hubbs, Clark. 1954. A new Texas subspecies, *apristis,* of the darter *Hadropterus scierus,* with a discussion of variation within the species. Amer. Midland Naturalist 52:211-20.

————. 1961. Developmental temperature tolerances of four etheostomatine fishes. Copeia 1961(2):195-98.

————. 1967. Geographic variations in survival of hybrids between etheostomatine fishes. Bull. of the Texas Memorial Museum, no. 13. 72 pp.

————. 1971. Survival of intergroup percid hybrids. Japanese J. of Ichthyology 18(2):65-75.

————, and N.E. Armstrong. 1962. Developmental temperature tolerance of Texas and Arkansas-Missouri *Etheostoma spectabile* (Percidae, Osteichthyes). Ecology 43(4):742-43.

————, and A.A. Echelle. 1972. Endangered non-game fishes of the upper Rio Grande basin. In: Rare and endangered wildlife of Southwestern United States, 147-67. Santa Fe: New Mexico Game and Fish Dept.

————, and M.V. Johnson. 1961. Differences in the egg complement of *Hadropterus scierus* from Austin and San Marcos. Southwestern Naturalist 6(1):9-12.

————, R.A. Kuehne, and J.C. Ball. 1953. The fishes of the upper Guadalupe River, Texas. Texas J. of Science 5(2):216-44.

————, and C.M. Laritz. 1961. Natural hybridization between *Hadropterus scierus* and *Percina caprodes.* Southwestern Naturalist 6(3-4):188-92.

————, A. Peden, and M.M. Stevenson. 1969. The developmental rate of the greenthroat darter, *Etheostoma lepidum.* Amer. Midland Naturalist 81(1):182-88.

————, and J. Pigg. 1972. Habitat preferences of the harlequin darter, *Etheostoma histrio,* in Texas and Oklahoma. Copeia 1972(1):193-94.

————, M.M. Stevenson, and A.E. Peden. 1968. Fecundity and egg size in two central Texas darter populations. Southwestern Naturalist 13(3):301-24.

————, and K. Strawn. 1957. The effects of light and temperature on the fecundity of the greenthroat darter, *Etheostoma lepidum.* Ecology 38(4):596-602.

Jenkins, R.E. 1971. Nuptial tuberculation and its systematic significance in the percid fish *Etheostoma (Ioa) vitreum.* Copeia 1971(4):735-38.

————. 1976. A list of undescribed freshwater fish species of continental United States and Canada, with additions to the 1970 checklist. Copeia 1976(3):642-44.

————, and N.M. Burkhead. 1975. Recent capture and analysis of the sharphead darter, *Etheostoma acuticeps,* an endangered percid fish of the Upper Tennessee River drainage. Copeia 1975(4):731-40.

————, and C.A. Freeman. 1972. Longitudinal distribution and habitat of the fishes of Mason Creek, an upper Roanoke River drainage tributary, Virginia. Virginia J. of Science 23(4):193-202.

————, E.A. Lachner, and F.J. Schwartz. 1971. Fishes of the central Appalachian drainages: Their distribution and dispersal. In: P.C. Holt, ed., The distributional history of the biota of the southern Appalachians. Part III: Vertebrates, 43-117. Research Division Monograph 4. Virginia Polytechnic Institute, Blacksburg, Va.

Jordan, D.S. 1889. Descriptions of fourteen species of freshwater fishes collected by the U.S. Fish Commission in the summer of 1888. Proceedings of the U.S. National Museum 11:351-62.

————, and A.W. Brayton. 1878. On the distribution of the fishes of the Alleghany region of South Carolina, Georgia, and Tennessee, with descriptions of new and little known species. Contributions to North American ichthyology, 3A. Bull. of the U.S. National Museum 12:3-95.

————, and B.W. Evermann. 1896. The fishes of North and Middle America: A descriptive catalogue of the species of fish-like vertebrates found in the waters of North America, north of the Isthmus of Panama. Bull. of the U.S. National Museum, no. 47, pt. 1. 1240 pp.

————, ————, and H.W. Clark. 1930. Checklist of the fishes and fishlike vertebrates of North and Middle America north of the northern boundary of Venezuela and Colombia. Appendix X to the Report of the U.S. Commissioner of Fisheries for the fiscal year 1928. 670 pp.

————, and C.H. Gilbert. 1886. List of fishes collected in Arkansas, Indian Territory and Texas in September, 1884, with notes and descriptions. Proceedings of the U.S. National Museum 9:1-25.

Karr, J.R. 1963. Age, growth, and food habits of johnny, slenderhead and blackside darters of Boone County, Iowa. Proceedings of the Iowa Acad. of Science 70:228-36.

————. 1964. Age, growth, fecundity and food habits of fantail darters in Boone County, Iowa. Proceedings of the Iowa Acad. of Science 71:274-80.

Keast, A., and D. Webb. 1966. Mouth and body form relative to feeding ecology in the fish fauna of a small lake, Lake Opinicon, Ontario. J. of the Fisheries Research Board of Canada 23(12):1845-74.

Knapp, L.W. 1976. Redescription, relationships and status of the Maryland darter *Etheostoma sellare* (Radcliffe and Welsh) an endangered species. Proceedings of the Biological Soc. of Washington 89(6):99-118.

————, W.J. Richards, R.V. Miller, and N.R. Foster. 1963. Rediscovery of the percid fish *Etheostoma sellare* (Radcliffe and Welsh). Copeia 1963(2):455.

Kneib, R.T. 1972. The effects of man's activity on the distribution of five stream fishes in Little Pine Creek, Pennsylvania. Proceedings of the Pennsylvania Acad. of Science 46:49-51.

Koch, L.M. 1978. Food habits of *Etheostoma (Psychromaster) tuscumbia* in Buffler Spring, Lauderdale County, Alabama (Percidae, Etheostomatini). Assoc. of Southeastern Biologists Bull. 25(2):56.

Kott, E., and G. Humphreys. 1978. A comparison between two populations of the johnny darter, *Etheostoma nigrum nigrum* (Percidae) from Ontario, with notes on other populations. Canadian J. of Zoology 56(5):1043-51.

Kuehne, R.A. 1955. Stream surveys of the Guadalupe and San Antonio rivers. Austin: Texas Game and Fish Commission, IF Report Series, no. 1. 56 pp.

————, and R.M. Bailey. 1961. Stream capture and the distribution of the percid fish *Etheostoma sagitta,* with geologic and taxonomic considerations. Copeia 1961(1):1-8.

————, and J.W. Small, Jr. 1971. *Etheostoma barbouri,* a new darter (Percidae, Etheostomatini) from the Green River with notes on the subgenus *Catonotus.* Copeia 1971(1):18-26.

Lachner, E.A., and R.E. Jenkins. 1971. Systematics, distribution and evolution of the chub genus *Nocomis* Girard (Pisces, Cyprinidae) of eastern United States, with descriptions of new species. Washington: Smithsonian Contributions to Zoology, no. 85. 97 pp.

————, E.F. Westlake, and P.S. Handwerk. 1950. Studies on the biology of some percid fishes from western Pennsylvania. Amer. Midland Naturalist 43(1):92-111.

Lake, C.T. 1936. The life history of the fan-tailed darter *Catonotus flabellaris flabellaris* (Rafinesque). Amer. Midland Naturalist 17(5):816-30.

Larimore, R.W., W.F. Childers, and C. Heckrotte. 1959. Destruction and re-establishment of stream fish and invertebrates affected by drought. Transactions of the Amer. Fisheries Soc. 88(4):261-85.

————, and P.W. Smith. 1963. The fishes of Champaign County, Illinois, as affected by 60 years of stream changes. Bull. of the Illinois Natural History Survey 28(2):299-382.

Layzer, J.B., and R.J. Reed. 1978. Food, age and growth of the tessellated darter, *Etheostoma olmstedi* in Massachusetts. Amer. Midland Naturalist 100(2):459-62.

Lee, D.S., and R.E. Ashton. 1979. Seasonal and daily activity patterns of the glassy darter, *Etheostoma vitreum* (Percidae). Assoc. of Southeastern Biologists Bull. 26(2):36.

————, C.R. Gilbert, C.H. Hocutt, R.E. Jenkins, D.E. McAllister, and J.R. Stauffer, Jr. 1980. Atlas of North American freshwater fishes. Raleigh: North Carolina State Museum of Natural History, North Carolina Biological Survey Publication, no. 1980-12. 854 pp.

Linder, A.D. 1953. Observations on the care and behavior of darters, Etheostomatinae, in the laboratory. Proceedings of the Oklahoma Acad. of Science 43:28-30.

————. 1955. The fishes of the Blue River in Oklahoma with descriptions of two new percid hybrid combinations. Amer. Midland Naturalist 54(1):173-91.

————. 1958. Behavior and hybridization of two species of *Etheostoma* (Percidae). Transactions of the Kansas Acad. of Science 61(2):195-212.

Lindquist, D.G., J.R. Shute, and P.W. Shute. 1981. Spawning and nesting behavior of the Waccamaw darter, *Etheostoma perlongum.* Environmental Biology of Fishes 6(2):177-91.

Loos, J.J., and W.S. Woolcott. 1969. Hybridization and behavior in two species of *Percina* (Percidae). Copeia 1969(2):374-85.

Lotrich, V.A. 1973. Growth, production and community composition of fishes inhabiting a first-, second-, and third-order stream of eastern Kentucky. Ecological Monographs 43(3):377-97.

Margulies, D., O.S. Burch, and B.F. Clark. 1980. Rediscovery of the gilt darter (*Percina evides*) in the White River, Indiana. Amer. Midland Naturalist 104(2):207-8.

Mather, D. 1973. Food habits and feeding chronology of the blackbanded darter, *Percina nigrofasciata* (Agassiz), in Halawakee Creek, Alabama. Transactions of the Amer. Fisheries Society 102(1):48-55.

May, B. 1969. Observations on the biology of the variegated darter, *Etheostoma variatum* (Kirtland). Ohio J. of Science 69(2):85-92.

Mayden, R.L., and L.M. Page. 1979. Systematics of *Percina roanoka* and *P. crassa,* with comparisons to *P. peltata* and *P. notogramma* (Pisces: Percidae). Copeia 1979(3):413-26.

Meek, S.E. 1891. Report of explorations made in Missouri and Arkansas during 1889, with an account of the fishes observed in each of the river basins examined. Bull. of the U.S. Fisheries Commission, 1889, 9:113-41.

————. 1902. A contribution to the ichthyology of Mexico. Field Columbian Museum Publication 65, Zoological Series 3(6):63-128.

————. 1904. The fresh-water fishes of Mexico north of the isthmus of Tehuantepec. Field Columbian Museum Publication 93, Zoological Series 5. 252 pp.

Menhinick, E.F., T.M. Burton, and J.R. Bailey. 1974. An annotated checklist of the freshwater fishes of North Carolina. J. of the Elisha Mitchell Scientific Soc. 90(1):24-50.

Metcalf, A.L. 1966. Fishes of the Kansas River system in relation to zoogeography of the Great Plains. Museum of Natural History, Univ. of Kansas, Publication 17(3):23-189.

Mettee, M.F., R.W. Yerger, and E. Crittenden. 1976. A status report on the Okaloosa darter in northwest Florida. Southeastern Fishes Council Proceedings 1(2):1-3.

Miller, R.J., and H.W. Robison. 1973. The fishes of Oklahoma. Stillwater: Oklahoma State Univ. Museum of Natural History Series, no. 1. 246 pp.

Miller, R.R. 1972. Threatened freshwater fishes of the United States. Transactions of the Amer. Fisheries Soc. 101(2):239-52.

Miller, R.V. 1968. A systematic study of the greenside darter, *Etheostoma blennioides* Rafinesque (Pisces: Percidae). Copeia 1968(1):1-40.

Moore, G.A. 1968. Fishes. In: W.F. Blair, A.P. Blair, P. Brodkorb, F.R. Cagle, and G.A. Moore, Vertebrates of the

United States, 21-165. 2nd ed. New York: McGraw-Hill. 616 pp.

———, and F.B. Cross. 1950. Additional Oklahoma fishes with validation of *Poecilichthys parvipinnis* (Gilbert and Swain). Copeia 1950(2):139-48.

———, and J.D. Reeves. 1955. *Hadropterus pantherinus,* a new percid fish from Oklahoma and Arkansas. Copeia 1955(2):89-92.

———, and C.C. Rigney, 1952. Taxonomic status of the percid fish *Poecilichthys radiosus* in Oklahoma and Arkansas, with the descriptions of two new subspecies. Copeia 1952(1):7-15.

Morris, M.A., and L.M. Page. 1981. Variation in western logperches (Pisces: Percidae), with description of a new subspecies from the Ozarks. Copeia 1981(1):95-108.

Mount, D.I. 1959. Spawning behavior of the bluebreast darter, *Etheostoma camurum* (Cope). Copeia, 1959(3):240-43.

Moyle, P.B. 1976. Inland fishes of California. Berkeley: Univ. of California Press. 405 pp.

Mullan, J.W., R.L. Applegate, and W.C. Rainwater. 1968. Food of logperch (*Percina caprodes*) and brook silverside (*Labidesthes sicculus*), in a new and old Ozark reservoir. Transactions of the Amer. Fisheries Soc. 97(3):300-305.

New, J.G. 1966. Reproductive behavior of the shield darter, *Percina peltata peltata,* in New York. Copeia 1966(1):20-28.

Nieland, D.L. 1979. Fishes of the Duck River. Assoc. of Southeastern Biologists Bull. 26(2):67.

Norman, C. 1981. Snail darter's status threatened. Science 212(4496):761.

O'Neal, P., and H. Boschung. 1980. Life history aspects of *Etheostoma coosae* (Pisces: Percidae) in Barbaree Creek, Clay County, Alabama. Assoc. of Southeastern Biologists Bull. 27(2):53-54.

Page, L.M. 1974a. The subgenera of *Percina* (Percidae: Etheostomatini). Copeia 1974(1):66-86.

———. 1974b. The life history of the spottail darter, *Etheostoma squamiceps,* in Big Creek, Illinois, and Ferguson Creek, Kentucky. Illinois Natural History Survey Biological Notes, no. 89. 20 pp.

———. 1975a. The life history of the stripetail darter, *Etheostoma kennicotti,* in Big Creek, Illinois. Illinois Natural History Survey Biological Notes, no. 93. 15 pp.

———. 1975b. Relations among the darters of the subgenus *Catonotus* of *Etheostoma.* Copeia 1975(4):782-84.

———. 1976a. The modified midventral scales of *Percina* (Osteichthyes; Percidae). J. of Morphology 148(2):255-64.

———. 1976b. Natural darter hybrids: *Etheostoma gracile* x *Percina maculata, Percina caprodes* x *Percina maculata,* and *Percina phoxocephala* x *Percina maculata.* Southwestern Naturalist 21(2):161-68.

———. 1978. Redescription, distribution, variation and life history notes on *Percina macrocephala* (Percidae). Copeia 1978(4):655-64.

———. 1980. The life histories of *Etheostoma olivaceum* and *Etheostoma striatulum,* two species of darters in central Tennessee. Illinois Natural History Survey Biological Notes, no. 113. 14 pp.

———. 1981. The genera and subgenera of darters (Percidae, Etheostomatini). Occasional Papers of the Museum of Natural History, Univ. of Kansas, no. 90. 69 pp.

———, and M.E. Braasch. 1976. Systematic studies of darters of the subgenus *Catonotus* (Percidae), with the description of a new species from the lower Cumberland and Tennessee River system. Occasional Papers of the Natural History Museum, Univ. of Kansas, no. 60. 18 pp.

———, and ———. 1977. Systematic studies of darters of the subgenus *Catonotus* (Percidae), with the description of a new species from the Duck River system. Occasional Papers of the Museum of Natural History, Univ. of Kansas, no. 63. 18 pp.

———, and B.M. Burr. 1976. The life history of the slabrock darter, *Etheostoma smithi,* in Ferguson Creek, Kentucky. Illinois Natural History Biological Notes, no. 99. 12 pp.

———, ———, and P.W. Smith. 1976. The spottail darter, *Etheostoma squamiceps* (Osteichthyes, Percidae), in Indiana. Amer. Midland Naturalist 95(2):478-79.

———, and R.L. Mayden. 1979. Nesting site of the lollipop darter *Etheostoma neopterum.* Transactions of the Kentucky Acad. of Science 40(1-2):56-57.

———, and D.W. Schemske. 1978. The effect of interspecific competition on the distribution and size of darters of the subgenus *Catonotus* (Percidae: *Etheostoma*). Copeia 1978(3):406-12.

———, and P.W. Smith. 1970. The life history of the dusky darter, *Percina sciera,* in the Embarras River, Illinois. Illinois Natural History Survey Biological Notes, no. 69. 15 pp.

———, and ———. 1971. The life history of the slenderhead darter, *Percina phoxocephala,* in the Embarras River, Illinois. Illinois Natural History Survey Biological Notes, no. 74. 14 pp.

———, and ———. 1976. Variation and systematics of the stripetail darter, *Etheostoma kennicotti.* Copeia 1976(3): 532-41.

———, and G.S. Whitt. 1973a. Lactate dehydrogenase isozymes, malate dehydrogenase isozymes, and tetrazolium oxidase mobilities of darters (Etheostomatini). Comparative Biochemistry and Physiology 44(B):611-23.

———, and ———. 1973b. Lactate dehydrogenase isozymes of darters and the inclusiveness of the Genus *Percina.* Illinois Natural History Survey Biological Notes, no. 82. 7 pp.

Petravicz, J.J. 1936. The breeding habits of the least darter, *Microperca punctulata* Putnam. Copeia 1936(2):77-82.

Petravicz, W.P. 1938. The breeding habits of the black-sided darter, *Hadropterus maculatus* Girard. Copeia 1938(1):40-44.

Pflieger, W.L. 1971. A distributional study of Missouri fishes. Lawrence: Univ. of Kansas Publications, Museum of Natural History 20(3):225-570.

———. 1975. The fishes of Missouri. Missouri Dept. of Conservation. viii + 343 pp.

Pigg, J., and L.G. Hill. 1974. Fishes of the Kiamichi River, Oklahoma. Proceedings of the Oklahoma Acad. of Science 54:121-30.

Putnam, F.W. 1863. List of fishes sent by the museum to different institutions, in exchange for other specimens, with annotations. Harvard Univ. Museum of Comparative Zoology Bulletin 1(1):2-16.

Radcliffe, L., and W.W. Welsh. 1913. Description of a new darter from Maryland. Bull. of the U.S. Bureau of Fisheries, 1912, 32:29-32.

Rafinesque, C.S. 1819. Prodrome de 70 nouveaux genres d'animaux découverts dans l'intérieur des Etats-Unis d'Amérique durant l'année 1818. J. Physique, Paris 88:417-29.

Ramsey, J.S. 1976. Freshwater fishes. In: Endangered and threatened plants and animals of Alabama, 53-65. Bull., Alabama Museum of Natural History, no. 2. 93 pp.

———, and R.D. Suttkus. 1965. *Etheostoma ditrema,* a new darter of the subgenus *Oligocephalus* (Percidae) from springs of the Alabama River basin in Alabama and Georgia. Tulane Studies in Zoology 12(3):65-77.

———, W. Wieland, R.K. Wallace, and T.J. Timmons. 1980. Sampling rare fishes in the Cahaba River, Alabama. Assoc. of Southeastern Biologists Bull. 27(2):58.

Raney, E.C. 1941. *Poecilichthys kanawhae,* a new darter from the upper New River system in North Carolina and Virginia. Occasional Papers of the Museum of Zoology, Univ. of Michigan, no. 434. 16 pp.

———, and C.L. Hubbs. 1948. *Hadropterus notogrammus,* a new percid fish from Maryland, Virginia, and West Virginia. Occasional Papers of the Museum of Zoology, Univ. of Michigan, no. 512. 26 pp.

———, and E.A. Lachner. 1939. Observations on the life history of the spotted darter, *Poecilichthys maculatus* (Kirtland). Copeia 1939(3):157-65.

———, and ———. 1942. Studies of the summer food, growth and movements of young yellow pike-perch, *Stizostedion v. vitreum* in Oneida Lake, New York. J. of Wildlife Management 6(1):1-16.

———, and ———. 1943. Age and growth of johnny darters, *Boleosoma nigrum olmstedi* (Storer) and *Boleosoma longimanum* (Jordan), Amer. Midland Naturalist 29(1):229-38.

———, and R.D. Suttkus. 1964. *Etheostoma moorei,* a new darter of the subgenus *Nothonotus* from the White River system, Arkansas. Copeia 1964(1):130-39.

———, and ———. 1966. *Etheostoma rubrum,* a new percid fish of the subgenus *Nothonotus* from Bayou Pierre, Mississippi. Tulane Studies in Zoology 13(3):95-102.

———, and T. Zorach. 1967. *Etheostoma microlepidum,* a new percid fish of the subgenus *Nothonotus* from the Cumberland and Tennessee river systems. Amer. Midland Naturalist 77(1):93-103.

Reeves, C.D. 1907. The breeding habits of the rainbow darter (*Etheostoma coeruleum* Storer), a study in sexual selection. Biological Bull. 14:35-59.

Reighard, J. 1913. The breeding habits of the log-perch (*Percina caprodes*). Annual report of the Michigan Acad. of Science 15:104-5.

Richards, W.J. 1966. Systematics of the percid fishes of the *Etheostoma thalassinum* species group with comments on the subgenus *Etheostoma.* Copeia 1966(4):823-38.

———, and L.W. Knapp. 1964. *Percina lenticula,* a new percid fish with a redescription of the subgenus *Hadropterus.* Copeia 1964(4):690-701.

Robins, C.R., R.M. Bailey, C.E. Bond, J.R. Brooker, E.A. Lachner, R.N. Lea, and W.B. Scott. 1980. A list of common and scientific names of fishes from the United States and Canada. 4th ed. Amer. Fisheries Soc. Special Publication 12. 174 pp.

Robison, H.W. 1974a. Threatened fishes of Arkansas. Arkansas Acad. of Science Proceedings 28:59-64.

———. 1974b. New distributional records of some Arkansas fishes with addition of three species to the state ichthyofauna. Southwestern Naturalist 19(2):213-23.

———. 1974c. An additional population of *Etheostoma pallididorsum* Distler and Metcalf in Arkansas. Amer. Midland Naturalist 91(2):478-79.

———. 1977. Distribution, habitat, variation and status of the goldstripe darter *Etheostoma parvipinne* (Gilbert and Swain), in Arkansas. Southwestern Naturalist 22(4):435-42.

———, G.A. Moore, and R.J. Miller. 1974. Threatened fishes of Oklahoma. Proceedings of the Oklahoma Acad. of Science 54:139-46.

Ross, R.D. 1959. Drainage evolution and distribution problems of the fishes of the New (Upper Kanawha) River system in Virginia. Part 4: Key to the identification of fishes. Virginia Agricultural Experiment Station, Virginia Polytechnic Institute Technical Bull. 146. 27 pp.

———. 1971. The drainage history of the Tennessee River. In; P.C. Holt, ed., The distributional history of the biota of the southern Appalachians. Part III: Vertebrates, 11-42. Research Division Monograph 4. Virginia Polytechnic Institute, Blacksburg, Va.

———, and J.E. Carico. 1963. Records and distribution problems of fishes of the North, Middle, and South forks of the Holston River, Virginia. Virginia Agricultural Experiment Station, Virginia Polytechnic Institute Technical Bull. 161. 24 pp.

Scalat, C.G. 1971. Parasites of the orangebelly darter, *Etheostoma radiosum* (Pisces: Percidae). J. of Parasitology 57(4):900.

———. 1972. Food habits of the orangebelly darter, *Etheostoma radiosum cyanorum* (Osteichthyes: Percidae). Amer. Midland Naturalist 87(2):515-22.

———. 1973a. Reproduction of the orangebelly darter, *Etheostoma radiosum cyanorum* (Osteichthyes: Percidae). Amer. Midland Naturalist 89(1):156-65.

———. 1973b. Stream movements and population density of the orangebelly darter, *Etheostoma radiosum cyanorum* (Osteichthyes: Percidae). Southwestern Naturalist 17(4):381-87.

Schenck, J.R., and B.G. Whiteside. 1976. Distribution, habitat preference and population size estimate of *Etheostoma fonticola.* Copeia 1976(4):697-703.

———, and ———. 1977. Food habits and feeding behavior of the fountain darter, *Etheostoma fonticola* (Osteichthyes: Percidae). Southwestern Naturalist 21(4):487-92.

Schwartz, F.J. 1965a. Densities and ecology of the darters of the upper Allegheny River watershed. In: Studies on the aquatic ecology of the upper Ohio River system, 95-103. Special Publication 3. Pymatuning Laboratory of Ecology, Univ. of Pittsburgh.

———. 1965b. The distribution and probable postglacial dispersal of the percid fish, *Etheostoma b. blennioides,* in the Potomac River. Copeia 1965(3): 285-90.

Scott, W.B., and E.J. Crossman. 1973. Freshwater fishes of Canada. Ottawa: Fisheries Research Board of Canada Bull. 184. 966 pp.

Sisk, M.E., and D.H. Webb. 1976. Distribution and habitat preference of *Etheostoma histrio* in Kentucky. Transactions of the Kentucky Acad. of Science 37(1-2):33-34.

Small, J.W., Jr. 1975. Energy dynamics of benthic fishes in a small Kentucky stream. Ecology 56(4):827-40.

Smart, H.J., and J.H. Gee. 1979. Coexistence and resource partitioning in two species of darters (Percidae), *Etheostoma nigrum* and *Percina maculata*. Canadian J. of Zoology 57(10):2061-71.

Smith, P.L., and M.E. Sisk. 1969. The fishes of west Kentucky. II: The fishes of Obion Creek. Transactions of the Kentucky Acad. of Science 30(3-4):60-68.

Smith, P.W. 1979. The fishes of Illinois. Urbana: Univ. of Illinois Press. 314 pp.

————, A.C. Lopinot, and W.L. Pflieger. 1971. A distributional atlas of upper Mississippi River fishes. Illinois Natural History Survey Biological Notes, no. 73. 20 pp.

Smith, R.F. 1950. A general discussion of lakes surveyed during the 1950 fisheries survey. New Jersey Fishery Survey, Division of Fish and Game Report 1:26-142.

Smith, R.J.F. 1979. Alarm reactions of Iowa and johnny darters (*Etheostoma* Percidae, Pisces) to chemicals from injured conspecifics. Canadian J. of Zoology 57(6):1278-82.

Smith-Vaniz, W.F. 1968. Freshwater fishes of Alabama. Auburn: Auburn Univ. Agricultural Experiment Station. 211 pp.

Spear, E.P. 1960. Growth of the central johnny darter, *Etheostoma nigrum nigrum* (Rafinesque) in Augusta Creek, Michigan. Copeia 1960(3):241-43.

Starnes, W.C. 1977. The ecology and life history of the endangered snail darter, *Percina (Imostoma) tanasi*. Knoxville: Univ. of Tennessee, Tennessee Wildlife Resources Agency Technical Report 77-52. 144 pp.

————, D.A. Etnier, L.B. Starnes, and N.H. Douglas. 1977. Zoogeographic implications of the rediscovery of the percid genus *Ammocrypta* in the Tennessee River drainage. Copeia 1977(4):783-86.

————, and L.B. Starnes. 1979a. Discovery of the percid genus *Ammocrypta* (Pisces) in the Apalachicola drainage, Florida. Proceedings of the Florida Acad. of Science 42(1):61-62.

————, and ————. 1979b. Taxonomic status of the percid fish *Etheostoma nigrum susanae*. Copeia 1979(3):426-30.

Starrett, W.C. 1950. Distribution of the fishes of Boone County, Iowa, with special reference to the minnows and darters. Amer. Midland Naturalist 43(1):112-17.

Stevenson, M.M. 1971. *Percina macrolepida* (Pisces, Percidae, Etheostomatinae), a new percid fish of the subgenus *Percina* from Texas. Southwestern Naturalist 16(1):65-83.

Stiles, R.A. 1972. The reproductive behavior of three species of darters (*Etheostoma*) of the subgenus *Nothonotus* (Osteichthyes, Perciformes, Percidae). Assoc. of Southeastern Biologists Bull. 19(2):103.

Strawn, K. 1955-56. A method of breeding and raising three Texas darters. Aquarium J. 26:408-12; 27:31-32.

Suttkus, R.D., and G.H. Clemmer. 1977. A status report on the bayou darter, *Etheostoma rubrum,* and the Bayou Pierre system. Southeastern Fishes Council Proceedings 1(4):1-2.

————, and J.S. Ramsey. 1967. *Percina aurolineata*, a new percid fish from the Alabama River system and a discussion of ecology, distribution, and hybridization of darters of the subgenus *Hadropterus*. Tulane Studies in Zoology 13(4):129-45.

Taning, A.V. 1952. Experimental studies of meristic characters in fishes. Biological Reviews, Cambridge Philosophical Soc. 27:169-93.

Thomas, D.L. 1970. An ecological study of four darters of the genus *Percina* (Percidae) in the Kaskaskia River, Illinois. Illinois Natural History Survey Biological Notes, no. 70. 18 pp.

Thompson, B.A. 1973. The relationships of the percid fish *Etheostoma (Etheostoma) blennius* (Gilbert and Swain) (class Osteichthyes, order Perciformes, family Percidae). Assoc. of Southeastern Biologists Bull. 20(2):87.

————. 1974. An analysis of sympatric populations of two closely related species of *Percina*, with notes on food habits of the subgenus *Imostoma*. Assoc. of Southeastern Biologists Bull. 21(2):87.

————. 1978. Logperches of the southeastern United States (Etheostomatini, *Percina*). Assoc. of Southeastern Biologists Bull. 25(2):57.

Trautman, M.B. 1930. The specific distinctness of *Poecilichthys coeruleus* (Storer) and *Poecilichthys spectabilis* Agassiz. Copeia 1930(1):12-13.

————. 1957. The fishes of Ohio, with illustrated keys. Columbus: Ohio State Univ. Press. 683 pp.

————. 1981. The fishes of Ohio. Revised ed. Columbus: Ohio State Univ. Press. 782 pp.

Tsai, Chu-fa. 1968a. Distribution of the harlequin darter, *Etheostoma histrio*. Copeia 1968(1):178-81.

————. 1968b. Effects of chlorinated sewage effluents on fishes in upper Patuxent River, Maryland. Chesapeake Science 9(2):83-93.

————. 1968c. Variation and distribution of the rock darter, *Etheostoma rupestre*. Copeia 1968(2):346-53.

————. 1972. Life history of the eastern johnny darter, *Etheostoma olmstedi* Storer, in cold tailwater and sewage-polluted water. Transactions of the Amer. Fisheries Soc. 101(1):80-88.

————, and E.C. Raney. 1974. Systematics of the banded darter *Etheostoma zonale* (Pisces: Percidae). Copeia 1974(1):1-24.

Turner, C.L. 1921. Food of the common Ohio darters. Ohio J. of Science 22(2):41-62.

Ultsch, G.R., H. Boschung, and M.J. Ross. 1978. Metabolism, critical oxygen tension, and habitat selection in darters (*Etheostoma*). Ecology 59(1):99-107.

Underhill, J.C. 1963. Distribution in Minnesota of the subspecies of the percid fish *Etheostoma nigrum* and of their intergrades. Amer. Midland Naturalist 70(2):470-78.

Wall, B.R., Jr., and J.D. Williams. 1974. *Etheostoma boschungi,* a new percid fish from the Tennessee River drainage in northern Alabama and western Tennessee. Tulane Studies in Zoology and Botany 18(4):172-82.

Webb, D.H., and M.E. Sisk. 1975. The fishes of Kentucky.

III: The fishes of Bayou de Chien. Transactions of the Kentucky Acad. of Science 36(3-4):63-70.

Wieland, W. 1980. Feeding periodicity and diet of the bronze darter, *Percina palmaris*. Assoc. of Southeastern Biologists Bull. 27(2):72.

Williams, J.D. 1975. Systematics of the percid fishes of the subgenus *Ammocrypta*, genus *Ammocrypta*, with descriptions of two new species. Bull., Alabama Museum of Natural History, no. 1. 56 pp.

————, and D.A. Etnier. 1977. *Percina (Imostoma) antesella*, a new percid fish from the Coosa River system in Tennessee and Georgia. Proceedings of the Biological Soc. of Washington 90(1):6-18.

————, and ————. 1978. *Etheostoma aquali*, a new percid fish (subgenus *Nothonotus*) from the Duck and Buffalo rivers, Tennessee. Proceedings of the Biological Soc. of Washington 91(2):463-71.

————, and D.K. Finnley. 1977. Our vanishing fishes: Can they be saved? Acad. of Natural Science of Philadelphia, Frontiers 41(4):21-32.

————, and H.W. Robison. 1980. *Ozarka*, a new subgenus of *Etheostoma* (Pisces: Percidae). Brimleyana 4:149-56.

Winn, H.E. 1953. Breeding habits of the percid fish *Hadropterus copelandi* in Michigan. Copeia 1953(1):26-30.

————. 1958a. Observations on the reproductive habits of darters (Pisces-Percidae). Amer. Midland Naturalist 59(1):190-212.

————. 1958b. Comparative reproductive behavior and ecology of fourteen species of darters (Pisces-Percidae). Ecological Monographs 28(2):155-91.

————, and A.R. Picciolo. 1960. Communal spawning of the glassy darter, *Etheostoma vitreum* (Cope). Copeia 1960(3):186-92.

Wiseman, E.D., A.A. Echelle, and A.F. Echelle. 1978. Electrophoretic evidence for subspecific differentiation and intergradation in *Etheostoma spectabile* (Teleostei: Percidae). Copeia 1978(2):320-27.

Wolfe, G.W., B.H. Bauer, and B.A. Branson. 1978. Age and growth, length–weight relationships, and condition factors of the greenside darter from Silver Creek, Kentucky. Transactions of the Kentucky Acad. of Science 39(3-4):131-34.

Yerger, R.W. 1978. Okaloosa darter, *Etheostoma okaloosae* Fowler. In: C.R. Gilbert, ed., Rare and endangered biota of Florida, 4:2-4. Gainesville: Univ. Presses of Florida.

Zorach, T. 1968. *Etheostoma bellum*, a new darter of the subgenus *Nothonotus* from the Green River system, Kentucky and Tennessee. Copeia 1968(3):474-82.

————. 1969. *Etheostoma jordani* and *E. tippecanoe*, species of the subgenus *Nothonotus* (Pisces: Percidae). Amer. Midland Naturalist 81(2):412-34.

————. 1970. The systematics of the percid fish *Etheostoma rufilineatum* (Cope). Amer. Midland Naturalist 84(1):208-25.

————. 1971. Taxonomic status of the subspecies of the tessellated darter, *Etheostoma olmstedi* Storer, in southeastern Virginia. Chesapeake Science 11(4):254-63.

————. 1972. Systematics of the percid fishes, *Etheostoma camurum* and *E. chlorobranchium* new species, with a discussion of the subgenus *Nothonotus*. Copeia 1972(3):427-47.

————, and E.C. Raney. 1967. Systematics of the percid fish, *Etheostoma maculata* Kirtland, and related species of the subgenus *Nothonotus*. Amer. Midland Naturalist 77(2):296-322.

Index
to Common and Scientific Names